Reprints of Economic Classics

CAPITAL AND FINANCE IN THE AGE OF THE RENAISSANCE

CAPITAL & FINANCE IN THE AGE OF THE RENAISSANCE

A STUDY OF THE FUGGERS
AND THEIR CONNECTIONS

by

RICHARD EHRENBERG

Translated from the German by
H. M. LUCAS

AUGUSTUS M. KELLEY, PUBLISHERS

First edition 1928

Reprinted 1985 by
Augustus M. Kelley, Publishers
Fairfield, NJ 07006

Library of Congress Cataloging in Publication Data

Ehrenberg, Richard, 1857-1921.
  Capital & finance in the Age of the Renaissance.
  (Reprints of economic classics)
  Translation of: Zeitlater der Fugger.
  Reprint. Originally published: New York: Harcourt,
Brace, 1928.
  1. Fugger family.   2. Europe—Economic conditions.
3. Finance—Europe—History.   4. Banks and banking—
Europe—History.   I. Title.   II. Title: Capital and
finance in the Age of the Renaissance.   III. Series.
HC51.5.E3813   332'.094   85-170
ISBN 0-678-00015-8

CONTENTS

CHAPTER 3

THE FLORENTINES AND OTHER TUSCAN FINANCIERS

BOOK II

THE INTERNATIONAL BOURSES OF THE SIXTEENTH CENTURY

CHAPTER 1

ANTWERP

CHAPTER 2

LYONS

CHAPTER 3

CAPITAL TRANSACTIONS ON THE INTERNATIONAL MARKETS OF THE SIXTEENTH CENTURY

CONTENTS

CONCLUSION

FROM THE AGE OF THE FUGGER TO THE PRESENT

PUBLISHERS' NOTE

THE rapidly growing interest in economic and social history has produced a general desire to know more of the manner in which the economic development of Europe has been interpreted by scholars of other nations. The aim of the Publishers is to meet that demand. With this object, translations of works on economic and social history by distinguished foreign authorities, which are likely to be of interest to English students, will from time to time be produced. The opening volumes of the series are *The Industrial Revolution in the Eighteenth Century*, by Professor Paul Mantoux, and *Capital and Finance in the Age of the Renaissance. A Study of the Fuggers and their Connections*, by Dr. Richard Ehrenberg. The books of Professor Mantoux and Dr. Ehrenberg hold a deservedly high place in economic and historical literature, and it is believed that the appearance of English versions of them will be generally welcomed. They will be followed in due course by translations of other foreign works, throwing light on different aspects of economic and social history.

PREFACE

THE book of Dr. Richard Ehrenberg, *Das Zeitalter der Fugger*, has long been known and valued by English students, and all who are interested in a critical period in the economic history of Europe will be glad that it has been made more accessible in the excellent translation of Mrs. Lucas. Certain chapters, of somewhat less general interest than the remainder, have been omitted. But the reader will find in the following pages a fuller study than is elsewhere available in English of the financial developments which were the prelude to the industrial expansion of the seventeenth and eighteenth centuries.

Much attention has been devoted in recent years by continental scholars to the investigation of the earlier phases of capitalist enterprise. The subject has been approached along several different paths and with varying conclusions. It is clear, however, that the mobilization of financial resources on a greater scale than in the past, which took place in the age of the Renaissance, is a phenomenon which lies near the centre of it, and it is this aspect of the problem which forms the theme of Dr. Ehrenberg's book. Though he selects for special examination the business of the Fugger, who were the greatest financiers of the period, his work is much more than a study of the activities of a single firm, however important. It is an attempt to show the causes which produced the increased demand for capital in the sixteenth century, the sources from which capital was drawn, and the financial machinery through which it was made available for commercial ventures, for industry and for the needs of States.

The Public Finance of the sixteenth century is a study which is largely pathological. There were degrees in the incompetence and immorality of Governments, but the practice of all was bad; and, if Elizabeth, with the aid of Gresham, had achieved by the middle of her reign a reputation which stood her in good stead as a borrower, it was due, it may be suspected, less to the virtue of the English Government than to the vices of its neighbours. The causes of the *impasse* lay deeper than the personal shortcomings of statesmen and their advisers. The essence of the difficulty consisted in the fact that an antiquated engine was being used to draw a load for which it had not been designed. The incompatibility of mediaeval systems of finance with the new military and administrative methods was making itself increasingly felt. The interest of Dr. Ehrenberg's introductory pages consists partly in the account which they give of the financial aspects of the recurrent political breakdowns, and of the attempts of Governments to draw upon the resources of the money-market in order to avert them.

13

The part played by the financier in the commercial and industrial life of the age was more fruitful and constructive. A steady flow of capital was needed to finance the movement of the produce handled on the world-market, such as the eastern spice-crop, copper, alum, the precious metals, and the cloth shipped by the English Merchant Adventurers. The supply of it came from productive enterprises, such as the silver and copper mines of the Fugger in the Tyrol and Hungary, the profits of trading ventures, successful investments and speculations on the part of the merchants themselves, and to a less extent – since the habit of lending money at call had already gone some way on the continent – from savings invested by the general public. Dr. Ehrenberg's account of the *personnel* and organization of the Antwerp money-market shows the machinery through which the financial resources of the age were mobilized. Its essence, as his description shows, was internationalism, freedom for every capitalist to undertake every transaction within his means, a unity which had as its symptom the movement of all the principal markets in sympathy with each other, and as its effect the mobilization of large resources at the strategic points of commerce.

The world of international finance described by Dr. Ehrenberg stood in intimate relation, therefore, both with the political and with the economic problems of the period. Its significance for the future was profound. Dr. Ehrenberg's concluding pages describe shortly the principal landmarks in the financial history of the seventeenth century. The story of English banking in the century before the foundation of the Bank of England contains several phases which are still obscure, and not every one will agree with his interpretation of it. But if the causes that produced the sensational changes which took place after the Revolution are to be understood, it is necessary that the English developments should be set in relation to their continental background. It is not the least of the merits of Dr. Ehrenberg's book that it assists the English reader to see the economic evolution of his own country as part of a general European movement.

TRANSLATOR'S NOTE

CERTAIN sections of Dr. Richard Ehrenberg's book have been omitted in translation. They are :

Vol I. Chapter IV (The Geonese Spaniards and Netherlanders). Chapter V (The Importance of the Financiers of the Sixteenth Century).

Vol II. Section III, entitled : The Time of the International Financial Crises.

The references contained in Dr. Ehrenberg's copious notes have been given. A note has been added on the Currencies mentioned in the text.

H. M. L.

NOTE ON THE CURRENCIES

The *gulden*, according to the Imperial edict of 1524, contained $37\frac{1}{8}$ English grains of fine gold (Del Mar, p. 339). The revolutionary government in Holland coined 'guilders' or florins of $160\frac{1}{2}$ grains fine silver (*Ib.*, p. 369).

The *Livre Tournois* in 1200 designated 98 grammes of fine silver, by 1600 it had fallen to 11 grammes (D'Avenel, Vol. I, p. 62). In the middle of the sixteenth century it was equal to $\frac{4}{5}$ of the Livre d'Artois or Cayolus gulden.

The *Flemish Pound* or Livre de gros de Flandres contained 20 schelling =240 grooten.

The *Carolus gulden*, also called the Livre d'Artois or florin de Brabant, was a Netherlands silver coin established by the law of February 22, 1542 (Shaw, p. 345). It was equal to 40 gr. or 20 stivers. Hence 1 pound Flemish=6 Carolus gulden.

The *ducat* was equal to 42 or 43 stivers and thus was rather more than 2 Carolus Gulden and rather less than $\frac{1}{3}$ of a pound Flemish.

The Spanish ducat was worth 375 maravedi.

The *Rhenish florin* was a gold gulden. 7 fl. Rh.=10 Carolus gulden= about 5 ducats.

The *Crown* or *Écu* was about $\frac{7}{8}$ of a ducat and in the middle of the sixteenth century was worth rather more than 5 shillings English.

BOOK I
INTRODUCTION

INTRODUCTION

MONEY CAPITAL AND PUBLIC CREDIT TOWARDS THE END OF THE MIDDLE AGES

V IEWS on Money Capital. Pecunia pecuniam non parere potest.
Money is essentially unproductive. Anyone, therefore, who demands fruits from it, sins not only against positive commandments of divine and secular law, but also against the nature of things. A man profoundly learned in this commercial law of the Middle Ages formulates in these words the first principle which for many centuries ruled undisputed in theory and even attempted to bring practice under its sway.[1]

This ecclesiastical view of money capital had its origin in the leading idea of Christianity directed against the materialism of antiquity – the idea that earthly things were only valuable in so far as they served as preparation for the life to come. It was based on a moral precept from the Bible, and a saying of Aristotle, which apparently was only the statement of an ideal, but which interpreted as a principle, appeared to deny productivity to money.

As the two highest spiritual authorities of the Middle Ages had both pronounced in the same sense, it was practically impossible to contradict the theory. On the other hand, the circumstances of ordinary life could not be made to harmonize with this view. So long as money was not yet used on a large scale as a medium of exchange, but served chiefly as a measure of value and so long as payments were chiefly made in kind, interest on money capital was comparatively rare. As soon, however, as the economic life of the European peoples outgrew this early stage of cultural development, especially since the time of the Crusades, the ecclesiastical ideal was thrust more and more into the background until finally even the doctrine changed.

The new doctrine no longer made moral claims, but for the first time since the classical period tried to treat economic facts from an economic point of view. Since Adam Smith it has borne the name of the 'mercantile' system. Like every other theory which has proved important in practice, it is the product of various interests and tendencies. Public opinion in the mass was chiefly influenced by the enormous production of precious metals in Spanish America. The news of these fabulous treasures which was spread abroad, not without the help of Spanish financiers, had a deep and lasting influence on the imagination of the masses; the more so as for some considerable time the power of Spain was actually strengthened by the American silver. It also influenced

---

[1] Endemann, *Studien in der romanisch-kanonist. Wirthschafts-und Rechtslehre*, 1874–83, II. 11.

21

many of the second- or third-rate writers, who after the devastating wars of the sixteenth and seventeenth centuries tried more or less systematically to develop their views of the State and economics. They spread the exaggerations of the mercantile doctrine, the over-estimation of the power of money, which Adam Smith fought against.

On the other hand, genuine mercantilism, important alike on the practical and scientific side, had arisen much earlier. It was chiefly the result of the experience in economic matters collected throughout many centuries by the mediæval cities. Since the end of the Middle Ages, this experience had been utilized by princes and statesmen in order to extend and establish their power and to form real States. It had also been used by writers of the first rank in order to support the princes at their work by advice which already bore the stamp of true science.

With seeming suddenness one principle becomes prominent at this time which expresses a new view of the essence and significance of money capital. This principle runs 'Pecunia nervus belli' (money is the sinews of war).

It is no theory but a principle based on experience. It was not framed in conscious opposition to the mediæval doctrine, and it holds no logical contradiction of it. It contents itself with a brief statement of an often observed fact. But it brings before us one of the most important consequences of the great spiritual revolution we call the 'Renaissance.'

The Renaissance means everywhere, but more especially in regard to social and civic life, a return in this last resort to Nature, to what is actually before us, here in this instance to human nature, which is once again regarded as a datum.

The Catholic Church of the Middle Ages with its effort to bring up men by its doctrine to the highest morality had itself long sunk to an outer hypocrisy and an inner moral corruption, without, however, renouncing its ideal claims on human nature. The Renaissance, on the other hand, gave up the idea of making men more noble and therefore directed its efforts all the more to bridling and ruling them.

The statecraft of the Renaissance did not, like the Ecclesiastical doctrine of the Middle Ages, erect a powerful structure of dogma clamped together with iron logic but resting on feet of clay. It preferred to embody its observations in short sentences. It turned to Classical times originally, not from a fondness to philosophy or archæology, but because it needed the classics. Where else could the young science of experience find authority to rival the wisdom of the schoolmen sanctified as it was by age and faith? Hence at first the passionate search for the remains of a vanished civilization, a search which degenerated all too soon with a meaningless heaping up of dead authorities and a learned pedantry.

The Renaissance, properly speaking, was only the high-water mark of the development, which had begun long before and which rose with increasing speed in the last centuries of the Middle Ages. So the old principle 'Pecunia nervus belli' did not reappear so suddenly after all.[1] Originating in this form in Aceio, it appears occasionally in mediæval literature. When, however, thousands of fresh experiences had demonstrated its truth, the statecraft of the Renaissance made it the central point of its economic discussion, and this came to pass first of all in that country and that city, where such experiences were the most abundantly forthcoming.

The Italians, and more especially the Florentines, towards the end of the Middle Ages could look back on a practice in handling money capital extending over more than three hundred years. They knew that money had become an indispensable weapon for the attainment of political power. They had had this fact perpetually before their eyes for hundreds of years, and each generation had handed it down with a steadily growing store of practical experience. Masters of language now gave it the stamp of universality, and with the help of the newly rediscovered classical learning made it the common property of the upper classes throughout Europe.

Both for theory and for legislation, however, the ban against interest on capital remained for a time unattacked and left to a gradual and spontaneous dissolution. It progressively lost influence on practical life, the experiences of which were elsewhere formulated into a scientific clearness.

Among Florentine statesmen and learned men of the fifteenth century the saying 'Pecunia nervus belli' had certainly long been current, before Machiavelli took it for his subject of a short but important polemic.[2] In opposition to the general view he there lays it down that money is not the sinews of war, that it is not sufficient of itself to obtain good soldiers; that, on the other hand, with soldiers money can often be procured.

---

[1] Davanzati, *Lezione delle monete in der Ausg. bei Argelatus* IV. 164, Note 1; Lipsius, *Polit. s. civ. doctr.* (1596) IV. 9. V. 6; Büchmann, *Geflügelte Worte.* 16. Aufl. (1889) p. 339 ff. Sansovino, *Concetti politici* (No. 388): Il nutrimento dell' essercito senz' alcun dubbio è il danaro. Questo dà misura ad ogni cosa e si converte in ogni cosa. Però disse quel savio antico, ch'i capitani, i soldati, l'arme, i cavalli e gli stromenti, l'artiglierie, ma non i danari, erano simili, ad un corpo, che havesse testa, braccia, collo, petto, gambe e piedi, ma non ventre; perche si come il ventre dà nutrimento al corpo, cosi i danari danno sostanza all' essercito, e quel Re di Sparta gli chiamò nervo della guerra; perche si come i nervi danno il moto al corpo, cosi lo danno i danari all' essercito.

[2] *Discorsi sopra le deche di Tito Livio* II. 10.

The fact that this principle was accepted in Machiavelli's circle as an axiom was sufficient to rouse opposition in his inventive mind, but this opposition had a much deeper root. Machiavelli hated the mercenaries and was enthusiastic for a militia system with extensive liability for service. He introduced this into Florence, without, however, much success. His friend, the great historian Francesco Guicciardini, who, though far from his equal in intellect, dialectic and political farsightedness, was far superior to him in practical insight into immediate political necessity, contradicted him here as he did elsewhere.[1] At present, he says, it is easier to get soldiers with money than money with soldiers. On this head Guicciardini knew his own times better than Machiavelli did. The saying 'Pecunia nervus belli' had in the time of the Renaissance already received the popular form which two hundred years later was usually ascribed to Montecuccoli. A trustworthy authority gives the story as follows: [2]

When King Louis XII, in the year 1499, formed the project of taking the Dukedom of Milan, to which he thought he had a claim, he one day asked in the State Council of the Condottiere Gian Giacomo de Trivulzio, a Milanese who had entered his service, what preparations were necessary for this great enterprise – Trivulzio, who as a Condottiere had the most exact information on this head, answered him, 'Most Gracious King, three things must be ready: money, money, and once again, money.' Here this saying has the character of a jest springing spontaneously from past experience. Montecuccoli, on the other hand, two hundred years later, in his memoirs,[3] joins this saying rather heavily to the well-known apothegms of the ancients, and calls money 'the tool of tools' and continues, 'What wonder hath brought forth the marvellous effects of which history is full? Hereon a certain man, being asked what were the things necessary for making war, replied that there were three: Money, Money, Money.' Here the empirical doctrine is turned once more into a kind of dogma with a claim to a universal application. On the other hand, a well-known military writer of the present states it in a strictly limited form – 'A full war chest may be worth an army corps, financial talent on the part of a leader in the field may be worth a good general.' [4]

The first great statesmen and publicists of the Renaissance did not wish to pursue either economics or finance. They spoke of money as the sinews of war, because money was more important for war than for any

[1] *Opere inedite* I. 61.
[2] Lodovico Guicciardini, *L'hore de recreatione*, in the German translation of Daniel Federmann von Memmingen, Basel, 1575.
[3] Montecuccoli, Lib. 1, cap. 2, tit. 5: del danaro.
[4] Von der Goltz, *Das Volk in Waffen*, p. 465.

other process that came within their purview. Within a few generations, however, their observations were generalized. Botero designates war as the most important eventuality for which a prince must keep money in reserve; and Bodinus Besold, Ammirato, and other publicists of the same epoch, use the same language. They are followed by the mercantilists proper.

The necessity of raising ready money for war first set the stone rolling, which – if we may adopt the saying of a modern Pope – shattered the Colossus of the scholastic teaching as to usury. The saying 'Pecunia nervus belli' has become a chief root of modern economic doctrine. Only one chief root, however. The other is found in Machiavelli's saying which attributes more importance in war to man-power than to money.

The controversy between Machiavelli and Guicciardini lasted long in literature without being decided. Even in mercantilism a tendency friendly to labour is often observable alongside of a tendency friendly to capital. The latter, however, prevailed. The significance of capital, under-estimated by the teaching of the Middle Ages, over-estimated by mercantilism, was first put in its right place by Adam Smith. This has not prevented his followers, however, from falling once again into both extremes. We are, therefore, justified in saying that the controversy between Machiavelli and Guicciardini already contains the germ of the latest problems of social science.

The Need of Capital for War. The system of dealing in kind prevalent in the early Middle Ages had been turning by degrees into a monetary and credit system, but this transformation went on with feverish rapidity at the time of the Renaissance. One chief symptom was the greed for the possession of money. Never since the time of the Roman Empire had everything been so easily bought with money: the highest ecclesiastical and worldly dignities, the blood of men, the honour of the greatest ladies, and eternal salvation itself. Gold and spices, but chiefly gold, was the goal of the Portuguese explorers, the goal of Columbus, his exalted patrons and his followers. Machiavelli was justified in speaking of the 'vileness' of human nature. The same age also produced characters of heroic self-abnegation, which shed their radiance across the centuries. These, however, did not occur among the great ones of the world, and the same great movement which showed the strength of faith and of conviction as opposed to the prevailing egoism was only made palatable to many rulers by the fact that it increased their revenues.

The general greed for money which seized on the upper classes in the epoch of the Renaissance concealed other and more far-reaching motive forces. The money so passionately desired by princes, high ecclesiastics and nobles, was used in the first place to satisfy the ever-growing general ostentation, the luxury in food, and other sensual gratifications;

but it also furthered the progress of art and science and the many passions they embrace, among which the most distinguished and the most costly was a gigantic love of building. In the case of princes other large forms of expenditure grew up which, unlike those already mentioned, had a non-personal character. First of all, those called forth by the transformation of the mediæval feudal state into the modern bureaucracy. The ever-increasing expenses of the state in administration, justice and diplomacy entailed claims on the princes which, as we have seen, they tried for a long time to pass on at least in part to others, but which nevertheless necessitated the payment of a growing number of professional officials. What the princes managed to save by allowing the officials to help themselves in other more or less legal ways, they must have had to pay out again in bribes to the officials of other princes. War, however, with its extraordinary demands ate up more money than all these other claims taken together. The same boundless ambition which expressed itself in the less powerful princes by gigantic building schemes, led the more powerful and a progressive foreign policy which could only be carried out by means of perpetual wars. Wars and armaments were the department among the princes' activities where the transformation of a system of dealing in kind into a money and credit system went forward most speedily.

The feudal system of defence had undoubtedly constituted an advance on the original German system where all free men were liable to bear arms. It had its origin in the increase of the claims, both technical and economic, which were made on the men under arms, and under the feudal system these claims were satisfied by distribution of labour. A special military caste was formed among the feudatories. But like all human institutions the feudal military system had from the beginning a fatal weakness. It recognized only a contractual obligation to bear arms. If the feudal lord failed to fulfil his duty to his vassal or asked more of him than his feudal due, the vassal could leave his lord. We know that this often happened and we know too that this fact largely helped the development of the mercenaries.

These developed at first chiefly in the cities, for here the general obligation of all citizens to serve under arms early proved incompatible with increasing economic development, and the feudal system in the nature of things could not be of importance in the organization of defence. Here too the use of money made such strides that it was soon possible to hand over the conduct of wars without the city wall to mercenaries. For a long time the princes could not do this owing to the smallness of their monetary revenue. It was only when the technique of war had been completely revolutionized by the successes of the cities and the Swiss Confederacy and the knightly armies had sustained repeated defeats that the princes saw themselves obliged to reorganize their military system. Service in arms, which under the feudal system had become a profession, developed in the thirteenth and fourteenth centuries, through the fact of payment into a form of manual labour; and finally in the fourteenth and fifteenth centuries, through the use of muskets and cannon it became an industry, requiring skilful direction and large capital. The princes were not yet capable to satisfying their claims on the technical side because they had no standing armies; and on the economic side, because their monetary revenues were insufficient.

Under these circumstances the conduct of war fell into the hands of professional private undertakers, the Condottieri, and they for the first time since the classical epoch created an art of war, a highly organized technique. Italy was the classic country of these general undertakers of war, and it was here too that the renaissance of the monetary system first made itself evident. The Condottieri themselves were at the beginning chiefly German or Spanish, and even when the leaders' posts had mostly been filled by Italians, the rank and file still remained chiefly Germans, Swiss, and Spaniards.

The Condottieri relieved the princes of the training and generalship of the armies, not, however, of their maintenance during the war. The economic difficulties connected with the size of the armies and their equipment continually increased and were at first a source of far worse evils than those of the mediæval system.

Like the feudal liability to service, the hire system only rested on contracts which the war lord made with leader of mercenaries, and the leader – usually through the agency of the captains – made with the soldiers. While, however, the feudal contract was largely based upon the public code, under the new system the contracts were only based on the civil code, and in particular on the rights of property – Blood for money; no money, no Swiss!

This relation, inherent in the system, gave the wars of the sixteenth and seventeenth centuries their particular character. It explained the unseemly and fatal influence which the badly paid troops brought to bear on the course of the world's history because they could not be trusted. How often the French Kings, or even more the German Emperors, have been left in the lurch by their mercenaries, or hindered in carrying out their war plans by the threat of mutiny and desertion! Think of such events as the storming of Rome by Charles V's unruly Germans, or the sack of Antwerp by the Spanish soldateska. The 'Ribauds' of the thirteenth century are reproduced in the 'Routiers,' 'Écorcheurs' and 'Retondeurs' of the fifteenth, and the mercenary armies of the Thirty Years War were no better. This war would never have lasted so long if at every opportunity for peace there had not been ambitious and greedy commanders and troops ready to fight against anybody for the money of any power which had a mind to fish in troubled waters.

The degradation of military service into a mere trade would not have led to the worst, had not the bad financial position of most of the war lords and the faulty organization of the monetary system in the princes' budgets led of necessity to forced 'deliveries in kind,' that is to say to robbery, murder, and arson. During the war the mercenaries were often actually forced to rob friend and foe alike; and when it was over they were not infrequently driven to maintain themselves by highway robbery till they found a new employer. This told adversely not only on the peoples, but also on the princes, who always had it before them that they would be ruined by the cruel maxim of the mercenary leaders that 'War must feed war.'

Machiavelli, who certainly had no tender feeling for the sufferings of the peoples, hated the mercenaries from the standpoint of the princes and their power.[1] The princes on their side, however, always sacrificed everything to the attempt to satisfy the indispensable mercenaries, because only so could they be prevented from deserting and committing atrocities.

In the fifteenth century Charles VII of France formed a small standing army. While, however, the first consequence of this measure was the transformation of the Taille into a permanent tax, yet for many centuries longer the further carrying out of this beneficent reform was prevented by the princes' insufficient money revenues. The foreign policy of the Great Powers of the sixteenth and seventeenth centuries could not yet rely to any large extent on standing armies.[2]

The meaning of this is best shown by a few figures. In the year 1532 Dr. Christopher Scheuerl calculated the cost of an average war equipment inclusive of pay for six months, but exclusive of provisions, baggage and other smaller costs, at 560,000 fl. A Spanish army corps which in the second half of the sixteenth century was sent to Southern Italy and had to be kept there half a year cost on an average $1\frac{1}{4}$ million ducats. The expenditure of the Spanish Crown in putting down the rebellion in the Netherlands averaged two to three million gold crowns a year, i.e. more than the yearly revenue of the Netherlands Government during the most flourishing trade period. Now let us consider that in the sixteenth century there were only twenty-five years, in the seventeenth century only twenty-one years, in which there were no

---

[1] Cf. Machiavelli, *Scritti inediti ed. Canestrini pref.* xxiv, & 281 ff. Canestrini, 'Documenti per servire alla storia d. milizia italiana ed. Canestrini' (*Arch. stor. tal.* XV), p. cviii ff. cxxiii ff.

Clément, *Jacques Cœur et Charles VII*, vol. I, 76 ff., 83, 107 ff.

war-like operations on a large scale. These facts should suffice to give some idea of the effect of the enormous demand for capital for war purposes on the financial arrangements of princes, more especially as in the absence of a regular army the irregular and incalculable nature of these requirements made impossible any orderly system of finance.

The capital needed for war belonged from its nature to extraordinary expenditure. Moreover, this very often occurred suddenly and demanded immediate satisfaction. Finally, it usually had to be met not in the places where revenue was raised, but in far distant countries. The principle that war must feed war often could not be acted upon, not only if the troops were on home territory, but even in the enemies' country, either from political considerations or because there was nothing further to fight. The armies needed reinforcements and fresh equipment. All this required money, and, as we see from the wars of Charles V and Philip II, often hundreds of miles from the place where it was to be found, and months or even years before the time when the revenues from the domains and taxes and other dues accumulating very slowly in the princes' coffers should have reached the required amount.

Finally we must bear in mind the dangers of the roads, the lack of transport and its extreme slowness and the great difficulties of moving large sums of money for any distance. It is only when all this has been brought before us that we can have a true picture of the anxiety with which the princes of the sixteenth and seventeenth centuries, even those who were financially the best situated, must have remembered in war-time the old saying, 'Pecunia nervus belli.'

Means of Meeting the Demand for Capital for War. The foreign policy of the European Great Powers in the period from the middle of the fifteenth to the middle of the seventeenth century was only to be successfully carried out if there were large supplies of ready money in an accessible form. This, however, was not by any means always the case. Though the princes recognized that money was the sinews of war, they were unable to act on this maxim. Their revenues were still mostly revenues in kind, and where they did consist of ready money, they were usually not found at the time or place when they could have been used for war. Above all, they were often quite insufficient to meet the war expenditure.

Neither the revenues from the princes' own domains, nor the old feudal dues which were mostly quite unproductive, could be increased to any considerable extent. Permanent taxes and taxes on transactions of the modern type were only just beginning and as yet amounted to very little. They only came into consideration for war purposes in so far as they could be farmed out or mortgaged. The customs were gradually increased, but inasmuch as they were too numerous and their aims were not economic, but fiscal, the attempts to increase them raised so much ill-feeling that they could not be carried far, when the home industry was insufficient for the requirements of the country or where trade was the most important source of income. England alone at this time enjoyed a highly productive tariff which was adapted to the furtherance of national economic ends.

The publicists of the Renaissance never failed to urge the princes to collect a war chest, but only in a few instances was their advice followed. The Emperor Frederic III, King Henry VII of England, Pope Julius II, the Duke Galeazzo Maria Sforza of Milan, and Alfonso I of Ferrara, had some of them laid in large stores of ready money and some large treasures in jewels and gold and silver plate, and in the case of the Italian princes we have mentioned how their policy profited to the full from their forethought. The same cannot be said of the more important princes outside Italy. If they were good managers they did not pursue an active foreign policy, and if they did so, they were not good managers. A careful prince always had for his successor a spendthrift who did not understand how to utilize his predecessor's financial policy. Thus Frederick III was succeeded by Maximilian I and Henry VII by Henry VIII. King Louis XI and Louis XII of France, and Ferdinand and Isabella of Spain held their property together with a firm hand, but did not go so far as to form a war chest. When such a treasure was collected in other countries it was never sufficient to carry on years of European war. Charles V and Philip II, who had enormous national treasures in gold and silver in their territories, used these to carry out their worldwide plans. All the treasures of Peru and Mexico proved inadequate in the long run, and in any case they were not easily accessible in Italy, Picardy, Flanders, or Germany.

The possibility of raising extraordinary war taxes depended in the first place on the power of the prince over his subjects. This power was of very different degrees in different countries, Germany and France being the two extreme points. In Germany the Emperor, when the Empire was in extremity, usually obtained little or no help from the Diet of the Empire, while in France the Crown was often able on occasions of far less urgency to obtain the grant of millions. But in France itself, the long wars could not be carried on by means of such taxes; they were insufficient and came in much too slowly. No European prince was as yet able to impose taxes in kind or grants,[1] and the prosperity of the agricultural mass of the people had not yet reached such a point that it was possible to get anything by turning the tax screw. The

---

[1] Philippe de Commines, *Mémoires*, V. 19: 'Y a il roy ne seigneur sur terre qui ait povoir, oultre son demaine, de mettre un denier sur ses subjects sans octroy et consentement de ceulx qui le doibvent payer, simon par tyrannie ou viollence.'

nobility and the Church, who were the greatest landowners, submitted themselves to taxation with a particularly ill-grace; the tax-paying capacity of the nobles, who themselves suffered from a chronic deficit, was usually not large; while the Church, which could have paid more, only did so when this served its own interest. The cities were able to pay and usually disposed to tax, or in case of necessity they could be compelled to do so. In fact they were heavily taxed, but the princes had to take care not to kill the goose that laid the golden eggs. In the case of a sudden urgent need of capital even in the cities it was as a general rule only possible to obtain the necessary sums as a loan.

Among financial prerogatives the Mint was far the most productive and it was also the only one whose yield could be increased at short notice. Many princes, both in the Middle Ages and later in the sixteenth and seventeenth centuries, did a roaring business in currency depreciation. Trade, however, learned to guard itself against bad coining on the part of the authorities, both by having its own particular trade currencies and by the development of money surrogates. This considerably diminished the profit to be made out of currency depreciation. The princes themselves also began to perceive that this barbaric financial expedient was in the last resort ruinous for themselves; and in the large states, at any rate, it was only adopted in the case of extreme necessity.

Its place was taken by another method of raising money still more objectionable from the political and economic point of view. This was the sale of offices. The growth in the number of officials led to the same step as the development of the army. The princes left the fulfilment of the new duties to private undertakers. We shall see this phenomenon more especially in the domain of financial administration, when in the Renaissance period the system of farming out the taxes came into extensive use. The sale of offices extended also to other branches of the administration and even to the judicature. It was the most prevalent in the French and the Papal administrative systems. In both instance new offices were created on a large scale, only in order to be sold. This process could, however, not be repeated sufficiently often, and on the whole was not productive enough to be of much weight in view of the continued increase of war expenditure.[1]

The most rough and ready of all financial expedients, the sale of the Crown lands, had even in the feudal state outrun the bounds of expediency. The enfeoffing of Crown lands had in most cases constituted a permanent alienation. It had been carried so far in Germany that towards the end of the Middle Ages there was no Imperial domain land properly speaking. The efforts of the German Emperors to get it back

[1] Cf. Woker, *Das kirchliche Finanzwesen der Päpste*, p. 6. For France cf. B. Picot, *Histoire des Etats généraux*, I, 434 ff., II, 117 ff.

were for long brought to nought by their pressing need of money and were turned in the contrary direction. On the other hand, the domains of the House of Hapsburg had increased largely; the same was true of the other states where the feudal system had produced the same consequences, the feudal lords had for a long time striven with growing success to get back the lost Crown domains. It was on this account that towards the end of the Middle Ages the sale of parts of the domains or their revenues was everywhere regarded as a desperate financial expedient. The mortgaging of portions of the domain lands (i.e. the sources of revenue) was rightly regarded as equivalent to sale, while the pledging of the revenues was a favourite and general expedient.

These methods of covering extraordinary monetary requirements were either no longer or not yet applicable. They were all more or less objectionable from a political or economic point of view. Moreover, even when they were sufficient for the requirements of war, they could not be applied with sufficient speed to meet the case, nor sufficient ease to meet the wishes of the princes, who accordingly were as a rule reduced to the use of credit.

The Beginnings and Bases of Public Credit. Public credit exists as soon as there is any public authority. The chief, who in return for services expected or received promised his subject or follower a service in return, was bringing public credit into play. If this return was to be periodic or annual, it assumed the character of a funded debt, this was also the case when one prince became liable to pay tribute to another. Every purchase, on the other hand, which a prince undertook without cash payment constituted a floating debt. The distinguishing sign of public credit is already present. The debtor who cannot, or will not, pay cannot be constrained by law (though he may be compelled by force) to fulfil his obligation, because the authority which is his as lord can prevent the compulsory application of the law.

A Nuremberg merchant of the sixteenth century, on an occasion when it was feared that the French Crown would cease to pay its debts, declared that 'Great lords do as they will.' The essence of public credit is already recognized here. It means that of the three conditions for any credit – the belief that the debtor can, will and must pay – the third condition is usually absent unless the creditor can assert his claim by the use of force. The growth of the general feeling for justice exercised a certain pressure on the debtor and made him keep his engagements even in the case of public credit, and the increase of economic insight told in the same direction. But even at the present day we often see that these motives are insufficient to prevent gross violations of public credit. In earlier times matters were even worse. Anyone who gave credit to a prince knew that the repayment of the debt depended only on his debtor's capacity and will to pay.[1] The case was very different for the cities, who had power as overlords, but were also corporations, associations of individuals held in a common bond. According to the generally accepted law each individual burgher was liable for the debts of the city both with his person and his property. Should the city fail in its engagements the creditor was entitled to recourse against the person and property of any burgher who fell into his power. The cities, even as late as the sixteenth century, expressly gave this right to their creditors, who on occasion knew how to take advantage of it. It constituted an effective means of compulsion, for the burghers were often forced by their trade to remain outside the protection of their city with a considerable amount of their property. From an economic point of view this motive was of great importance. The general principle that the holder of public authority could not have the law he had broken enforced against him, was not infringed but confirmed by this right of the creditors of cities.[2]

Connected with this is a still more far-reaching and fundamental difference between the debts of princes and cities. The fact that all burghers were liable for the debts of their cities, while this was certainly not the case without more in regard to the subjects of princes was decisive for the chief basis of any credit, the ability to pay. The princes' capacity to pay depended first of all on the amount of the revenues from their domains. As these were never sufficient to pay the interest on large debts, or even to repay the capital, the most important consideration in a prince's capacity to pay was his power over the purses of his subjects. This power, as we saw, had various degrees, but never went so far that the subjects were liable without more to meet the prince's debts.

Towards the end of the Middle Ages in some countries princes had the right of raising forced loans from their subjects. They could also, as we shall see, use the credit of the cities for loans for their own expenditure. For the loans, however, which they themselves raised the sole guarantee besides their domains was the taxes expressly granted by their subjects. If the subjects were themselves to be liable for such debts, a special grant by Parliament was needful; and in order to obtain this the princes usually had to make some concession in return, e.g. to

---

[1] Too much importance is attached to primal rights in regard to public credit. This is true, e.g. of the otherwise excellent work of A. v. Kostanecki, *Der öffentl. Credit im Mittelalter* (Schmollers Staats- und socialwissenschaftl. Forschungen 1889, IX. 1). P. 11 ff. especially do not sufficiently distinguish between public and private credit.

[2] Gierke (*Deutsches Genossenschaftsrecht*, II, 383 ff. 770), cf. Kostanecki l. c. p. 12. (*Remembrancia* 1579–1664, *Analyt. Index.* London, 1878, p. 189 ff. and *Fugger Archiv*, 48, 6.)

make over some definite revenues of their own for the interest and repayments of the debt. This was usually the condition imposed before
the princes were allowed to avail themselves of the credit of the cities.
The princes, however, strove with increasing success to convert the
voluntary contractual liability for certain of the princes' debts on the
part of their subjects into a general and compulsory liability arising
from the authority of the princes. Long and violent struggles were
necessary to attain this end. Meanwhile loans at high interest were
greatly hated by the people, and this naturally hampered the princes in
their financial operations. In the case of the debts of princes there was
never any question of unlimited solidarity, as in the case of the city
debts.

Even in the cities the burghers often forbade the council to burden the
city with debt without their consent. While therefore the princes after
centuries of struggle extended their power, which had been strictly
limited by contract, the authorities in the towns had their previously
unlimited powers restricted in this way. Even at this later time, however, there were hardly any city loans for which the whole community
was not liable, while even at the time when the princes' power had
reached its highest there were always some princes' loans for which the
subjects were not responsible.

Even when the subjects had to meet the debts of their princes, this
did not result in such a large increase of capacity to pay as that which
the cities enjoyed through the personal liability of their burghers. The
burghers were the class of the population economically the soundest
and possessed of the most capital, while among the princes' subjects
there were very few of this type.

In regard to the will to pay, also, conditions were not usually very
favourable in the case of princes. Lending at interest continued to be
strictly forbidden both by ecclesiastical and secular law, and though
certain princes in the sixteenth century transformed the ban on interest
into a interest tax, the doctrine of usury offered them a most useful
handle for breaking the most solemn promises to pay, if their ceaseless
money difficulties became specially pressing. The princes and their
advisers seldom had sufficient economic foresight and insight to be
deterred by higher considerations from the momentarily desirable
state bankruptcy. Such considerations weighed the less with them as
the creditors were very often not of the country, but foreign merchants
or bankers; and also because princes were less affected by the economic
weal or woe of their subjects than they now are.

In the cities ruled by merchants, whose creditors were as a rule
their own citizens or those of a friendly city, the situation was entirely
different.

If a prince died, his successor as such was not bound to take over his predecessor's debts.

Though as a matter of fact they were mostly taken over in the sixteenth century, this was less due to a sense of justice than because the successor in his monetary requirements was usually dependent on his predecessor's creditors.

Even in the second half of the eighteenth century the jurists were by no means agreed on this point whether a prince was bound to recognize the debts of his predecessor; and examples are not wanting to show that this was not invariably the case.[1] In any change of government the creditors of the Crown were in great anxiety on account of their claims, if they had lacked the foresight to get the heir as a co-signatory.

While the legal principle that 'le roi est mort, vive le roi' was not applied automatically to the prince's debts, the cities were perpetual persons in the present legal sense that though the holders of public authority might change it remained unaffected thereby.

We see accordingly that the three first principles of all credit – the belief that the debtor can, will and must pay – were weak in earlier times in the credit given to princes, but strong in the case of that given to cities. The cities accordingly enjoyed much better credit than the princes. In fact, even towards the end of the Middle Ages the latter had, properly speaking, no credit, that is no personal credit at all. About the middle of the eighteenth century it was considered necessary to remind the capitalists of the old saying, 'Lend not to him who is mightier than thou; or if thou lendest, look upon thy loan as lost.' [2]

This held good of all loans the repayment of which the prince promised 'in verbo principis' without other security than his princely word. As Cardinal Granvella was credited by his contemporaries with the proverb in regard to such financial obligations that 'There is a time to promise and a time to keep,' so in Germany in the previous century the saying went, 'The noble makes promises and the peasant keeps them.' [3]

Loans of Princes. As the princes, as such, had very little personal credit, they had regularly to give security for their loans. Only one kind of loan formed an exception, the forced loan, and this played an important part. Since the thirteenth century the princes more and more contracted the habit of obtaining forced loans from those among their subjects who relied on their protection or were in some other way dependent on them, and who also had liquid capital at their disposal. These, how-

---

[1] Cf. e.g. Joh. Frd. Kobii, *Commentatio juris praesertim germanici – de pecunia mutuaticia tuto collocanda* (Göttingen 1761), § 37.

[2] 'Noli foenerari fortiori te, quod si foeneraveris, quasi perditum habe,' *Ecclesiasticus* viii, 15, quoted in Kobius l.c. § 36).

[3] Granvella's saying is quoted by a representative of the Welser in 1547 (*Ztschr. d. histor. Ver. f. Schwaben* 1875, p. 131). The second cf. Kobius l.c. § 24.

ever, were regarded by the princes themselves, still more by their subjects, not as real loans, but as a kind of tax, and actually they were for the most part indirect taxes.

The princes anticipated taxes which had been already passed, but which did not come in sufficiently fast, by the method of forcing their rich subjects to advance the amount of the tax according to an arbitrary estimate. No special charge on the tax was given for the most part, and there was no interest.[1] Such forced loans were often imposed before the taxes from which they were to be repaid had been granted. The object was then clearly to render illusory the right of the States General to grant the taxes. In any case, forced loans were most in favour with princes of absolutist tendencies, chiefly with Louis XI and his successors on the French throne, until from the time of Richelieu the Crown no longer sought to cover itself by the device of the forced loan, but could levy direct taxes of every kind without calling the States. In England, on the other hand, under Henry VIII, Elizabeth, and James I, the forced loan had at times been very common, but in 1628 the Crown was forced, owing to the growing resistance of Parliament, to renounce a financial expedient which the people had always bitterly hated.

In other countries, also, the subjects did all they could to ward off forced loans; and even in France the Crown was not sufficiently powerful in the sixteenth century for it to be able to cover all its extraordinary monetary requirements by such loans. In view of the crushing burden of interest due to the undue extension of credit through voluntary loans in the second half of the sixteenth century, a writer like Botero [2] with absolutist tendencies might be disposed to praise forced loans without interest; and the princes themselves found it advisable in time of great monetary requirements to make use as far as possible of voluntary loans. These moreover often contained an indirect compulsion, e.g. the creditors were induced to lend again by the fear of losing their old claims, and foreign merchants were threatened with the withdrawal of their privileges if they declined to help the King with advances – and other terrorism of the same kind.

There were, on the other hand, some forced loans which, from the fact that they were called for at a moment of general patriotic emotion, had the character of semi-voluntary loans – e.g. in France after the battle of St. Quentin in 1557, or in England in 1588 when the country had to be defended against the Spanish Armada. When the French

[1] Royal appeals for forced loans: Louis XII of France (1513) (in *Régistres des deliberations du Bureau de la Ville de Paris* I, 201 ff.); and James I of England in 1625 (Rushworth, *Histor. Coll.* I, 124).

[2] *Ragion di Stato*, II, 7. Cf., on the other hand, Diomede Carafa (about 1470), in Fornari, *Teor. econom. n. Prov. napolit.*, p. 59.

Crown demanded loans from the cities, and the citizens had their shares compulsorily allotted to them, this was not a forced loan proper, since capital and interest were secured on certain definite revenues. In the case of the true variety, the creditors regularly ran the risk of losing their capital, without getting high interest as a compensation for the risk incurred. Owners of capital had usually to be brought to make loans of this kind by compulsion.

In voluntary loans, on the other hand, they demanded not only high interest, but also security in the form of a guarantee or pledge.

We have already spoken of the guarantee of the heir apparent. Next to this stood that of the highest officials and dignitaries, which was very general in the Netherlands in the sixteenth century. The Diet of a province sometimes guaranteed the loan contracted by the prince, but much the most general form was the guarantee of a respected city, e.g. London in the case of the loans of the English Crown, or Antwerp in the case of the loans of the Court of the Netherlands.

If the prince promised himself to defray the interest and repayment, the surety was only liable if he was in default. In many cases, however, the loan was not contracted by the prince, but in the name of the official, noble, Diet or city on the prince's account. This was a different relation from a legal point of view, but from an economic standpoint it came to the same thing. It is not the credit of the prince, but that of the high official, or city, which was the decisive factor. The most important of the intermediaries who gave their credit for the prince were the financial officials and the cities.

The chief difference between the financial administration of the modern state and the older system is the prevalence under the latter of the system of farming out the revenues. The cities as well as the princes farmed out their revenues, and the system extended as the increased use of money made the financial administration a special art. The princes had not the necessary staff of officials, and it would have been the height of foolishness to have the many small monetary revenues collected by poorly paid venal officials. It was very important for the princes to have their revenues at their disposal in large sums at the place and time when they needed them. They accordingly made over the collection of many revenues to private undertakers, who were able to make advances on them. In the case of the cities, the first reason was not equally cogent. If nevertheless they employed the system, it must have corresponded to some general need.

The entire revenues, however, were not farmed out, and the princes and cities accordingly needed their own financial officials. The same causes, however, which made it necessary to employ tax farmers caused the officials to be chosen from the class which alone was technically and economically qualified for the duties of their position, that is the merchant class. There was no radical distinction between financial officials and tax farmers. The farmers were for the most part the agents and the sleeping partners of the officials. They formed one class which we will consider in detail later.[1]

These financiers who administered the princes' revenues enjoyed good credit, both from their position and because in general they were rich merchants. They employed this for a consideration – for the princes, either making advances themselves or obtaining them in their own names from other capitalists. Their credit was therefore the most important of the various elements from which the state credit was afterwards formed.

The princes, as we see, could only cover their extraordinary monetary requirements through voluntary loans by availing themselves of the credit of their magnates and high officials, diets, cities, or financiers. This was only done by their giving a security to those who allowed them to use their credit, as the lenders proper greatly preferred this to the mere guarantee. The security might be a pledge as was the case when it consisted of jewels or other valuables. Only loans of small amount could be raised on pledges of this description, and therefore since the end of the Middle Ages they ceased to be important. The same holds good of the mortgaging of individual Crown lands, a process which the princes held to be equivalent to sale and therefore disliked. The most usual form of security was the mortgaging definite revenues. Not only in the case of loans, but in all the prince's debts, even in the case of small purchases of commodities on credit or pensions to servants, as well as for periodic payments to foreign princes, the creditor expected to have his claim secured on a definite branch of the prince's revenue. By means of such warrants (assignations, consignations, libranzas, tallies) the creditor received a legal title to the payment of his claim, and this often contained the authority in case of necessity to satisfy himself directly from the revenue upon which he had been given security.

This authority, however, only constituted a sufficient security when the income accrued direct to the creditor without the agency of the prince's officials. This was often expressly stipulated, especially in the case of larger loans, either in connection with the leasing of the revenue in question; or by collecting the yield of the revenue without taking over the lease until the creditor had obtained satisfaction both for capital and interest; or finally by a formal purchase of the princely revenues, which then became the property of the lender.

---

[1] *Lettres et mémoires de Colbert ed. Clément II*, p. cxcix. Colbert enunciated the principle that 'Un financier doit estre auprès d'un surintendant ce qui est un soldat auprès de son capitaine; il ne doit l'abandonner qu'avec la vie.'

The necessity for giving security on definite revenues, or for pledging or selling them to creditors is a chief cause of endless subdivisions, which, along with the system of farming out the revenues, was a characteristic of the old financial system of the princes as opposed to the modern system. This necessity it was which brought to naught the attempts of princes to reorganize and unify their finances, so long as there was a load of debt which could be lightened by farming the taxes or splitting them up.[1]

The system exemplifies a vicious circle. Excessive indebtedness on the part of the princes was made necessary by the conditions we have seen. It could not be borne without the system of farming out the taxes or the pledging of individual branches of revenue. This led to a frightful degeneration of the financial system, which was unavoidable while the circumstances lasted, which led to the repeated heaping up of debts.

Incurable financial disorganization, corruption of the whole of public life, dependence of the Government on the financiers, exhaustion of the people – these ills, which proved the ruin of many states, sprang immediately from the farming out and splitting up of the finances of the princes. They would have been impossible without an undue extension of credit. They were, however, rooted most deeply, on the one hand in the princes' passion for war and glory, and on the other in the progress, especially the irregular progress of an economic system based on the use of money.

The loans of princes were usually at first 'anticipations,' floating debts. These could never be entirely avoided, and we can prove that they existed already in the earliest Middle Ages. Nevertheless French publicists, from Bodin to Boisguillebert, are not wrong when they put the real beginning of the regular large anticipations in the last years of the reign of Francis I and the time of Henry II of France.[2] For it was at this epoch that the interest-bearing floating debt became a necessary part of the princes' budgets. These could not have existed without the debt, which, however, proved their ruin.

The floating debt had a fatal effect in the first place because of the enormous interest, and secondly because in the excessive subdivision of the whole financial system; the individual parts of the princes' revenue were often burdened with charges far in excess of the total income.

An extensive system of mortgages without a register gives only

---

[1] Adler, *Die Organisation der Centralverwaltung unter Kaiser Maximilian I.* Cf. e.g. for France: R. Brown, *Calendar of State papers*, VI, 956, 1557; for Spain: Brit. Mus. Cott. MSS. Vespasian C. VI, fol. 133 ff , 1575.

[2] Bodin, *Les six livres de la république.* Paris 1583, VI, 2. Boisguillebert, *Factum de la France en Da"re*, p. 297 ff.

a weak analogy for the state of confusion and fraudulent over-indebtedness which perpetually characterized the finances of most princes.

Funded loans at the end of the Middle Ages were still relatively un-important for the princes in comparison with the floating debt. Most princes did not raise any funded debt, and we shall see that even those who apparently did so, really concluded transactions of a rather differ-ent kind. Here we must distinguish between funded debts in the wider and funded loans in the narrower sense, between the loans raised by the princes themselves and those which their parliaments and cities raised for them or took over from them. From early times the princes had secured on separate parts of their income both non-recurrent expendi-ture and also recurrent expenses such as official salaries, pensions, donations, annual payments to the Church. To the extent of this burden these portions were pledged during the lives of the officials, pen-sioners, etc., or permanently alienated; for quite apart from the per-manent payments made to the Church, it early came about that persons who were granted payment or pensions as an act of grace were given the right of handing them on to their heirs.[1] These grants already approxi-mated closely to our state 'rentes' or annuities, except for the fact that they were always 'situated' on some definite branch of the princes' revenues and also they originated, not because the recipients had handed over capital in return for the annuity, but because they had served or were about to be serviceable to the prince in some other way.

The conception of the 'perpetual debt' had therefore been introduced in practice with the financial system of the princes long before a per-petual authority of the state was recognized in principle. The separate branches of the princes' revenues were regarded as real property which could be burdened with perpetual rent charges in the same way as land.

Probably the princes had always known how to obtain, not only other services, but also capital by securing life or perpetual annuities; for the cities had done so from very early times. The first certain instance of such a transaction, however, in the case of a prince, occurs only in the second half of the fifteenth century, and then only in the case of the Kings of Castile. Even the Popes, whose property and income were cer-tainly well established, did not begin till the year 1526 to get money for themselves by funded loans ('monti') on the model of the Italian city

---

[1] For such changes in revenues of Counts of Champagne *see* de Joubainville, *Histoire des Ducs et Des Comtes de Champagne*, V, 849. For the burden on the revenues of the French Crown 'tam ad vitam quam perpetuo' in 1316 cf. Vuitry, *Etudes sur le Régime Financier de la France*, New Series, I, 4,

states.[1] In France the first rentes began to be issued by the cities in 1522, especially by the city of Paris on behalf of the Crown, and it was long before the Crown could dispense with the cities as intermediaries. The English funded debt starts with the revolution of 1689. In the Middle Ages the rulers of the Netherlands frequently adopted the expedient of the sale of annuities. But in this case also they employed as intermediaries the diets or the individual cities which 'lent their seal' to the prince. The diets or cities concluded the arrangements for the loan and the princes pledged themselves to pay the annuities for them. Later as the power of the rulers increased, they ceased to ask the diets or cities for their consent and issued annuities on their own account. They then funded them on the individual provinces or cities, transferring revenues to them for the payment of the annuities. During the sixteenth century many annuities on a large scale were issued in this form. The next step forward was that revenues were no longer assigned. But even in the Netherlands in the sixteenth century there is no instance of a prince selling annuities without charging them on a province or a city.[2]

A prince, as such, had not the power of raising large funded loans, if he had not at his disposition the credit of the corporately organized diets or cities. It is characteristic that the funded debt of the Spanish Crown in the sixteenth and seventeenth centuries increased chiefly through the repeated state bankruptcies. These always ended by the Crown undertaking a compulsory funding operation of its gigantic floating debt, i.e. it reduced the interest by 100–200 per cent. and did away with the obligation to repay the capital.[3] The Crown could not obtain the enormous sums it required directly by funded loans. It therefore first contracted floating debts at a high rate of interest and every twenty or thirty years converted this compulsorily into funded loans. These, however, were only saleable at a large discount, as though they were always charged on definite revenues. This was only a nominal security as each head of the revenue had long been over charged, and moreover was almost as a regular thing withdrawn from the creditors in case of need. In this the Church lent ready aid to the Crown by means of the ban of usury.

[1] *Codigos Españoles*, VI, 446; VII, 275. *Mem. de la Real Acad. de la hist.* VI, 141 ff. Molina, *De justit. et jure*, II, *Disp.* 383, No. 15. Cf. Coppi, *Finanze dello Stato Ponteficio*, Roma, 1855, p. 3 ff.; Ranke, *Fürsten und Völker von Südeuropa*, IV, 10 ff.; Vührer, *Histoire de la dette publique en France*, I, 15 ff.; Sinclair, *History of the Public Revenue of the British Empire*, II, 57.

[2] Cf. Blok in *den Bijdragen voor vaderl. geschied.* 3, part, 124; and for later times the State Archives at Brussels, *Chambre des Comptes*, No. 434.

[3] Peri, *Il Negotiante*, about 1640, calls the Juros 'Una sorte di pagamento dato e ricevuto da qualch' anni in qua per necessità.'

We must now shortly discuss the practical significance of the ecclesiastical ban against interest on loans, towards the end of the Middle Ages. We must here make clear a point which has given rise to many errors, namely the relation between interest and annuity.

The Practical Importance of the Ecclesiastical Doctrine of Usury. In spite of the ban of the Church interest-bearing loans had at the end of the Middle Ages been for centuries an everyday legal transaction. It was nevertheless regarded as a gross sin. In the Papal indulgences money gained through usury was put on a level with stolen goods. Jurisprudence also held strictly to this view.[1] Whether the 'usurers' themselves, that is the whole body of merchants, had uneasy consciences when they received interest, is not easy to say; but certainly this was true of not a few of them. In the twelfth and thirteenth centuries merchants often, or perhaps regularly, directed in their wills that their heirs should restore their gains from usury or should employ them for the salvation of the testator's soul.[2] By the end of the Middle Ages this was no longer a general custom. Even in the sixteenth century, however, it often happened that merchants took a legal opinion as to whether this or that undertaking was permissible under canon law. In the year 1577 an agent of the Fugger in Spain writes of a Genoese Lazaro Doria recently dead: 'He was of so ticklish a conscience that he dealt not in bills or commerce against which the preachers and theologians here write and rage.' He had added in his will, where mention was made of the restoration of forbidden profits, that he had no load upon his conscience, for he had never had his own capital nor yet paid it into a business partnership, but had borrowed on bills all the money he had used for such dealings. The hair-splittings of the doctrine of usury had had such a distorting effect on the feeling of merchants, reputed conscientious, that they regarded it as a sin to 'commit usury' with their own but not with borrowed money. Nevertheless a feeling of this kind did still exist, and even when the voice of conscience was silent people knew that the loan at interest was forbidden both by the ecclesiastical and the secular law, and that therefore law could not be invoked on behalf of the creditor. The doctrine, however, excepted from its ban the loans of princes and cities, declaring that such loans served the common weal. This, however, was an uncertain reservation, and all 'usurers' moved, if not by fear of eternal punishment, then by the dread of losing their capital, tried to find a cloak for their operations. It was this that gave rise to the

---

[1] Woker, *Das kirchl. Finanzwesen d. Päpste*, p. 105. Endemann, *Studien in der romanisch-kanonist. Wirthschafts- und Rechtslehre*, II, 378 ff.

[2] Mandelli, *Il commune di Vercelli nel medio evo*, II, 135. A will of this kind occurs, e.g. *Histor. patr. monum.* VI (Chart II), 829.

many fine phrases used from ancient times down to the sixteenth, or even seventeenth, century in place of the objectionable word.[1]

Commerce of course found many ways of getting round the ban on interest. The interest was added directly to the capital, or in what appeared as a bill transaction the interest was smuggled into the price of the bills; or commodities were lent in place of ready money and then charged at a high rate; or the loan was made in the form of a deposit, which was permissible, and so forth. The Church and the Law recognized many of these forms, thus opening the door for the evasion of their own bans. The distinctions which were made were, however, so numerous and fine-drawn, and the views of the ecclesiastical and legal experts differed so widely as to what was permissible, that in the centuries between the first lightening of the ban on usury and its removal by legislation commerce was never free from uncertainty. Owners of capital were always learning afresh from experience that this ban on usury would be involved by any debtor who could not pay, but more especially by bankrupt princes, not only to get out of their financial obligations with greater ease, but to give an air of legality to the proceeding. They knew moreover that this was passionately desired by all the prince's subjects who were not his creditors, and that the fact that a princely bankruptcy was a popular act made it so much the easier.

These circumstances all combined to raise still further the interest on the princes' loans, which was in any case not low. This again increased the princes' financial difficulties and the popular hatred against the ' usurers'. There was no escape from this vicious circle. This situation lasted in most countries throughout the sixteenth century.

There was only one permissible form of credit business, and this was permissible because it was not considered as credit – the purchase of annuities. In the times when dealing in kind was the prevalent system this custom originated from the necessity of finding a form for the alienation of rights to revenue in kind, and with the development of the use of money the purchase of rentes became the most usual form for the investment of capital. At this stage it was not the need of capital, but the need of investment which was most powerful in making general the purchase of annuities. This can be proved from facts, but is quite obvious if we compare the purchase of an annuity with a loan.

In the case where credit is sought and obtained, this is usually in the form of a loan where the lender reserves the right to demand the return

---

[1] A selection of these phrases: Latin: Lucrum, fictum, damnum, interesse, donum, guiderdonum, remuneratio, premium, costamenta. Italian: Dono, prode, bene, guadagno, gracie, civanza. French: Don, frais, finance. English: Reward, interest, consideration, gratuity. German. Abnützung, Verehrung, Pension, etc.

of his capital. In the case of a purchase of annuities, however, the lender expressly renounces this right. He buys an annual sum, and if he wants his capital back, he cannot apply to the recipient of the purchase money, but must resell the annuity to a third party. This important distinction made it possible for the Church to justify the principle of the purchase of annuities – a fact which strengthened its general popularity.[1] This could only come about because the need for investment was general and continually increasing among circles which were not accustomed, like the merchants, to lend and borrow at interest. Owners of capital who were not merchants only occasionally felt the need to raise capital and were usually concerned to find a profitable investment for it. What they wanted was not a temporary investment like the merchants, but something permanent. This they found in the purchase of annuities.

The chief sellers of annuities in the Middle Ages were the cities, whose credit, from the reasons we know, was so good that any owner of capital was glad to buy an annuity from them. Hence it arose that the annuity was at a lower rate of interest in the purchase price than the interest on loans, even when the loan was secured on real property and the annuity was not; for we shall see that the annuity loans of the cities as a rule were not secured on any particular property.

The sale of annuities became very early for the cities, and later for the princes, a means of procuring capital for any special requirements. Annuity loans of this kind approximated, in fact, to ordinary loans; but in form they remained sales of annuities. The annuity was the return for a permanent and irrevocable transfer of capital, interest for a temporary and revocable one. The conceptions of interest and annuity were therefore distinct.[2] We shall discuss later how they were related in practice.

Loans of the Cities. Towards the end of the Middle Ages an increasing indebtedness descended on the cities as well as on the princes. The *independent cities* had not only to carry on many wars as they had done before, but had to put forth all their strength to resist the attacks of the princes on their liberty. The citizens had long ceased to take the field themselves, and the mercenary system was nowhere more fully developed than in the cities. The growth of the use of fire-arms had forced them to surround themselves with stronger fortifications, and their regular revenues, often very large, were never sufficient to produce the enormous

---

[1] Endemann, l.c., II, 125, does not sufficiently stress this distinction. Cf. for the opposite Bodin, *Les Six Livres de la République* (1583), VI, 2.

[2] This distinction was drawn even in the seventeenth century, and the commercial world. Cf. Van Neulighem in his Boeckhouden (1630) distinguishes: 1. Geld op renten geven op huysen oft lant; 2. Geld op deposito oft interest geven.

sums needed. The credit of the cities therefore was accordingly their most powerful weapon in the struggle for their freedom.

Those cities, moreover, which had either lost their freedom or had never been free were forced by their lord to strain their credit ever increasingly for his benefit. It was, however, as we have seen, so good, and the need of an investment in the cities themselves so great, that they usually had little difficulty in satisfying their credit requirements. Only when the demand was very sudden and large, the cities also had to resort to forced loans, which were quite differently conditioned from those of the princes. They were assessed on the citizens like taxes; interest was paid and the public revenues were given as security. Nevertheless there was in later times an increasing disinclination to resort to forced loans, e.g. in Florence, where there had been frequent forced loans since the beginning of the fourteenth century, the historian Guicciardini at the beginning of the sixteenth century advised their discontinuance on the ground that they were tiresome and intricate and disturbed the city as much as new taxes. In place of them he recommended floating loans, anticipations, which cost more, especially if they lasted some time so that they had to be renewed several times. The fact, however, that the community had to raise a few thousand ducats was less important than the discontent caused by taxes or forced loans.[1]

We must regard this as the view prevailing among those responsible for the cities' financial policy, for as a matter of fact forced loans lost their importance in the cities towards the end of the Middle Ages. The republic of Florence, if we keep to one chosen example, returned to them in the exigencies of its last struggle. After the fall of the republic the Medici used them on a large scale, though now no interest was paid nor definite revenues given as security.[2]

Apart from sudden demands for capital on an unusually large scale the cities were easily able to raise the capital they required by means of voluntary loans and sales of annuities. Indeed, so great was the disposition to invest money with them that they often carried on a regular banking business. At the beginning of the seventeenth century George Obrecht writes: 'In our times certain cities borrow large sums of money at 5 per cent. and lend them out again at 8 per cent.'[3]

The oldest city loans were everywhere floating loans, anticipations of

[1] Guicciardini, *Opere inedite*, X, 351. He calls forced loans 'Accatti universali da' ricchi.' Originally every 'accatto' was a forced loan.

[2] Varchi, *Stor. fiorent. ad. a.* 1530. Albéri, *Relaz. d. ambasc. venet.* II, 32 ff., 346. Reumont, *Gesch. Toskanas*, I, 114.

[3] Obrecht, *Polit. Bedencken und Discurs von Verbesserung Land und Leut.* 1617, p. 128. For the fourteenth and fifteenth centuries cf. Schönberg, *Finanzverhältnisse der Stadt Basel*, p. 102 ff. Kostanecki, *Der öffentl. Credit im Mittelalter*, p. 41 ff.

definite revenues. It had been the custom from early times that should these revenues prove insufficient, the whole city with all its citizens should be liable for the debt.[1] A development took place in two directions: On the one hand, the floating debts were to an increasing extent replaced by funded loans; and on the other, the charge on definite revenues was abandoned and replaced by the primary liability of the whole city and all its individual citizens.

Towards the end of the Middle Ages the sale of annuities in its various forms was the most usual method for the cities to raise capital. The annuities were mostly sold, to use the apt phrase of the Netherlands, 'Opt corpus der stadt.' [2] Besides this, however, there were frequent cases of mortgaging definite revenues and real property belonging to the cities, even in the case of funded loans. This was even more frequent in the case of the floating debts which no city could entirely dispense with. Even Venice in the beginning of the sixteenth century had to resort to the pawning of jewels. At the end of the Middle Ages as a general rule princes raised money by anticipations and cities by the sale of annuities.

The organization of the debts of the cities was naturally most highly developed in Italy. Great attention has therefore been paid to the Italian Monti of the Middle Ages, without, however, arriving at a satisfactory conclusion. An attempt has been made to import modern conceptions and classify the Monti accordingly. Were they state loans or banks, syndicates of state creditors and tax-farmers, or limited liability companies? The truth is that they contained the germs of all these modern arrangements, which developed from them at a later time.[3]

We cannot look for the chief root of the Monti in the tax-farming system, which since Roman times had never really died out in Italy. It was already very general in the cities at an extraordinarily early date.[4] The lease of the taxes was designated as a 'sale,' though the cities originally never intended permanently to alienate their revenues. This came

---

[1] For example, Vercelli, *Hist. patr. monum.* VI (Chart II), No. 1516. Manelli, *Il commune di Vercelli nel medio evo*, II, 104. Troyes in Champagne. D'Arbois de Joubainville, *Histoire des Ducs et des Comtes de Champagne*, IV, 729.

[2] 'Opt lichaem der stadt' or 'op heure ende op alle heure ingesetene goeden,' or 'pour le corps de la ville et pour chacune manière de gens non labourans et labourans,' Gilliodts, *Inventaire*, I, 389, *Antw. Arch. Bl.* I, 36 ff.

[3] Morpurgo, *La critica storica e gli studi intorno alle instituz. finanz.* 1877. Goldschmidt, *Universalgesch. d. Handelsrechts*, p. 291 ff. Endemann, *Studien in d. roman. kanonist. Wirthsch.- u. Rechtslehre*, I. 431 ff. Rezasco, *Dizionario d. ling. ital stor. ed amministr. s. v. monte, luogho, compera*. Cecchetti, *La vita d. Veneziani fino al* 1200, p. 71 ff. Cuneo, *Mem. sopra l'antico debito pubblico di Genova*. Lobero, 'Mem. stor. d. Banca di S. Giorgio,' *Lib. jur Genuens.* I, 171, 176, 177 ff.

[4] For this farming-out system of the city of Genoa, *see Liber. jur. Gen.* I, 77, 139, 141, 144, 159 ff.

about in the course of things.[1] The extraordinary requirements of the cities necessitated anticipations of the farmed revenues, which were regularly asked and granted at the time of the contract. Need of money once again brought about a renewal of the connection and the grant of further advances. Finally there was a definite funding of the floating debt. This also happened many times in the case of forced loans which it was not possible – or more usually, was not held expedient – to repay; [2] for the need of a means of investing capital, which we have already emphasized, made itself increasingly felt in the Italian cities.

Originally the lease of the city revenues and the making of advances upon them was a commercial undertaking, which, however, could not be carried on by individual merchants on account of the large amount of capital required. It was accordingly necessary to form companies for this purpose. So, for example, the first voluntary loan we hear of for the Venetian Republic was taken up in the year 1164 by a company constituted as follows: two persons with two shares apiece, two with one, one with a half-share and two with a quarter-share; and it is possible that other unnamed persons may have been interested under the names of these chief partners. At any rate, this was so in later loans of a similar character. This method of participation was a favourite means of finding a safe and interest-bearing investment for the capital of the citizens, their widows and orphans, the Church, etc., which was not employed in trade.[3]

Meanwhile the Italian city states had consolidated their many floating loans into great Monti, either, as in Genoa, selling to the Monti for its own administration a portion of the state revenue, or, as in the case of most other republics, keeping the revenues themselves and giving the Monti a charge on some or all of them. The right to the repayment of the loans was reserved, but could no longer be demanded. The interest was for the most part reduced.[4] The persons who before had held subsidiary shares in the tax-farming companies were given equal rights with the rest, and became accordingly immediate creditors of the state. Their shares (Luoghi) were entered in great registers (Cartularies), could be inherited or sold and were subject to fluctuations of value in

---

[1] Vgl. Rezasco, *Dizionario d. ling. ital stor. ed amministr. v. comperare, vendere.*

[2] The development prior to the fourteenth century is not clear. No consistent account exists of the origin of the Camera degli Imprestidi and the Monte vecchio in Venice and the Officium assignationis mutuorum and the first consolidated comperae in Genoa. Cf. the first monti in Florence.

[3] In 1546 the Republic of Genoa reduced the rate of interest on the debt and deferred payment. It sought the sanction of the Pope for this because many Luoghi were in the hands of the Church (Cuneo, pp. 190, 298 ff.; Lobero, p. 159).

[4] For Genoa see Cuneo, pp. 26, 77, 124 ff.; Lobero, pp. 16, 93 ff. For Florence, Rezasco, p. 650. For Pisa, Morpurgo, p. 156 ff.

accordance with the state's credit or the money market and the prevalence of war or peace. In the case of the Monti carrying on their own
business for profit the value of the shares also varied with the amount
of the dividend.

In Genoa there was the most highly developed system of partial
obligations and shares. Here the Luoghi were always expressed in the
same round figure, were a perfect fungible commodity like money and
were often used, in fact, as a means of payment.[1]

Finally in later times the Monti were used, not only for permanent,
but for temporary investment. Owing to the use cf their shares as
currency their character approximated to that of the Giro and Deposit
banks with which they have often been confused.[2] The feature which
distinguished from all other similar institutions of the Middle Ages was
the stable organization which they placed at the disposal of the towns
for the satisfaction of any extraordinary call for money and at the service of the capitalists for the investment of their free capital.

Lenders of Money Capital. It came about early in the Middle Ages
that rich monasteries, or even, in exceptional cases, secular lords and
gentlemen, were able to lend money;[3] but the class which was first able
to do this on a large scale was the merchant class. Long before this was
necessary for tradesmen or landowners, merchants had had to keep at
their disposal money capital on a larger or smaller scale. This meant
that they were disposed to lend this capital for other purposes if they
could get a larger profit than in their own business, or obtained advantages which they required for their business. Hence the money loans
which the city burghers made, not only to their own overlords, but also
to the rulers of the countries where they carried on business as foreigners
for the sake of obtaining rights and privileges, without which it was impossible to live securely or to carry on an undisturbed and profitable
trade. Originally the foreigners had no rights, and the burghers, who in
the first place were not all freemen, had even in their birthplace to
struggle for centuries for their rights – the freedom of the city, the rights
of merchants.[4]

In the Middle Ages only a part of the European merchant class engaged in moneylending as a trade. This was early taken up by certain
classes of merchants, first of all the Jews. So long as they lived among
Germanic races, the Jews had from early times always occupied themselves first and foremost with trade. This they were forced to do, for

---

[1] Chiefly within the territory of the city. Cf. *Liber. jur. Gen.* II. 471, 498, 1076.
[2] Even Italians did this in the sixteenth century. Cf. Capmany Mem. I, 214;
Narino Sanuto Diarii, II, 377, 391.
[3] Lamprecht, *Deutsches Wirthschaftsleben*, I, 1446. Von Inama-Sternegg,
Deutsche Wirthschaftsgeschichte, II, 444 ff.
[4] Goldchmidt, *Universalgeschichte des Handelsrechts S.* 112 ff.

though for centuries they were allowed to buy land, yet in actual fact there was little room for them either in the old District Associations (Markgenossenschaft) nor among the great landowners, who were the ruling class in Carlovingian times. In the few towns of the early Middle Ages, on the other hand, the Jews occupied a highly privileged position. Their trade was indispensable to the German peoples, who had little of their own.[1]

Meanwhile, however, the Romans and the Germans had given rise to new peoples whose trade activities began to gather force from the ninth century onwards, especially since the epoch of the Crusades. The trade of South Germany developed in connection with this Romanic movement, while in the north a further independent trading area was created by the Frisians and Saxons. The Jews ceased to be indispensable as merchants, while at the same time the Church let loose popular fury against them. They lost their privileged position, or rather they became dependent on the pleasure of the overlord, who could protect them or leave them in the lurch as suited his interest. They now first began to to occupy themselves with dealing in money.[2]

Here they occupied at first a position similar to that they had before in the trade in commodities. They were at first indispensable both to the people and more especially to the princes, whose need of money had increased greatly since the time of the Crusades. They were the first professional moneylenders of the Middle Ages. The princes often chose a shorter and cheaper way of using the Jews' capital: they confiscated their property. Other people who needed money could not use this method so frequently. On the occasions when this method was employed, it was on a grand scale, the Jews were killed, their houses were plundered and burnt. Religious hatred here combined with the natural hatred of the oppressed debtor for his creditor. Persecution forced the Jews to buy the ruler's protection with new loans of money, in which they paid themselves for the great risk of loss by charging correspondingly high interest.

The Jews were gradually driven from this position by the progress of the Christian merchants. The ban of the Church on usury had at first made professional money-lending difficult for Christians, while in practice, if not in law, the Church had left the Jews a free hand for a long time, all the while, in fact, that it could not do without them. In the

---

[1] Stobbe, *Die Juden in Deutschland während des Mittelalters*, S. 6 ff. Goldschmidt, l.c. p. 108 ff. Heyd, *Geschichte d. Levantehandels*, French later Edition, I, 125 ff.

[2] The first general persecution of the Jews began in 1096. The first mention of their moneylending is in the year 1096, Vita s. Annonis (ca. 1100) Mon. Germ. S. S. XI, 502. Ut. v. Inama-Sternegg, l.c. p. 445. Stobbe, p. 103 ff.

D

course of the thirteenth century the Church learnt that it was more profitable in all money affairs to employ the Italian merchants who could serve them in recovering the ecclesiastical dues. The Papal collectors were the first professional Christian moneylenders.

The inhabitants of the cities of Piacenza and Asti in North Italy, and of Cahors in Southern France, were the first who began to drive the Jews out of dealing in money in the regions north of the Alps. In the course of the thirteenth century they in their turn were replaced by the Tuscans, then by the people of Bologna and Siena, and later by the Florentines; but the name of Lombards or Caorsins still cling to all professional moneylenders who were Christians.

The process by which the Jews were driven from the higher kind of money-lending – which alone concerns us here – took a very different course in different countries. In Italy it must have been over so early that there is no historical tradition of it; perhaps there the Jews never played a leading part as moneylenders. In England, France and the Netherlands they were driven out of the larger money business before the end of the thirteenth century. Throughout the larger part of North Germany in the Middle Ages they do not seem to have been tolerated. Their expulsion in South Germany and Spain was not completed till the end of the Middle Ages. At this time, however, the Jews in all the chief countries in Europe had sunk to be pawnbrokers and money-brokers. All the higher branches of the money business, especially financial dealings with princes, were in the hands of Christian capitalists.

Among these the Florentines held the first place since the fourteenth century. Their inland situation put them at a disadvantage for dealing in commodities as compared with the cities on the sea. It was only in 1421 that they obtained in Leghorn a serviceable port of their own, and they had hardly had time to make use of it when the Mediterranean trade began to decay. Therefore, besides silk and wool manufactures, their chief trade was dealing in money. They soon drove out of large international finance the inhabitants of the Lombard cities, and after them those of rival Tuscan cities (Siena, Lucca, Pisa). Their importance as financiers reached its first high-water mark in the first half of the fourteenth century under Philippe le Bel of France, and his three sons and Edward III of England. In both countries they were then economically supreme. They overstrained their strength, however, and at the same time incurred popular hatred.

A series of catastrophes overtook them. In 1339 King Edward III of England ceased to pay his creditors, among whom far the most important were the Florentines, Bardi and Peruzzi. They in their turn suspended payments and brought down with them in their fall most of the other Florentine banking houses.[1] In Florence itself a rising of the Guilds in 1343 overturned the rule of rich patrician families, who were exiled and their property confiscated. This misfortune overtook them again two years later in France; and in England the resistance of the people against the Italian moneylenders grew in strength.

In the subsequent long period of continued exhaustion on the part of Florentine finance, the Kings of England and France helped themselves as best they might, mostly by means of forced loans from their subjects.

The discontent thus evoked necessitated the return to voluntary loans at high interest, and now native merchants came forward as lenders of money in the grand style: William de la Pole in England, and later, in France, Jacques Cœur. This was, however, only an episode. The native merchants were not nearly powerful enough financially, and the Florentines, who had now regained strength, once more had the upper hand.

The second great period of Florentine finance is associated with the name of the *Medici*. Three generations of this family had to collect capital and lend it out before they succeeded in getting the first place in their native country; and it was only in the fifth generation that their influence became powerful in the other countries of Europe. Averardo, called Bicci de Medici, who lived in the second half of the fourteenth century, had as yet no considerable property. His son, Giovanni, was always regarded by his descendants themselves as the founder of the family fortunes.

Giovanni de Medici stood in close relation with Pope John XXII of infamous memory, whose money affairs he managed. Giovanni's son, Cosimo, accompanied the Pope to the Council of Constance. When Pope John was a prisoner in Germany Giovanni de Medici had him ransomed with 38,500 florins, gave him shelter in Florence, and when he died had him buried with great pomp.

The often repeated assertion that the Medici owed their riches to the treasures left by this Pope has been disproved. When John, now merely Balthasar Cossa, died he left a considerable burden of debt, and the mitre which he had pledged to the Medici was demanded back from them under threat of excommunication by Pope Martin V. It goes without saying that Giovanni de Medici made a great deal of money out of his large dealings with the Curia, not only under John XXII, but also under his successor, Martin V, for the Medici seemed to have remained the chief bankers of the Curia till the year 1476.

When Giovanni died in 1428 he left property amounting to 178,221

[1] Cf. especially Ammirato, *Istor. fior.* I, 495: — — 'l'ultimo fallimento de Bardi che quasi assorbi tutte le ricchezze de privati.'

gulden. According to the tax lists there was only one citizen who had a larger income – Palla Strozzi.[1]

Under Giovanni's sons, Cosimo and Lorenzo, the riches of the family reached their highest point, for Lorenzo in 1440 left 225, 136 fl.; and Piero, Cosimo's son, left 237,988 fl. in 1469, so that their total fortune, about the middle of the fifteenth century, can be put at half a million gulden. Cosimo (Pater Patriæ) had already begun to give effective support to his struggle for political power by means of well-calculated munificence. (This may even have begun in the time of Giovanni.) The family spent on public buildings, taxes and works of charity, between 1391 and 1434, 36,000 fl.; between 1434 and 1464, 400,000 fl.; between 1464 and 1471, 263,000 fl. Lorenzo the Magnificent, Cosimo's grandson, finally treated the state finances as his own and his own as the state finances. Because in this case the idea of making profit had become entirely subordinate, he could use his capital and the state credit all the more energetically for the attainment of political power. The Medici hardly ever had more influence over the course of the world's history than that which they exercised in the time of the struggles between Louis XI of France, Edward IV of England, and Charles the Bold of Burgundy.

In Europe, towards the end of the Middle Ages, there were no financiers to compare with the Medici in international importance. Some other Florentine families like the Portinari, the Sassetti and the Guidetti were closely connected with the Medici both in business and in politics. Two families, the Pazzi and the Strozzi, who were repeatedly at variance with the Medici, played a considerable independent rôle as moneylenders; but outside Italy they were scarcely mentioned in large undertakings, and at this period only came in contact with credit-brokers of more or less local importance.

This is also true of most of the banks in the proper sense of the word. Banking business had developed from money changing in Italy itself in the thirteenth century, and in many centres outside Italy in the fourteenth and fifteenth centuries. There were business men who made it their business to receive deposits either with or without interest, and acted as agents for payments in the market by giro transfers and for local payments through bills of exchange. These business houses, called 'tabulæ, tavole, banchi, bancherii,' from the pay tables indispensable in their occupation, used the capital entrusted to them in active credit operations; in addition, they usually traded in commodities on a more or

---

[1] Canestrini, *La scienza e l'arte di stato,* p. 153. Income tax paid 1427–32: Palla Strozzi, 507 fl., Giovanni de' Medici, 397 fl., Gabrielo Panciatici, 391 fl.

less large scale. Their credit business usually served the needs of their own market. The Florentines, whose banking had international importance, were exceptional. Even they, however, carried on a considerable business in commodities, a sure sign that there was not yet enough money business to keep employed the capital – either their own or other people's – which they held. The demand for money capital had, however, begun to grow rapidly, and the same is true of the holdings of money. Both, however, were spread over an enormous district with bad means of communication; and the few branches which the Florentines had outside Florence were insufficient to link together supply and demand. We see, accordingly, that the princes and cities everywhere, in the event of a call for money, put themselves into communication with any capitalists who happened to be at hand, or with agents of merely local importance, and borrowed capital from nobles, charitable or religious foundations, clerics, officials, and burghers, the princes also borrowing on occasions from other princes, and a great deal from the cities. This borrowing was often in very small sums, and frequently on hard terms which did not always consist in the promise of interest in money.

The princes, if they had money to lend – which was rare – the nobles, the charitable institutions, and the monasteries, gladly used opportunities of this kind to buy land, which was mortgaged to them as a rule and redeemed; the cities, on the other hand, preferred customs, the Mint, highways, and other royal prerogatives as securities.

But the clerics and, to a greater extent still, the burghers knew how to appreciate the advantage of interest in money, which came in as a sure regular income with no exertion on their part, whether called interest or annual payment, and whether the process by which it was obtained was called a loan or purchase of annuity.

The rentier, towards the end of the Middle Ages, was a not infrequent phenomenon in the cities. Besides the corporations and foundations there were everywhere widows and orphans whose incomes consisted solely of annuities. It seems that in many of the cities of the Netherlands, as early as the fourteenth century, the manual workers (Ambachts-Luyde) nicknamed the rentiers as a class apart, Ledichganghers or 'the idlers.'[1] The chief families, apart from trade, lived on annuities. We know that the cities carried on a kind of banking business for this purpose, and we can easily see how they in this way collected capital,

---

[1] *Annales de la Société d'émulation de Bruges*, 1873, XXI. A Netherlands Mint order of 1489 distinguishes Prélats, nobles, RENTIERS, bons marchans. Cf. Gilliodts van Severen, *Invent. des archives de Bruges*, VI, 495 (Verzeichniss von Leibrenten 1264–1332).

not only from their own citizens, but also from those of neighbouring and friendly towns.[1]

Such an organization for dealing in capital soon showed its effect in a low and stable rate of interest. But even this organization was as yet very imperfect. It only served to bring together the monetary requirements of the city community with the need of its citizens for an investment.

There is to-day an economic institution which is used to organize both national and international credit, and puts all the many credit agents of the second and third rank into communication with one another. Such an institution, the capital exchange, was only present in the Middle Ages in a very rudimentary form.

The Beginnings of the Capital Exchange. A bourse or exchange is an assembly meeting at frequent intervals, usually daily, consisting of the merchants and other persons, who meet for the purpose of dealing without exhibiting, delivering and paying for their goods at the same time. Bourses or exchanges arose from a tendency inherent in trade from the outset to concentrate as far as possible, from the necessity of bringing supply and demand as far as possible together. This requirement had long before called into being markets and fairs. They, however, satisfied it far less perfectly than the exchanges, from which they were distinguished in two important particulars. Markets and fairs – especially the latter, which are, practically speaking, alone important for trade on a large scale – occur at longer intervals than the assemblies of the exchange or bourse. Secondly, in these cases the commodities must regularly be taken to the place where the business is concluded and tested as to its quantity and quality, and finally transported to the districts where they are to be disposed of. It is evident that this procedure is a great hindrance to trade concentration, while the long intervals at which markets and fairs recur, though it calls forth trade concentration, is at the same time a sign of a poor trade development.

It is accordingly obvious that exchanges are a product of a higher stage of economic culture, and that they do not arise except under

[1] Cf. for Basle, Schönberg, *Finanzverhältnisse der Stadt Basel im 14. u. 15. Jahrh.* p. 102 ff.; Mainz: *Deutsche Städtechroniken*, Bd. XVII, p. 93 ff.; Hamburg: Koppmann, *Hamb. Kämmereirechnungen*; Ghent: Gaillard, *Archives du conseil de Flandre*, p. 92, *Rekeningen der Stad Gent*, 1336–49, ed. de Pauw u. Vuylsteke; Bruges: Gilliodts l.c. Bd. I–VI, *passim*. Cf. *Bibl. de l'Ecole des Chartes*, 1884, p. 259 ff., Gaillard l.c., Gilliodts, I, 5, 32, 67, V, 520, VI, 493. Geneva paid in 1480: 10 Scudi 'duobus mercatoribus corrateriis (brokers) pro ipsorum laboribus et expensis perquirendi in Argentina (Strasburg) pecunias mutuo secundum consuetudinem patrie illus ad racionem de quinque pro centenario per annum, de undecim millibus scutis tunc ad solvendum restantibus quas repererunt, eciam ad sciendum si pecunie erant ad aliquid minus de quinque pro centum.' (*Mém. de la soc. d'histoire de Génève*, VIII, 430.)

certain conditions. First, the wholesale trade must be so considerable that two or four fairs a year cannot deal with it. Next, the commodities must be so far standardized that they do not have to be seen at the time of the transaction. There is also a third factor. Exchanges and fairs presuppose a high degree of commercial liberty. Where these are only an exception from the rule of general restriction of trade, only fairs and not a daily exchange can be formed.

This already tells us that for the wholesale trade of the Middle Ages the fair was the characteristic form of business concentration, as the exchange is for the wholesale trade of modern times. There were, however, exchanges in the Middle Ages, but they were not used for dealing in commodities, but in bills of exchange. Exchange of coins could never be the object of exchange (bourse) business in the proper sense.

In order to conclude a bill transaction both parties needed an accurate knowledge of the currency conditions involved, and the bill buyer needed to be sure that the seller was a person of sound credit. All the other requirements of ordinary dealing in commodities are absent. The bill does not have to be transported, warehoused and inspected. At the beginning it was necessary after the preliminary agreement to register bill transactions before a notary. The trade in bills could accordingly be carried on in the fairs of the Middle Ages in the manner characteristic of exchange business; and in the markets where there was enough of it for the trade to be regular and continuous, real exchanges then arose.

These fall into two classes in accordance with their origin, with perhaps an intermediate class. In the markets with a considerable home trade, especially in the trading cities of Italy, they arose from the business which developed at the banks of the money-changers native to the city, when the notaries likewise had stalls in the open air. Here there arose, on the one hand, money-changing to facilitate the local payments of the giro and deposit business; and, on the other, in order to facilitate payments between places near the traffic in bills of exchange. The latter, in the important markets, had the characteristics of exchange business as early as the fourteenth century.

The development was somewhat different in the markets without much home trade, where foreigners controlled most of the business and where, above all, the Italians had dealing in bills entirely in their hands. The fact that this form of business was introduced by them does not need further proof. In the countries north of the Alps bill business, therefore, developed in the closest connection with the factories of the Italians. The streets and market places where they lived, and more especially where they had their consular houses or Loggias, were the localities where bourse business first developed. Hence the bourse itself was often called Loggia or Loge. The present term 'Bourse' is taken from the square in Bruges, the greatest mediæval foreign market, where the Florentines, Genoese and Venetians had their consular houses.

In the markets of Southern France and Northern Spain, which already had bourses in mediæval times, these seem to have arisen partly from the concourse round the tables of the money-changers and partly to have been connected with the factories of the Italians.

Like ordinary commodities and bills of exchange, capital to be lent can be an object of exchange, dealings in which always tend to have the character of bourse business. A bourse develops when the traffic is sufficiently important and when the capital to be lent takes on certain standardized forms. Neither of these factors were fully present in the Middle Ages, and therefore bourses, where capital was dealt in, were not then very important. Nevertheless, this form of business existed and took its rise from the bourse dealings in bills of exchange.

The bill of exchange originally only served as currency, but it soon developed into a credit instrument. In fact the use of the bill as currency is indissolubly connected with the credit given to its drawer; for if the drawer needed in market A money which perhaps was already in a distant market B, but could not be brought quickly and safely to A because of the bad communications and the dangers of the roads – a frequent case in the Middle Ages; or if the money was only ready at B one, two or three months later – as was the rule when the drawer of the bill had taken the initiative in the transaction – it is obvious that business of this kind is really a credit transaction.

Transactions of the following sort were very common. In 1266 the Governor of Saint Louis of France in Palestine found himself in monetary difficulties. The King thereupon empowered him by a kind of letter of credit to borrow money and promised anyone who lent him this money, and presented the letter in Paris, to pay him the equivalent fifteen days afterwards, 'apud templum.' The governor then concluded with the Western merchants, or their agents in the Levant, a bill transaction, which was also a loan.

Similar operations are also reported of Richard Cœur de Lion and John Lackland in the twelfth century.[1] Quite at the end of the Middle Ages, ordinary credit business began to take on the form of bills in order to free itself from the character of 'usury.'

In short, wherever there was a bourse for bills of exchange, there

----

[1] *Bibl. de l'école des chartes*, XIX, p. 116 ff. Papa d'Amico, *I titoli di credito* p. 69 ff. *Bond in Archæologia*, XXVIII, p. 216 ff. Cf. also Huillard-Bréholles, *Hist. docum. Fred. II.* V. 385, 456, 471, 498, 549, 603, 605 ff. Cecchetti, *Vita dei Veneziani fino al* 1200, p. 72. Blancard, *Docum. inédits*, I, 403 ff., *Arch. stor. ital.*, Ser. 3. t. III, parte 1, p. 118. *Scelta di curiosità letterarie*, No. 116, p. 15.

must have been a bourse for capital without our being informed of this in all instances. Reliable information in the absence of business documents is extremely scanty. It is, however, established that in the thirteenth century the merchants had to maintain in many markets a sort of bourse for loan capital, both to meet their own requirements and on account of the needs of princes and cities. From this something similar to a 'market rate of interest' seems to have developed here and there.

So in the year 1260 the Sienese trading company of the Tolomei writes to their agent, who was at the Champagne fairs, that they have sold bills in Siena for the next fair because in this way they could raise most cheaply the money they needed for prosecuting the war against Florence. The letter adds that it was not so profitable to borrow in Siena, for the rate of interest for merchants to each other (da uno mercatante ad altro) was 5 or 6 pf. a pound (probably for two months, making an annual rate of about 12½ per cent. to 15 per cent. a year); for people other than merchants, twice this rate; also that the sale of bills on England was not so good as bills on the Champagne fairs. At the same time the lords of the country, the Counts of Champagne, borrowed at the fairs, and the interest on these loans – which was high – was calculated like commercial debts from fair to fair. An agent of Edward I reports that he had borrowed money for his master, in 1274, from a Lucca merchant in the Champagne fairs. Philippe le Bel borrowed from the Florentines, who themselves obtained capital on loan at the same fairs. He allowed the interest to be deducted on the loans contracted at the Champagne fairs 50 sous on 100 livres per fair (two months) the equivalent of 15 per cent. a year; and in the case of the other loans 1 denier from each pound per week, 4 denier per month, 4 sous per year, or 20 per cent. per annum. All this already makes the impression of a fairly regular business in lending capital; as we are told that in the Champagne fairs there were special places for the money-changers, we must suppose that it was here that the business in capital was chiefly concentrated.[1]

We gather from Giovanni da Uzzano that the Florentines, in the middle of the fifteenth century, knew accurately when to expect the recurrent periods of tight and easy money in the various markets. Here it was not only trade conditions which came into play, but also government requirements, especially the pay of the soldiers. We get the impression of regular dealings in capital, which, however, were chiefly in the form of bill transactions or very closely connected with them. On

---

[1] Sceltà di Curiosità Letterarie l.c. Arbois de Joubainville, *Historie des Ducs de Champagne*, IV, 840 ff. Bond, *Archæologia*, XXVIII, 273. Vuitry *Etudes sur le Régime Financier de la France*, New Series, I, 179. Bourquelot, *Etudes sur les Foires de Champagne*, II, 13, 129 ff.

this account, therefore, it must have had the character of bourse business.[1]

We know also that the shares of the Italian monti were dealt in in the manner of bourse business. The fluctuations in the quotations were already considerable in the fourteenth century, and the larger extent of the transactions caused the introduction, both in Florence and Genoa, of a special turnover tax. Theologians and jurists disputed whether it was permissible to buy such shares below their face value, the Dominicans in Florence declaring in favour of this proceeding, while the Minorites asserted the contrary. We must also remember that at any rate the Public Debt Office was in the market, the Rialto; and Luca Pacioli, in 1494, speaks expressly of the daily transactions which took place in the Rialto in shares of this Camera d'Imprestidi.[2]

Finally, from Bruges we have an example of a bourse transaction of the fiscal kind. It is not large and is not a loan proper, but a bill transaction. In 1475 the city of Bruges lent £908 10s. to 'Te Wissele Jegens Diversche Cooplieden ter Buerze.'[3] There cannot, however, have been regular direct dealing in capital on account of the city in the Bruges Bourse itself, or we should have record of more transactions of this kind.

If we consider this scanty information, one fact is fairly clear. In the Middle Ages princes and cities – if we exclude Italian cities – could not cover their own requirements directly on the bourse, but needed merchants at any rate as agents. They, on their side, took advantage of the low market rate, but charged their debtors a far higher rate than those of the market or bourse. Only a small proportion of the loans of princes or cities had any relation to a money market. Most of them were transacted on their own, so to speak, from house to house.

The capital bourses of the Middle Ages were only important for merchants. They were a convenience both to native and foreign merchants in certain markets in concentrating their trade in bills and the business in lending capital, which was closely connected with it.

The far-reaching and international importance of the bourse is a modern product.

Review of the State of Public Credit at the end of the Middle Ages. At the Renaissance European culture turned from unattainable ideals to Nature and reality. The precept of the Church, 'Take ye not interest from loans,' had proved impracticable, and experience had given the

[1] Uzzano in (Pagnini), *Della Decima*, IV, cap. 47 u. 48.

[2] Luca Pacioli, *Trattato de' computi e delle scritture ed. Gitti*, p. 77. Rezasco, *Dizionario Art. Monti*. Cuneo, *Banca di S. Giorgio*, p. 107 ff., 127, 180, 307. Canestrini, *La scienza e l'arte di Stato*, p. 424 ff. Fabronius, *Magni Cosmi Medici Vita Adnot*. 35. Villani, *Stor. fior. lib*. 3, cap. 106. Ammirato, *Stor. lib*, 14. Endemann, *Studien*, I, 434, 441 ff.

[3] Gilliodts van Severen, *Inventaires*, VI, 82.

principle, 'Money is the sinews of war,' such importance that finally a new political system, 'Mercantilism,' took its rise from it.

In the last centuries of the Middle Ages the system of dealing in kind among the European peoples broke down in some places, remaining untouched in others. The public budgets of princes and cities showed an increasingly monetary character on the expenditure side, especially in regard to the largest item, the cost of the army. The receipts, on the other hand, in the case of the prince at any rate, continued to be chiefly in kind. General experience showed that it was impossible to increase receipts of this sort proportionately to the increase of the expenditure. They were, moreover, not generally available at the time and place where the expenditure had to be met. Hence the necessity for a large and increasing amount of credit, though this also presented considerable difficulties.

In many places, it is true, there were small amounts of monetary capital which the owners wished to invest. The sale of annuities by the cities also gave an opportunity of this kind without conflicting with the ban on usury. On the other hand, it was very difficult for princes in need of money to avail themselves of credit: first, because they had little or no personal credit, and also because the bad state of their revenue organization greatly restricted the use of real credit – i.e. the mortgaging of revenues – a disorder which at the same time had a ruinous effect upon their budgets.

Above all, the credit organization was, on the whole, very poorly developed. Commerce had made a system for itself, and in Italy there was already an elaborate system for satisfying the credit requirements of the cities and the need of investment on the part of their citizens.

The princes, on the other hand, concluded their loans like private individuals with any owners of capital who presented themselves, without any systematic agency. To measure the advance of modern times in this respect we will state briefly how, towards the end of the Middle Ages, the individual princes of the more important states acted. It is, however, important to get rid of the idea that there is any definite line of division between the Middle Ages and modern times. Then, as always, the different degrees of development co-existed, but the process whereby the more backward conditions gave place to others was then comparatively rapid. This is the characteristic of an age of transition.

The simplest method of raising money for war, which is also the crudest and the most ruinous, was still employed towards the end of the Middle Ages by the chief secular lord of Christendom, the Emperor. Frederick III was a careful manager, but in this respect, as in all others, so limited and pettifogging that his economy was no good to him. In any case, his revenues as a feudal lord were inadequate, and as Emperor quite insignificant. He might have been able to increase his receipts from his own country by the use of greater energy and foresight. Instead of this he believed, like the kings of the Old Testament, in the collection of gold and silver plate as a provision for the future. In the course of his long reign he must often have experienced the inadequacy of this method, for at every large call for money he had to resort to selling or pledging offices, estates, annuities, etc., and, since he was never able to redeem his pledges, they became permanent alienations. He was perpetually in debt, not only to his own Diet, but to every kind of individual, clerics, merchants, Italians, and Jews, and he owed numerous sums, often quite small ones, to his own counsellors, court servants, and mercenaries, so that he was driven from one scandalous situation to another.[1] Under his son, Maximilian, matters were even worse. Whereas Frederick was a miser, his son was prodigal to the verge of madness. A contemporary Augsburg chronicler has left us a picture of the finances of the knightly Maximilian:[2] 'He was pious, not of great wit, and was always poor. In his land he had mortgaged many cities and castles, rents and rights (Gülten) so that he kept little for himself. He had knavish counsellors who ruled him in all things. They all became rich and the Emperor poor. If a man desired aught from the Emperor, he must give gifts to his counsellors, who thereupon brought it to pass. If later his opponent came they took gifts from him also, giving in return letters which said the contrary to the former ones. The Emperor suffered this to be so. He would always make wars and yet had no money. At times when he wished to set forth to war, his servants were so poor that they together with the Emperor could not pay their reckoning at the inn.' We shall learn later other details of this shameful form of finance.

Maximilian, in all his monetary difficulties, kept the collection of gold and silver plate which he had inherited, and even increased it by expensive additions. Since, however, it was for the most part never out of pawn, he cannot have had much pleasure from it. He had, on the contrary, to pay interest at usurious rates for the possession of this dead capital. Against this we must set off the progress in the goldsmiths' art which may have resulted from the Emperor's patronage. This primitive method of raising money ceased under Charles V – a few exceptions apart – chiefly because the loans to be raised on valuables were insignificant in proportion to the enormous amounts of money now required.

---

[1] Cf. Chmel, *Geschichte Kaiser Friedrichs IV*, z. B. I, 403 ff., II, 106 ff., 173. *Archiv f. Kund. österr. Geschäftsquellen*, X, 183 ff., 370 ff.

[2] Greiff in *den Anmerkungen zu dem Tagebuche des Lucas Rem*, p. 100. Cf. z. B. Brewer, *The reign of Henry VIII*, vol. I, p. 132 ff. *Négoc. dipl. de la France avec la Toscane*, II, 429, 513.

Maximilian was as backward in his financial management as in all other respects, so that for him, as it had been for his father before him, it was a matter of insuperable difficulty to obtain financial grants from his parliaments, either the Imperial Diet or the diets of the separate states. Nobles and clergy contributed practically nothing to the regular state taxes. The city of Vienna brought in almost as much to the Emperor Frederick III as the whole of Styria.

If, on the other hand, the diets were asked to grant extraordinary taxes, they haggled over every gulden, and in the end only granted the barest minimum in return for ruinous concessions on the side of the Crown. The Emperor could not dream of raising forced loans. Maximilian once attempted to raise one from the great trading companies, but had to give it up.

The financial system of the kings of France was a very different story. There is a well-known saying of Maximilian's that he was a King of kings, for no man felt bound to obey him; the King of Spain was a king of men, for though people reproached him, they yet did his bidding. But the King of France was a king of beasts, for no man dared to refuse to do his bidding.[1]

Translate this into financial language. The French Crown had levied on its subjects, and the clergy also since 1438, a regular direct tax, the taille; it also regularly raised heavy dues from its feudatories, and even the greatest vassals were not quite tax free. The indirect taxes, though very oppressive, produced an increasing yield. In the interests of defence or some other pressing call, it was not very difficult to obtain the grant of extraordinary taxation from the states general. Above all, towards the end of the Middle Ages the forced loan was a favourite expedient, especially a forced loan on the well-to-do. They grumbled, but were compelled to pay, the methods employed being mediæval, as we shall see.

In 1473 Louis XI, wishing to raise money in haste, demanded from Lyons – as well as from other cities – a forced loan of 20,000 livres, to be raised from the richest inhabitants, to whom the King sent a letter. The citizens thereupon met and recognized the King's need and the reasonableness of his demand, for it was in his power to take everything.[2] The sum, however, was too high. The city had already on several occasions made large advances to the King, whereof nothing had been repaid. Bargaining then began between the King's commissioners and the citizens. Finally they agreed on 8,000 livres, from which the commissioners, apparently without having powers so to do, remitted a further 2,500 livres. The King gave himself no further trouble as to the

[1] Ranke, *Franz. Geschichte*, 1, 125.

[2] '. . . que de son auctorité il pourroit prandre de fait, quant son bon plaisir seroit ainsi le fere' (*Bibl. de l'école des Chartes XLIII*, p. 462).

manner of raising the money, he cared only about getting it as soon as possible. This all happened under the economical Louis XI.

No interest was paid on forced loans, and they were often not repaid. It was only in 1522 that the cities began to receive definite royal revenues for the interest on their compulsory advances. They, in their turn, sold perpetual annuities on these, and this was the beginning of the present French 'rentes.'

In the case of voluntary loans at interest, to which the Crown only resorted in cases of extreme urgency, and which were, as a rule, on a very small scale, the financial officials at the King's direction put themselves in communication with a business house, pledged revenues, and on occasion also jewels, or became personally liable both for capital and interest. In short, these transactions were still of a mediæval type, and the French Crown at the end of the Middle Ages often had its policy checked from the want of a little ready money.

The case was very similar with the loans of the English Kings. Forced loans played a chief part when Parliament was not sitting. In the letters under the Privy Seal which the King, in the event of a special call for money, sent to certain, or even many, capital owners, it is stated that the regular thing was in such cases for the Crown to demand from Parliament, should it be sitting, the grant of a general tax, that otherwise the Crown must be assisted by loans from individuals. This must be the case in the present instance, as the financial necessity brooked no delay. The King doubted not that the person named would show his loyalty by the advance of the sum demanded of him.[1]

Besides, there were also in England voluntary loans of Italians and others, but since the end of the Civil Wars these had been unimportant. Henry VII got together a large treasure which enabled his son to lend money not only to other princes, but even to merchants.

Among the larger European countries, Castile was the one whose rulers at the end of the Middle Ages had far the best developed system of loans. The Crown there had actual annuity loans, as yet, however, funded on separate branches of revenue, not on the whole country. They were regularly used and were regularly dealt in. In 1438 the Parliament demanded that the full amount should not be paid to persons buying up the royal annuities at much below par. In 1480 Queen Isabella revoked a part of the sales of annuities of her predecessor, Henry IV. She distinguished between the annuities bought at low prices and those bought at the right price, i.e. between those bought direct from the King and those obtained from third persons.[2]

---

[1] Cf. Stubbs, *Constitut. History*, III, 91, 253.

[2] *Codigos Españoles*, VII, 275. Colmeiro, *Hist. de la econom. polit. en Espana*, I, 502.

There were also, of course, floating loans – those which Guicciardini, in an ambassador's report of 1513, called 'permute,' i.e. bills: though at that moment they were of subordinate importance in Castile. In 1489, when Ferdinand and Isabella were in pressing need of money for the war against the Moors, they sent invitations to all cities and also to numerous individuals, asking them to make advances. These were similar to those sent by the Kings of England and France, except that Ferdinand and Isabella granted 10 per cent. annuities for the sums so obtained. When this was no longer enough, the Queen pawned her jewels.[1]

In her last will, Queen Isabella advised her successors never to sell perpetual annuities, and ordered that all the free revenues of the kingdom of Granada should be applied before anything else to the repayment of the loans. These orders, however, were not carried out. Spain in the sixteenth century fell into a state of the most hopeless indebtedness.

The Netherlands finance accounts give us a clear account of how floating loans were contracted at the end of the Middle Ages.[2] The Brussels Court, if any one, should have been able to get the advantage of bourse dealings for its loans. Instead of this, however, it borrowed, usually from the same Florentine merchants – mostly the Frescobaldi and Gualterotti, first in Bruges and then in Antwerp – larger or smaller sums, as required. It paid high interest and gave its creditors a charge for the repayment on available revenues. It took all possible guarantees from officials and citizens, and even pledged jewels. In urgent cases it did not shrink from selling large parts of the domains to cities, nobles, churches, monasteries and private persons, though it would have been able to give instead annuities on the domain, or to have such annuities sold through the towns – a financial expedient which was actually used at the same time as the sale of the domains.

In short, though the loan system of many princes towards the end of the Middle Ages had developed many new features, yet, even at its highest point of development, the system still showed a preponderantly mediæval character.

[1] Colmeiro, II, 578.
[2] *Comptes de la recette générale des Finances* (Archives départementales de Lille).

CHAPTER 1

THE FUGGER [1]

I

THE RISE OF THE FUGGER TILL THE DEATH OF JAKOB II (1525)

ORIGIN and Beginnings. The Fugger did not belong, as did the Welser, the Herwart, the Langenmantel, and others, to the 'old' families of Augsburg. Their ancestor, Hans Fugger, came to Augsburg from the village of Graben in the year 1367. He was a weaver, but he also traded, and he left, what was a considerable fortune for those days, 3,000 florins.

A year after he came to Augsburg the Guilds obtained a share in the management of the city, which hitherto had been exclusively in the hands of the old families. The most distinguished Guilds were the Weavers and Merchants, and they accordingly profited the most by the change. Hans Fugger's sons were already respected members of both guilds, and one of them, Jakob, was Master of the Guild of Weavers, though he himself had ceased to weave. Other families, however, were rising in the world, and there is nothing to show that the Fugger were already specially prominent. Like most of the Augsburg merchants they still dealt exclusively in 'spices, silk and woollen materials,' a trade where long established relations with Venice as yet played the chief part.

Andreas was the richest and most respected of Hans Fugger's sons. He married a daughter of one of the old families and was the ancestor of the Fugger vom Reh, so called from the doe in their coat of arms. Some of his sons largely increased the scope of the business, and had relations with the Netherlands, with Leipzig, even, it is said, with Denmark. Incautious giving of credit, however, proved their ruin, and when Lucas, the last son of Andreas, died in 1494, he left behind him more

[1] There have been several attempts to write a history of the Fugger.

1. A member of the family, Hans Jakob Fugger, composed in 1546 the *Gehaim Erenbuch des Fuggerischen Geschlechtes*, of which the MS. [is in the German National Museum in Nuremberg.

2. A MS. from the end of the sixteenth century, 'Cronica des Gantzen Fuggerischen Geschlechtes.'

3. A printed work, *Fuggerorum et Fuggerarum Imagines*, Aug. 1618.

4. *Pinacotheca Fuggerorum*, Oct. 17, 1754. *Later works.* Dr. Dobel, the Archivist of the Fugger Family Archives, published two treatises: 'Uber den Bergbau und Handel der Fugger in Kärnten und Tyrol' and 'Der Fugger Bergbau und Handel in Ungarn' in *Ztschr. d. histor. Vereines f. Schwaben u. Neuburg*, VI, 33 ff., IX, 193 ff. Cp. also Wenzel, *A Fuggerek jelentösége Magyarorszag történetében*, Budapest, 1882; Häbler, 'Die Fugger und der spanische Gewürzhandel' in *Ztschr. d. histor. Ver. f. Schwaben*, XIX, 25 ff.; and 'Die Finanzdekrete Philipps II und die Fugger,' *Deutsche Zeitschr. f. Geschichtswissensch*, XI, H. 2, p. 276 ff. Aloys Geiger, *Jakob Fugger*, Regensburg, 1895.

debts than assets. The branch of the Fugger vom Reh continued to sink, so that many of them became handicraftsmen, or had to enter the service of their more fortunate cousins, the Fugger of the Lilies (Gilgen) as clerks.

This chief branch of the Fugger von der Gilgen sprang from another son of the original ancestor, Jakob I, a modest man, who was, as we have seen, master of the Weavers Guild, but who was looked down on by his proud brother Andreas. He married a daughter of the master of the Augsburg Mint. This man, Bäsinger, had 'great business with every kind of merchant,' and in 1444, when his debts amounted to 24,000 florins, had to cease payment. His son-in-law went surety for him and he compounded with his creditors, who got 75 per cent. of their claims. He then went to Tyrol and once again became a mint master, this time in Hall, the centre of the growing Tyrolese mining district. Apparently it was through him that the Fugger had their first connections with the Tyrolese mining industry.[1]

Jakob II. When 'Old' Jakob Fugger died, his sons, Ulrich, George, and Peter, carried on the business. Two other sons had died before their father, and two more, Marcus and Jakob, were intended for the Church. In 1473 Peter also died, and on the request of Ulrich and George, Jakob abandoned his clerical career and became a merchant. The family came rightly to consider this a great stroke of luck; for Jakob 'the second' showed a real genius for business, and it is almost entirely to him that the Fugger owe their importance in the world's history.

Jakob Fugger was just fourteen when he became a merchant in 1473. He learned his business, like many other young South Germans of that day, in the great business house of the Germans in Venice, the Fondaco dei Tedeschi, where his elder brothers had a permanent warehouse. When he became a partner and the three had carried on the business together for some time, they made an agreement that their male heirs and descendants should leave their property in common in the business, but that the daughters should be given money down in dowries 'so that the Fugger business may remain in every wise undivided.'

This principle was observed as far as possible as long as the house prospered, and it was only given up after the war of Schmalkalden. Of the three brothers, George died first in 1506, and Ulrich followed him four years later. Jakob, who had no children of his own, then took his nephews, Hieronymus, Ulrich, Raymund, and Anton, into partnership. He managed the business, which was now styled 'Jakob Fugger and Nephews,' till his death.

New Business Methods. When Jakob II entered the business the

[1] Cf. for Bäsinger: *Die Chroniken d. deutschen Städte*; Augsburg, II, 99 ff., *D. Archiv. f. Gesch. u. Alterth.-Kunde Tirols*, V, 50.

Fugger's trade had not yet struck out into new paths. It is true that as early as 1473 Ulrich Fugger had done business with the Hapsburgs, but this transaction was still on the old lines. In the year 1473 the Emperor Frederick III was preparing to go to Trier to make an agreement with Charles the Bold of Burgundy as to the marriage of his son Maximilian with Charles's daughter Maria. For this expedition the Emperor wished his train 'to be habited in plain coloured cloth and furnished forth right merrily, and Ulrich Fugger was commended to him by the Chancellor, Hans Rebwein, as an honest and sound man to furnish His Majesty with good cloth and silks.' Ulrich Fugger lived up to this description, 'whereon the Emperor made him as a free gift without payment his coat of arms of the lilies, and this' – Hans Jakob Fugger says in conclusion – 'was the first Trade and Businesse which the Lords of Austria had with the House of Fugger.'[1] This transaction did not, however, lead to a continued connection. This began first at the time when the silver mines of the Tyrol were becoming increasingly important, and under Maximilian I the Hapsburgs' struggle to obtain the position of a world power made itself openly felt. The Fugger, who knew how to forward this effort, then entered on their period of importance in the world's history.

It was not, however, Ulrich Fugger who brought new undertakings of such wide scope into the business. It was, as the oldest family records show, Jakob who had left the trade in spices, silks and woollens,and had 'betaken himself to various undertakings of greater profit, such as bills of exchange and mines.' The first beginning of this kind had been made as we have seen by 'Old' Jakob in the middle of the fifteenth century. The first decisive movement in this direction, however, was in 1487, when Jakob Fugger the Second – we do not hear of any one else – together with the Genoese Antonio de Cavallis, advanced the sum of 23,627 florins to Siegmund, Archduke of Tyrol, who in spite of his rich silver mines was always in dire straits for money. They received as security a mortgage on the best of the Schwatz silver mines and the whole province of Tyrol, under which, if the money were not punctually repaid, the silver due from the mines to the Archduke should be handed over. The next year, 1488, saw business on a still grander scale. The brothers, Ulrich, George, and Jakob Fugger, advanced to the Archduke 150,000 florins, and till this debt was paid the whole silver production of the Schwatz mines had to be handed over to the Fugger at a very low price.

[1] This tale is told in the greatest detail by Hans Jakob Fugger in an MS. of 1555, in *Kgl. Staatsbibl.* in Münich (I, 319), and more concisely in the *Gehaim Erenbuch des Fuggerischen Geschlechts.*

It was through transactions of this kind that the mines which the Fugger themselves owned in Tyrol and Carinthia [1] became increasingly important.

Similarly in Hungary the trade in copper, which the Fugger had begun in 1495, was soon extended by working the large copper mines in Neusohl and elsewhere. In this case the Fugger were helped by the influential Austrian family of Thurzo, with whom they often intermarried. In the years 1498 and 1499, they, together with other business houses in Augsburg, formed powerful syndicates to get control of the copper market in Venice, while at the same time they shipped Hungarian copper through Danzig to the Netherlands. As early at any rate as 1494 they had a connection with Antwerp.

Business with the Emperor Maximilian I. When in 1490 Archduke Siegmund handed over the government of Tyrol to Maximilian I, the latter, who was the worst manager of all the Hapsburgs, immediately approached the Fugger for a loan. This happened for the first time in 1492, a year when Maximilian was so hard pressed, owing to the cessation of the English subsidies, that he could not pay Duke Albert of Saxony the sums promised to him for the military service he had rendered. It is uncertain whether the Fugger did as Maximilian wished and made fresh advances on the Tyrolese silver production. In any case, in 1494 they had still a claim of 40,000 florins on the silver. Nevertheless Maximilian tried to pledge the Tyrolese silver production yet again to a Nuremberg consortium under Heinrich Wolff. The Fugger meanwhile declined to release their mortgage, and the Nurembergers had to content themselves with a bad security. [2]

The Fugger at this time were still remarkably cautious about satisfying Maximilian's perpetual claims. When, however, his need was most acute, they gave in. In 1496, when there was no money for the expedition to Italy and even the loyal cities of the Empire, in spite of the most urgent entreaties, would lend nothing to the King on the security of the Poll tax, 'Gemeine Pfennig,' the Fugger lent 121,600 florins on the security of the output of the Tyrolese copper mines. They deducted from this almost half to satisfy their remaining claim on the silver, and as the State Government kept back a further large sum for its own use, the warlike Maximilian was to find himself left with only 13,000 florins. Finally, however, the Fugger agreed once again to lend him 27,000 florins on the silver. [3]

The war with Switzerland in 1499 once again rendered acute Maxi-

---

[1] Cf. for the Fugger business in Carinthia, the Tyrol and Hungary, Dobel and Wenzel.

[2] Cf. Chmel, *Urk. z. Gesch. Maximilians*, I. p. 41 ff.

[3] Chmel l.c. p. 95. Ulmann, *Kaiser Maximilian I*, vol. I, p. 438 ff.

milian's chronic money troubles. After ceaseless efforts on the part of the Emperor's trusted servant George Gossembrot (whom we shall hear more of), the Fugger declared themselves ready to make a fresh advance on the Tyrolese copper. Shortly afterwards Gossembrot came into violent collision with the Fugger, who wanted to have sole control of the copper market, and the syndicate in which he was interested had to dissolve.

Trade in silver and copper was in these years certainly the Fugger's chief occupation since the feudal lord's share of the copper and silver production had always been the best security the needy Hapsburgs could offer. This it was too that made the Fugger, who could not tear themselves away from the profitable copper and silver trade, more and more the most important helpers of Maximilian in his money difficulties. This became apparent during the Ten Years War in Italy (1508–1517).

When in the summer and autumn of 1507 Maximilian asked the Imperial Diet at Constance for the grant of a general tax of the Empire for the Roman expedition, the States at last declared themselves ready to give him 12,000 men and to raise 120,000 florins by taxation. For the moment, however, this was no good to the King, for the Imperial taxes came in slowly, while cash was immediately necessary to pay the Swiss 'Die Freien Knechte der Eidgenossen,' who otherwise would have gone over to France.[1]

The Diet at Constance recommended Maximilian to raise a loan from the great business houses. This came to nothing, as did the attempt to get prepayment of subsidies from the Italian cities which were expecting armed help. The King's credit was *nil*, and even the Fugger would lend nothing except on a mortgage of the Crown lands; for he had no other security to give. In July, 1507, Maximilian had to bring himself to mortgage his revenues as Count of Kirchberg and Lord of Weissenhorn to the Fugger for 50,000 florins. The mortgage was never redeemed, and these lands, apart from a few older parcels of land in Graben and Augsburg, form the beginning of the Fugger's afterwards very extensive possessions in real property.[2]

This money was a drop on a hot stone. In his extremity the Emperor bethought him of turning to account the growing feeling against the great business houses. He attempted, against the advice of the Diet, to raise a forced loan from the business houses in Augsburg, Nuremberg,

[1] Maximilian wrote to his daughter Margaretha about the Swiss: 'Il sount mechans, villains, prest pour traïre France on Allemaignes.' Cf. Janssen, *Frankfurter Reichscorrespondenz*, II, 712 ff., 741, 745.

[2] Cf. Report of the Venetian envoy Quirino from Augsburg (Albéri, *Relaz. d. ambasc. venet.* XIV, 28 ff.).

Memmingen, and Ratisbon. All the firms resisted to the uttermost. They made use of Dr. Conrad Peutinger as their agent with Maximilian, and after months of fruitless negotiations, the companies advanced 'a mighty sum,' apparently 150,000 florins, but once again on the Crown land. The King, moreover, had to bear witness that this was a voluntary act and to promise never again to try to impose a forced loan. The Fugger bore a large share of this loan.[1]

The year 1508 saw further advances made by the Fugger; a small advance of 8,000 florins on the right to farm salt ('Salt Meieramt') at Hall in Tyrol in January, later another of unknown amount on a large and valuable collar, and yet a third of 128,750 florins on the security of the copper and silver production.[2]

The League of Cambrai gave the Emperor – he attained this title in 1508 – the promise of large subsidies from his allies, 170,000 ducats in all. The payment had moreover to be made at the most widely distant place, Rome, Florence, and Antwerp, and was very slow, while Maximilian as usual required money immediately and the whole amount in Germany. Jakob Fugger was able to get the money to Augsburg, some in a fortnight and the rest within six weeks, by means of bills of exchange. A bill transaction on such a scale between such distant localities, carried through in such a relatively short space of time, was regarded in those days as a great feat. The fame of the Fugger grew mainly through business of this kind, which they carried on later on an even larger scale. Without running any great risks they were able to make a large profit from a skilful use of the price of bills – 'arbitrage' as it is called now, 'cambrio arbitrio' in the language of that time.[3]

In 1511 the Emperor conceived the crazy notion of making himself Pope. The idea itself and the plan for its execution are very characteristic of Maximilian.[4]

His agent Paul von Lichtenstein was to borrow 300,000 ducats to bribe the Cardinals from Jakob Fugger. He was to pledge as security 'the four best caskets with Our jewels together with Our robes of state.'

---

[1] Cf. for the negotiations about the Forced Loan cf. Jäger, *Ulm im Mittelalter*, p. 677, Herberger *im Jahresber. d. histor. Ver. f. Schwaben*, Neuburg, 1849–50.

[2] Le Glay, *Corresp. de Maximilien et de Marguerite d'Autriche*, I, 177, and also Dobel, *Zisschr. d. histor ver. f. Schwaben*, IX, 199.

[3] Cf. Hans Jakob Fugger's *Spiegel der ehren des Erzhauses Osterreich in der Ausg – des Sigm. v. Birken.* 1668, 12, S. 9, and the rather different version of v. Stetten, *Geschichte der Augsbg. Geschlechter*, p. 202. In 1509 the 'marchans allemans nommez les Fouckers, demourans en la ville d'Anvers' (*Comptes de la Trésorerie de la guerre 1506–11 und Comptes de la Recette générale des Finances 1510*, Archives de la Chambre des comptes in Lille) make a first appearance in the accounts of the Court of the Netherlands.

[4] Cf. Goldast, *Polit. Reichshändel*, XII, 4, p. 428, and Geiger, p. 22 ff.

The interest was to be 100,000 ducats for which Jakob Fugger was to be given a lien on:

(1) The Imperial subsidy 'the which we will obtain in the next Diet from the States of the Realm.'

(2) On subsidies and taxes in the future on the Austrian Crown lands.

(3) On the annual Spanish subsidies.

(4) Should all this prove insufficient the Emperor will assign a third of all the revenues he will draw from the Holy See in order to pay the debt. Further, he undertakes to appoint any one whom Jakob Fugger shall designate as the keeper of the Imperial treasures. The Fugger bank in Rome is to pay over the loan to the Emperor's envoys, so that they can use it as they want it. Lichtenstein is to spare no pains to bring about the loan, 'and though the Fugger deny thee more than once, still shalt thou trye yet again.'

The whole business throws light on the adventurous fancy and unscrupulous policy of Maximilian's oddly compounded character; and it is also an important piece of contributory evidence as to the election of Charles V. Needless to say, it all remained a pious wish.

In spite of these unbusinesslike attempts to bleed them, the Fugger apparently lent the Emperor money in the years following, but we have no further information till 1514. In that year Jakob Fugger lent the Emperor 12,000 florins on the revenues of Tyrol, and 32,000 florins on the security of the lordship of Biberbach. When in October, 1515, Maximilian pressed him for a new loan Jakob Fugger replied that 'in past time and in this very year he had advanced great sums, close upon 300,000 florins to His Majesty on silver and copper, whereof the greater part had not been repaid.' After the loan which as a loyal subject he had at great pains to himself made to His Majesty but lately on his journey from Vienna to Augsburg, he had not thought him so soon to be entreated for a new loan. The King's silver was pledged already for seven and eight years to come and the copper for four years. The getting of silver had sunk to the half, whereby the repayment of the debt was mightily delayed. He knew not how long he had to live now, nor how he should stand by reason of the wars a few years hence. He had besides much business and such increased unto him daily, wherefore those came to him at home whom in years past he had gladly ridden to seek. Nevertheless he quit himself of them, for he was now of a good age and had no child. He would therefore content himself with his business as it was and undertake nothing new.

Only after much persuasion Jakob Fugger consented once more to advance in conjunction with the Höchstetter 40,000 florins on the security of the Schwatz copper for the years 1520–1523 at $4\frac{1}{2}$ florins the hundredweight; and in addition as 'a favour' on each hundredweight of silver 5 marks of silver at the price of 8 florins 27 crowns the mark. Finally Jakob Fugger consented to a further loan of 10,000 florins on the security of silver and the grant of customs privileges.[1] All this shows two things, first that the Fugger remained in close connection with the Emperor, and secondly that their position was now very important.[2]

At this point we begin to hear of fairly large financial transactions on the Fugger's part in Antwerp. Hitherto the factory [3] there (which first had a house to itself in 1508) had really only been used for dealing in commodities, a business where pepper figured alongside of copper and silver. In 1505 the Fugger had shared in a large undertaking of German and Italian merchants in the East Indies, but this does not seem to have been repeated. Nevertheless they kept their own agent in Lisbon, and he made at regular intervals large shipments of pepper to Antwerp, where the Fugger played a leading part in the pepper market for several decades.[4]

In 1515 the Emperor was granted a lump sum of 100,000 florins in return for releasing his grandson from his tutelage and thereby ceased to interfere in the government of the Netherlands. The Fugger agency in Antwerp was commissioned to receive this money. Soon after they acted several times as agents for transferring English subsidies to Maximilian. In this matter the Florentine Frescobaldi had played the chief part at first, but as they proved unequal to the task the Fugger had to step in. In April, 1516, they advanced 20,000 florins to the Emperor through the Cardinal von Sitten, and in May the Frescobaldi, who had failed to send the money punctually to Trent where the Emperor lay with his army, were themselves driven to borrow 60,000 florins from the Fugger. Maximilian's credit, whether financial or political, had now fallen so low through the failure of the English subsidies and his own heedlessness that the English envoy could write home that the Emperor behaved like a boy in his nonage. It was this very envoy whom Maximilian asked to assure Jakob Fugger that the friendship between the Emperor and the King of England was as firm as ever and that the King would continue to support the Emperor.[5]

In the summer of 1516 the Court of the Netherlands borrowed from Bernhard Stecher, the Fugger's agent in Antwerp, for the period of one

[1] Dobel, l.c. IX, 200 ff.
[2] Augsburger Stadtarchiv, Herwartiana Suppl. III.
[3] Factory is used in the eighteenth century sense of a depot.
[4] For details of the Fugger factory cf. Thys, *Histor. d. straten v. Antwerpen 2. Aufl.* (1893), p. 548 ff. Antwerp factors of the Fugger were: 1507 Conrad Meuting (Mutinck), 1510-13 Felix Hanolt, 1513-20 Bernhard Stecher, 1517-22 Wolff Haller, 1521 Anton Hanolt u. s. f.
[5] Brewer, *Calendar of State Papers*, vol. II, No. 2310, 1231, 1384.

year under the guarantee of the city of Antwerp, 27,000 pounds at 40
pfennigs of Flemish money (i.e. 27,000 Carolus gulden).

For this the Fugger received 3,000 pounds in interest, about 11 per
cent., no means a high rate for those times. The agent received in
addition 100 pounds for his trouble and expenses. At the end of the
year the repayment of capital and interest was found impossible on
account of the large expenditure for Charles' projected journey to take
over the government of Spain, the war in Friesland and so forth.
The loan, which now with accrued interest amounted to 30,000 pounds,
was prolonged from Midsummer Day, 1517, till Christmas in the following year. The Fugger meanwhile had other outstanding claims on the
Emperor for 42,000 pounds, making a total of 72,000 pounds. When
the loan was extended, the Antwerp agent, Stecher, received a further
100 pounds from the Finance Ministry of the Netherlands. Finally to
end the story of the Antwerp business we should mention that the
Fugger in 1518 lent 38,000 pounds in order to pay the Frisian garrisons
for three months and to meet other pressing needs. For this loan several
receivers-general of provinces and cities had to make themselves personally responsible. The interest was 4,000 pounds for thirteen months,
or not quite 10 per cent.[1]

The Fugger and the Reformation. The next great dealings of the
Fugger with the House of Austria refer to the time of Charles' election
as Emperor. Before we enter on these, we must turn to the connection
between the Fugger and the Roman Church.

They had a factory in Rome which Dr. Christopher Scheuerl speaks
of as early as 1500 as 'the Fugger Bank,' and by its means they had large
financial dealings, not only with the Papal Curia, but with individual
princes of the Church. They were interested in the lease of the Papal
Mint, and when a prominent cardinal died in 1505, it was said that Jakob
Fugger had large claims against him. In 1507 Pope Julius II had deposited 100,000 ducats in their bank in Rome and in 1509 he had the
monies produced by the Year of Jubilee paid in to them.

In the year 1510 they sold to this Pope at the price of 18,000 ducats
a diamond which they had had to take over at 20,000 ducats from the
liquidator of the Venetian banking firm of Agostini. The Fugger were
the first and with the Welser the only German firm which fell into the
old category of merchants called in the Middle Ages 'Campsores
Romanan curiam sequentes.' [2]

---

[1] *Lille, Comptes de la Recette Générale des Finances.* Cf. Brewer l.c. No. 2721,
2866 and *passim.*

[2] Pauli, *Lüb. Zustände im Mittelalter*, II, 106. Reumont, *Geschichte der Stadt
Rom*, IIIa, 441, IIIb, 398, 423. Marino Sanuto, *Diarii*, VI. 231, VII, 197, VIII,
11, 87, X, 283. Janssen, *Frankfurter Reichscorrespondenz*, II, 762.

In this way the Fugger became connected with Albrecht of Brandenburg when he was made Archbishop of Mainz. At least since the beginning of the fourteenth century the Archbishops had had to pay the Curia in hard cash for their confirmation and the sending of the episcopal pallium. Albrecht had to pay 30,000 ducats, most of which he first had to borrow. On the day following his consecration, the 15th May, he wrote an acknowledgment of indebtedness in which he acknowledged that Jakob Fugger had lent him 21,000 ducats for defraying these expenses and had paid them over to the new Archbishop's representative in Rome through his agent there. Albrecht promised to repay this loan at the term in good Flemish gulden at the rate of 140 gold gulden for 100 ducats as well as 500 Flemish gold gulden for 'Trouble, Danger and Expense.' [1] The usual periphrasis for interest.

From his regular revenue the Archbishop would never have been able to pay back such a sum. He therefore obtained from Pope Leo X, on payment of another 10,000 ducats, the right of being General Commissioner for Saxony and other parts of Germany of the new Jubilee Indulgence which the Pope had just declared. It seems that the Fugger helped in this arrangement, which for them was merely a means of getting their money more quickly. At any rate there is no ground to transfer the indignation against the traffic in indulgences to the Fugger. The whole business had been quite usual with bankers in Italy for centuries and the trafficking which appeared so markedly in Germany at the time of the Indulgence had been described, for example in Florence, as early as the fourteenth century. Then, too, honest men had denounced it with righteous indignation. The only novelty was that the man who now roused the whole people against the Indulgence should call forth a general response.

The Pardoner Tetzel was accompanied everywhere by an agent of the Fugger, who kept in his hands a key of the Indulgence chest. When the chest was full, it was opened in the presence of the Fugger's agent and its entire contents were then paid over to him and sent to Andreas Mattstedt, the Fugger's agent in Leipzig. Finally half the proceeds were paid over to the Curia by Engelbert Schauer, the Fugger's agent in Rome, and the other half was used to pay the instalment of interest and capital due on the money lent to Archbishop Albrecht. Such was the business which led to the Reformation. [2]

The Fugger's fortunes were now climbing faster and faster towards

---

[1] Hennes, *Albrecht von Brandenburg*, S. 5 ff. Körner, *Tezel der Ablassprediger*, S. 44 ff., 61 ff. Cf. Woker, *Das kirchliche Finanzwesen der Päpste*, S. 99 ff.

[2] For Engelbert Schauer cf. Loose, *Anton Tuchers Haushaltungsbuch*, S. 124, 150, S. 24; Roth, *Geschichte des Nürnbg. Handels*, I, 359 ff. He is here called Angelus Saur.

the zenith. The moment approached when they threw their gold into the scales in the struggle for the first place between the Houses of the Hapsburgs and the Valois and thereby gave the Hapsburgs the crown of King of the Romans.

The Fugger and the Election of Charles V as Emperor. The election of Charles of Spain to be King of the Romans is the event of this age which most clearly illustrates the power of money and is sufficient in itself to justify the phrase 'the Age of the Fugger.' The German Electoral princes would never have chosen Charles had not the Fugger helped his cause with their cash, and still more their powerful credit. This is evident throughout the whole transaction.

The Emperor Maximilian spent his last years in indescribable straits for money. In 1518 Jakob Fugger had to lend him 2,000 florins, and again, as the result of ceaseless pressure, another 1,000 florins, because otherwise His Majesty would literally have had 'nothing to eat.' This, however, did not prevent the Emperor at this very time from helping his grandson's election as Emperor by every means in his power and especially by large promises of money. He could not, of course, engage money of his own, nor yet directly money belonging to his grandson, but he could offer the promises of the Fugger, who in their turn lent their signature, not to Maximilian, but to his far more solvent grandson.

The Fugger had already had many money dealings with Charles when he ruled only the Netherlands. The Fugger's Antwerp agent, Wolff Haller, must even then have been in high favour with the young Prince and his counsellors, for Charles declared afterwards that when he took over the government of Spain (in 1517) he had received most important services from Haller and also at the time of the election as King of the Romans.

As Haller, we know, made a journey in 1519 from Antwerp to Spain to carry out some large monetary transaction between the King and the Fugger in connection with the election, it is probable that he had acted for the Fugger in these dealings, a fact which would explain the great affection with which Charles continued to remember him in later years – in 1526 he speaks of him as 'Our Counsellor from Our youth up.'

Of these first negotiations we know no details, only the result. In August, 1517, when Charles was setting out to Spain, he gave his envoy Courteville and the Imperial Treasurer Villinger bills on the Fugger for 94,000 florins in order to bring the electors to elect him. This, however, was no use, for the money was to be paid after the election. The old Emperor knew better. He wrote to Charles that there must be immediate payment in cash and not 94,000 florins, but 450,000 florins in addition. Then began a bargaining which lasted for years with each separate elector, a proceeding made all the more scandalous by the fact that the electors kept raising their terms owing to the French King's candidature.[1]

When Charles declared that he wished to become King of the Romans, cost what it might, Francis let it be known that he was prepared to spend on it half his year's income, which was thought to be three million livres. Francis was no despicable rival, though less dangerous than his own skilful boasting made him appear to his contemporaries. His situation with regard to ready money was far less brilliant than his envoys and friends boasted, and he would have had great difficulty in paying his engagements, had he intended to pay them, which he did not. The German electors, however, had no use for such promises, they wanted money down, or else the guarantee of first-rate German merchants.

King Francis first approached the Republic of Genoa for a loan of 80,000 scudi. In view of Genoa's wavering position between the two great camps in Europe, we cannot wonder that this was refused. He had no greater luck with an attempt to raise a large loan in Lyons. The money of the Florentines who set the tone for Lyons was not then as it was afterwards at the disposal of the French Crown. Indeed some of the most important Florentines who had their main business in Antwerp even supported Charles. It was only from his mother, the rich Duchess of Angoulême, that Francis received any considerable sum of money, but this was not nearly enough to decide the election.[2]

Charles meanwhile discovered even richer sources of money. As a result of Maximilian's advice he looked out for fresh means, and as the Fugger's terms proved too hard, he entered into relations with other merchants.

In September, 1518, negotiations were carried through in Antwerp with the great Florentine banker Filippo Gualterotti. At the same time or shortly after relations were established with the most important Genoese merchants and with the next largest firm to the Fugger, the South German house of Anton Welser and Company, who sent to Spain two special representatives for this purpose, Heinrich Ehinger and Sebastian Schopel.[3]

These negotiations were concluded at the beginning of January, 1519. The Welser contributed 110,000 florins as well as 25,000 crowns. Filippo Gualterotti, 55,000 florins, the Genoese Benedetto and Agostino Fornari, 55,000 florins ; and another Geonese firm Agostino and Nicolo de Grimaldi and Company (who were represented by

---

[1] Gachard, *Rapport sur les Archives de Lille*, p. 149, 152; De Quinsonas, *Marguerite d'Autriche*, II, 250.

[2] Marino Sanuto, *Diarii*, Vols. XXVI and XXVII *passim*. Casoni, *Annali di Genova*, p. 66. Brewer, *Calendar*, III, 84 and 116.

[3] Cf. Brewer, *Calendar*, II, No. 4440.

Lorenzo Vivaldi), 55,000 florins. They all gave the Spanish Government bills on Augsburg and Frankfurt am Main pledging themselves to pay over the amount of the bills during April either to Charles' new special representative Paul von Armstorffer, or according to Armstorffer's directions to the German electors, only, however, in the case that Charles should be elected King of the Romans. Paul von Armstorffer himself took the bills to Germany and handed them over to Jakob Fugger to keep for the time being.[1]

Meanwhile negotiations with the German electors continued. They were going favourably for Charles, but were by no means concluded when on 12th January, 1519, the Emperor Maximilian died.

King Francis now redoubled his promises, causing the electors and their counsellors (who also had to be bribed) to increase their demands on Charles. These to his sorrow he was forced to concede, for as we see from his letters the crown of King of the Romans grew in importance in his eyes as its price rose.

At this point the extent to which the Fugger backed the House of Austria becomes evident. Charles' representative reported over and over again that the electors would only sell their votes for cash or the Fugger's promises to pay.[2] Francis, therefore, tried at first to bring them over to his side. He had the Fugger asked to accept a bill of 300,000 écus for him, and as Jakob Fugger told one of the Spanish representatives at the end of February he could have been able to make 30,000 florins over this transaction. But the Fugger wished, as the Dutch Finance Minister Hoochstraten said in their praise, to remain 'good and loyal subjects of Our Lord the King.' Probably also the security offered by Francis did not seem good enough. In any case the result of their reflections was unfavourable to the French.[3]

In February, 1519, the Hapsburg party in the Empire was very nervous lest the South German merchants should transfer their good offices to the King of France.

The Swabian League then wrote on 16th February to the Council of Augsburg that it had learnt that certain foreign Kings, the King of France amongst others, had sought to obtain bills from the companies and merchants. As this was in the interests of the opponents of the Alliance, the Council were to forbid the merchants to undertake such business on pain of death. The merchants moreover were to declare on oath what had already taken place in the matter. The Council imparted the contents of the letter to the merchants, who answered that of late

[1] See Jakob Fugger to Paul v. Armstorffer, Feb. 11, 1519 (Archives of German Nat. Museum).
[2] Letter of the Envoy to Charles in the State Archives in Lille.
[3] Mone, *Anzeiger*, 1836, Sp. 36. Le Glay, *Corresp. de Marguerite d'Autriche*, II, 203,

they had done no business of this kind with the King of France; certain of them moreover, both shortly before and after the Emperor's death, had refused the request of the French King to accept bills for him.[1] Nevertheless the merchants were still not considered perfectly safe. They were, therefore, expressly forbidden to undertake business in bills for the French, whereupon one of Charles' election agents wrote home that now through the help of the Fugger and the Swabian League the French Court could get neither credit nor bills. A few days later, however, the Statthalterin Margaretha wrote from Brussels to Charles that some merchants wished to pay only after the election and reserve themselves the possibility of using the money in certain eventualities for the King of France. It is expressly stated of the Welser that they seemed to wish to withdraw from the business on the plea that war had broken out between Nüremberg, where they had an important branch, and the Margrave of Brandenburg.[2]

Even though it proved possible to keep the merchants to their promise, French competition continued to drive up the price of the crown. In the beginning of March this was only a little over 500,000 florins, and of this amount only a very little remained to be raised. A few weeks later, however, Charles' agents had to report that a further sum of 220,000 florins was necessary. Charles at first was very unwilling, the whole business seemed to be getting too expensive. Finally he gave in and again applied to the Fugger for new loans.[3]

Jakob Fugger moreover was not by any means always ready to satisfy requirements on this increasingly gigantic scale. He found at the same time that he was asked to lend hundreds and thousands of fresh money, comparatively small old payments due to him remained in arrear.

He repeatedly complained of this as well as of many other wrongs he suffered. He was so indispensable that it was necessary to meet his wishes. Finally the Fugger lent the whole sum on bill acceptances and notes of hand given by Charles, who wished at all costs to become King of the Romans.[4] As all this did not satisfy the greed of the electors and one of them, Joachim of Brandenburg, really did go over to the French at the eleventh hour, the total loan now rose to over 850,000 florins, of which the Fugger lent 543,000 florins, the Welser 143,000 florins, the Genoese and the Florentines together 165,000 florins. The merchants' acceptances were handed over by Charles' representative piecemeal in

[1] *Augsburger Stadtarchiv, Litteralien.* (Le Glay, *Négoc. diplomat.* II, 244, 322, *vgl. damit auch*, II, 302 ff.).

[2] Mone, *Anzeiger*, 1836, Sp. 36. Le Glay, *Négoc. dipl.* II, 316 ff., 322.

[3] Mone, l.c. 1835, Sp. 286, and unprinted letter in Lille Archives. Sanuto (*Diarii*, XXVII, 252). Le Glay, *Négoc. dipl.* II, 288.

[4] Le Glay, *Négoc. dipl.* I, 220, II, 264, 437, 445. Mone, *Anzeiger*, 1836, Sp. 27–32.

return for the votes. This with many other curious details appears from an account bearing the title 'Expenses incurred by the Emperor Charles V for his election as King of the Romans.' It is neatly drawn up with entries for the electors with their counsellors and servants and their many other princes, counts, and other nobility. A considerable sum is spent for the upkeep of the Spanish Commissioner and his train, and for the Württemberg War, the Swabian League, Franz von Sickingen, etc., this entry amounts to 171,360 florins. Then come the previous advances that year of Jakob Fugger and Hans Paumgartner with the addition of 30,000 florins for interest, then the monies paid to the cities of the Empire, officials of the Court and so forth, 29,000 florins for payment of the Swiss mercenaries, and finally 17,500 florins difference in exchange to the Fugger and the Welser. Charles' envoys dealt so open-handedly with money that they scarcely noticed that while repayment was demanded from them in effective gold gulden, the merchants had only engaged in Flemish gulden, so that there was an agio of 2 kreuzer on each gulden.[1] The whole bill was paid in an honest and honourable way, Charles covering a small deficit from his own resources. He was now King of the Romans. The electoral act itself with its ceremonious speeches was only a comedy meant for the people.

In the last hour before the decision a very characteristic difficulty had arisen. The German princes refused the acceptances of the Italian merchants, who on their side would not deposit cash with the Fugger, on the ground that the Fugger had tried to spoil their business. Finally the matter was settled by the Welser going surety for the Italians.[2]

When the news of the election reached Augsburg, some of the most prominent citizens, Jakob Fugger among them, wanted to light bonfires. As this had never hitherto been the custom, the Council preferred to do it at the expense of the city.

'There were many hidden charges therein,' says the chronicler, 'that shot off in the fire. It was right fairly done and cost much money.' This might have been said of the election itself. Charles had reached his goal, but was it worth such a heavy sacrifice? One of his most active agents had written to him at the last moment that it was true the votes cost much money; on the other hand, they would give great security and quietness to Charles' rule in all his states. There has never been a greater political mistake. The Roman crown proved itself in every direction a fatal gift to its wearer.

Charles' election brought considerable expense for the splendours of

---

[1] Greiff *im Jahresberichte d. histor. Vereins f. Schwaben und Neuburg* 1868, S. 19 ff.

[2] Le Glay, *Négoc. dipl.* II, 336 ff.

his coronation progress to Aix and the coronation itself.[1] This, however, was a small thing in comparison. It was far more serious that the people of Spain showed no inclination to pay the price of the Crown, and when Charles' ministers tried to exact payment immediately after Charles' departure the fearful revolution of the citizens broke out, one of its main causes being the large export of money.[2] The worst effect, however, of Charles' election was that it brought him the undying hatred of the French King, and with it a series of wars which, though they brought Italy under Hapsburg influence, led to the loss of Metz, Toul, and Verdun, cost Charles' subjects streams of blood, and made Charles himself even more incurably bankrupt. Immediately after the election his finances were so exhausted that he could not meet a great part of his engagements and could still less arm against his defeated rival who was pushing on to war. Francis outbid him for the Swiss mercenaries, and also drew over to his side a mass of German troops.[3]

Some German princes who had contented themselves with the guarantee of the cities of Antwerp and Mechlin for the payments promised them by the Emperor, had to come upon their guarantors, who did not pay. Hereupon the princely creditors sent challenges to the cities with threats against their lives and property. The cities in their turn complained to the Emperor and he, having great need on his own account of Antwerp's powerful help, took some time to raise the money to satisfy the claims of the most influential of the German princes, the Archbishop of Mainz.

The Count Palatine, on the other hand, could not obtain payment, and other German princes fared no better, a fact which loosened their dependence on the Emperor and in many cases helped on open rebellion.[4]

Charles V and Jakob Fugger. The business houses which had helped Charles' election and had promptly discharged the engagements it had entailed were to find that the Emperor broke his solemn promises to pay. In the beginning of the year 1521, in the Diet of Worms, he made an agreement with Fugger under which their claim was transferred in part to Tyrol and in part to Spain. At that time he received a large new loan from the Welser. A few months later, in order to raise money for the French war, there were large sales of Crown property both in Naples and in the Netherlands which he had lately occupied. It was the Welser who bought the largest share. Next year also, though large amounts of money were raised in the Netherlands, Spain and Germany and sent to

[1] Lille Chambre des Comptes, B. 2294.
[2] Häbler, *Die wirthschaftliche Blüthe Spaniens im* 16. *Jahrhundert,* S. 53, An m. 13.
[3] Baumgarten, *Geschichte Karls V,* t. II, 28 ff. (Lanz, *Aktenstücke,* S. 453).
[4] Lanz, *Correspondenz Karls V,* t. I, 123, 129 ff., 453.

Italy for the maintenance of the Imperial forces, these proved insuffici-ent, and the payments to the merchants fell increasingly into arrears.[1]

The Emperor's credit was so bad in 1522 that Lucas Rem, who was interested in Jakob Fugger's large advances to the Emperor to the ex-tent of 18,310 fl., would have been glad to sell his share at half price. The Fugger in March, 1523, had received very little of the claim of 415,000 fl., for which they had been given a charge on Tyrol; and, more-over, nothing had been paid on the claims transferred to Spain amount-ing to 152,000 ducats, which, including interest and new advances, reached the total of 198,121 ducats at 375 maravedis to the ducat.

At last Jakob Fugger lost patience, and he wrote a letter to the Emperor which will be noteworthy for all time as evidence of the tone in which a merchant – the foremost of his time, of course – dared to adopt towards the most powerful monarch of his day:[2]

'Your Imperial Majesty doubtless knows how I and my kinsmen have ever hitherto been disposed to serve the House of Austria in all loyalty to the furtherance of its well-being and prosperity; wherefore, in order to be pleasing to Your Majesty's Grandsire, the late Emperor Maximilian, and to gain for Your Majesty the Roman Crown, we have held ourselves bounden to engage ourselves towards divers princes who placed their Trust and Reliance upon myself and perchance on No Man besides. We have, moreover, advanced to Your Majesty's Agents for the same end a Great Sum of Money, of which we ourselves have had to raise a large part from our Friends. It is well known that Your Imperial Majesty could not have gained the Roman Crown save with mine aid, and I can prove the same by the writings of Your Majesty's Agents given by their own hands. In this matter I have not studied mine own Profit. For had I left the House of Austria and had been minded to further France, I had obtained much money and property, such as was then offered to me. How grave a Disadvantage had in this case accrued to Your Majesty and the House of Austria, Your Majesty's Royal Mind well knoweth.'

We do not hear how Charles took this letter, which was delivered to him in Valladolid on 24th April, 1523. At any rate, it did the Fugger no lasting harm. In the subsequent years the repayment of these loans made more progress, though in 1530 there were still 112,200 fl. owing on the 415,000 fl. charged on Tyrol. In the meantime the Fugger had rendered many new services to the House of Austria.

The year 1524 brought great vicissitudes in the state of the Emperor's

[1] Spinelli in Brewer, *Calendar III*, App. 22. For 1522 cf. Lanz, *Correspondenz Karls V*, t. I, 70 ff.

[2] For Lucas Rem cf. v. Greiff *im Jahresber. d. histor. Ver. f. Schwaben* 1860, p. 73. For Jacob Fugger's letter see also von Greiff, l.c. 1868, p. 49.

finances. At the beginning of the year his lack of money and credit reached such a pitch that even in the Netherlands he could raise no new loans.

In the spring there was a distinct improvement for no very obvious reason. The complaints of the princes whose payments were in arrear were, it is true, particularly loud, but the armies in Italy and the South of France – Bourbon was besieging Marseilles – had plenty of money as late as August. Probably the Fugger had already provided money under the Spanish agreements, which we shall discuss later. At the end of August, however, means gave out altogether, and the army before Marseilles was in great straits.[1]

The position was identical with that of Maximilian before Milan in 1516. Now, as on the former occasion, negotiations were carried on with Henry VIII of England about the payment of subsidies. Now, again, the fact that the subsidies came too late caused the hasty withdrawal of the Emperor's forces. Thereupon King Francis descended suddenly on Italy and took Milan.

In February, 1525, the famous event occurred which appeared so brilliantly to justify Machiavelli's dictum that it is easier to get money with soldiers than soldiers with money. The Emperor had in Northern Italy a splendid army, but it had received no pay for three months, and was in such straits that it must either be disbanded or attack. The Emperor's marshals chose the latter alternative, and their success equalled their hopes. The battle of Pavia was fought, King Francis was taken prisoner, and money poured in from all sides. The King of England, the Republics of Genoa and Venice, the Pope and the Duke of Milan paid rich subsidies to the Emperor who had so suddenly risen to power.[2]

Throughout this period the Fugger are rarely mentioned in connection with the Imperial finances, and in the succeeding years the Emperor's policy, which was entirely centred on Italy, seems to have drawn him to the Genoese rather than the South German merchants. The point, however, which we have now reached is most important for the relations of the Fugger with the Hapsburgs, for now began their lasting connection with Spain and Naples.

Spain. In the year 1524 the Fugger for the first time took a lease, for the three years 1525–7, of the revenues of the Spanish Crown from the three great ecclesiastical Orders of Knights – those of Sant Jago, Cala-

---

[1] Baumgarten, *Geschichte Karls V*, vol. II, p. 256 ff., 269. Brewer, *Calendar IV*, 421, 463, 510, 589, 607, 761, etc. (Bergenroth, *Calendar II*, 651, 662).

[2] See Brewer, *Calendar IV*, Nos. 1064–1237. Cf. also Villa, *Italia desde la batalla de Pavia hasta el saco de Roma*, pp. 29, 73. Lanz, *Correspondenz*, I, 152. G. de Leva, *Stor. docum. di Carlo V*, t. II, 238 ff. Baumgarten, *Geschichte Karls V*, II, p. 291 ff.

trava and Alcantara – whose Grand Master was the King of Spain. With a few interruptions the famous lease of the Maestrazgos was in the Fugger's hands for more than a century. It formed the basis of their enormous Spanish business.

The leased revenues consisted chiefly in dues in money and kind from the lands of the orders. Later, the products of the quicksilver mines of Almaden and the silver mines of Guadalcanal were added. The Fugger had temporarily to take over the management of the mines as well as of many of the farms. In order to collect and manage revenues and properties – both extraordinarily various and scattered profits and properties – the Fugger kept representatives in the different districts under a chief agent at Almagro. Later on there was also at the Court a permanent agent, who was chief director of all the Fugger business in Spain. A particularly experienced man was always put in this post, which was both difficult and of cardinal importance for the fortunes of his employers.

It has been asserted that the Emperor intentionally drew the Genoese and the Fugger into Spanish affairs in order to chain them indissolubly to the fortunes of his house. This is not impossible, and in any case circumstances always tended to make the Fugger increasingly dependent on the state of their Spanish business.

The annual rent which the Fugger paid for the Maestrazgos was at first 135,000 ducats, or about 50 million maravedis. At the end of the first three years their total profit for the period was put at 2,200,000 maravedis, which, if correctly stated, was scarcely sufficient to pay interest on the capital. Nevertheless, the Genoese made a bid of 10,000 ducats more for the annual lease. This time, however, the newly discovered quicksilver mines were included.

The Genoese accordingly obtained the lease for five years, during which the rent amounted to about 54 million maravedis. The Maestrazgos then returned to the Fugger, who held the lease until 1634, with the intermission of the years 1557 to 1562, and perhaps also of the years 1615 to 1624. The rent for the period 1538–42 was 57 million maravedis; for 1547–50, 61 million; for 1563–72, 93 million; for 1573–82, 98 million; for 1583–94, 101 million; from 1595 onwards, $110\frac{1}{2}$ million. The lessees always had to prepay the rent often for several years ahead. Perhaps this was what happened in 1524 when the Fugger first took over the Maestrazgos, a fact which would explain the sudden, though temporary, cessation of the Emperor's money troubles. The Maestrazgos certainly served at that time to pay off the part of the old election debt which had been transferred to Spain.

Naples. The same time saw the beginning of the Fugger's lasting connection in Naples. It was, however, not the Emperor's finances, but those of his brother Ferdinand that gave the first impulse to this extension of the Fugger's business relations.

In 1521 the Emperor had transferred to Ferdinand the rule over the German dominions and with it a heavy load of debt dating back to the time of the Emperor Maximilian and the election of Charles. The revenues of this most important domain, Tyrol, had been in great part mortgaged to the Fugger for years ahead. Ferdinand, nevertheless, had to raise money for his brother for the war with the Turks, the suppression of the peasants' rising and many other pressing needs. He tried on all hands to raise money. His brother supported him by handing over important revenues in Naples which he could mortgage to the Fugger. They lent him accordingly, in 1524, 25,000 fl. and 20,000 ducats, and the next year 59,562 ducats.[1] Later, they had engagements in Naples for large amounts, sometimes as much as 400,000 ducats. The delays in repayment in Naples, however, always caused them great annoyance, so that in 1546 they cut their losses, and their rivals the Genoese held the field.

Jakob Fugger's Death. His Importance. About 1525 the Fugger were, beyond dispute, the most influential financiers of their time. Their busness relations reached from Hungary and Poland to Spain, from Antwerp to Naples. In the words of the contemporary chronicler of Augsburg, Clemens Sender, 'The names of Jakob Fugger and his nephews are known in all kingdoms and lands; yea, among the heathen also. Emperors, Kings, Princes and Lords have sent to treat with him, the Pope has greeted him as his well beloved son and embraced him, and the Cardinals have risen up before him. All the merchants of the world have called him an enlightened man, and all the heathen have wondered because of him. He is the glory of all Germany.'

At this high-water mark of their development the Fugger were to learn the constant peril of their position. In June, 1525, the machinations of their enemies caused them to be accused of delivering base metal to the Royal Mint; and at the order of King Ludwig their mines, their stores and other property were seized, and their people put in prison. Though Anton Fugger was able to disprove these charges and to annul the confiscation, the Fugger lost over this affair more than 200,000 gulden.[2]

It is undeniable, moreover, that the Fugger in many countries were hated by the people. Envy and misunderstanding contributed not a little to their unpopularity. In popular language their name was used as

---

[1] Oberleitner *im Archiv. f. Kunde österr. Geschichtsquellen XXII*, 19, 22 cf. *Augsberger Stadtarchive Herwarth. Collect. Suppl. Band II*, 414,

[2] Cf. Dobel, Bergbau und Handel der Fugger in Ungarn (*Ztschr. d. histor. Ver. f. Schwaben u. Neuburg*, Bd. VI) S. 42. Wenzel, *A Fuggerek jelentösége Magyarorszag történetében*, p. 28 ff., 138 ff., 147 ff., 155.

a generic term for a great monopolist. The Fucker, Fokker, Fucar, and so forth, have ever since become in many different countries the name for the financiers which the people held responsible for every evil.

Jakob Fugger, the man to whom the Fugger owe their greatness, died on the 30th January, 1526.[1] He is depicted as a handsome man, clean-shaven, wearing, as in his portraits, a cap of cloth of gold. He was of a merry disposition, pleasant to every one. Though modest in his bearing, he was on occasion a plain speaker, even to the most highly placed. He himself had few wants, but was hospitable in the grand style of his age and position. He gave many mummings, skating parties and dances to the most select society of Augsburg, the Herrentrinkstube. He would have rebuilt this clubhouse if he had been allowed to add the Fugger coat of arms. He was a true son of his time in his love of building. He had one of the existing Fugger houses in the Winemarket built and decorated with the utmost splendour. He had the church of St. Ann enriched with splendid statues and erected a wonderful family tomb. When, however, this church came into the hands of the Lutherans, he asked his nephews to have him buried elsewhere, for he was a good true Christian and quite against Lutheranism. He also contributed largely to the building of other churches and founded them on his own account.

The best known of his many charitable works is the Fuggerei alms-houses. A significant trait is his proposal to the Augsburg City Council that it should make an arrangement (no details of which are given) whereby the sheaf of rye should never cost the poor man more than a gulden. This proposal, as the Ehrenbuch says, went no further, owing to the counsels of the goddess Avarice.

The most interesting for us, however, is the little that is known about Jakob Fugger's personal relation to his business. He was a financier of the first rank 'of high understanding.' Even to the last he was a very keen man of business. When his nephew, Georg Thurso, urged him to give up the risky Hungarian business, he rejected such timorous counsels, saying that he 'would win so long as he was able.' Yet, when the catastrophe came, his cautious generalship was strikingly evident. In spite of the distant aims and enormous extent of a business scattered over Europe, he suffered so little from nerves that, as he often told his nephews, he never had 'any hindrance to sleep, but laid from him all care and stress of business with his shirt.'

We see the effect of Jakob Fugger's work if we compare the balance in the Fugger archives (2-1-22) for the year 1527 with the state of the property in 1511.

---

[1] The best source is the MS. copy of the Chronicle of Clemens Sender in the Augsburg City Archives. For his buildings and charities cf. Aloys Geiger, *Jakob Fugger*, p. 68.

		Florins
On the 14th February, 1511, the Fugger property in land, houses furniture and plate amounted to		70,884
Of this the male line received a third in advance		23,628
This left for the joint account of Jakob and the heirs of Ulrich and Georg in the business		47,256
To this were to be added various assets (goods, book debts, money, or its equivalents)		213,207
	Total	245,463
This was distributed as follows:		
Jakob Fugger		80,999
Heirs of Ulrich		87,583
Heirs of Georg		76,881
	Total	245,463
Different members of the family received from this		48,672
	Total	196,791

The remainder formed the capital with which the firm recommenced its operations.

At the end of 1527 the firm owned in –		
Land, houses, etc.		127,902
Goods, book debts, etc.		1,904,750
	Total	2,032,652
Of this a deduction was made for a charitable foundation		11,450
	Total	2,021,202
If we deduct the capital of 1511		196,791
we get the profit for 17 years		1,824,411

i.e. 927 per cent., or an average of $54\frac{1}{2}$ per cent. for each year.

Jakob Fugger died childless, and the Fugger business passed to the nephews, who had been his partners since 1510. Jakob's second will, executed a few weeks before his death (on the 22nd December), contained the following provisions: 'As the eldest nephew, Hieronymus, had not hitherto shown himself useful in the business and had not shared in the management, and as Jakob opined that this state would not alter, his two surviving nephews, Raymund and Anton, who had helped in his lifetime, were, on his death, to take over the management of the business. As, moreover, Raymund was not strong enough to undertake business journeys and much other work, Anton was to be empowered to manage the business at his own will and pleasure as Jakob had done. Thus the monarchical principle in force since the death of Jakob's brothers was confirmed for the next generation. The family history turned a new leaf, inscribed *Anton Fugger*.

II

HEYDAY UNDER ANTON FUGGER (1525-1560)

Anton's Cautious Policy in the Early Years. When Anton took over the direction of the business he was thirty-two – young enough, it might be supposed, to wish to launch out on his own rather than to maintain what his uncle had won. At first, however, he showed no great enterprise and was, on the whole, more intent on liquidating his present undertakings than in entering on new ones. This fact is the more remarkable in view of the extraordinary opportunities which immediately came his way. The financial position of the Hapsburgs was desperate. What this meant in politics is best illustrated by reference to two events: the defeat of Hungary by the Turks at Mohacs and its consequent need of protection by the Hapsburgs; and, secondly, the formation of the 'Holy Alliance' of Cognac, in which Pope Clement VII forged the hatred and revenge of the French King and the riches of the English into a weapon with which to break the power of the Emperor.

We can understand that Anton Fugger was none too ready to give unlimited credit to Ludwig, the King of Hungary, who had robbed him with violence a year before. Nevertheless, he helped him in his extremity with 50,000 fl., which, however, proved insufficient. After the battle the Fugger's agent said to the English agent, John Hacket, that King Ludwig would not have been defeated if he had had 150,000 ducats more in cash.[1] The King lost his life in the battle, and in the consequent struggle for the Hungarian crown, Ferdinand of Austria won a victory over the national candidate Zapolya. This proved an expensive business, and there was once more danger from the Turks. The Emperor, moreover, asked his brother to raise troops for Italy, but sent no money to pay them as he himself was in great straits.[2]

The Emperor's Italian army left unprovided laid waste Northern Italy. His credit in Venice and Genoa was ruined, because the Neapolitan Government did not pay the bills which the Emperor's com-

---

[1] Wenzel, l.c. p. 156. Brewer, *Calendar IV*, No. 2485.
[2] Lanz, *Correspondenz*, I, 218, 238. Villa, *Italia desde la batalla de Pavia hasta el saco de Roma*, pp. 110, 116, 126. Gayangos, *Calendar III*, 1, 509.

mandery had drawn on them and because the Italians generally began to hate the Emperor's rule. In short, the world power policy of the House of Hapsburg was once again irreconcilably at variance with the sorry state of its finances.

The Fugger helped over and over again, but they demanded adequate security, which was not forthcoming in the summer of 1526. In August Ferdinand sent a trusted agent to Augsburg to raise money, which neither the city nor the merchants disposed to lend. The latter, not only the Fugger, but the Hochstetter, Paumgartner, Pimel, etc., declared that their money was tied up in the Tyrolese mines, that they had incurred severe losses in Hungary and had had their business greatly hampered elsewhere, and that therefore they could raise no ready money themselves. Attempts were made to raise loans in Strasburg, Ulm and the Netherlands. At length, by pledging the Crown jewels, Georg Frundsberg was able to raise some money and hire some mercenaries whom he marched to Italy, though there was no more money for their pay. The following year, 1527, the Emperor had to resort to the shadiest methods in order to keep his mutinous army. Ferdinand's situation in Hungary was no better.[1]

In Italy this chapter was closed by the sack of Rome by the Emperor's troops, who paid themselves by this means. In order to ward off the peril from the East, the necessary money was always raised at the last moment. The Fugger took a leading part in this again in 1527, and their claims on King Ferdinand reached a large total.[2]

The Fugger Balance Sheet in 1527. In order to get a better insight into the extent and nature of the Fugger business at this time, we will examine their balance sheet for 1527, stated in round numbers. The assets amounted to 3 million gulden. This was distributed as follows:

	Florins
Mines and mining shares	270,000
Other real estate	150,000
Goods	380,000
Cash	50,000
Book debts	1,650,000
Private accounts of the partners for sums taken from them since 1511	430,000
Unconcluded business	70,000
	3,000,000

[1] Villa, l.c. pp. 126, 166, 187, 190–91. Oberleitner, pp. 30, 121. Thorsch, *Materialien z. einer Gesch. d. österr. Staatsschulden*, p. 24.

[2] Guicciardini (C. III). Ferdinand's loans with the Fugger in 1527, cf. Oberleitner, p. 33, 45; Thorsch, p. 25–26.

The mines were apportioned 60,000 fl. to Tyrol and 210,000 fl. to Hungary; the real property was 57,000 fl. plots of land in and around Augsburg, 70,000 fl. of farms, 15,000 fl. for the house in Antwerp and its appurtenances, 6,000 fl. for the house in Rome.

The goods consisted chiefly of copper (of which there was a store worth 200,000 gulden in Antwerp alone), silver, tin, and a small amount of cloth, damask, and other textiles.

The ready money is distributed between the chief office in Augsburg and fourteen factories. In the whole of Spain the Spanish agents held only 1,541 fl., in Augsburg 7,262 fl. (as against 10,376 fl. in Nuremberg and 12,844 fl. in Breslau), but this has no significance.

Among the book debts the largest items are those in the 'Courtbook' containing the claims against King Ferdinand and his estates, including the amounts he had drawn on Naples. The total was 651,000 fl. We note the following items:

161,840 fl. remainder of the 415,000 fl. charged on Tyrol from the sums due on the Emperor's election.

156,000 fl. bond on Naples, 7th January, 1526 = 108,662 ducats to be paid off before 1530.

86,090 fl. = 60,063 ducats repayable in instalments, also transferred to Naples.

40,000 fl. on the salt pans at Hall at interest at 8 per cent., etc.

King Ferdinand also owed 60,619 fl. over and above the 'Courtbook.'

The Spanish book debts amounted to 507,000 fl., but these were set off against liabilities amounting to 337,000 fl., so that capital in Spain amounted only to 170,000 fl. These Spanish transactions were mostly connected with the lease of the Maestrazgos.

A considerable number of doubtful claims were written off as bad debts, e.g.:

206,741 fl., claim on King Ferdinand for losses for robbery of the Fugger business in Hungary by King Ludwig.

113,122 fl., divers claims on Alexi Thurzo.

20,938 fl., claim on the Pope, arising under Pope Leo, for insufficient security (jewels).

The liabilities amount only to 870,000 fl., distributed as follows:

	Florins
Spain (already mentioned)	340,000
Bills	290,000
Hungary	54,000
Various	186,000
	870,000

The bills ('Billbook') were numerous entries, mostly belonging to friends or kinsmen. They were interest-bearing deposits, which the Fugger took partly out of kindness, partly to increase their liquid capital against acceptances or bills with one name. The interest varied very much, large items being as little as 2–3 per cent., rising to 30 per cent. or more for small entries. (The latter, apparently, are instances of benevolence.)

The factories and other branches besides the head office were as follows:

(1) Bozen: A small depot for goods.
(2) Hall in Tyrol: Real estate, reserves of copper, silver, as well as 26,000 fl. of outstanding debts and 3,134 fl. in cash.
(3) Schwatz: Mine 74,000 fl. worth of ore, 45,000 fl. of outstanding debts.
(4) Fuggerau: Mining shares and 31,706 fl. of outstanding debts.
(5) Vienna $\Big\}$ unimportant.
(6) Leipzig
(7) Smelting works : Hochkirch in Silesia.
(8) Breslau: House and mine on the Reichenstein.
(9) Neusohl in Hungary: Mine and houses, stock of silver.
(10) Nuremberg: Factory with 34,000 fl. of outstanding debts.
(11) Frankfort-on-Main: Small factory for the fairs, only some furniture and some unfinished business.
(12) Cologne: Quite unimportant.
(13) Antwerp: Large factory with house, barns, garden, stabling much furniture and important stocks of goods.
(14) Amsterdam: Unimportant.
(15) Denmark: Only business connected with forwarding Hungarian copper from the Baltic to Antwerp.
(16) Venice: Chambers and magazines with much furniture and stocks of copper and tin.
(17) Rome: House, some furniture, 26,000 fl. of outstanding debts.
(18) Spain: A considerable number of factories (already described).

Such was the state of the Fugger business after two years of Anton's management. It was extensive, and the number of outstanding liabilities was very large; but, on the other hand, the securities were good and the whole business situation was sound. The liabilities counted for very little.

Cautious Policy of the Fugger till 1530. Anton Fugger still did not allow himself to be lured away from his cautious principles. In the autumn of 1527, however, he undertook to get by various methods 100,000 crowns for the Emperor from Spain to Germany, where the money was used to procure new troops for Italy.[1] There was, however, little risk involved. At the same time, the lease of the Maestrazgos was to be renewed, and Anton Fugger let himself be outbidden by the Genoese. The last named became at that time increasingly important in supplying the Emperor with money, and the Antwerp money market proved so good a source of supply that it was not necessary to apply to the Fugger, who had not yet begun to use the Antwerp Bourse for their large financial operations. A little earlier the condition of the Imperial troops in Italy was much what it had been before Pavia. But in the summer and early autumn of 1528 so much money flowed in from all sides that the Emperor was able to bring over the great Andrea Doria, whose claims Francis had left unsettled. We shall see later the details of this affair, where finance played the chief part. All we know of the Fugger at this time is the fact drawn from Dr. Christopher Scheuerl's letterbooks, that they had paid the half of the 90,000 ducats which the King of Portugal had advanced to the Emperor. The Welser had paid the rest. King Ferdinand, too, received from the Fugger only small amounts, less than from the Herwarts and Pimels.[2]

In the beginning of the year 1529 the Emperor found himself once again in such straits that he announced that he would not shrink from selling Toledo to raise money. He failed to understand why no one now would lend to him. In May Andrea Doria echoed the same plaint, and by August things were no better. There was nothing to do but to make peace, for King Francis was no better situated. The money question played an important part in the case of both parties at the Peace of Cambrai. Throughout this whole year there is no mention of the Fugger.

The Hapsburgs and the Fugger in 1530. The Emperor now enjoyed a long period of peace with France, but this did not mean rest for him. He immediately betook himself to other tasks, entailing considerable expenditure. The chief motive of his leaving Spain in 1529 was to reduce Italy to order, that is, by the subjugation of Florence to obtain grants of money from the Medici Pope Clement VII. This last step was necessary in order to obtain the election of his brother Ferdinand as King of Rome and to give him help against the Turks; lastly, too, the German heretics had to be chastised.[3]

All this meant troops and ready money; the first was forthcoming, but not the second. The Emperor, however, at the Peace of Cambrai had stipulated enormous ransoms for the French princes amounting to 1,200,000 gold crowns. This sum, however, was not paid till 1530 and

---

[1] Brewer, *Calendar IV*, Nos. 3597, 3885, *Papiers d'Etat du Cardinal de Granvelle*, I, 347.

[2] Thorsch, p. 28.

[3] Lanz, *Correspondenz*, I, 360 ff. *Coleccion de documentos ineditos*, vol. XIV, and Heine, *Briefe an Karl V*. Gayangos, *Calendar*, vols. III and IV.

1531, and the Emperor reserved the greater part of it for some undisclosed purpose, probably for the various eventualities entailed by his policy.[1]

The Cortes, at the end of 1528, had granted him extraordinary taxation, and we shall see later how skifully he used this to raise ready money in Genoa. But, as he wrote to his brother, the Spaniards detested all expenditure for Italy, and accordingly he could take very little money with him from Spain, and even at times could not have it sent after him for fear of rousing Spanish discontent.

The Netherlands granted new 'aides,' on which the Statthalterin Margaretha borrowed large sums, part of which were transferred through the Genoese to Italy, part through the agency of the Fugger, Welser and Herwarts to Germany, in order to recruit new troops for Italy.[2] This money, however, did not last long. Though the Genoese helped once again in the summer of 1530, in October the pay of the troops was again 70,000 ducats in arrear, so that looting and mutiny set in once more.[3]

The Emperor not only kept his army together, but increased it, thereby furthering the Pope's dearest wish – the overthrow of Florence. Charles, however, always kept before the Pope the necessity of defending Hungary against the Turks, which he considered the common duty of all Christendom, and so was not willing to bear the sole cost. His envoys also hinted at the possible chastisement of the German heretics. By these means it was hoped to induce the Pope to make large grants from his well-filled treasury.

The Emperor before coming to Italy had obtained from Clement an important grant, the Cruzada. This was the name for the Crusade bulls which the Popes had granted in earlier times to the Kings of Castile to cover the cost of the war with the Moors. Under it any one could buy indulgences. When the struggle against the unbelievers ceased in Spain only the traffic in indulgences remained. The Cruzada was meanwhile seldom granted by the Popes.[4]

Since 1522 the Emperor had often applied first to Pope Adrian and then to Clement for the grant of a Cruzada General en Toda la Christianidad for a great war against the Turks. It had been granted him in 1523, but only for his own dominions and for one year, because the Pope was

---

[1] Gayangos, IV, 1, 840, IV, 2, 83. Le Glay, *Négoc. dipl. entre la France et l'Autriche, precis histor.* CCVII.

[2] Lille, B. 2351 (1529): 'Deniers paiez es mains de l'empereur par mandemens: 41,000 fl. d'or aux Fockers, Velser et Herwarders.'

[3] Heine, l.c. pp. 12, 24. *Col. de docum. ined.* XIV, 85, 92 ff.

[4] Häbler, p. 113. Philippson in Sybel's *Histor. Ztschr.*, vol. 39, p. 281. Gachard, *Corresp. de Charles V et d'Adrien VI*, pref. CII, CX, 2, 61, 170, 181, 190, 199, 221. Gayangos, III, 1, 240, 302, 325, 419, 456, 529.

afraid of competition for the jubilee year 1525. On Adrian's death a short time after, Clement refused to grant the Bull, and, as open enmity then broke out between the Emperor and the Pope, there could be no further question of it. It is probable that the Emperor's desire for the Cruzada was an important motive for his making peace with the Pope, who on his side demanded as his price the restoration of the Medici in Florence. The Cruzada became once again a burning question, and in February, 1529, the Emperor's envoys managed to obtain the grant. Difficulties ensued, however, and it was still some time before the Bull could be published. The Emperor failed to obtain further grants till after Florence had fallen.[1]

When Charles came back from Italy to Germany in the spring of 1530, for the purpose of settling its religious confusion and obtaining his brother's election as King of Rome, he was at any rate sure of the Cruzada and was about to get in the French ransoms. All the same, he had to remain some time in Innsbrook as he had no money for continuing his journey. He had to bring himself to touch a small part of the French ransoms, and as he needed money at once he applied to the South German merchants, who gave him the help he needed.[2]

He had sent from Spain 200,000 crowns of the French ransoms and 150,000 ducats from the subsidy previously granted him by the Cortes. The equivalent of these amounts was in part paid over by the Fugger and Welser to the Emperor himself, and in part used by them for the election of Ferdinand as King. The money was brought secretly to Fuentarabbia on the Spanish frontier and there received by an agent of the Fugger. The Fugger had been promised that the export of the money from Spain should be made as easy as possible for them; it had to be carried out secretly, however, because otherwise the Spaniards would not have let it go.

This, however, was not all that the Fugger and Welser lent the Emperor. We know that together they advanced large sums on the Cruzada, but we know no details of the transaction.[3] We are, however, exactly informed as to the sums lent by the Fugger to Ferdinand for his election as King of Rome by a contract in the Fugger Archives, dated 25th October, 1530, between the King on the one part and Raymund, Anton and Hieronymus Fugger on the other, 'on account of a sum of

---

[1] Gayangos, III, 2, 893; (III, 2, 975). *Bulletin de la commission d'histoire* 3, ser. VII, 33. *Compte-rendu* 4, ser. XVI, p. 261 ff. (IV, I, 117). Heine, p. 35, Gayangos, IV, 1, p. 146.

[2] Heine, l.c. p. 10. Gayangos, IV, 1, 478, 492, 742–43, 746 ff., 776, 783 ff., 840 (also IV, 1, 183), IV, 2, 83. Lanz, *Correspondenz*, I (6.–12, 1531).

[3] Lucas Rem, *Tagebuch*, p. 75. Virck, *Polit. Corresp. d. Stadt Strassburg I*, No. 762.

money, should Your Majesty need it, for His election as King of Rome.'

According to this agreement, the Fugger had to pay out on Ferdinand's account 275,333 fl. 20 kr. (20,000 fl. gold to the Archbishop of Mainz on the spot, 32,000 fl. to him in 1531, 16,000 fl. to the Elector of Brandenburg, 100,000 fl. in two yearly instalments to the Count Palatine, and the remainder, 98,000 fl., direct to the King's treasurer, Pfennigmeister). The whole bore interest at 10 per cent. As, moreover, the Fugger 'in the present heavie courses' had had themselves to borrow part of the money from their friends and other merchants at extremely high rates of interest, while their other business had had to suffer the lack thereof (in return both for their great trouble and the risk that the Fugger had incurred by raising the money in so short a time and because they had had to send it to their loss by bills from the most various places). On all these grounds and of his special favour the King assured a special 'refreshment and token of honour of 40,000 fl.' Including this high extra charge and the interest Ferdinand's whole liability upon his election amounted to 356,845 fl. 37 kr. Of this amount 100,000 fl. were to be repaid in the Netherlands in five yearly instalments of 20,000 fl.; 173,333 fl. 20 kr. were secured on a Neapolitan annuity of Ferdinand's, amounting to 160,000 ducats a year, so that this part would be paid off (with 120,930 ducats) in seven or eight years' time; 73,512 fl. were to be repaid from the Schwatz silver. For the remaining 10,000 fl. the Fugger were to be allowed to take over the Mark of Burgau for the sum at which the Bishop of Augsburg then held it. Further, they had to pay an annuity of 7,000 fl. to the Archbishop of Mainz, and repay themselves for this from the revenues of the Joachimsthal mines and the salt pans at Hall.

Perhaps, in view of these extensive repayments, the extra charge of 40,000 fl. is not really excessive.

A balance sheet of 1530 shows that King Ferdinand owed the Fugger not less than a million gulden, *inter alia*:

112,200 still due on Charles' election as Emperor.

249,000 fl. on the income in Naples.

258,400 fl. old Hungarian debt.

The last named item, however, is perhaps the sum which had been written off as irrecoverable by the Fugger in 1527. They now added interest to the total without much hope of getting anything. It continued to figure in later balance sheets under 'doubtful debts outstanding.'[1] In spite of these enormous loans, the Fugger made others in the same year. Italian affairs were now settled. The Germans had, at any rate, come to a provisional settlement with the Diet of Augsburg and the election of Ferdinand as King of Rome.

[1] Oberleitner, l.c. p. 45., also p. 48; Thorsch, p. 32.

The retreat of Soliman from Vienna had made the Turkish danger less pressing for the moment. The Emperor could therefore allow himself leisure to settle his finances. He set up a commission to investigate the titles of the old claims, some dating back to his grandfather, which encumbered him, and he used the French ransoms, the grants from the Pope and other sources to pay off his debts in grand style. King Ferdinand made an attempt at any rate to consolidate his burden of debt.[1]

On 14th November, 1530, the Emperor ennobled Raymund, Anton and Hieronymus Fugger, gave them great immunities, and allowed them to choose whether and when they wished to take the title of Count or Freiherr. They did not, however, do so at this time.[2]

The Balance Sheets of the Fugger in 1533 *and* 1536. At this period the business capital of the Fugger did not increase so rapidly as under Jakob. In 1527 it had amounted to 2 million gulden, of which, however, 400,000 fl. had been taken out by the partners, so that only 1,600,000 fl. remained. New balance sheets were drawn up in 1533 and 1536, and the latter shows 1,800,000 fl. as business capital. We can state the profit only for the period 1534–6. It amounted to 120,000 fl. – i.e. only $2\frac{1}{5}$ per cent. per annum.

The assets in 1536 amount to 3,811,000 gulden. The liabilities had nearly doubled between 1527 and 1536. They now amounted to 1,770,000 gulden. In other words, the increase of the business since 1527 had only been made possible by outside capital. The bill engagements had risen from 290,000 fl. to 703,000 fl. The 'Billbook' now contains a large number of large and small entries, interest-bearing deposits mostly in the names of friends and kinsmen, though other names occur, showing that these were in part real loans. Most items are under 10,000 fl., the largest single item being 34,000 fl.; the average rate of interest is $4\frac{1}{2}$–5 per cent.

In Spain, too, the Fugger owed large sums, which appear to have been closely connected with the outstanding debts due to them.

We may mention:

	Million Maravedis
New lease of the Maestrazgos	25
Sebastian Neidhart	$12\frac{1}{3}$
Christopher Herwart	$3\frac{1}{6}$
Jakob Welser & Sons, Nüremberg	$8\frac{1}{4}$

In Antwerp we may note as large creditors Lazarus Tucher with

[1] Lanz, *Correspondenz I*, 421. Thorsch, p. 30. Brussels Archives (*Papiers d'Etat et de l'Audience* No. 873).
[2] Geiger, p. 23.

21,000 £ fl. (against which are to set off 4,700 £ fl. owed by him) and Erasmus Schetz with 5,000 £ fl.

Taking it all in all, while the state of the business was not so sound as nine years before, there was yet no cause for anxiety.

Subsequent Period till 1546. We have little information as to the Fugger's financial dealings in the following decade.

In 1536, when the Emperor again entered on war with France, the Fugger instantly took a leading part in raising the necessary money. On the 14th April they granted the Emperor a loan of 100,000 ducats, payable in two instalments in May and June, to be repaid at the end of the year with 14 per cent. interest from the first gold or silver from India. For still greater security they were granted a privilege, whereby they received an annuity of 26,526 ducats from the revenues of the crown of Castile with the right to sell it, if the debt had not been repaid before January, 1537.[1]

The supply of gold and silver 'from India' was this year so plentiful that the mints did not know how to deal with it. Nevertheless, the Emperor's war-chest suffered from permanent emptiness, so that after the unsuccessful expedition to the South of France, the Emperor's counsellors recommended him to cease hostilities for want of money.[2]

On 26th February, 1537, the Fugger again lent the Emperor 100,000 ducats, payable in two instalments in May and June, to be repaid from the first Spanish revenues of the year 1538. For greater security the Fugger were allowed to hold back the rent of the Maestrazgos.

The loan was to begin to bear interest at 14 per cent. two months before the payment of the instalments, an increase of the interest which was fairly usual. The reason adduced was the difficulty of raising money, which forced the lender to make arrangements some time before paying over the loan, so that large sums were lying at home without interest, or bearing no interest while on their way from other countries.

Moreover, in 1537 the Turkish danger made new armaments necessary and King Ferdinand had to borrow 83,000 florins from the Fugger.[3]

In the years 1538 and 1539 the Emperor continued to have large amounts of money brought from Spain and the Netherlands to Germany and Italy, though the war with France had long been over. People puzzled over what this money was meant for. Was it for a new expedition against the Barbary pirates, against the Turks, or against the German Protestants? The last named began to regard the

---

[1] Fugger-Archiv. 44, 1.
[2] Lanz, *Corresp.* II, 265, 656 ff. Scheuerl's MS. letterbooks, June, 1534.
[3] Thorsch, p. 33.

Fugger, who were once again largely interested in these affairs, with special distrust.[1]

We have again a Fugger balance sheet for the year 1539, though only a rough profit and loss account. Once again the extensions of the Spanish business is noteworthy.

The book debts now amount to $1\frac{1}{4}$ millions, against which the liabilities are 542,000 fl.

Among the debts due we note:

His Imperial Majesty

			Million Maravedis
Bill of	30,000	ducats	10·8
,, ,,	50,000	,,	6·7
,, ,,	70,000	,,	32·2
,, ,,	65,000	,,	17·2
,, ,,	150,000	,,	46·6
,, ,,	476,000	,,	105·0
Maestrazgos $a/_c$			75·2
			293·7

This is more than 780,000 ducats.

Among the Spanish liabilities may be instanced:

	Million Maravedis
Alonso de Santa Gadea	11
Hans Welser and Brothers	29
Sebastian Neidhart	8·2
,, $a/_c$ of 476,000 ducats	21·5
,, various $a/_c$	9

These 79 million maravedis of over 200,000 ducats are apparently shares in the Fugger's large transactions with the Emperor.

At Antwerp, also, the book debts had grown, and now amount to 202,000 fl. The King of Portugal owes 22,100 £ fl., the Statthalterin Maria 7,000 £ fl.

The 'Courtbook' is considerably reduced and only amounts to 417,000 fl. This reduction is to some extent only apparent, as the Neapolitan engagements are kept in a separate account, amounting to

[1] Scheuerl's letterbook, March, 1538. Letter of Anton Welser in Augsburg to Lienhard Tucher in Nürnberg, 7 April, 1539 (Tucher-Archiv). State papers, King Henry VIII, vol. I, 608, 16 April, 1539. Lanz, *Corresp.* II, 307.

362,000 fl. There is nevertheless a slight fall in the outstanding claims, inconsiderable, however, in comparison with the increase of the Spanish investments.

The bill liabilities have increased still further to 804,000 florins. For the years 1540 and 1541 we know only of two rather unimportant loans granted to King Ferdinand by the Fugger; these were followed at the beginning of 1542 by business on a larger scale.[1] A new period of large financial operations began, but unfortunately our information is very imperfect.

The progress of the Turks in alliance with France forced the Hapsburg brothers to war on two fronts and to extraordinary financial efforts. With the help of the international money-market of Antwerp, they raised loans on a larger scale than ever before. In this the Fugger played the leading part. We shall see later how these loans were raised in Antwerp. Unhappily the Netherlands finance accounts, in other respects very instructive, do not give the names of the individual lenders, but only those of the financiers who acted as agents for the court of Brussels.

Accordingly the Fugger's exact share is not clear. From another source we learn only that the Queen Statthalterin Maria in 1542 borrowed from the Fugger and Welser 250,000 crowns within six weeks for the Emperor, while he himself borrowed 600,000 crowns in Spain, and that he raised a loan from the Fugger for Italy amounting to 100,000 ducats. In 1544 King Ferdinand received 109,105 ducats and 108,645 fl. from Queen Maria. We do not know who lent her the money.[2]

Period of the War of Schmalkalden. The period we now enter is fateful for the Fugger. At this time their business reached its highest point, but the seed of corruption was now sown and was shortly after to show itself.

The firm had already undergone an important change. Raymund Fugger had died in 1535, and Hieronymus in 1538. In this year Anton had taken his nephews, Hans, Jakob, George, Christopher and Raymund, into the business which henceforth bore the name of 'Anton Fugger and Nephews.' Anton retained complete control of the concern. He had to give no account of profits and losses to his nephews, and they on their side had to render unquestioning obedience to him.[3] It is doubtful whether he used this absolute power invariably for the good of the family. The business, however, which proved the most unlucky

---

[1] Thorsch, p. 34. Gairdner, *Cal. XVIII*, No. 292.

[2] Lanz, *Correspondenz*, January, 1542. Thorsch, p. 39.

[3] Cf. the Gesellschafts-Vertrag of 1538 in the Fugger-Archives, 2, 1, 14, fol. 45.

was not undertaken till the last years of Anton's life when his hold on the reins was somewhat loosened.

The force of money in determining the course of the world's history meets us at every turn at this period. Up to 1546 we have been able to trace it very imperfectly from lack of detailed information, but from the outbreak of the war of Schmalkalden we can follow more closely again.

In April, 1546, when the Emperor's decision to make war on the Protestants was not yet known, he sent orders to his son Philip in Spain to raise the money for the war.[1]

The first step was to be the raising of a loan of 150,000 to 200,000 ducats at the lowest possible interest from the Fugger or the Welser on the pretext that it was for the maintenance of the Imperial Court. Next, a message was to be sent to Genoa to the Imperial envoy Figueroa ordering him to raise as best he could a further 150,000 ducats by means of a charge in the Papal grants and on the rent of the Maestrazgos. Finally, 200,000 ducats were to be raised in Antwerp, if possible on 'finance,' i.e. by short-term borrowing on the bourse, which the Emperor thought more advantageous and easier than bill transactions. This was perfectly true, for we know from other sources that in Antwerp bills on South Germany were only taken with difficulty, the uncertainty of the political situation having made the merchants nervous. The attempts to raise money must be distributed in this way, the Emperor said, because it would be impossible to raise so large a sum in any one place, and because by so doing it was easier to conceal the aim of the operation. The letter gives further instructions for the execution of the different financial undertakings and emphasizes the necessity of having all the money ready for use in Germany at the beginning of June.

These arrangements, however, proved in part impossible to carry out, first because of the difficulty of getting the money so quickly from Spain, then because the Pope left the Emperor in the lurch. He withdrew the grants he had originally promised and in the end took sides against Charles,[2] who accordingly could get no money in Italy. He was therefore thrown upon the Catholic business houses of South Germany, and on the Antwerp Bourse. At first, however, these partially failed him, so that his state was for some time critical, and it was only in July that he could raise sufficient troops. His opponents, the Protestant princes, fared scarcely better.

[1] This important document is published in v. Döllinger, *Dokum. z. Geschichte Karls V*, p. 44 ff.

[2] Lanz, *Correspondenz Karls V*, vol. II, 490. Maurenbrecher, *Karl V und die deutschen Protestanten*, p. 120 ff., 128, and Appendix, p. 75.

In Augsburg the prevailing party was the Protestant democratic party, under the Burgomaster Jakob Herbrot, who kept the city on the side of the Schmalkaldian League. A middle party under another Protestant Burgomaster, Hans Welser of the Nüremberg Welser, strove in vain for neutrality, while the great Catholic patricians mostly left the city because they were discontented with the present rule and did not wish to be involved in the confusion. We shall see later how some of these kept a wavering attitude between the parties. The Fugger, however, once again proved faithful to the House of Austria.[1]

The support which the Emperor received from his great Catholic merchants roused the greatest bitterness among the Schmalkaldians. They, too, were ceaselessly embarrassed for money. Though the King of France advanced 100,000 crowns and the cities belonging to the League contributed, the Elector of Saxony, Johann, had still, after the outbreak of the war, to try to raise money in small sums, 1,000 to 6,000 florins at a time, in order to pay his troops. The League in July demanded accordingly that the Augsburg merchants, who had raised a large sum to help the Emperor in this ruinous purpose, and had encouraged and even incited him to it, should now do the same for the opposite party and cease to lend to the Emperor. They even demanded that the Augsburg Council should *force* its burghers to lend all their ready money, jewels, and silver plate, for the League. When, in August and Spetember, there was talk of new dealings of the Fugger with the Emperor, the letters of the Catholic business houses, the Fugger, Paumgartner, Neidhart, Herwart, Meuting, and of the companies of Bartholomew Welser and Hans Herwart, were seized and opened. The Fugger had promised the Augsburg Council to| deliver the wheat harvested on their lands at Augsburg. They were, however, forced by the Schmalkaldians to send it to their head-quarters at Ulm.

The Augsburg Council held it their duty to protect the interests of their citizens against such demands. This they successfully did, and Anton Fugger showed his gratitude later by interceding for his native city with the Emperor. In September the bitterness of the Schmalkaldians against the Fugger reached its climax. They told the Augsburg' envoy, Matthew Langemantel, that they knew that the King of England was just about to repay 60,000 fl. to the Fugger and Welser, who must lend this money to the League. Should they decline,

---

[1] Cf. Hecker in *d. Ztschr. d. histor. Vereins f. Schwaben*, 1, 34 ff. Also Litteralien in the Augsburg Archives, and the correspondence of Sebastian Neidhart, Hieron. Seiler and Anton Fugger. For the finances of the League of Schmalkalden, cf. Kius, *Das Finanzwesen Ernestin. Hauses Sachsen im.* 16 *Jahrh*, p. 75 ff.

in spite of having lent the Emperor another 200,000 fl., they must be treated as open enemies, 'as those who by their loans and bills had furthered the Emperor in this war, which else he had been unable to bring to pass.' The Landgrave of Hesse threatened to destroy the Fuggers' farmhouses. When the Augsburg Council informed Anton Fugger, who was in Schwatz, offering him to take care of his interests, he replied that he had no money which he could lend the Schmal-kaldians and that he had to use the money repaid him by the King of England (which was much less than had been alleged) for the payment of his debts and the maintenance of his family. He thanked the Council for their offer and promised again to deserve it. Accordingly the Council now decided to take definitely the side of its burghers against the Protestant princes, and showed its solidarity by regretting that it must bear the displeasure of the princes in common with them.

This did not fail to happen. The Elector of Saxony said, 'How comes it that the men of Augsburg wish to bite the nut with the Fugger, when before they kept Raymund Fugger in prison, merely for offending against a poor man?'

It appears that in the end the democratic party were able to obtain forced loans from the Catholic merchants, but we are ignorant of the details. In any case, the Schmalkaldians' complaints as to their financial difficulties never ceased, while the Emperor now had plenty of money. He accordingly played a waiting game, while the League tried to force him to a battle. The invasion of Duke Maurice of Saxony into the domain of the Elector forced the Elector Johann Friedrich to separate himself from the League, and so the Emperor, at the end of 1546, became master of South Germany.

The South German Protestants now had to entreat the Emperor for mercy and buy it with enormous contributions. Anton Fugger under-took to act as mediator for his native city with the Emperor, who had then pitched his head-quarters at Ulm. By the gift of a golden drinking-vessel valued at 3,000 kronen, Anton Fugger gained the favour of the Duke of Alba, who helped in his turn to get a reduction of the Augsburg contribution.[1] In the whole negotiation, Anton Fugger appears as the sole intermediary and as a great man who often had to deal severely with the Augsburg Council, when they tried to cheat over trifles.

The Welser, who at the same time also had a representative in the Imperial camp (we shall see later what forced them to this), had to be content with hard treatment, because their behaviour at the beginning of the war had been very uncertain. Anton Fugger was held up

[1] *Ztschr. d. histor. Vereine f. Schwaben*, I, 57, 294.

before them as a model. He, on his part, was not at all edified by the violence and low cunning which were manifest both in the Emperor's policy and in the conduct of these finances, as is shown by many passages in his letters. He decided very unwillingly to help again with ready money, which was needed for the upkeep of the army and the coming campaign in Saxony, for the forced contributions were not paid immediately. On the 27th January he lent the Emperor 122,477 fl. and on the 15th February a further 20,000 ducats. On the 26th February, however, the Welser's representative, Christopher Peutinger, reported to Augsburg that 'the Fugger were tired of Imperial loans; they had already let themselves in so deep that they had to wait a long time before they could get their money again.'

In further surmising that they would have to come in again, he was right. On 15th May, when Charles had conquered the Elector of Saxony, he concluded negotiations with the Fugger for a loan of 60,000 fl. in the camp at Wittenberg. Anton Fugger, meanwhile, had betaken himself from Ulm back to Schwatz, where he spent the greater part of the year in low spirits and poor health.

We learn from his letters and his will that the Fugger had had serious thoughts of giving up their business. Had they done so, it would have been fortunate for them.

Wish of the Fugger to give up their Business – Its state in 1546.   In his will, dated the 22nd March, 1550, and also in the last codicil of 1560 which deals with the business, Anton Fugger says that he had hoped that his nephews would follow in his footsteps and those of their forbears and become merchants, but that he had seen that none of them were disposed so to do. He had accordingly agreed with them to bring the business 'to an end and retire.' This decision must have been made in the year 1547 or the beginning of the next year, for the general balance sheet drawn up for its execution was closed at the end of the year 1546, and the first great distribution undertaken under this was made on 31st July, 1548. We must next consider the balance sheet for 31st December, 1546. It is perhaps the most important which has remained for us.[1]

	Florins
The landed estate valued at	729,331
The other assets, after deducting liabilities	4,382,552
Total	5,111,883

[1] In the Fugger-Archives, 2, 1, 22a, there are several copies of the balance sheet of 1546. The differences are explained by the different methods of calculation.

	Florins
The capital in 1539 had been	2,197,740
The amount made in the seven years was therefore an annual average of 19 per cent.	2,914,143
This profit was not, however, distributed in full. The money used in improvements on the landed property was written off at	210,443
The male line received on the remaining value of the landed estate preferential payment of ⅓	169,346
Anton Fugger received for his management ⅛ of the final profit also as a preferential payment	309,627
Finally the receipts from certain old outstanding debts were distributed separately	133,288
Total amount deducted	822,704

So that only 2,091,439 fl. was actually distributed.

It may be stated here parenthetically that the total, after allowing for these deductions, was held as follows:

	Florins
Anton Fugger, founder of the Fugger-Babenhausen branch	2,436,790
Raymund Fugger's heirs	1,526,251
Jakob and Hieronymus Fugger's heirs	758,202

Further, we must consider an 'Audit of the General Balance Sheet of 1546,' which was meant to show the profit and loss of the different branches of the business. According to this the gross profit for the period 1539–46 was:

	Florins
Spanish business	1,515,565
Hungarian business	1,258,744
Neapolitan revenue	259,378
Silver trade	144,914

The expenses were: In Augsburg, 81,193 fl.; in Spain, 54,050; in Antwerp, 37,717; in Hungary, 85,350, and the interest paid on this, as shown in the Bill-book, as 208,641 fl.

This statement shows the importance of the Spanish and Hungarian business for the whole situation of the firm. If we deduct the expenditure from the gross profit, these two branches show a net profit of 2,634,000 fl., i.e. nearly 90 per cent. of the total profit.

The assets in round figures are as follows:

	Florins
Landed property and mines	800,000
Stock-in-trade	1,250,000
Ready money	250,000
Book debts	3,900,000
Private accounts of the partners	400,000
Various	500,000
Total	7,100,000

Among the landed property Babenhausen, valued at 156,000 fl., is the largest; Weissenhorn, with Maverstetten and Buch, are down for 61,000 fl. Kirchberg, 59,000 fl.; Biberbach, 44,000 fl.; Donauwörth, 56,000 fl.; the Augsburg property, 63,000 fl.; and there are various others. Copper and fustian are the only considerable stock. The stock of fustian was valued at 125,000 fl., and more than a million gulden's worth of copper, half of which was in Antwerp.

More than half the outstanding claims were in Spain, but the statement as to the Spanish debtors is far from clear. It is specially striking that the two largest claims against the Emperor (447,429 ducats lease of the latest revenues of the Maestrazgos and 219,159 fl. for bonds (libranzas) on the Maestrazgos which the Fugger had paid) are not included in the sum total of the Spanish debts. These, nevertheless, amount to two million in round numbers, nearly all claims against the Emperor.[1]

The next large item among the book debts are the Antwerp debtors. Among these we note:

	£ Flemish
The city of Antwerp note	21,746
Caspar Ducci for (Flemish) bonds of the Receivers General	44,517
King of England	83,900
Queen Maria Statthalterin of the Netherlands	30,739
The King of Portugal	6,252

These large items amounted to 187,000 £ Flemish, or 790,000 fl., the total of the Spanish and Antwerp outstanding claims amounted to 2¾ million as compared with 1½ million in the year 1539.

The 'Courtbook' which contains King Ferdinand's debt is closed at 443,108 fl., only 26,000 fl. more than in the year 1539. The old Neapolitan entries have disappeared. Ferdinand, however, had shortly before sold to the Fugger a perpetual annuity of 11,000 ducats yearly

[1] Rymer, Foedera, Ed. v. 1704–27, XV, 101. (Fugger-Archiv. 2, 1, 22a, Augsburger Stadtarchiv (Litteralien) and Acts of the Privy Council, I, 488 ff.)

on his revenues from Calabria in return for a cash payment of 110,000
ducats. The Fugger drew this rent direct from the collectors in twenty-
eight cities and estates. This business is entered in the books at
150,000 fl.

The liabilities amount to 2 million gulden, not specially much if we
consider how the earning assets had grown. The Spanish creditors in
fact are less than in 1539, 342,407 ducats or 490,000 fl. (as against
542,000 fl. in 1539). Of this sum 200,000 is only a book entry on the
Emperor's side, so that the actual liabilities of the Spanish business
are only 290,000 fl., shares in the Consortium held by the Nüremberg
Welser and some others. The Fugger's bill liabilities, too, have fallen
since 1539, they amount now to 694,000 fl. The Antwerp business,
on the other hand, is indebted to the extent of 110,234 £ Flemish, or
about 460,000 fl. in thirty-five different entries, mostly to other South
German houses. In order to carry on their large Antwerp business, and
to get money relatively cheap, the Fugger had begun to borrow on
the Antwerp Bourse from quarter to quarter, or for two quarters, of
the kind euphemistically called 'Deposits.' For these they paid $1\frac{3}{4}$–$2\frac{1}{2}$
per cent. per quarter, $4\frac{1}{2}$–5 per cent. per half-year, about 9 per cent.
a year, while they on their side made about 12–13 per cent. on their
money in Antwerp.

The 'Fugger bills' became at this time an article of current trade,
an innovation which was only to show its dangerous consequences
at a later time. At first the Fugger bonds were considered as safe as
gold.

The balance sheet of 1546 shows the following new factories: Krem-
nitz in Hungary, Teschen, Cracow, Danzig, Erfurt, London, and
Florence, mostly small branches for the dispatch and sale of copper
and fustian. The financial situation of the firm, as shown by this
balance sheet of 1546, must still be regarded as sound in spite of the
large increase of investments in Antwerp and Spain. In view of the
ever increasing difficulty of getting money from Spain these last constituted a grave risk.

The firm of 'Anton Fugger and Nephews' held at this time a business
capital of about 5 million gulden, the largest it had ever held, and
certainly the largest ever held till then by one firm.

On the 31st July, 1548, as we have seen, a considerable part of the
business capital was distributed to the partners. It was hoped to share
out the rest before the end of the year 1550, and so the Fugger business
would have been brought to an end. But, as Anton Fugger says in his
will, 'On account of long wars, matters have gone right heavily, so
that not only were we unable to bring our own business to an end
and collect the monies owing to us, but we have been constrained, in

order to serve the Emperor and the King, to make fresh loans, ourselves borrowing money and getting into debt.'

New Business – Seeds of Decay. During all the ensuing period, the last years of Anton Fugger, it is quite clear that an effort was made to liquidate the existing undertakings and begin no new ones. The fact that new business was forced on him he seems at first to have taken hard. As soon, however, as he started on the inclined plane, he seems to have lacked energy to apply the brake with force. His Antwerp agent, Matthew Oertel, was chiefly responsible for the gigantic increase of the new financial undertakings. Anton Fugger himself, however, cannot be exonerated for this and its evil consequences. Like his Uncle Jakob, he seems not to have been free from the wish 'to "make" money as long as he might.' This wish, fully justified in 1525, would only have been justifiable a quarter of a century later had Anton Fugger had a successor of his own pattern. The Fugger might then have remained the first financiers of Europe. As it was, the third generation lacked the business genius of the first and second, and had not only to yield up the first place to the Genoese, but to see their credit, once so unimpeachable, severely shaken.

The Fugger in the years when they were liquidating their affairs undertook large new business which was not forced on them. This is plain from the history of their relations with the English Crown, of which we saw the beginning in the years 1545 and 1546. In 1547 the Fugger were still owed on this amount 83,900 £ Flemish, 639,000 L. on the money lent and 20,000 L. for copper. The first of the sums was paid back, the second still further deferred.[1]

In September, 1549, William Damsell, the financial agent of the English Crown in Antwerp, had tried for months in vain to raise a loan in Antwerp, and the Fugger finally agreed to advance for a year 54,000 L. = 328,800 Car. fl. At the end of the year the loan was prolonged at 12 per cent., and though a payment of 127,000 Carolus gulden was made in February, 1551, the Fugger had had to make several other large loans in this time.

In the beginning of the year 1552 Thomas Gresham, the new financial agent of the English Crown, went to Antwerp to borrow money to pay the Fugger. Their claims amounted to 123,047 L., of which 77,577 L. was paid off in two instalments (63,577 L. and 14,000 L.) The rest, 45,470 L., was then prolonged, but appears to have been paid back shortly afterwards, as the Fugger balance sheet for 1553 shows no claim on the English Crown. They needed all their money for the Emperor. In November and December, 1553, Christopher Dawntsey, a new English agent, repeatedly approached the Fugger's Antwerp agent for a

[1] Acts of the Privy Council, II, 80, 159.

loan, which was refused on the ground that the Fugger had already lent all they had to lend to the Emperor.[1] Their relations, however, with the English Crown were not yet at an end. On 1st August, 1548, the Fugger lent the Emperor 150,000 ducats in return for a charge on the Neapolitan revenues, at 12 per cent. interest. We hear of no further loans till 1551. This is connected with the increasing difficulty with which they collected their outstanding debts. The three loans granted at Ulm and Wittenberg during the war of Schmalkalden were still in arrears in 1551. On the occasion of the grant of a new loan, apparently they were formed into a consolidated debt, which, inclusive of interest at 12 per cent., up to the end of February, 1552, amounted to 273,161 ducats. This was secured partly on Antwerp and partly on Spain.

In April, 1551, the Emperor at Augsburg demanded fresh loans from the South German merchants. Probably for the sake of collecting their old claims the better, the Fugger and the Welser agreed. They advanced no ready money, however, but issued bonds which were discounted by Wolff Haller von Hallerstein in Antwerp at 11 per cent. The Fugger's share amounted to 100,000 Carolus gulden or 70,000 fl. Rh.

In October, 1551, the Emperor again borrowed in Augsburg 76,000 ducats at 12 per cent. in return for a charge on the gold and silver expected from 'India.' The firm of Anton Fugger and Nephews was interested in this to the extent of 33,000 ducats, and Anton Fugger on his own account with 20,000 ducats. The large undertakings which Anton Fugger repeatedly undertook for his private interest prove clearly that the passion for money-making was not yet dead in him. But at the moment we have now reached, it was not very great, if we may judge from the comparatively small sums which he contributed to the loans. Towards the end of the year 1551, when the Emperor again needed money to pay his army before Magdeburg, the Augsburg merchants declined to grant him any more loans, and it was only with the greatest difficulty that he extracted 25,000 thalers from the city of Nüremberg.[2]

Charles V and Anton Fugger in 1552. We have now reached the important turning-point in the reign of Charles V, and we meet once again a striking instance of the power of the Fugger's money. It is the last time that they had the Emperor's fate in their hands. Both the

[1] The English sources are not to be trusted as to figures. Cf. Turnbull, *Calendar of State Papers*, foreign series, Edward VI, No. 193, 198–99, 207; Queen Mary, No. 69, 104. Acts of the Privy Council, III, 26, 33, 219, 505, IV, 27, 29, 40, 99. Nares, *Memoirs of Burghley*, p. 405 (caution). Burgon, *Life and Times of Sir Thomas Gresham*, I, 80 et seq.

[2] Manuale der Herren Eltern in the Kreis Archive in Nüremburg, 1551, Wednesday after Christmas.

beginning and the end of his reign leave the mark of their name. Next to the election of Charles as Emperor the negotiations of Anton Fugger with Charles in the sad days of Villach are the clearest proof of the close ties of common interest which bound the Fugger to the Hapsburgs.[1]

In January, 1552, the Elector Maurice of Saxony had bought the financial help of the French King by handing over Metz, Toul, and Verdun. In February he came out openly against the Emperor. Charles was in Innsbruck without money and troops, and his first attempts to raise money were fruitless. The merchants knew only too well, as Charles himself stated in his letters, that the Emperor could no longer give them security or safe revenues. Perhaps they feared 'those who have weapons in their hands,' or were affecting to do so, as the Emperor suspected.

'It seems,' he says, 'as if the merchants were agreed together to serve me no longer. I find neither in Augsburg nor elsewhere any man who will lend to me, howsoever large a profit be offered to him.' Such was the result of this violent financial policy of the time of the war of Schmalkalden.

Nevertheless in March Queen Maria of the Netherlands succeeded in getting from the Fugger's Antwerp agent a small amount of money. But there was not much to be had in the Netherlands either. During the early part of the year the Emperor was unable to oppose his enemies, who were actually masters of Germany, and his letters show that his helplessness was entirely due to lack of money.

For a considerable time he had been negotiating with Anton Fugger for a large loan and had even had it promised to him. The financier delayed the fulfilment of his promise, alleging that the warlike disturbances in South Germany, the failure of the Frankfort Easter Fair, and the prevailing tightness of money, made it impossible for him to raise the necessary large sum himself. In vain the Emperor urged that 'in haste lies the use of this affair.' At the end of March Anton Fugger was bidden by an autograph letter from the Emperor to come to Innsbruck in all haste. 'This is what I now most greatly desire,' Charles wrote.

Anton Fugger in reply to this urgent appeal did not delay in setting out. The negotiations in Innsbruck as to financial help on a large scale were feverishly carried on between the Emperor's secretary Erasso and Anton Fugger; but this time also they proved very difficult. The small forces which the Emperor had already recruited, having received no pay, were threatening to disband. The garrisons of the

---

[1] Here, besides the Fugger Archives, I have only used Lanz, *Correspondenz Karls V*, vol. III, pp. 100 seq.

fortresses which prevented the Elector Maurice from destroying the Emperor altogether were insufficient in numbers and badly provisioned. Accordingly Maurice reduced Emberg on the 19th May; and the Emperor and his Court, including Anton Fugger, had to flee in haste to Villach. On the 23rd May, the Elector invested Innsbruck. Charles tried in vain to play off the former Elector Johann Friedrich against Maurice. Money was lacking for this as well as for munitions. Attempts were made to raise money in Augsburg, Ulm, Nüremberg, Strasburg, and even in Venice, but the South German merchants and their Venetian agents were on the side of the Emperor's enemies. Anton Fugger was the last hope of the Emperor, now old, ill, and hard pressed. It is not too much to say that Anton Fugger saved him, for without money and troops he would have had to agree to all the conditions proposed by the German princes in the negotiations which opened at Passau on 26th May. Charles expressly declared that he was raising the money in all haste in order to negotiate with more authority at Passau and in order to destroy the impression that he was powerless. There is a striking and sudden change of tone in June when his arrangements with Anton Fugger were concluded. He now took his time examining the conditions of the intermediaries, and Maurice did not get nearly all that he aimed at.[1]

Anton Fugger lent the Emperor the enormous sum of 400,000 ducats. Of this sum 100,000 ducats were to be paid over in Germany to the Queen of Bohemia (60,000), the Cardinal of Trent, etc., and 50,000 ducats in Venice. The Emperor kept at his own disposition the remaining 250,000 ducats. He owed the Genoese about this amount, and had originally intended to pay it by drafts from Spain. He himself, however, was now in need of money, and Anton Fugger was to try to induce the Genoese to extend the period of the loan for one or two years longer, and if necessary himself to act as guarantor.

In telling his eldest nephew, Hans Jakob, of this contract, Anton Fugger added that it was to be hoped that the business with the Genoese would come to nothing. Never yet had a business been concluded with so little hope of profit. The nephews were to consider whether they would agree that it should be for the firm. Their agreement was necessary because it had been settled to break up the firm. In fact the nephews did not come in, so Anton Fugger took over the business on his own account.

The Fugger's guarantee did not, however, prove to be necessary for the Genoese. Meanwhile the Emperor was in need of money north of the Alps in order to ward off an invasion by the King of France. He was therefore easily able to use the 250,000 ducats which had not yet

[1] Lanz, l.c. III, 237 and v. Döllinger, *Dokumente z. Geschichte Karls V*, p. 20.

come into his disposition. The Queen-Regent of the Netherlands made an agreement on the 8th August with Matthew Oertel, the Fugger's agent in Antwerp, that the 250,000 ducats should be paid over then. This payment, which constituted a remarkable achievement for that time, was carried out on the 10th November. A short time before unusually large cargoes of silver had arrived from America in Antwerp and Genoa, and the Fuggers had also managed to extract a considerable sum from Spain. Generally speaking, they remained determined to liquidate their business, and were not at all displeased that at this juncture the Genoese helped the Emperor with still larger advances. The loan of Villach nevertheless constituted a large increase of their investments and especially of the unpopular Spanish investments, for the repayment was to take place exclusively in Spain. This, however, was a source of extra profit, which was welcome in view of the very moderate interest (12 per cent.), but it considerably increased the difficulties of liquidation.

Anton Fugger and the Antwerp Bourse. The Emperor's war with France, which needed financing on a scale hitherto unknown, threw all the Fugger's good resolutions about retirement to the winds. From the year 1553 we hear again of several large dealings with the Emperor. Matthew Oertel lent the Court at Brussels sums of 195,000 and 18,000 ducats, and these, together with the Villach loan, were secured in Spain, so that the Spanish revenues were mortgaged up to 1557. In April, moreover, Anton Fugger bought for 300,000 Carolus gulden a 10 per cent. annuity on the revenues of Brabant and Flanders. In the same year their further engagements are mentioned – one of 85,000 ducats, one of 164,926 Rh. fl. and one of 173 million Maravedis – all of which seem to have been concluded in the Netherlands. Anton Fugger repeatedly complained in his letters to Matthew Oertel that 'no Resolution as to our debts will come from the Court. Verily in these heavy times they have much else to do, but it is yet hazardous and these affairs are tedious.' Anton Fugger had already had to borrow in Augsburg and Nüremberg in order to fulfil these large new engagements. Towards the end of the year, when one of these payments matured, he gave orders that it was to be prolonged even at 10 per cent., 'for if I lay the money on finance (short term loans) it bears 12 per cent.'

In those times this was a dangerous principle. It shows Anton's continual zeal for money-making that in this year 1553 he bought from Duke Cosimo of Florence, for 100,000 ducats, an annual sum of 10,000 ducats from the Duke's Neapolitan revenues. The negotiations were carried on between the Fugger's Venetian agent and a ducal official according to the instructions of Anton Fugger. He seems to have been unwilling, but to have been tempted by the large profit, which overcame his dislike of the Neapolitan connection and his mistrust of his correspondent. He seems to have feared, not without reason, that he was going to be cheated; and we get the impression that the Venetian agent, who was himself interested in the affair, promoted it on his own account and that Anton Fugger let himself be over-persuaded. From the last months of 1553 and the beginning of the next year letters of Anton Fugger to Matthew Oertel have been preserved which show that he already regarded the financial situation with great anxiety.

He complained, above all, of the difficulty of obtaining money from Spain. All would come right in the end, but the state revenues were already pledged far ahead. If Erasso could still find people to deal with him, it could only be on the most unfavourable conditions. 'It is in truth a great harm to his Imperial Majesty that His Majesty will make war and borrow money on finance. These great lords might well lay aside their delight in wars.' Soon after he complains 'that in this Court no man considers aught and the debts which have been agreed with a binding promise are not paid. I hold that the Bishop of Arras should be spoken to touching this matter. A gift of 1,000 fl. should be made to Erasso, for thereby matters will be quickened. But to lend yet three or perchance four times in addition, at 80 kreuzer to the ducats, that is not to be done.' Then, again, he says: 'As to the negotiations touching Spain, I hold that great profit is to be made, the cause wherefore I withhold myself ye will have understood. I have no desire for such dealings, therefore enough of this. As to Erasso, he has so acted that I think not to deal with him and it is certain that he does ill service to his master, who, however, will have it so.' But these new good resolutions were once more to be thrown to the winds.

There are also plenty of expressions of disapproval as to the German policy of the Emperor. 'It is not good that His Imperial Majesty cometh not (to the Empire) and that the Diet falls into the water and Germany becometh a bears' den where each man doeth what he listeth.'

Matthew Oertel had raised much money at interest in Antwerp in order to cover the large advances of the year 1553. Anton Fugger, too, owed large sums in South Germany on his private account. In February 1554, 30,000 fl. fell due for payment, and we note with astonishment that there is difficulty in raising the money for this. Anton Fugger repeatedly ordered Oertel to raise the money to send to Augsburg at any price 'for my credit stands thereon,' and, again, 'I think as much on men's mockery as on the money itself.' This was a threatening symptom of the coming ruin. There was no escape from debt except by bringing money from Spain, which needed special arrangements. Before dealing with this we must briefly consider the whole situation of the firm as shown in the balance sheet drawn up at the end of 1553. We must bear in mind, however, that a part of the pending business was undertaken on Anton Fugger's private account and does not appear in the balance sheet of the firm.

According to the balance sheet of 1546 a capital of about $4\frac{1}{2}$ million gulden was brought forward. Since this time, however, more than 2 millions had been paid out to the members of the firm, so that the balance sheet of 1553 shows only 2,327,276 fl. as capital brought forward. As the assets of the firm now amount to 3,248,794 fl., the profit for seven years amounts to 921,518 fl., or about $5\frac{5}{8}$ per cent. per annum. We note the following items under the heading 'Debtors':

	Florins
The members of the firm	1,500,000
Spanish business	1,200,000
The Treasury of the Netherlands	400,000

Other outstanding claims:	
In Antwerp	100,000
In Lisbon	300,000
King Ferdinand	270,000

The liabilities amounted only to 1,100,000 fl., distributed as follows:

	Florins
Antwerp	360,000
Augsburg	200,000
Spain	320,000

These are all relatively small sums, and the whole situation of the business appears accordingly in a very favourable light. Apart, however, from Anton Fugger's new private undertakings, the old arrears were probably paid partly in kind, so that the actual state was not nearly so good. However, the family might well have been thankful if their property had remained at the 1553 level.

Anton Fugger's ceaseless efforts to get money out of Spain were chiefly in respect of his private undertakings, which had grown to a gigantic size since Villach. When Charles' son Philip was expected from Spain in the Netherlands, Anton Fugger ordered that a great quantity of silver should be sent secretly with him on his ships, and this appears actually to have been done. At any rate, at the end of 1553, 200,000 ducats of silver arrived for the Fugger in Antwerp; and in the following year it was hoped to extract a further sum of 300,000 ducats, though it was extraordinarily difficult to obtain permission from Spain.

It was lucky for every one who had outstanding claims in Spain that Philip was marrying Queen Mary of England. She needed money, and Gresham, who was sent to Antwerp to raise it, found this extremely difficult owing to the prevailing tightness. He was therefore overjoyed when some Genoese and also the Fugger's agent, Oertel, promised him a loan of 300,000 ducats, if provided with the Emperor's permit. He himself would collect the money in Spain. The business materialized because the Emperor wished to oblige Queen Mary. Anton Fugger was interested to the extent of 12,750 ducats.

In 1554 the Fugger do not seem to have done much business. They lent the Duke of Florence 75,000 scudi at 12 per cent., selling him at the same time a jewel for 23,600 scudi, which the Duke continued to owe them. They also helped King Ferdinand with 56,000 thalers. These were undertakings when the money had to remain out several years, but they are not of the unmanageable type of the Spanish and Netherlands loans.

We shall see later, in 1555 and 1556, how fearfully the war increased the debts of the Spanish Crown and the Netherlands. In 1555 Erasso came from England, where King Philip then was, in order to borrow money in Antwerp, which after much trouble he succeeded in doing. The Fugger lent the largest sum – 200,000 crowns.[1] We do not know how Erasso managed to induce Oertel to undertake this business, and whether the consent of Anton Fugger was obtained. Anyhow, this transaction opened for the Fugger an area of new large loans in which there seems to have been no holding back. The Antwerp Bourse proved fatal to them, as it had to many other merchants.

Antwerp had steadily grown in importance for the Fugger in the half-century in which they had done business there. In the first few decades they had mainly used it for selling spices and Hungarian and Tyrolese copper. This, however, did not mean that financial transactions were excluded, but for a long time these were confined to bills and certain dealings with the Antwerp agent of the King of Portugal, mostly on a basis of copper and pepper. It was only in the 'forties of the century that the Fugger began regularly to borrow money on the Antwerp Bourse on 'deposit,' and this method had become more and more indispensable to them as a means of raising money. At the same time, there is an increase of active credit business in Antwerp; since 1545 there had been many such transactions with the Court of the Netherlands, the city of Antwerp, and the English Crown. All the large loans which were critical for the situation of the firm were at that time always managed in South Germany by the head of the firm himself. This arrangement was

---

[1] Cf. R. Brown, *Calendar VI*, 48.

now first altered, the year 1552 being the first of this new phase. Matthew Oertel is now repeatedly mentioned as the independent agent for large loans to the Brussels Court; and when, after the Villach loan, the 250,000 ducats promised by Anton Fugger to the Emperor were to be used in the Netherlands and not in Italy, negotiations as to the settlement of this business were carried on with Oertel. The large undertakings of the year 1553 were all concluded in Antwerp, and this remained the usual way for some considerable time.

Charles V made over the government of the Netherlands to his son, in October, 1555, leaving him such severe financial difficulties that, as Philip said later, it was impossible to fulfil his engagements, which he would gladly have done, 'even with his own blood.' The war with France, moreover, continued to require an ever increasing amount of money. In the following two years, as we shall see, the debts of the Netherlands rose to a crazy height. The Antwerp Bourse was seized with a credit mania of the worst type, which did not leave Matthew Oertel exempt. How far Anton Fugger himself was affected we have not sufficient material to show. It is, however, scarcely conceivable that the agent should have concluded loans on such a scale without the consent of his chief.

We have the German and French text of a deed, dated 1st February, 1556, under which Matthew Oertel, agent for Anton Fugger and Nephews, undertook to pay King Philip in ready money a sum not exceeding 400,000 ducats, payable in Spain, so that the King might pay his Spanish soldiers and so prevent their excesses. Oertel had promised this on condition that the King should give a bond on secure revenues for everything he owed the Fugger, inclusive of interest at 12 per cent. The highest officials of the Netherlands were guarantors in their own persons for the repayment, and for greater security the first 'aide' which the States General of the Netherlands should grant the King was pledged to the Fugger.

In the beginning of April, 1556, the Fugger accordingly took over more than 1¼ millions' worth in Carolus gulden of Netherlands bonds of the Receivers General, for which the King did not give security in the first place, but which bore the signatures of the Receivers General of the different provinces, so that the creditors had recourse against the Receivers, while the King's promise, which was not secured on any definite revenues, was quite valueless.

These bonds had for some time been considered an unsafe investment, and the Fugger now staked on them 600,000 ducats, i.e. 50 per cent. more than Anton Fugger, after months of negotiation in Villach, had lent the Emperor in his extremity on security of much greater value.

This, however, was not yet all. The 400,000 ducats which Oertel had advanced for payment in Spain proved to be not nearly sufficient. They grew to 540,000 ducats. Besides this the Fugger had already lent the King 112,000 ducats in the autumn of 1555; and in the year 1556 sums of 30,000 and 40,000 ducats were advanced in addition, the last sum being secured on the rich silver mines of Guadalcanal, which were then just discovered. In the beginning of 1557, Oertel, in the Netherlands, advanced 430,000 ducats for repayment 'from the first gold and silver that shall come from India.'

So the thing went on. Instead of the Fugger having their old advances repaid, they had to lend the House of Austria, in a space of one and a half years, more money than they had ever lent before in so short a time. Erasso fairly pumped them dry; and they got no thanks for this either from him or his master.

In April, 1557, Oertel wrote to Anton Fugger: 'I wot not how to bring it about to make Erasso our friend, for I have never yet met his like, for he speaks a man fair to his face and behind his back saith ever the contrary. He agreeth with no one in Summa save with his own agents whom he hath created that they may do his pleasure in all things. Now that is not your Honour's way, and from us he hath had little in gifts and the like. This brings upon us more disfavour and weary running to and fro than ought else; for he and his men say to all men that from no one do they have so much trouble and so little profit as from us.'[1]

As Erasso was already a rich man from the bribes he had taken for fourteen years, he paid no attention to small 'gifts.' Oertel, nevertheless, tried to win him over; but Erasso accepted the services with thanks and did exactly as he pleased. He could easily, Oertel writes, make all quits again, 'though his nature seldom or never allows it to him.'

The Fugger and the Financial Crisis of 1557. In the spring of 1557 the over expansion of credit in Antwerp had reached the danger-point. The quarterly payments were deferred by the King's Order; and even the city of Antwerp, which had strained its credit to the utmost, availed itself of this means of escape, which was the equivalent of a moratorium. We must deal next with the Fugger's share in the events which, in the course of the years 1557–62, shook the finance and trade of Europe to its foundations.

In the summer of 1557 King Philip ordered that no further payments were to be made to his creditors either in Spain or the Netherlands, and he confiscated two Spanish cargoes of silver for Flanders, valued at 570,000 ducats, for the Fugger. The anger and anxiety of old Anton

---

[1] *Papiers d'Etat du Cardinal de Granvella V*, 683.

Fugger knew no bounds, and Oertel tried in vain to quiet him. When all that was known was the delay in the King's payments he wrote to Anton Fugger: 'As in South Germany people make so much ado and hold our King for bankrupt and have served France again with 300,000 crowns, I would gladly hear what the evil speakers say now that the Frenchman has met with a reverse of fortune before St. Quentin.' Oertel had entreated the King to keep his engagements to the Fugger, saying that he would undertake for his masters that they should again serve the King if he needed money. Erasso had, however, replied that Anton Fugger had already prayed the King to trouble him no further for loans, because he would have peace.

To this Oertel made the rejoinder: 'That the Fugger had never deserted His Majesty in his need, but in the space of 1½ years had served him with 1½ million of gold.'

All this, however, availed nothing. The King told the agent twice that he did it with as great unwillingness as he had ever done anything yet, but his great necessity forced him thereto, lest people took hurt from the armies. Nevertheless, Oertel says in the same letter that the whole thing was chiefly due to Erasso, who had never been willing that the Fugger should be paid what was due to them in Spain. He added, it was now too late to win Erasso with money, 'the matter had gone too far.'

Anton Fugger bitterly reproached the agent for his arbitrary behaviour which had led to such great losses. He had written to him many times that he was not to trust the Court. 'The devil thank you for this agency.' In order 'to sleep in peace' he withdrew from Oertel his power to lend money on his account or that of the firm, and soon after dismissed him from his service. Oertel, however, asserted that he had always acted with his master's consent; but he is not to be exonerated of an undue optimism, and his view must have determined that of Anton Fugger, who was at a distance and getting old. If he had undertaken the new large business only under the impression that he was securing the Fugger's old claims, he might be less severely judged. It is, however, probable that he was interested largely on his own account, for he left the service of the Fugger a rich man, while his masters had suffered enormous losses.

Anton Fugger wanted to come himself to Antwerp. Instead of doing so, however, he sent his son Hans, who together with the agent, Sebastian Kurz, had the difficult task of saving what it was possible to save, especially getting in the outstanding claims in order to pay off the debts. 'The creditors are many,' Anton Fugger wrote in 1558. 'A man might shudder to think of them.' At first, however, there was no possibility of paying them off.

In the following years the Fugger had themselves to seek more credits. They borrowed large sums in Antwerp, usually at 8–10 per cent. per annum, and their credit was so good that in the general mistrust and the absence of 'good borrowers' every one 'looked out for the Fugger Bonds.' This state of things only changed with the death of Anton Fugger.

We have a general statement of the year 1558 of the Fugger claims against King Philip in Spain only, that is exclusively the Netherlands claims. These amounted to a total of 1,660,809 ducats. To this was to be added the silver which had been taken from them, the value of which on the 25th May, 1559, the King promised to pay. Inclusive of 14 per cent. interest the amount was to be 762,262 crowns (100 crowns = about 94 Spanish ducats of 11 reals). There was, however, no prospect of repayment. The credit of the Fugger remained good and they borrowed considerable sums during the year 1560, both in Antwerp and Nüremberg, at the moderate rate for those days of 7–8 per cent.

As the promised repayment of the confiscated money did not take place, the Fugger's Spanish claim, inclusive of interest at 12–14 per cent., rose at the end of 1560 to almost 3 million ducats or 4 million gulden.

As the Fugger's own capital only amounted to 2 million, the house was already in a highly dangerous state. In addition it had outstanding claims in the Netherlands amounting to about 1½ million gulden. The debt of the Netherlands Receivers General, amounting to 900,000 gulden, must, however, be regarded as practically worthless, as the States General refused to be responsible for it.

The Court of Spain made the Fugger a proposal for a composition of their Spanish claim. Under this arrangement the interest was to be reduced to 5 per cent., and great losses of capital would have resulted in addition. The Fugger accordingly did not agree, in the hope that their help would again be needed and their original contracts would then have to be confirmed. This hope, however, was not fulfilled, for – as the Venetian envoy Tiepolo wrote in January, 1560, from Spain – the Genoese were more resourceful and enterprising than the Fugger. They had for the most part had their claims repaid during the war on the occasion of new loans, while the Fugger meanwhile had had to stand idly by while their claims grew with the added interest. Accordingly, Anton's eldest nephew, Hans Jakob Fugger, was sent to Spain to make an agreement, which, however, did not come about till two years later.[1]

We note with astonishment that at this critical moment the Fugger allowed themselves to begin new loan business. In February, 1559, Hans Fugger in Antwerp lent Queen Elizabeth, through the agency of Gresham, about 10,000 £ fl. for one year, this being the only financial

Brown, *Calendar VII*, 142.

dealings which the Fugger undertook with the heretic Queen.[1] In the same year they advanced to the Duke of Alba 11,853 £ fl., and to the Emperor Ferdinand in 1560 a loan of 40,000 fl. without interest, secured on the salt offices of Vienna and Aussee; and to Ferdinand's son Maximilian 30,000 fl. at 10 per cent.

The Fugger were so closely linked with the Hapsburgs that even at such a time they could not escape from their demands for money. It is, however, to be supposed that Anton Fugger himself no longer troubled as to the details of the business, while his younger kinsmen viewed the situation with a more optimistic eye.

Anton Fugger's End. His Importance. On 11th July, 1560, Anton Fugger, then old and in ill-health, added a codicil to his will made ten years earlier making special dispositions as to the future management of the Fugger business. He had spoken seriously to his eldest nephew Hans Jakob, asking him to take over the direction of the business. He had, however, declined on the ground that the business of the city and his own affairs gave him so much to do that he could not act as head of the business. Thereupon Anton had turned to Hans Jakob's brother, George, and had received a blunt refusal. 'He could not do the work,' he said, 'and would far rather live in peace.' Anton fared no better with his third nephew, Christopher, though he represented to him very pressingly that in his youth he had been most employed in trade in Tyrol, Antwerp, and Spain. Anton Fugger, in his codicil, speaks with some bitterness of these vain attempts. His fourth nephew Raymund had bad health, and therefore was no use in business, and Anton's own sons were too young to direct the business on their own account. He therefore laid it down that Hans Jakob must take up the burden together with his (Anton's) eldest son Marx. They must bear in mind the liquidation of the business as soon as possible; they must leave the name of the firm unaltered for six years more; and after the business was brought to a close they must carefully keep the most important business papers 'for the good of our Posterity in case of need.' The directions for the preservation of these papers and for all the circumstances connected with the business are extraordinarily detailed. In another codicil he forbade his successors to sell any of the landed estates. All this clearly shows that at the time of his death, on 14th September, 1560, he was full of anxiety for the future of his house.

His nephew, Hans Jakob, in the *Secret Book of Honour* of the family which he composed in 1546, is not able to tell us much about Anton. He

---

[1] The text of Elizabeth's promissory note in the Fugger archives (48/6). The interest is added to the capital and is designated 'dicto Joanni (Fucker) in remuneratione et premium (sic!) laborum suorum ex nostra mera liberalitate et favore donavimus.'

was 'as the eldest of the Fugger house right active and diligent in the guidance thereof, soft of speech, great in counsel and apt knowledge-ableness.'

We learn from another source that his motto was 'Silence is golden.' These traits are insufficient for us to judge the character of the man who worked in the Fugger business for almost half a century and was its sole director for thirty years. It is a proof of his extraordinary intelligence that he was able throughout this long period to keep his house, at least to the outward eye, in the pre-eminent position to which Jakob Fugger had raised it, so that the Florentine Guicciardini, in a description of the Netherlands which appeared soon after Anton's death, describes him, with reference to the respect paid him in Antwerp, as 'a real prince among the other merchants.' Though he may have lacked the commercial genius of Jakob Fugger, yet his 'knowledgeableness' proved a still more precious quality in a far more difficult time and in the work of keeping what had been already won. This quality only deserted him in his last days, or, rather, the weariness which had seized on a nature in any case not sufficiently energetic to deal with the difficulties of the situation, deprived him of the power of withstanding the speculative tendencies of his Antwerp agent, Matthew Oertel.

The Fugger had to pay dearly for the too intimate connection of their fate with the over-speculation of the Antwerp Bourse.

The Alleged Burning of the Notes of Hand of Charles V. We may here mention the anecdote of Anton Fugger's burning one of Charles V's notes of hand in his presence. This story is not mentioned either in the Fugger business papers or in the 'Description of the Fugger' drawn up from the family papers at the end of the sixteenth century. The versions of the story differ in time and place, and are also recounted of many other rich merchants. For instance, the same story is told by Casoni of Centurione; and in the Netherlands, not only in connection with Anton Fugger, but also with the Antwerp merchant Jan Daem, and of the Florentine Gaspar Ducci. The story is first told of Anton Fugger in a magazine called the *Journal des Savans* of the year 1685, and the other versions also seem to have arisen in the seventeenth century, a poverty-stricken time which was inclined to embellish the now legendary riches of the financial princes of the sixteenth century with such romantic tales.

In the Fugger archives I found a short statement drawn up by Dr. Holtzapfel, an administrator of the Fugger property in Spain. This was evidently meant as part of a memorandum setting forth the services of the Fugger to the House of Austria in an attempt to get some payments on enormous sums due from the Spanish Crown and thus to check the further decline in the fortunes of the house. This statement says: 'As

Emperor Charles (after the taking of Ingolstadt in 1546) came again and once more desired money of Master Anton, the same answered him that he had means in the Netherlands wherewith he would and could serve His Majesty, which was most fortunate; but in Germany he had no other means save certain bills of His Majesty, which he had torn up or burnt in order that His Majesty might see that he was jealous to serve him with all his substance.'

In this form the anecdote seems more probable, especially if we suppose that it was a case of a clever *coup de théatre*. We know that after the taking of Ingolstadt in September or October, 1546, Anton Fugger advanced to the Emperor the necessary means for the overthrow of the South German Protestants, bringing money from the Netherlands for this purpose. The Emperor, on the other hand, may have demanded immediate payment in South Germany. It may be that Anton Fugger took this drastic step as a means of making more impressive his assertion that payment in South Germany was impossible. The story would be more credible, however, if it had been placed a year later, when he was already 'weary.'

III

THE PERIOD OF DECLINE FROM THE DEATH OF ANTON FUGGER TO THE END OF THE FUGGER BUSINESS

The Third Generation. Hans Jakob Fugger. The Fugger business had now arrived at the critical third generation, which was to prove fatal in this case also. Hans Jakob Fugger, the eldest nephew who under Anton's will had to take over the direction of the business in conjunction with Marx, Anton's eldest son, was by no means equal to his task. A patron of art and learning and a passionate collector, he was much occupied with such pursuits and his personal relations with princes, especially the Dukes of Bavaria. These preoccupations and a more cavalier conception of the nature of business prevented him from devoting himself to details, in the manner which, in view of the situation of the house, was then doubly necessary. Anton's eldest son, Marx, later showed himself at least a cautious man of business; but even when he was set free from the unlucky influence of Hans Jakob, he did not understand how to bring to bear sufficient caution nor yet sufficient brilliance and energy in the introduction of new business. Moreover, even before Anton Fugger's death the Genoese had known how to render themselves indispensable to the Spanish Court, while the Fugger, tied by their past and their lack of enterprise, were kept to the Spanish business and the old markets, and were prevented from making use of the fresh centres of trade and finance which were then developing. The decline of the house and its riches was therefore inevitable.

The name of the firm 'Anton Fugger and Nephews' remained at first unaltered, much longer indeed than the period laid down in Anton's will; but their credit fell with striking rapidity. While in 1560 in Antwerp 'the Fugger Bond' was considered the safest of investments and they had to pay less for their loans than any other firm, or even the city of Antwerp itself, in the following year it was reported that the Fugger were making continual efforts to remit money from Antwerp to South Germany in order to pay their debts there, for they had previously borrowed money wherever they could and paid off long-standing creditors who were already pressing them. In the beginning of September, 1561, some South German merchants, who had lent the bankrupt Courts of Spain, France and Portugal more than they themselves possessed, had to cease payment; and, as Sir Thomas Gresham reports from Antwerp, anxiety was felt there on the Fugger's account.[1] Their credit only improved again when in 1562 they came to an arrangement with the Spanish Court as to the gradual paying off of the gigantic sums due to them. Even then, in order to fulfil their obligations, they had to borrow large amounts on unfavourable conditions. The most important and characteristic transaction of this kind may be mentioned here.

In 1563 the Fugger borrowed from the Spanish usurer Juan de Curiel della Torre 300,000 crowns at 10 per cent. per annum – not a very high rate for those days of monetary shortage. Juan de Curiel gave the Fugger 100,000 crowns of Spanish annuities, which were then worth only half their normal value. The Fugger had accordingly to write off so much, which made the real rate of interest much higher. It is not clear for how long they continued to owe this money; if for two years, they lost on the 250,000 crowns in each year 55,000 crowns, i.e. 22 per cent. This was the more scandalous as the creditor had then, through Erasso's agency, forced the Fugger out of the lease of the Maestrazgos.[2]

The composition which the Fugger made with the Spanish financial administration as to their outstanding claims on 26th August, 1562, was considerably less favourable than the arrangements with the other creditors, who had come to an agreement earlier. Their interest was cut down and they were given a charge on Spanish annuities and landed estates, on which they inevitably lost heavily. Moreover, they were compelled to take over the lease of the Maestrazgos at an extremely high price. The worst point, however, was the long time over which the repayment was distributed.

State of the Business in the year 1563. We have a balance sheet of the Fugger of 1563.

---

[1] Kervyn de Lettenhove, *Relat. polit.* II, 618, III, 113.
[2] Fugger-Archiv, 2, 1, 1 fol. 260; 2, 5, 13, 21 January, 1576.

The assets are as follows:

		Ducats
I. (1) Spanish claims against the King		2,975,797
(2) Juros at 5 per cent. taken from Juan de Curiel as part of the loan mentioned above		100,000
		3,075,797

To be written off:

	Ducats	
$\frac{1}{3}$ of the Juros (which, however, entailed a greater loss)	226,492	
$\frac{1}{4}$ of the landed estate	144,869	371,361
Leaving		2,704,436
		= fl. 3,605,913
Interest to the end of 1563		839,222
Total	fl.	4,445,135

II. Other Assets in Spain:	Florins
(1) Cash	27,774
(2) Old arrears still regarded as good from the lease of the Maestrazgos, 15/8/50	58,877
(3) Other good debts	97,933
Total	184,584

III. Antwerp Assets:	£ fl.
(1) (a) Seven cities in Flanders	29,583
(b) 'Must pay daily together all Interest, but because we do not know the rate, we only reckon by Rentas, $6\frac{1}{4}$ per cent. Easter Market, 1560, to Pamas Market, 1563,' therefore interest	6,470
(2) (a) Duke of Alba, 1559	11,853
(b) Duke of Alba, 1561	18,494
(3) King of Portugal of 1561	2,508
(4) City of Antwerp	7,354
(5) States of Brabant	4,100
(6) Hans Jakob Fugger	75,943
(7) King Philip	9,405
(8) Duke of Alba, once again	3,110
(9) Other Debtors	4,305
(10) Cash	1,476
Total £ fl.	174,601
	= fl. 782,694

IV. Augsburg Assets: Florins
   (1) Emperor Ferdinand, 1560, lent without interest   40,000
   (2) King Maximilian   30,000
   (3) Archduke Ferdinand   4,680
   (4) Members of the Fugger family   24,700
   (5) Various debtors   23,101
   (6) Cash   41,435

                                               fl. 163,816

                                              Florins
V. Nüremberg and Vienna Assets   28,616

VI. Assets in the 'Chief Book':
   (1) Landed property in Antwerp   15,000
       Goods and stock   9,000
       Goods in transit   32,548

                                         fl.   56,548

                             Total Assets   fl. 5,661,393

This total does not contain: (i) the amounts already written off as losses on the Spanish and other assets amounting to 613,000 fl.; (ii) the Netherlands bonds of the Receivers General to the amount of 95,314 £ fl. = 430,000 fl. It should be noted that a great part of the Exchequer bonds had already been distributed to different members of the family.

The *Liabilities* fall into the following chief categories:

I. Shares in the business: Florins
   (1) Anton Fugger's heirs   1,246,350
   (2) Hans Jakob Fugger   562,065
   (3) George Fugger   28,092
   (4) Christopher Fugger   38,738
   (5) Ulrich Fugger   66,981
   (6) Raymund Fugger   77,998

II. Spanish Creditors:
   (1) Christopher Fugger   ducats   306,602
   (2) Duke of Alba   24,000
   (3) Juan de Curiel della Torre   335,250
   (4) Various   29,698

            Ducats   696,550 = fl. 928,734

III. Creditors in Antwerp:
Deposits repayable in the course of 1563   Florins 1,967,805

IV. Creditors in Augsburg:

	fl.	
Schwatz trade	59,158	
Deposits	38,000	
		97,158

V. Creditors in the 'Chief Book':
Unsettled bills and deposits   301,000

VI. Other creditors   84,267

Total Liabilities fl. 5,399,188

The chief heads of the balance sheet are therefore:

ASSETS.	Mill. fl.	LIABILITIES.	Mill. fl.
King Philip in Spain	4·44	Business Capital	2·00
Other Spanish Assets	·18	Deposits of members of the family	·40
Other claims on Princes and Cities	·50	Deposits of strangers	2·70
Claims on members of the Fugger family	·37	Other liabilities	·30
Other assets	·17		
	5·66		5·40

If we compare this balance sheet with those of 1546 and 1553 we first miss the 'Landed Property,' then notice the absence of dealings in commodities. We notice, thirdly, the relative smallness of the business capital and the general unhealthy state of affairs, financially speaking. Fourthly, we see that the Spanish business is now all important, only Antwerp being at all considerable besides, all other business connections having ceased or become quite unimportant.

The Netherlands Bonds of the Receivers General held by the Fugger had amounted in 1556 to the huge sum of 200,000 £ fl., or 600,000 ducats. In 1557 the Receivers General ceased payment, which was not resumed, because the States General would not recognize the debt. The bonds were therefore worthless. The Fugger allotted to Hans Jakob Fugger 32,103 £, to George and Raymund Fugger 45,877 £, and so on, while the firm only kept 95,314 £, and these, as we have seen, were not entered among the assets.

Marx Fugger and Brothers. At this time there were dissensions among the partners. Hans Jakob Fugger had borrowed enormous sums both on his own account and that of the firm and had begun several risky new undertakings. As a result, in 1563 he found himself in great difficulties, so that on account of his debts he had to leave Augsburg for his castle of Taufkirchen and afterwards to hand over to his creditors, not only this castle, but all his other property. Among his property was his interest in the Fugger business, amounting to 400,000 fl. The total of his debts on his own account amounted to more than a million. After much quarrelling an arrangement was made with the other partners under which Hans Jakob left the firm, which in its turn took over his debts in Augsburg. He had not enough left to bring up his large family properly, so he entered the service of Duke Albert of Bavaria and removed to Munich. He died in 1575, and his descendants never came back into the business.

Hans Jakob's disappearance from the firm did not, however, mean the healing of the breach between him and the other members of the family: it even grew wider. His brothers George and Raymund died in 1569, while Christopher, the last brother, in 1572 took up Hans Jakob's part and also left the firm after a quarrel. He owned a considerable amount of capital which had in great part to be paid over to him. (At his death, in 1579, he was regarded as the richest of the Fugger.) The firm was, therefore, considerably weakened by his leaving it. Anton's sons, who remained as chief partners, were forced to bring in again a considerable part of the private fortune which their father had with-drawn from the business. Before this Marx Fugger, the elder son, had had to assume the sole management, as his brothers refused to give him their support.

After the death and departure of the four nephews of Anton Fugger his three sons, Marx, Hans, and Jakob, remained as the only partners, and the firm assumed the style of Marx Fugger and Brothers. In 1591 Marx Fugger, on account of his advanced age, handed over the management to his brother Hans, who handed it down to his son Marx in 1597. The years 1597 and 1598 saw the deaths of Anton Fugger's three sons. After this it is unimportant who directed the business, which continued to decline. Even during the period when it was under Anton's sons it is not necessary to follow the course of events in detail. We will only mention a few outstanding facts.

In 1572 King Philip II asked the Fugger for a loan of a million ducats. After a long resistance their Spanish factor said that his masters would advance 300,000 ducats. The Genoese Tommaso Fiesco came to Augsburg from Antwerp as a representative of the King to try and induce the Fugger to make further advances. He pressed them so hard that they consented first to 50,000 £ fl., then to 80,000 £ fl., and finally to

100,000 £ fl., on condition that they were allowed to give in payment
the 19,244 £ of Netherlands bonds of the Receivers General which belonged to them personally. The Genoese, however, wanted more. The
Fugger pointed to the great services they had rendered and the bad
treatment they had often received, but Fiesco rejoined that the King
was in great straits and must have more money. When he had finally
succeeded in bargaining for the 100,000 £ fl. he turned the screw and
demanded that the Fugger should give up their condition as to the bonds
of the Receivers General which had been already more or less agreed,
and that they should advance the 300,000 ducats at 12 per cent. unconditionally. This demand called forth from the Fugger the following
characteristic expression of opinion as to their Antwerp agent Jakob
Mair: 'He is a sly cat, but doing business with Germans has a different
sense from business with the English or Genoese, for at this time our
affairs and all other businesses make as much ado to serve with 100,000
crowns as with a million a few years since.'

This is a clear indication of the situation of the house and of that of all
the South German merchants. In Spain the Genoese had now taken the
place of the Fugger, who, however, made many fresh advances to the
King, though the Genoese produced incomparably larger sums. The
Spanish bankers, too, began once more to be important, though they
imposed harder conditions than the Fugger had done. The King obtained money, however, while the Fugger abstained as far as possible
from fresh undertakings. Only by the threat that their old claims would
remain unpaid could any money be squeezed out of them. On the other
hand, the Fugger needed to bribe perpetually in order to obtain some of
the promised repayments. Finally, in the general mistrust, the Spanish
reserves of ready money, which could not be sent *in natura*, ceased to be
able to be remitted by means of bills to Antwerp, Italy, and South Germany, so that the Fugger could not pay off their large burden of debt in
those places.

The Fugger and the Spanish Financial Crisis of 1575. We will deal
later with the bad state of affairs prevalent at this time in Spain which
resulted in the fearful catastrophe of the state bankruptcy of 1575.
In the greatest extremity, when the Spaniards and Genoese themselves
were bankrupt, the Fugger came once more to honour, for their credit
at this time was not really shaken. They served the King over and
over again with sums of from 100,000 to 150,000 crowns, which was
then an extraordinary feat. Their reward for this was that they were
better treated than the other creditors at the state bankruptcy – only,
however, from the hope of further advances. Moreover, this roused the
other creditors against the Fugger, so that they tried to do them at
Court all the harm they could.

The King urgently required to send money to the Netherlands, to satisfy the starving and mutinous troops. It was too dangerous to send large sums in cash, and there was no solvent business house except the Fugger who could do this through bills. They too were for long unwilling, for they did not know how they were going to get the money out of Spain or into the Netherlands. Finally their Spanish agent gave a hint that if the King would take the risk the matter might be considered. This caused great joy, though only 100,000 crowns were in question. The King said that he 'would take it as a great favour.' The Fugger, however, ordered their agent, in order to keep up their credit, neither to borrow in Spain nor to have borrowing undertaken in Antwerp.

The agent was in a tight place. When, in accordance with his instructions, he refused to conclude the transaction, the King's Contador Garnica, who was otherwise exceedingly well disposed towards him, began to 'play a wild game and to say that the agent could not make it plainer that the Fugger had no wish to serve the King, and like the rest only sought for enormous profits.' Finally the agent had to agree to send 70,000 crowns to the Netherlands 'for (as he said in his letter to another agent) here a man may not conclude a bargain without more and go care-free home again, but must bear ever in mind that the masters have stuck fast almost 3 million of gold at the King's back without counting the wheat and debts in the Maestrazgos.'

The money was packed in chests, sealed with the King's seal, and sent through Lisbon to Antwerp.

Direct bill transactions between Spain and Antwerp were now absolute; but the Fugger were very nervous about using the new markets, especially the Genoese bill fairs, but also Lisbon, Lyons, and Florence. In the case of the necessary remittances from Spain their attitude, which was a cautiousness understandable at such a time, gave the Spanish agent many sleepless nights. Finally he decided to act against his instructions and make use of the new markets. In this way he managed, between the winter of 1575 and the spring of 1578, to remit through bills about 2 million crowns, which enabled the Fugger to pay off part of their debts. In other ways as well the agent, Thomas Muller, showed himself a business man of exceptional ability. He was able to check those who hated and envied the Fugger at Court and to keep the King's favour for his masters. This, however, was only to be achieved by means of fresh services, so that the Fugger perpetually reproached him.

In the beginning of August, 1576, dangerous mutinies of the Spanish troops were reported from the Netherlands. The Contador Garnica immediately asked Thomas Muller to send 200,000 crowns to the

Netherlands, for the Fugger should not desert the King in his hour of need. If the troops were not satisfied, the Netherlands provinces would be lost and the Fugger would be responsible. In vain the agent declined, Garnica pressed for immediate consent. As soon as the soldiers saw the Fugger bills, he said, they would be quiet and wait till the money was collected. He said he must have an answer next day, and he even sent his agent the same night, saying that the Fugger must help or they would know what to expect. When Muller announced that the Fugger had always been faithful servants of the King and he did not know, therefore, what should happen to them, the Spaniard made a cross, kissed it, and cried out, 'I swear on the Holy Cross, if Flanders is lost from lack of money, the blame will be yours.' The interview continued for some time in this passionate tone, but the agent stood his ground. Late at night he paid a visit to President Hopperus, 'an upright, trusty man,' as he wrote to his masters, 'my kind master and well affected towards your Honour.' The President, however, said the same as the Contador and entreated the agent for Heaven's sake to prove that the Fugger were true servants of the King. Not only he, but the whole Netherlands would owe their eternal gratitude.

The same night the King wrote to the agent and said in full Council that no one but the Fugger could help him in his extremity, and that this would be the last service of the kind that he would require of them.

Muller tried first and foremost to protect his masters against the danger which threatened more and more, of being drawn into the state bankruptcy, or 'Decree' as it was called. This danger was one of the chief reasons, he said, why the Fugger should not commit themselves more deeply with the King, 'chiefly in view of the little money at the disposition of the merchants of all nations, for though the Fugger be great, yet can they not make money out of stone.' Finally, however, 'in order not to spill the soup,' he had to say, without, however, giving a binding promise on account of the Decree, that he would send 200,000 crowns to Flanders, which he was able to do in roundabout ways through skilful bill transactions.

The King was greatly pleased by this service; he wrote that he 'held it a great matter.' But it did not suffice to stay the catastrophe then threatening the Netherlands. On November the Spanish armies sacked Antwerp, thereby ruining its commercial prosperity. Many merchants had recently left the city. The Fugger's agent had to remain in order to guard the money for the Spanish bills drawn for the King. When the mutinous troops stormed the city, the Fugger house was surrounded by Alvarez Juan Giron and his men. In order to guard against further losses the agent had to pay him 11,000 crowns, his original demands having been more. Moreover, the troops stole more than 2,000 £ out of a larger sum of money committed to them for safe keeping by a friendly firm. To crown all, the Colonel Carl Fugger, a kinsman, who had brought there in 1573 a regiment recruited in Augsburg for the Duke of Alba, came to the Fugger house threatening to plunder if he were not bought off with 50,000 crowns. He was with difficulty got rid of through the agency of a friendly member of the State Council.

The great services they had rendered in the face of danger and the ceaseless efforts of their Spanish agent successfully kept the Fugger out of the Decree in spite of the machinations of their enemies. Towards other princes they held back as much as they could in the matter of loans. So, for example, in 1577 they refused a loan to Duke William of Bavaria on the ground that since the sack of Antwerp business was ruined, many bankruptcies were expected at the approaching Frankfurt Fair, and a great change in the general situation. They had, they said, no spare cash, and were themselves in great difficulties owing to the impossibility of getting in their outstanding claims, so that they had to give their whole attention to maintaining their own credit. The Duke was then owing them more than 100,000 fl. The Fugger also soundly declined to make any further advances in Spain.

Balance Sheet of 1577

We give here the balance sheet for 1577, the last we shall quote. The assets are as follows:

	Good Florins	Doubtful Florins
Spanish Debtors	5,026,000	785,026
Antwerp Debtors	120,128	232,470
Emperor Maxmilian II	220,674	—
Archduke Ferdinand	12,874	—
Archduke Albert in Bavaria	11,909	—
„ „ for his son William	1,116,611	—
Duchess Anna in Bavaria, loan without interest	4,000	—
Sundry Debtors in Augsburg	270,767	40,239
„ Debtors in Nuremberg	29,204	2,222
„ Debtors in Vienna	9,094	18,444
Debtors in the Chief Book:		
Emperor Ferdinand has owed since 1547 on Kirchberg and Weissenhorn	—	30,000
Interest on this sum, 1557–77, 20 years, at 5 %	—	30,000
Old arrears from the Maestrazgos	1,336	37,650
Various (mostly unsettled bill transactions)	494,380	68,855
Cash	241,082	—
Total	fl. 6,558,059	fl. 1,244,906

Liabilities.

	Florins
Shares in the business	1,270,399
Deposits by members of the family	3,398,000
Spanish creditors, to be taken in connection with the assets (in round figures)	1,000,000
Other pending transactions	277,806
Deposits of friends, employés, etc.	591,150

Total fl. 6,537,355

This is a very different picture from the balance sheet of 1562. Instead of having to pay interest on 3 million of borrowed money, the members of the family had about this amount in outstanding claims. The soundness of the house had been re-established, though at great cost. Anton Fugger's heirs, besides their shares in the business, amounting to more than a million gulden, had had to advance on loan almost 2 million. The capital on deposit belonging to Christopher Fugger, amounting to 700,000 fl., was soon after paid out for the Spanish bills for the Netherlands, so that the frightful burden of the Spanish business fell entirely on Anton's sons. But the fact that 1¼ million gulden must be classed as doubtful was still hidden in the future.

Last Phase of the Fugger Business. There is in existence a letter of the year 1581 from the Fugger brothers to their brother-in-law Hans Khevenhüller, who owed them 45,000 fl. They warned him very seriously about the repayment of this amount, saying that they had soon to lend a large sum to the Emperor, but from lack of ready money had themselves been compelled to borrow, and that they had to repay the loan. Moreover, they had to pay out 100,000 fl. to Georg Fugger's heirs. Money was as hard to come by in Augsburg as in other places and could not be brought from Spain without great danger and expense. In the years 1584 and 1585 the situation was the same. The Genoese had won the first place as international financiers. The Fugger complained that the Genoese 'everywhere brought the water all to their own mill.' A different story, indeed, since the Genoese at the time of the election of Charles V had complained of the harsh treatment they received from the Fugger.

Nevertheless the Fugger did a considerable business till the end of the century, e.g. in the period 1594 to 1600 the profit made amounted to 575,397 fl.; in the next ten years, however, the loss amounted to about the same sum. The Spanish claims refused to diminish. In the year 1604 they amounted to about 5¾ million ducats, of which 5 million were debts of the Spanish Crown – these were, however, set off against liabilities amounting to almost 3 million, the King's account being 2 million.

In the year 1607 there was a Spanish State bankruptcy for the third time, in which the Fugger were interested to the extent of 3¼ million ducats. At this time they had paid out the greater part of the business capital, and the deposits of the different partners had been repaid to them. They owed 2 million to persons outside the firm, so that the situation of 1562 recurred. As in the first quarter day in Spain after the Decree there was 'a great run' of creditors, and there were even 'executions.' The King helped with a moratorium, and when the Fugger represented to him that their whole capital was comprised in the claims on the Spanish Crown and that their honour and credit were in the greatest danger, if the charges on the state revenues, of which they had been deprived, were not restored, they got off once again with nothing worse than a fright. In the subsequent period, however, their situation became the more unsafe, because they made new advances to the Spanish Crown, and that for this purpose they themselves contracted new loans; the most dangerous point of all being that these loans were met by means of advances from their now all-powerful rivals, the Genoese. Their assets in Spain amounted in 1622 to 5½ million ducats and their liabilities to 4¼ million, a most risky position, which would prove fatal if the equilibrium so painfully maintained were to be destroyed. This happened once more in the year 1626. The powerful minister Olivarez, who hated the Fugger, demanded of them that they should take over the payments of 50,000 ducats a month for the maintenance of the Court, the so-called Mesadas.

Andreas Hyrus, the Fugger's agent, made unavailing representations, and was himself at last intimidated or captivated. Olivarez said, 'The Asiento must come, even if the Fugger are ruined.' With great lack of consideration he demanded the continued payment of the Mesadas, although the assignments which had been given to the Fugger in return had not, for the most part, been realized. The Fugger had, moreover, to pay 200,000 ducats for annual interest on their debts in Spain and Italy. This was a state of things which could not continue.

In the beginning of the year 1630, Octavio Centurione dared to say of the Fugger that their supposed riches were pure imagination. A few months later the Spanish agent had to write that he was in such dffii-culties on account of a debt of 34,000 ducats which had fallen due that he had thought that there would be 'a general break-up.' Finally, after many entreaties and promises, he induced the Genoese, Bart. Spinola, to take over the debt, so that the worst was staved off. Shortly after, however, the agent could only realize a bill of 5,000 crowns if Spinola added his signature. In the same year the agent Hyrus was removed.

Next year the King again granted a moratorium in order to shield the Fugger from their creditors, and this was further prolonged in 1632. In 1637, however, the Fugger estate in Spain came under the administration of the Genoese, among whom Bart. Spinola was chief creditor.

As this administration only made matters worse, in 1639 Hyrus was sent back to Spain and remained there as liquidator till 1644, when another representative was sent out. A statement of the year 1641, which puts matters in too favourable a light, states the Spanish assets of the Fugger at 2,100 million maravedis, the liabilities at 1,250 millions, a surplus of 850 millions. If we examine these figures, it is plain that the assets, i.e. the claims on the Crown and on others, amount to 1,327 million maravedis at most, or $3\frac{2}{3}$ million ducats, while the liabilities amount to $4\frac{1}{4}$ million ducats, leaving a deficit of over half a million ducats. This calculation assumes that all the outstanding claims would be paid, which was far from being the case.

The Fugger business in Spain had reached this sad state through acting as we have seen. It had already had claims on the Spanish Crown amounting to over 3 million ducats, none of which was ever repaid. The loss incurred, including the sums already written off, amounts to at least 4 million ducats. The Spanish line of the Hapsburgs remained in debt to the Fugger for this amount. To this must be added the Netherlands bonds of the Receivers General, the debt of the States of Brabant, which also was in fact never repaid, the so-called Friesland debt, an annual payment secured on the revenues of the Crown lands in Friesland which was not paid after the separation of this province. Other annual payments were continued by the provinces after their liberation, but the Fugger's was discontinued owing to the support which they were known to have afforded to the Spanish Crown. Many efforts were made to re-establish it, and Article 24 of the Treaty of Westphalia seemed to offer some hope of this, but this never materialized. In 1673 the arrears of the payment with interest and expenses amounted to 2 million gulden.

In conclusion the Fugger had still in 1650 a claim against the Imperial line of the Hapsburgs amounting to 615,600 fl. – a debt which had originated in the years 1574 to 1617. The original capital had only been 144,000 fl., the rest being due to arrears of interest, though only 8 per cent. was charged up to 1603, and after that date only 5–6 per cent. The total loss which the Fugger sustained on their claims against the Hapsburgs up to the middle of the seventeenth century is certainly not put too high at 8 million Rhenish gulden. We shall scarcely be wrong in supposing that the greater part of the Fugger's earnings in the course of a hundred years was lost in this way. At their most brilliant period, i.e. about the middle of the sixteenth century, the family had never owned more than 5 or 6 millions of the money of that day, even including the private fortunes of their individual members. In the following half-century, in spite of the work of Anton Fugger and his sons, the property had not really increased. Only its nominal value grew through the general monetary depreciation. What remained after another half-century was only some landed property which had been laid waste in the wars and was heavily mortgaged. The family laws as to inheritance, under which it descended in the male line and none of it could be sold, kept the lands more or less together in spite of the enormous families of many of the Fugger. (In 1619, for example, the family numbered a hundred persons.)

CHAPTER 2

THE OTHER GERMAN FINANCIERS

THE BUSINESS HOUSES OF SOUTH GERMANY

IT was the rapid development of the silver mines of Tyrol, about the middle of the fifteenth century, which first induced the other South German business houses like the Fugger gradually to leave the old track of laborious but solid trade which centred in Venice. Perhaps it would be more accurate to express this change as follows: The decline of the profits of trade with Venice, etc., induced them to look for other means of gain, so they went into finance and mining in Tyrol and by the capital they put in brought the latter to a flourishing state. Further research is needed to show which of these two views is the correct one.

The Meuting. As early as 1456 the Meutings of Augsburg lent 35,000 fl. to Duke Sigmund of Tyrol, who was known as 'the Münzreich,' but, all the same, was continually in need of money. Until it should be repaid the Duke made over to them, at the price of 7¾ fl. per mark (Vienna weight), all the silver produced from the works and delivered to him. Thereupon the Meuting must have gone into the business of money changers; for in 1475 the Bishop of Augsburg lodged a complaint to the Council there 'of the exchange, which Ulrich Meuting is in the habit of carrying on there, by reason whereof a master of the mint and his associates were impeded in their rights,' and in the next year, in addition to Meuting, he named Ulrich Mayr and some others who had been guilty of the same trespass. In this department the new power of capital was already breaking through the barriers of the Middle Ages.[1]

In 1474 Ludwig Meuting already had business relations with the Emperor Frederick III, and as he soon afterwards got at variance with the town of Augsburg he obtained a safe conduct from the Emperor. This Ludwig Meuting is the first of the South German merchants to be mentioned in Antwerp. As early as 1479 he had to get in some outstanding debts there. Finally, George Meuting settled in Antwerp, married there in 1516, and in company with the well-known Gillebert van Schoonabeke went in for large speculation in real estate. Later, he carried on important financial business with the Court of Brussels, which appears to have brought him down in 1537. The family, however, lasted on in Antwerp till 1820.[2]

---

[1] Ladurner *im Archiv. f. Gesh. u. Alterthumskunde Tirols,* vol. V. Also cf. *Augsburger Stadtarchiv, Grosse Rathsdekret-Sammlung,* VII, 30 u. 52, and von Stetten, *Gesch. d. augsburger Geschlechter,* p. 186.

[2] Chmel, *Aktenstücke z. Gesch. d. Hauses Habsburg,* III, 540, 609; also Actes scabinaux in Antwerp Stadtarchive, 1479, 25/10. Cf. *Annuaire de la noblesse de Belgique,* 1883, p. 332 ff.; *Bulletin de la Propriété,* 1887, p. 92.

The Meuting who had remained behind in Augsburg played a not insignificant part in international finance for some decades longer than their relatives in Antwerp. Bernhard Meuting in 1543 took a share of 29,000 pounds in the Antwerp loan to the Court of Brussels. The Meuting were one of the Augsburg business houses who were suspected of supporting the Emperor in the Schmalkaldian war. King Ferdinand got a loan of 25,000 fl. from Jacob Meuting in 1549 and another of 100,000 fl. in 1551. On the other hand, in 1553 Bernhard and Philip Meuting took a share of 43,735 crowns in Lyons in the great loan to the King of France. In this they appear as citizens of Berne. Bernard Meuting was one of the first victims of the great credit crisis of 1557–62. It appears, nevertheless, that other members of the family carried on business after this, for in 1566 the Emperor Maximilian II obtained a loan from the Meuting.[1]

Mining, Smelting and Iron Works. The business houses of Nuremberg and Augsburg took an early part in the silver mining of Saxony. From the records in the Archives of the Imhof families we learn that by 1479 Cunz Imhof and Heinrich Wolff in Nuremberg, and Lucas Welser in Augsburg, held some shares in the silver mining works at the Schneeberg. Soon after we come across the Nuremberg families of Führer and Schlüsselfelder as undertakers of the copper mining works at Eisleben with which was connected the important Saiger smelting works at Armstedt in Thuringia. In 1511 there are mentioned as undertakers of ironworks the Nuremberg merchants Hans Kress, Paul Heymer, and Sebald Ketzel. Further, at that time Peter Rümmel carried on silver mining in Tyrol, and Lucas Semler smelting works in Silesia; Mathias Landaur and Hans and Gregory Schütze also carried on smelting works. In 1482 George Holzschuher and Ulrich Erkel of Nuremberg had the monopoly of supplying silver to the town of Berne, whose mint Holzschuher managed through his people.[2] We shall see later that the Welser, too, then already carried on similar businesses.

The Emperor Maximilian and the South German Merchants. There is a certain homely romantic charm in the relations of Maximilian to the burghers of the imperial towns of South Germany. It still gives us pleasure to read how the Emperor lived among his true burghers and danced with their wives and daughters at the town hall. But on both sides the very real basis of these beautiful relations was a monetary one. A contemporary chronicler says: 'The Emperor was favourably disposed towards the men of Augsburg. There were many merchants there who

[1] Lille, B. 2436; Augsbg. St.-A. Litteralien 1546; Thorsch, pp. 40, 41, 49; v. Stettin, *Geschichte v. Augsburg*, I, 551.

[2] Akten der Freiherrl. von Imhofschen u. von Scheuerlschen Familien Archive in Nuremburg. Cf. also v. Haller, *Schweizerisches Munz u. Medaillen Cabinet*, II, 88; Lohner, *Münzen der Republik Bern*, p. 257.

did business with him. If he wanted money they lent him a large quantity on the silver and copper from Schwatz. These merchants got a lot of profit out of him, for he was an honourable man and kept his promises. So the merchants could fleece him. And if the Emperor carried on business in copper and silver with them, the Emperor's councillors likewise took part secretly under the names of merchants.'[1]

But this is by no means a correct description of their relations. The Emperor Maximilian by no means always conducted himself so honourably towards the burghers. We find, indeed, indications of a financial behaviour which appear to justify the scorn with which the Italians in particular judged these beggarly acts of the Emperor. Indeed, the Emperor was perhaps only personally responsible so far as he made a bad choice of his financial officials. But in reference to this it is again very noticeable that he preferred to make use of Augsburg and Nuremberg merchants to manage his finances. The most celebrated of these men of business were Heinrich Wolff and his son Balthasar from Nuremberg, and George Gossembrot, Lucas Gassner, Hans von Stetten, George Ilsung, and Hans Paumgartner from Augsburg.

How the Wolffs came to serve the Emperor deserves to be told in greater detail. In 1494, Heinrich Wolff, who by that time 'was almost his good friend,' agreed to lend to the Emperor 'a goodly sum of money' on the silver from Schwatz. He paid this sum and obtained a written promise from Maximilian that for four years all the Tyrol silver that was to be delivered to the Mint at Hall should be handed over to him at a definite price. But this silver was, as we know, already mortgaged to the Fugger, and they naturally would not give up their security. The Emperor was even prevailed upon to assign the silver to them for a longer period. He relegated Henry Wolff to his claim against Lodovico il Moro, Duke of Milan, who still owed him a part of his marriage portion. But Wolff got nothing from him, and in order to save his outstanding debt allowed himself to be drawn in to lend more and more to the Emperor till at last the whole of his very considerable property had gone. To compensate him Maximilian appointed him to his Council and then elevated his son Balthasar to be royal chamberlain and head treasurer to the patrimonial dominions, as well as ennobling him. But this son, when he stood in such high favour with the Emperor, began to be ashamed of his father who had been ruined. This broke his father's heart.[2]

Gossembrot was the first burgher of Augsburg who entered into the service of Maximilian. He had already done business with Duke Sig-

[1] Cf. Greiff in d. Anmerkungen zu Lucas Rems Tagebuche, p. 100, and v. Stetten, Geschichte Augsburgs, I, 245 ff.

[2] These details are from the Scheuerlbuch of Dr. Christof Scheuerl. For Balthasar Wolff cf. Adler, Die Organisation der Centralverwaltung unter Kaiser Maximilian, I, p. 83; Chmel, Urkunden z Gesch. Maximilians, I, p. 180 sq.

mund of Tyrol, with the result that in 1477 he was mortgagee of the guardianship of Ernberg, and in the same year was appointed an unpaid counsellor of the Duke. When Maximilian took over the government of Tyrol in 1490 he confirmed Gossembrot as guardian of Ernberg and employed him then in his many financial affairs, in which Gossenbrot appears on the one side as the Emperor's representative, but on the other as his banker. Thus in 1492 he procured for him 35,000 fl. on a tax granted by the province of Tyrol. In 1494 he tried to get money from the Fugger for the Emperor. But in 1495 he personally lent him 29,000 fl. at his pressing request. These, however, are only particular examples. Doubtless he developed a much more important business activity. In particular, in conjunction with his brother Sigmund, he had a large interest in the trade with Tyrolese copper, since in 1483 1,000 centners of copper were delivered to him as an instalment of a claim against Duke Sigmund. His peculiar position is perhaps best character-ized by the fact that in conjunction with his brother he had a large interest in the big syndicate which in 1498 and 1499 wished to keep up the price of copper in Venice.[1]

Hans von Stetten, too, was in 1491 empowered by Maximilian to get money by trading, exchange, and other ways, as should be necessary. Later, he was appointed Counsellor and Chamberlain of Lower Austria. In 1506 the Emperor informed him that he had served him truly for six-teen years, that in this time of pressing occasions, wars, etc., he had obtained for him or lent to him large sums of money by himself or his relations at least 200,000 fl. in all, which had been very useful to him, the Emperor, and had preserved him from harm. Further, for this he had never charged 'interest, compensation, or anything else,' and had re-ceived no pay, but into the bargain had neglected his own business and had used up of his own property 3,000 fl. more than was shown in the accounts. For this the Emperor now granted him once for all 10,000 fl., and mortgaged certain estates as security for the payment.[2]

All we know of Lucas Gassner is that from 1502–4 he was active as a financial official of Maximilian,[3] and we are not much better informed about Hans Paumgartner, although he played a very important part. Meanwhile, we will state here the little that we know of him and add a few details of the further fortunes of his family.

The Paumgartner. From early time the Nuremberg merchant Hans Paumgartner must have had a considerable interest in Tyrol mining,

[1] For Gossembrot cf. Ladurner *in d. Ztschr. d. Ferdinandeums*, 3, Folge, 15, Heft, p. 105; Chroniken *d. deutschen Städte: Augsburg*, II, 394; v. Stetten, *Geschichte v. Augsburg*, I, 246, 256; v. Beckh-Widmanstetter, *Die ältere Art der Geldbeschaffung im Kriege*, p. 19, Anm. 24.

[2] von Stetten, *Geschichte d. augsburger Geschlechter*, pp. 413, 417,

[3] Adler, l.c. p. 116 ff,

especially in copper mines. On this account he lived for a considerable time, at any rate from 1491 to 1499, at Kuffstein, and in the years 1498–9 with his partners, one of whom, Hans Knoll, was a conspicuous member of the copper syndicate. On the death of George Gossembrot in 1502, he, together with Lucas Gassner, for some years on behalf of the Emperor, took care of the businesses which till then Gossembrot had managed and succeeded him in the guardianship of Ernberg, which he held as security till 1523. But before 1511 he had already gone to live in Augsburg.[1]

His son, Hans Paumgartner the younger, married one of the Fugger in Augsburg, and in 1518, at the end of the Emperor Maximilian's life, was expressly mentioned as the man who paid money to the Hapsburgs. He at that time lent the Emperor 10,000 fl. In 1524, 75,000 fl. were paid out to him for old claims against Maximilian. In 1530 he lent the Emperor 42,000 fl.; it was, however, paid back after three months with 17 per cent. per annum interest to his representative, Wolff Haller, in Antwerp. In 1543 he also helped King Ferdinand with 10,000 fl., and in November, 1544, in conjunction with the Fugger and the Haugs, lent him 100,000 fl. on silver. In the Schmalkaldian war he remained on the side of the Catholics, and consequently was much hated by the Protestants. For a long time he was an Imperial counsellor and was ennobled in 1539. He was accounted among the richest merchants of his time. But serious misfortune quickly came on his sons. One of them, David, left Augsburg in 1552, became a partisan of William of Grumbach, and through his senseless vanity became involved in his fall and perished on the scaffold in 1567. He had already lost his fortune. His brother, John George, got into financial difficulties in 1565, and was for five years in a debtor's prison. Then he made over all his assets to his creditors, whose claims amounted to 104,471 fl., and went abroad.[2]

The Welser. Unfortunately we are not so well informed about the fate of the second largest of the German trading houses of the sixteenth century as is necessary, considering its all-embracing and many-sided importance. While the Fugger preserved their archives the Welser, after the fall of their business, lost theirs, and it is only recently, through the piety and labour of individual descendants, that the scanty remains of these treasures have again been collected. The information we have is, however, sufficient to let us recognize the fundamental difference from almost every point of view that existed between the two largest trading houses of South Germany.

Origin. The Welsers belong to one of the oldest families of Augsburg;

---

[1] Cf. Ladurner, *Ztschr. d. Ferdinandeums*, 3, Folge (1870), p. 107. Adler l.c.

[2] Cf. v. Stetten, *Geschichte v. Augsburg*, I, 564, 590; v. Stetten, *Gesch. d. Augsburger Geschlechter*, p. 198.

but about their business – which for a long period, like the other burgher families of South Germany, they would have chiefly carried on with Italy – we first hear in 1473, when the brothers Bartel, Jacob, Lucas and Ulrich Welser together founded a trading company, whose importance was increased through their connection with Hans Vöhlin of Memmingen. This Hans Vöhlin, who was one of the line founded in the fourteenth century by Vöhlin von Ungerhausen, appear with his associates in 1490 as having a part in the Tyrol silver business. The connection of the Welser with the Vöhlins was doubtless already established, for Anton Welser, one of the sons of Lucas, had in 1479 married a daughter of Hans Vöhlin. Lucas Welser was the ancestor of the three chief branches of the family named after his sons Anton, Lucas, and Jacob. The Lucas branch was extinct by 1628; the Jacob branch (the Nuremberg main branch) became extinct in 1878; while the Anton branch still exists in its Ulm offshoot.

For some time Anton Welser lived in Memmingen, where his father-in-law, Hans Vöhlin, was burgomaster; but about 1496 he returned to Augsburg, and in conjunction with his brother-in-law, Conrad Vöhlin, formed the firm of Anton Welser, Conrad Vöhlin and Company, which quickly became of great consequence. It also at once engaged in the silver trade. They induced the town of Berne to have coined the unpopular 'Rollenbatzen.' In this apparently they enjoyed the support of the Emperor.[1]

Development till 1517. We have already seen many times that the Welser took a part in the great financial transactions due to the policy of the Hapsburgs. But at the same time they carried on an extensive trade and tried to adapt themselves to the new conditions in this department. That is a great difference between the basis of their business and that of the Fugger. While Jakob Fugger early gave up trading, Anton Welser founded an important factory at Lisbon, and in 1503 his agent, Simon Seitz, succeeded in obtaining the first privileges for the German merchants. The Welser then took a prominent part in the great expedition to the East Indies, which was equipped by the German and Italian merchants in 1505. Their share amounted to 20,000 fl.; that of the Fugger, on the other hand, was only 4,000 fl.; and that of the Genoese and Florentines together only 29,400 fl. The enterprise produced a profit of 175 per cent. per annum; but in consequence of Portuguese chicanery it was so long before it was divided and such difficulties were put in the way of the Germans and Italians trading directly that to go on with it was not to be thought of.[2] For this reason, after this the

[1] Ladurner, p. 101; Löhner, p. 259.
[2] *Mitth. d. Ver. f. Geschichte d. Stadt Nürnberg Heft,* 1, p. 100; Heyd, *Gesch. d. Lavantehandels,* II, 523 ff. (new French Ed. II, 530 ff.).

Welser carried on the highly speculative business at second-hand with East Indian spices from Lisbon to Antwerp and South Germany on a large scale. For a long time fortune smiled on them so that for the time being they made considerable profits.[1]

We learn from Lucas Rem, who with his brother Andreas then had a share in the profits, that his share amounted to:

31 per cent. from 1502 to 1504, or $10\frac{1}{3}$ per cent. per annum.
39 ,, ,, ,, 1505 ,, 1507, ,, 13 ,, ,, ,, ,,
15 ,, ,, ,, 1508 ,, 1510, ,, 5 ,, ,, ,, ,,
11 ,, ,, ,, 1511 ,, 1512, ,, $5\frac{1}{2}$,, ,, ,, ,,
16 ,, ,, ,, 1513 ,, 1515, ,, $5\frac{1}{3}$,, ,, ,, ,,
30 ,, ,, ,, 1516 ,, 1516, ,, 15 ,, ,, ,, ,,

We also hear that the result of the business chiefly depended on the state of the business with Portugal. For the whole period of sixteen years there was an average annual profit of 9 per cent., which is quite respectable, but cannot be compared with the profits of the Fugger, who, as we have seen, earned an average annual profit of $54\frac{1}{2}$ per cent.

Certainly it may be that at times the profits of the Welser were higher than appears from the accounts and dividends, and here again we come upon a great difference between the Fugger and the Welser.

The business house of the Fugger never had more than a few persons interested except near relations, and since the death of the brothers of Jakob Fugger the management was always in one hand. The factories therefore must, as a rule, have been managed by carefully chosen paid assistants who did not belong to the family. The house of the Welser, on the other hand, had a large number of persons interested, part of whom either did not belong to the family or were only distant relations. They worked at the factories, but at the same time they were entitled to a share in the profits. So they did their best to carry on the business well. But the whole system led repeatedly to great disputes as to the way in which the business should be carried on and the profits reckoned, so that in 1517 part of the company left believing that they had been cheated by the others.[2]

The articles of partnership of 1508 contain no less than eighteen names, and in the course of the next year some others must have joined the firm: Anton Welser the elder, Conrad Vöhlin, Ludwig Reyhing, Wolf Pfister, Jacob Welser, Marx Pfister, Hans Pfister, Conrad Imhof, Anton Lauginger, Peter Heintzel, Hans Lauginger, Narciss Lauginger, Ulrich Hanold, Simon Seitz, Hans Heintzel, Wilhelm Heintzel, Andreas Rem, and Bartholomew Welser. Lucas Rem is not mentioned, but no doubt he had an interest in the business.

[1] *Tagebuch d. Lucas Rem*, edit. v. Greiff, p. 30.
[2] Lucas Rem (l.c. p. 19).

In 1517 Jacob Welser, Ulrich Hanold and Andreas and Lucas Rem retired from the business; possibly some others did, too, whom the Welser wanted to get rid of. Jacob Welser founded a new firm in Nuremberg.

About the development of the Welser business before this great alteration it may be added that in 1507 the Welser were mentioned in Antwerp; yet it was only in 1509 that they bought there a large house which had just been built, called 'De Gulden Roose,' near the cathedral, where the head post office is now.[1] Lucas Rem repeatedly acted as agent of the firm at Antwerp at that time; in 1521 Gabriel Studelin is mentioned as agent, and in 1525–30 Alexius Grimel, whom we shall come across again later.

At this time, besides those in Antwerp and Lisbon, the Welser had well-established factories in Nuremberg, Danzig, Venice, Milan, Rome, Genoa, Freiburg, Berne, Zurich, Lyons, Saragossa, and possibly in other places, which were regularly visited by individual members of the firm in order to inspect the factories. In 1512 the Welser gave up the shipping trade and closed down the factory at Danzig.

A new period in the development of the house begins with Jacob Welser leaving the firm in 1517, and the death of Anton Welser which followed in the next year. After this there was an increasing amount of purely financial business, without, however, displacing the trading in goods and the other undertakings. The Welser remained the second largest business house, though their capital, which never approached that of the Fugger, was considerably weakened by the division in 1517.

The Nuremberg Welser. Anton's brother, Jacob Welser, in 1493 was managing the Nuremberg branch of the house, but also from time to time was in partnership with Conrad Imhof, and when his father-in-law, Hans Thumer, died in 1500 carried on this business till 1502. In one of the lists of Nuremberg merchants attributed to the year 1511, it is said of him, 'He carries on a large trade in all countries such as no merchant of Nuremberg has ever done.' But the real direction of the business was then concentrated in Augsburg. In 1517, Jacob left the firm and founded his own business in Nuremberg. He took in as partners his sons Hans, Jacob and Sebastian, and Hieronymus Fütterer; and later on, from time to time, Hans Fütterer and Wolff Harstörfer as well; but the firm was never particularly large. The capital amounted to 66,000 fl. in 1527; 92,000 fl. from 1529 to 1535; 243,000 fl. in 1543; but so much was taken out by the partners that only 86,400 fl. remained in the business. In the following two years this increased again to 281,000 fl.[2]

---

[1] Thys, *Bulletin de la Propriété*, 1890, p. 8.
[2] *Register der Rattschleg in unsser Versamlung* (Freiherrl. von Welsersches Familien-Archiv in Schloss Neunhof).

The Welser of Nuremberg had factories in Genoa, Venice, Aquila (in South Italy, for buying saffron), Milan, Antwerp, Lyons, Vienna, and Schlackenwald in Bohemia; in the last-named place in order to carry on their participation in the mines there. In 1516, not far from the tin and silver mines of Schlackenwald, there was discovered new rich silver deposits, and with the help of the Counts Schlich, who owned the land, the flourishing town of Joachimsthal soon grew up. The Counts made use of an old privilege and began at once to strike coins there. The first genuine thalers, which at first were called 'Joachimsthaler,' came from the mint there. The Welser of Nuremberg, in conjunction with Hans Nutzel, lent the Counts a great deal of money, and also took a part in the mining at Schlackenwald, which they extended.[1]

The main business of the Welser of Nuremberg was pure trade, but this did not debar them at times from carrying out very important financial transactions; their operations at first, however, were on a very solid basis corresponding to the ruling business principles in Nuremberg. Thus, in the resolutions of the partnership in 1529, it is stated: 'Agreed that in Antwerp or the Netherlands no credit over 25,000 fl. 'shall be given, and when such a claim falls due and the debtor wishes the advance continued the interest shall be got in; no interest shall be allowed to run on interest; also no bonds of the Receivers General shall be taken; but it shall always be required that the ruler of the land shall enter into a written engagement jointly and severally, and finally promissory notes shall not be accepted unless they are acknowledged by the drawers.' Further, in 1545, it was decided not to lend the King of France more than 24,000 crowns.

These were wise principles, but unfortunately they were soon abandoned. By the end of 1546 we find Jacob and Sebastian Welser taking part to the extent of almost 100,000 ducats in no less than six great loans, which the Fugger had granted to the Emperor against bills on Spain. But it was much more dangerous that they decided in 1551 'to venture 100,000 fl. on short term loans in the market and bonds of the Receivers General.' Such a spirit of enterprise in critical times could not fail to result in great losses, and so, since this time, the welfare of the Welser of Nuremberg soon went downhill.

Of the sons of the founder of the Nuremberg firm, Jacob the younger managed the Antwerp factory since 1530, Hans the Augsburg branch, which soon became more important than the main business. In his father's lifetime Hans already seems to have been the soul of the business, for in 1531 his brother Jacob, who is expressly described as Hans' agent, was paid 10,800 livres, whose value Hans Welser in Augsburg had in 1530 handed over against bills of exchange of the Emperor. The

[1] Scheuerl Buch and Sternberg, *Geschichte d. Böhm. Bergwerke*, p. 322.

firm was changed to Hans Welser and Brothers before 1537, although their father, Jacob, did not die till 1541.

Hans Welser attained to great consequence in Augsburg, and even became Burgomaster. Contrary to his cousins in Augsburg, he was a Protestant, but a moderate one, and did not wish to know anything of the war against the Emperor. He died in 1559, five years after his brother Jacob. The third brother, Sebastian, remained in Nuremberg and carried on the business after the death of his brothers till he gave up the ghost in 1566. His sons, Jacob and Hans, then gave up trade which no longer paid. At the time of their father's death their claims on the French Court amounted to 55,245 livres Tournois. So much for the Welser of Nuremberg.[1]

The Augsburg Welser under Bartholomew. Of the other sons of Anton Welser, Bartholomew, after his father's death, took over the management of the head business at Augsburg, while Franz deserves mention as the father of Philippine Welser. Bartholomew Welser is especially celebrated for his attempt at colonization in Venezuela which, however, regarded – as it rightly should be judged – as a business enterprise, does not deserve the praise lavished on him for it. It was an adventure on the Spanish model. Begun without serious intentions of business profit, and in spite of the system of exploitation equally on the Spanish pattern, yet in essentials only by warlike means carried through as a genuine 'Conquista,' it was finally wrecked for want of sufficient power as well as by the hostile disposition of the Spaniards. Yet the Welser expedition to Venezuela will always remain memorable as the first and only attempt of the Germans in America – even though under a foreign monarch, for Charles V ruled there as King of Spain, not as Emperor – to acquire such an extensive territory.[2]

By the end of Anton Welser's life the business had acquired a somewhat new character by the large participation in the loans for the election of Charles V as Emperor. We must refer to the previous chapter for the details of this big affair. It was concluded in Anton Welser's lifetime; but as he died soon after it fell to his son to carry it out. With it the Welser stepped into the first rank of the great financiers. Again the Emperor at the Diet of Worms received from them a considerable loan, and in the same year they also took a prominent part in the great sales of the Neapolitan domains.

Of the following decade, apart from the Venezuela enterprise which began in 1527, we only know that during the years 1525–8 the Welser,

---

[1] Lille, B. 2363. Hecker *in der Ztschr. d. histor. ver. f. Schwaben*, I, 52.

[2] The latest description of the Welser enterprise in Venezuela is Schumacher in the *Festschrift z. Erinnerung an die Entdeckung Amerikas*, Bd. II (Hamburg, 1892). Häbler has, however, discovered some new sources.

with Hans Ebner in Nuremberg, carried on a large trade in copper, which is described as monopolistic, and that with the Fugger they participated largely in the great loans which the Hapsburg brothers had to take up in 1530; but of the details of this participation we know just as little as of that of the Fugger.

Now came the time when the Welser, too, thought it necessary to give a new splendour to their old burgher patriciate; in 1532 the Emperor ennobled the brothers Bartholomew, Anton and Franz Welser two years after the same elevation in rank had happened to the Fugger. These Augsburg Welser remained Catholic; they did not, however, keep so unwaveringly true to the house of Hapsburg as the Fugger did. During the agitations preceding the election of Charles V their attitude had been vacillating, and once they even wished to draw back altogether. In contrast with the Fugger they had in Lyons a factory which was very important for them, and their interests there compelled them to a see-saw policy between the two parties into which Europe was then politically separated. Their attitude towards the religious conflicts was a similar one.

In 1527 their agent at Rome was thrown into prison because he would not lend the Pope 1,000 ducats. In 1532 there were mutterings in Lyons that the Welser had taken a part in the exchange business by means of which, it was said, the King of France would support the Evangelicals; and in 1534 they begged the Emperor to take back the money he had deposited with them, presumably to use it against the Protestants in case of need; for the Welser were frightened of being involved in the religious conflict.[1] It is consistent with this ambiguous behaviour that Bartholomew Welser, on the 6th April, 1541, obtained for himself, his children, his partners and the employees in his business an express letter of protection. The Fugger had never considered such a thing necessary.

During the whole period the Welser were, it is true, repeatedly mentioned in connection with large financial transactions of the Emperor but never without the Fugger, so there is no need for us here to repeat the details of these transactions. On the other hand, it is important that the Welser participated with 50,000 livres in a loan which the King of France, after the outbreak of the fourth war with the Emperor in 1542, took up in Lyons; certainly they were half compelled to do this, and they had nevertheless to pay for it later.

Here we may allude to the correspondence in 1542–5 between Hieronymus Seiler (Bartholomew's son-in-law, who earlier had represented the firm in Spain, but had gone out of it) and Alexius Grimel, formerly the Welser's agent in Antwerp. It appears from this correspondence, which will repeatedly occupy us, that even then the Welser in monetary

[1] Gayangos, *Calendar III*, 2, 76. Lanz, *Correspondenz*, II, 121, 159.

matters did not always make towards their own relatives the advances that these hoped for. Seiler observes 'they wanted to have too much.'

The Time of the Schmalkaldian War. During the Schmalkaldian war we see that in their business practice the Welser strove more and more to be neutral, which is an essential difference between them and the Fugger.[1] In the previous chapter we have already seen that at the beginning of this war the Welser probably participated in the exchange transactions concluded for the Emperor by the Court of Brussels. But the Emperor also wanted a large sum of cash in South Germany at once. The Fugger were ready to help him there too, but the Welser, on the other hand, decidedly refused, although, as the Emperor knew, they had a large sum to receive at the next Antwerp fair. The Emperor was bitterly offended at this refusal, and the Welser had to pay heavily for it later.

In order to remain neutral as far as possible in the whole conflict, Bartholomew Welser, on 13th June, 1546, asked for permission from the Augsburg Council to be allowed to remain away from the town for three years. Permission was given, on which he betook himself to Arbon, on the Lake of Constance, where apparently he remained until the end of the war. In fact, the Welser do not appear to have lent any more money to either party. This reserve doubtless was mostly due to the conviction that the house was already more than sufficiently engaged in relation to its strength. In particular, the large capital which remained in Spain and could not be withdrawn, and the unluckly enterprise in Venezuela, caused Bartholomew Welser much anxiety. He therefore, in February, 1547, sent his nephew Christopher Peutinger to the head-quarters of the Emperor to beg for an order to pay on account of the outstanding claims of the Welser in Spain.

But the Emperor, who then was already Lord of South Germany, wanted to punish the Welser for their former refusal to help him. By this time Charles' tendency to despotism, which till then had been held back from political considerations, had broken out. Bartholomew Welser was quite right when he sorrowfully said 'that the evening is no longer just.' We have a picture by Titian of the Emperor dated shortly before the Schmalkaldian war; he sits in an arm-chair, bent, oppressed by gout, with his forehead full of wrinkles and an angry, piercing look in his eyes. That was what 'the evening' looked like. Yet his counsellors were more to blame than he was for the arbitrary proceedings which now began both in the politics and in the financial methods of the Emperor.

[1] The basis of the following are the business letters of the Welser written by Christof Peutinger from the Emperor's head-quarters at Ulm. These are in the Augsburg Stadtbibliothek, *Peutingeriana*, vol. I.

In finance, in addition to the influence of the son of Granvella, Bishop of Arras, that of the Imperial secretary, Francisco Erasso, was disastrous. We will later give an account in its place of the mysterious activity of this man, whom we have already met in the previous chapter. Here we only repeat the observations that Christopher Peutinger made about him.

When Peutinger came to Erasso to make representations about the payment of the older Spanish loans, he was informed that the Emperor must again have money, and that he would give Netherlands bonds of the Receivers General for it. As we have already seen, people then did not like to take this kind of security, because they were only a personal obligation on the Receivers General to pay. So Peutinger did not agree, and when Erasso observed that the charges on Spanish revenues could be given and Peutinger asked 'on which?' the Spaniard answered 'Sobre qualquiera cosa.' From this and other expressions of Erasso, Peutinger perceived that he 'was up to some bad tricks.' When Peutinger represented to him that formerly the Welser had been given good securities and had been well treated, Erasso answered, 'Time changes things'; the Welser had made a lot of money out of the Emperor, now they must lend him at least 100,000 ducats. Peutinger became quite 'confused and sorrowful' at this, and observed that Erasso had the Emperor on his side and access to him at all times, while everything that he, Peutinger, said vanished like foam, however well it may have been justified. He thought that Erasso's expression, 'El tiempo muda las cosas,' had somewhat the same meaning as what Granvella was reported to have said, 'There is a time to promise and a time to keep one's promise.' The chief aim of the Emperor's Spanish Council, and of Erasso in particular, was to prevent the Emperor making use of Spanish income in the German war. This is why the saying now ran, 'Eat bird or die.' Peutinger's impression was strengthened when he talked with the Bishop of Arras, who said 'even more shocking things' to him.

First of all the Bishop reproached the Welser that they had left the Emperor in the lurch in his need at Regensburg. Peutinger answered that at that time the firm did not know themselves what would happen to them and their property. They had much money to demand from the King of Portugal's agent in Antwerp and from the Court of the Netherlands, but they could not get any. This was why it had not been possible to serve the Emperor except in Spain against repayment outside of Spain. But this had not suited the Emperor.

Then the Bishop explained that the Emperor knew that the King of France had raised large loans in Lyons in which the Welser had participated with at least 40,000 crowns, and under another name with yet more. Peutinger replied that this was not correct. The Welser had only

K

once been compelled to lend the King 12,000 crowns in order to be allowed to go on carrying on business in Lyons, which was necessary for them in order to be able to serve the Emperor further; they had not done it to get a profit. We must interpose here that this was not strictly accurate. From the Seiler correspondence we know that the Welser, under Seiler's name, took part in the large arbitrage transactions of the Florentine Ducci in Antwerp with Lyons and served the financial needs of the French Court. But from the Tucher business correspondence, to which we shall return later, we see that also in 1545 they wished to participate directly in the great loan at Lyons. At that time there was no talk of any compulsion being used, but somewhat later it appears that pressure certainly seems to have been employed to make the German merchants in Lyons more accommodating towards the financial needs of the French Court.

Thirdly, the Bishop of Arras blamed the Welser for having repaid claims and paid interest to the German opponents of the Emperor, although he had expressly forbidden this. The excuse that the Welser had not known of this prohibition would not do. It was a 'cosa publica,' and the Emperor had nothing to do with the Welser blinding themselves. Peutinger explained that no repayments worth mentioning had been made, but that it was necessary to pay interest to keep up the credit of the house. Moreover, the Fugger had paid interest to the Emperor's opponents. To this the Bishop replied that this had been done only with the express permission of the Emperor; the Fugger had behaved well and not abandoned the Emperor in his great straits. 'This Bishop,' bemoans Peutinger, 'is more disastrous for us than his father, resolute as the devil; and they now mean to hold us tight.'

It did no good that Peutinger begged with tears that the Welser should not be ruined. The Emperor treated him in a kindly way, but referred him again to Erasso; and after he had bribed both him and the Duke of Alba handsomely, he had to be thoroughly satisfied that they were content with a loan of 100,000 fl. on the Emperor's mere note of hand, without any particular income being allocated for repayment.

The arrangement which the Welser then made to get this money, the way in which everywhere they collected small sums, how anxiously they calculated the unfavourable course of exchange, shows clearly, especially if we compare the large scale arrangements of the Fugger, how tight and difficult the financial position of the second largest German trading house had become at bottom. The whole conduct of the Welser at this period further shows that they were no match for the Fugger in political insight and mercantile acuteness. Yet Bartholomew Welser must be described as a man of business acumen. But its kind was a different one and not so suitable as that of the Fugger for the practical management of a business house of the first rank. This can be seen from the letter in which Bartholomew Welser renders the impression which the Emperor's conduct made on him.

If the Emperor's counsellors, he writes, reproach us that we are 'inutiles en tiempo de necesidad,' they should reflect how thoughtless it was to begin a war without having supplied themselves with money and troops, with the result that almost 'they and all of us together had gone to destruction.' 'It is easy for Erasso and his people to succeed in cutting straps out of other people's skin!' And what will be the result of the present procedure? The 'hotheads' will bring everything to ruin; the Emperor will soon be aware of the harm done. Already now we see that in the Netherlands, where the Regent, through her financial agent Ducci, will compel the merchants according to her will. The merchants who must arrange their affairs in the most orderly way cannot endure that longer than they must. Already much money was taken from the Court of the Netherlands and sent to the French: 'in time perhaps things will be yet more disastrous there'; in fact, *nolite confidere in principibus.* Some day credit will not be forced: 'for who will trust him in such large sums to another and particularly to such a powerful lord as the Emperor, a lord with whom he cannot deal by question and answer; he will only do it of goodwill and no longer on compulsion, cost him what it will.' If the Emperor does not consider this it will come to such a point that in all his kingdoms he will no longer have any more money or credit.

Bartholomew Welser gave formal orders to his Spanish agent 'in these times' to go into no new lending business, however high the profit may be, and though by this the profits of the business are much diminished, and also not to spend so much on bribes and other expenses, and generally slowly and carefully to reduce the whole business, but before all to make use of every opportunity of remitting money to Germany.

This was just the same resolution as that at which the Fugger also arrived somewhat later. The Welser too failed to carry it out. Anton Fugger, thanks to the favour he had won of the Emperor by his true services and, further, thanks to his own skilful management, succeeded in a short time in drawing out of the business at least considerable sums and bringing them into safety before new demands came on him. The Welser did not succeed in doing this.

The Later Period till the Crisis of 1557. In 1549 we again find Bartholomew Welser's Company taking part in loans which the Court of Brussels had raised on the Antwerp Bourse. Paul Behaim, who then went to Antwerp as the Imhof's agent, was instructed to implore the Welser's agent there as far as possible to prolong the participation which the Imhof had in that loan under the name of the Welser. In this year the Welser sent to Antwerp a new agent, Conrad Bayr, who formerly had been in the service of the Imhof. As soon as he came to Antwerp he informed Paul Behaim 'he had entirely turned round; he associated on the Bourse with no Germans except the Schetze (who were treated as Germans), Lazarus Tucher, Jacob Welser and Oertel (the Fugger agent), in short – very grave and important.' The persons mentioned were the heads or representatives of the the most prominent business houses, to which class the Welser still uncontestedly belonged. A Venetian Ambassador, reporting from Germany in 1548, names the Augsburg Welser with the Paumgartner as the richest German trading company after the Fugger.[1]

Bartholomew Welser participated with 70,000 Netherlands Carolus gulden in the loan which the Emperor took up in Augsburg in April, 1551. But, like the Fugger, did not pay ready money, but only gave promissory notes of his firm, which then were discounted at 11 per cent. per annum in Antwerp by Wolff Haller von Hallerstein.[2]

Soon after Bartholomew Welser retired from business, but he lived on till 1561. His sons Christopher, Leonard, and Hans, with his nephews Matthew and Marx Welser and Bartholomew May, carried on the business under the style of Christopher Welser and Brothers, which later was changed to Christopher Welser and Company. In June, 1552, we find this firm in Antwerp taking part in large loans which were taken up to send a fleet to Spain to fetch American silver. The city of Antwerp took charge of the loan in the interest of the merchants, who were in pressing need of silver. The Welser participated with 81,085 Carolus gulden, for two fairs (a half-year) against interest at 6½ per cent. *pro rata temporis*.[3]

We have now arrived at the third generation which had to conduct the business of the Welser since it had grown to be of European importance. It proved to be just as critical for the wealth of the family as we have seen in the case of the Fugger. In Antwerp, as in Spain and Lyons, the Welser allowed themselves to be drawn on to new risky financial business, and when the frightful financial crisis of 1557 overtook them their shares were:

	Florins
1. Unpaid Claims on the French Court	39,215
2. Netherlands Bonds of the Receivers General	20,523
3. Spanish Loans	122,461
Total	182,199

of which nothing was to be got.[4]

[1] Paul Behaim's (I) *Correspondence in the Germanisches Museum* and *Fontes Rerum Austr.* Abth. II, Bd. XXX, p. 71.

[2] Departemental-Archiv. in Lille (*Chambre des Comptes*, B. 2493).

[3] Brüsseler Staatsarchiv (*Chambre des Comptes*, No. 23470).

[4] Welser-Archives at Schloss Neunhof.

It is less dangerous, but characteristic of the enterprising spirit of the Welser that in the great loan which the town of Nuremberg had to take up through the Fugger in 1554 to carry on the war with the Margrave, they participated with 60,000 fl. (the whole amount was 110,000 fl.). In this their Antwerp agent, Conrad Bayr, played the chief part, just as the Antwerp agent of the Fugger at that time had perhaps more influence on the management of the business than Anton Fugger himself.[1]

After the state bankruptcy of 1557, the Welser received for their claims on the Spanish Crown 5 per cent. Spanish Rentes (juros), on which they must in any case have lost 40–50 per cent. In settling their claims they showed so little business ability that the remarkably efficient Spanish agent of the Fugger, in reporting home about it, critically shook his head.[2]

The claims on the French Court and the Netherlands bonds of the Receivers General remained for the most part unpaid.

Decline and Final Catastrophe. In the period that follows we have not sufficient information about the business activities of the Welser to be able to obtain a just picture of the increasingly rapid decline of the house. There is little point in repeating here the separate pieces of information of which we can get possession.

In the hard times of 1562, when the South German business houses suffered their first shock, the credit of the Welser remained at first unshaken; it was even for a time better than that of the Fugger. In 1566, when the Fugger and most of the other South German houses had enough to do to keep up their credit, the Welser could help the English Crown with a very welcome loan. Gresham writes from Antwerp: 'For these Welsers I could never get in, untill now; which be men of great name and fame throughout all Christendom, and through the death of his old factor (which was a dog and a ranke papist), and his factor, being nowe, is one that I have dealt muche in times past for myne own affairs, when I did occupie merchandise being in Spain xii yeres past, who hathe persuaded his masters to enter.'[3]

Yet with the progress of the confusion in the Netherlands and the general credit crisis the credit of the Welser, too, must have quickly declined in proportion. Their Antwerp property was sold in 1580. About this time Christopher and Hans appear to have completely retired from the business. Leonard had already died in 1557 and Matthew in 1578. Christopher's son of the same name founded the Ulm line of the house, the only one which still exists.

The conduct of the business then passed to Marcus Welser, who took

---

[1] Imhof and Welser Family Archives.

[2] Fugger Archives, 2, 5, 12. Letter from Valladolid of 23rd April, 1558.

[3] Burgon, *Life and Times of Thomas Gresham*, II, 156.

into partnership his nephew Matthew (son of the Matthew who died in 1578), and the business had the firm name of Marx and Matthew Welser and Company. It was by then already so weakened that it got into serious difficulties in 1587, and would like to have dissolved in 1590 if this could have been done in face of the difficulty of getting in the large Spanish and other outstanding debts. So the business was carried on further. Other attempts were made at oversea trading on a grand scale. These are very interesting in themselves, but cannot be followed out further here.[1]

After the death of Marcus Welser in 1596 Matthew carried on the business for another eighteen years in conjunction with his brothers, Marcus and Paul. In 1603 he became Imperial Treasurer (Reichspfennigmeister), but after three years had to give up this position and, as a result of his administration, remained a creditor of the Emperor for considerable sums – a fact which will have hastened the downfall of the house. Paul became Burgomaster of Augsburg. Marcus became a well-known polyhistorian, Chamberlain to the Treasury of the town of Augsburg and Imperial Counsellor. He died in 1614, and on the day after his death his brother was declared bankrupt. 'If Marcus Welser had remained alive,' says an Augsburg chronicler,[2] 'the dreadful, terrible bankruptcy would not yet have been made public, which has caused great harm to the whole town.'

There are many statements of the assets and liabilities of the house at the time of its collapse. They differ among themselves, but allow the hopeless position to be clearly seen.

The Welser themselves stated that their assets amounted to 372,000 fl.

	Florins
Of this amount claims on the Emperor were	181,000
On the Elector of Mainz	39,040
On the States of Brabant (in arrears since 1576)	30,000
Landed property is given as	46,600

But according to an expert valuation not more than 55,600 fl. out of this 372,000 fl. was unquestionably good. All the rest was doubtful or quite worthless. The liabilities, according to one compilation, amounted to 586,575 fl.; to another, 509,992 fl. Among these are:

The Fugger   131,000 fl.

According to another probably more correct statement, 74,666 fl.

[1] Dobel, Pepper Trade of the Fugger and Welser, 1586–91 in *Ztschr. d. hist. Ver. f. Schwaben*, XIII, 125 ff.
[2] Augsburger Stadtbibliothek, *Chronik der Jahre* 1546–1617 (*Augustana* No. 96 fol.).

The rest are sums under 100,000 fl., mostly belonging to relations and friends of the house. In the days just before the bankruptcy the Welser had taken up money which increased the general bitterness against them. At the suit of Hannibal, the chief creditor, both the surviving brothers were imprisoned and finally set in irons. They offered, if they were set free, to make over to their creditors all their assets and deal with them as directed, and also to make over to their creditors all property they might acquire later. The creditors, however, regarded this offer only as an attempt to deceive.

Paul Welser died in 1620, probably still in prison. Marcus spent his last days in complete poverty, so that he had to be supported out of the family trust. He died at the age of eighty in 1633.

Thus the world-wide business of the Welser came to an inglorious end. They had never, like the Fugger, influenced the course of history by their financial transactions. Their chief importance lies in their repeated attempts to secure for themselves, as South German merchants, a share in the trade of the world, even after the great discoveries. These attempts will always remain memorable.

The Hochstetter. In the first decade of the sixteenth century the Hochstetter was the most important business house in Augsburg after the Fugger and Welser. Ambrosius Hochstetter was the soul of the business. He carried it on with his brothers Hans and George and some other partners, and later on took his sons Ambrosius and Joachim into partnership. The firm changed from time to time. The Hochstetter were among the first South Germans to set up a branch in Antwerp. In 1486 they bought a large piece of land in the Kipdorp Strasse, which they built upon and rounded off. This was divided up after the collapse of the house, and a street was made through it which still bears the name 'Hochstetter Strasse.'[1]

In 1489 – so the Augsburger chronicler Clemens Sander relates – Ambrosius Hochstetter visited the Archduke Maximilian, who was held in prison by the burghers of Bruges, provided him with the means of subsistence, and also lent him money which enabled him to appease the men of Bruges. This story is not improbable, for the Hochstetter, even at the time of their fall, enjoyed the quite special favour of the house of Austria, and Clemens Sander was apparently informed of their relations.

The chief business of the firm was concentrated in Antwerp, where as a rule a member of the family lived. In 1505 they participated with 4,000 fl. in the great expedition of the South German and Italian merchants to the East Indies; and since then carried on an extensive trade at second-hand in spices between Lisbon and Antwerp. The Hochstetter were the most hated monopolists of their time. They acquired, it was

[1] Thys, *Histor. de straten en openbare plaatsen van Antwerpen,* Ed. 1893, p. 272.

said, their capital in small sums as deposits, and employed it to control
the market of individual commodities. Clemens Sander informs us:
'Princes, Counts, nobles, burghers, farmers, serving-men and women
have deposited the money they had with Ambrosius Hochstetter, and
he has paid them 5 per cent. Many farmers' boys, who had not more
than 10 gulden, have given it to him in his business, and thought it was
in good hands. For a time he must have paid interest on a million
gulden. But it was common talk that he lied freely. No one has known
that he paid interest on so much. *He was a good Christian and entirely
against the Lutherans.* But in his business he has often oppressed the
poor man, not only in the large articles of the world market, but also in
small wares. Thus he bought up ash wood when the roads were good and
brought it to market when the roads had become bad. He did the same
with wine and corn. He has often bought up the whole stock of one commodity at more than it was worth, so that he could squeeze at his
pleasure the other merchants who could not do this. Then he has raised
the price of goods in all lands and sold them at his pleasure.'

His own partners, too, made heavy complaints against Ambrosius
Hochstetter. In 1517, the year in which the great trading business of
the Welser split up on account of similar disputes, Bartholomew Rem, a
partner in the Hochstetter Company, complained to the town bailiff of
Augsburg and then, as he did not give him justice, to the Emperor and the
Empire that the Hochstetter had fraudulent balance sheets. Rem had
only 900 fl. in the business. He claimed 30,000 fl. as the profit on this
for six years, while the Hochstetters would only pay out 26,000 fl. to
him. If these figures are correct, the firm during the six years had made
an average annual profit of 500–600 per cent., which is quite incredible.
But in any case the suit was a perfect godsend, for the public opinion,
which was embittered against the large companies apart from that, and
particularly for the nobility who powerfully supported the discontented
Rem. Finally there was an arbitration, presided over by Jakob Fugger,
which awarded him part of his claim. Yet he considered his claim just,
wished to take the law into his own hands and pay himself out of the
Hochstetter's goods. For this he was put in prison, where he died. This
is Clemens Sander's account.

The Hochstetter speculated far beyond their resources. As it afterwards appeared, their own capital was by no means very large, which
again tells against the enormous figures for profits. For even if, as was
said, the business had lost a ship and other goods had been stolen in
transit by street robbers, and if in addition the sons and son-in-law of
Ambrosius Hochstetter were gamblers and wasters, yet after such fabulous profits the capital could not possibly have been so much diminished
by these means as it is stated to be in 1528.

In the years 1511–17 the Hochstetter obtained a considerable part of the output of the Tyrolese silver and copper. But the business with which the firm chiefly occupied itself in the last years of its existence was a large speculation in quicksilver. They had bought up some for 200,000 fl. and thought they could control the market, when new rich deposits were discovered in Spain and Hungary. In vain they tried to get hold of these. The speculation failed and the Hochstetter lost a third of the price they had paid.[1]

Yet, in September, 1526, an agent of the English Crown in Antwerp says that the Hochstetter are as rich and capable of performing their undertakings as the Welser, on which the payment of the English subsidies to the hard-pressed King of Hungary was transferred to them.[2] Yet some months later in merchants' letters, written from South Germany to Antwerp, there appear mysterious hints that the credit of the house no longer appears to be secure. It appears now that the Hochstetter plunged into a whirlpool of new business to escape the threatened destruction. In April, 1527, Joachim Hochstetter, one of the sons of old Ambrosius, obtained from the English Government permission for ten years to import goods into and export goods from England. Hitherto no South German merchant had ever done this. As immediately after there was a great rise of prices in England he imported a considerable quantity of wheat. In doing so he came into business relations with Richard Gresham, a highly respected member of this celebrated merchant family.

In March, 1528, Richard Gresham recommended him to Wolsey, as one of the richest merchants in the Netherlands and having much influence both at the Court of Brussels and in Germany. Hochstetter had been very helpful to Gresham and other Englishmen when they had been imprisoned in the Netherlands. But soon he himself needed their help. Just then there were five or six ships loaded with grain for the Hochstetter to be sent to England. Differences arose. The corn was seized in Holland, and the Hochstetter, who had sold it to Richard and John Gresham for delivery against English cloth, could not fulfil their contract. In July, 1528, Joachim Hochstetter himself travelled to England, where he had often been before. There he accused the Greshams, saying that during his last journey to England they had scorned him as bankrupt in the Netherlands and done him harm in every way, so that the credit of his house had been shaken in all Europe and he would be compelled to sell a quantity of quicksilver under value only to obtain ready money to pay his creditors. He demanded compensation from the Greshams

---

[1] Here again our principal authority is Clemens Sander. Cf. Gayangos, *Calendar III*, 2, 337, for the Spanish quicksilver mines.

[2] Brewer, *Calendar IV*, No. 2485, and 2652.

for the damage he had suffered.[1] Soon the house was completely ruined.

In August, 1528, the Hochstetter concluded the following transaction with the Court of Brussels.[2] The Imperial troops in Guelden had then to be paid at once, or they would scatter. The Hochstetter declared themselves ready to lend 200,000 Carolus gulden to the Court of Brussels. They handed over no cash, but 350,700 pounds of quicksilver and 60,760 pounds of cinnabar, which the Government on their side had to sell. The sale was entrusted to Lazarus Tucher, a Nuremberger who had settled in Antwerp, who already had carried on big transactions, especially in pepper, for the Hochstetter, the Welser and Manlich, and at that time was the chief agent for South German speculation in Antwerp.

Lazarus Tucher explained to the Government that he had only been able to get 126,000 Carolus gulden instead of 200,000 for the quicksilver and cinnabar; also these articles were not saleable; and since he had not been able to find buyers for the whole parcel, he, too, could not pay the 126,000 Carolus gulden in ready money, but only in instalments extending over many months. So the Government lost 74,000 Carolus gulden, which appeared very excessive to the chief Receiver General of the Netherlands, but was agreed to by the Emperor in view of his pressing need for money. Through this transaction Lazarus Tucher came into continued business relations with the Government of the Netherlands. That Antwerp agent of the Tucher of Nuremberg, but who had no business relations with Lazarus, reports of him in November, 1528: 'Since the Hochstetter have got into bad repute he does not talk so loud and is almost bankrupt himself, and conceals himself behind them, but each day extricates himself, and alleges that they still owe him 1,400 pounds Flemish for commission alone, on account of which he has now quarrelled with the Hochstetter, who won't pay it him. He is blamed for having brought them in and got them into ill repute. But he is clever enough, and will know how to carry the matter through.' In July, 1529, the same agent further states: 'He now stands very well, but much is said behind his back. Financing the Court had profited him and destroyed others.' This last refers to the Hochstetter who were then in a very bad way: 'They have got a bad repute; no one is here (in Antwerp) on their behalf except two servants; many fear that they will go to smash completely next quarter day.'

In Antwerp Lazarus Tucher was considered responsible for the fall of the house. Joachim Hochstetter himself blames the Greshams for having ruined his credit; and in Lyons there was another scapegoat. By March,

---

[1] Brewer, l.c. No. 3087 (22), 3863, 4018, 4147, 4552, 4662. Gairdner, *Calendar V*, No. 1774, belongs here. The date 1532 is certainly wrong.

[2] Lille, *Chambre des Comptes*, B, 2345, and 2357.

1528, the Tucher's agent sends information from Lyons 'that this quarter day the Hochstetters have almost lost their credit, so that nobody was willing to let them have money on bills.' 'The servant of the Manlich did them a lot of harm by speaking too loud about them, and has let them have nothing on bills, so the brokers were induced to warn one another of them. They had to pay a balance of 26,000 crowns here, but they could only get 6,000 crowns without giving security. Finally they induced Hans Welser and Marcus Lauginger to back their bills. Further, Matthew Rem – this was their agent in Lyons – had assigned to Wolff Harstörfer his body and property, and also all the quicksilver, cinnabar and copper belonging to the Hochstetters in Lyons, together worth 14,000 fl. If this had not been done they must have failed, for they had accepted all bills of exchange. In Augsburg, too, there was a powerful 'run' on the house, which, in fact, in a short time paid out some 400,000 fl. At the last moment they made over a claim of 200,000 Carolus gulden on the Court of the Netherlands to the Fugger and Jean Marcelis in Antwerp; this was disputed later on by the unpaid creditors.

In the spring of 1529 the old Ambrosius Hochstetter implored the Fugger to help him in his need. He proposed that the creditors might choose representatives to whom he should disclose the whole of his assets and liabilities. This actually appears to have been done. But the further proposal, that 100,000 fl. should be collected to maintain the house, was not carried out. The chief creditors preferred to be satisfied at once, which naturally made the catastrophe unavoidable.[1]

At the beginning of June, 1529, Lazarus Tucher took over claims of the Hochstetter in Portugal and Antwerp, as well as a large quantity of pepper that they had to receive from the King of Portugal. Further, in discharge of a debt which the Hochstetter had only contracted in February of the same year, he took over all their extremely valuable real property in Antwerp.[2]

The liabilities of the Hochstetter amounted then to over 400,000 fl., of which more than 150,000 fl. had already been called in. Certainly they themselves estimated their assets at 661,000 fl., but, according to a sober estimate, they were only worth 180,000 fl., and could not with certainty be reckoned at more than 70,000 fl. In these circumstances the collapse could not be kept off. Only after long efforts, in which King Ferdinand through his own commissioner took an active part, was an agreement come to in February, 1530.

The family never recovered from this blow in Augsburg. But one of the two sons of the old Ambrosius, the Joachim whom we have often mentioned founded a new branch of the family in England, which

---

[1] Fugger-Archiv. 2, 2, 1.
[2] *Antwerpener Schöffenbriefe*, 2 and 8 June, 1529.

flourished for a long time. Before the catastrophe Henry VIII had appointed him 'Principal Surveyor and Master of all Mines in England and Ireland.'[1] With his help the King wished to assist the English mining, which was then in its infancy. Joachim Hochstetter, with six other Germans, had offered to work all the mines discoverable in England, and as a start to introduce 1,000 miners from Germany. How far these high-flying intentions were then realized is quite uncertain. But in any case Joachim's son, Daniel, lived in England and was the chief agent of that large South German Company which under Elizabeth, as we shall see, appears, in fact, to have given a strong impetus to English mining. In the seventeenth and eighteenth centuries we come across his descendants in Hamburg as members of the Merchant Adventurers Company who had their chief factory there; this was the same Company which, under Elizabeth, had ruined the active trade of the Hansa towns with England There are certainly remarkable intricacies of industrial developments.

The Herwart. The Herwart of Augsburg are one of the most interesting of the South German families, which makes it all the more regrettable that we know so little of their business. In 1498 and 1499 we find George Herwart and his brothers, one of whom was Christopher, participating together in the often-mentioned copper syndicate with the Fugger, Grossenbrot and the Paumgartner. This implies that their business was then already of importance. In 1511 Clais de Clerc, in Antwerp, is mentioned as agent of Christopher Herwart, and the latter with the Florentine, Filippo Gualterotti, was a creditor of the Netherlands Government, which had obtained loans from the two totalling 29,000 livres Artois (at 40 gr. Flemish) for the war in Guelders, at a rate of interest about 20 per cent. per annum.[2] This is the first purely financial transaction that we hear of from a South German merchant from the Netherlands. Later on, too, we find the Herwart participating earlier and more largely in the financial transactions of the Netherlands than most of the other South German trading houses. In 1522 Marcus and Hans Herwart Brothers acquired a house in Antwerp. Their agent there then and in 1524 was Andreas Smut. In 1522 they paid out 10,000 livres Artois in Antwerp for the account of the Netherlands Government.

In the same year, 1522, we come across in Antwerp another firm of the family – Christopher Herwart and Company – which lent the Court of Brussels 64,000 livres Artois at about 20 per cent. This loan was many times renewed and not paid back until 1525. Lucas von Stetten appears as agent of this firm. For the period from October, 1523, to December, 1525, he claimed the sum of 10,251 arrears of interest, since the loan

---

[1] Brewer, *Calendar IV*, 5110. Also Ehrenberg, *Hamburg und England im Zeitalter der Königin Elisabeth*, p. 5 ff.

[2] Lille, B, 2218.

was mostly paid off in small instalments during this period: that would have been at the rate of 12 per cent. per annum. But the Netherlands financial administration was not willing to pay so much; finally, they agreed on 8,000 livres, which corresponds to interest at about 9 per cent. per annum. In the year 1529–31, too, Hans, Marcus, George, Christopher and Erasmus Herwart participated largely in the big financial transactions of the Netherlands Government. Once Marcus appears in conjunction with George, at another time with Christopher; while Hans and Erasmus are mentioned alone. George Meuting is mentioned as the Antwerp representative of Marcus, Christopher, and Erasmus.[1] In 1542 the city of Antwerp took up a loan from the heirs of Hans Herwart. It is certain that some members of the family had settled in Antwerp.

King Ferdinand, too, repeatedly obtained large loans from the Herwart. Thus in 1528 45,000 fl. (of which 20,000 fl. was in linen and cloth) from Christopher Herwart in conjunction with Pimel; 13,000 fl. in 1541; 95,000 fl. in 1546; 100,000 fl. in 1547; and 199,442 fl. in 1549.[2]

Part of the family remained true to the Catholic faith. In particular, Hans Herwart was one of those whose letters were opened by the Protestants in the Schmalkaldian war; while George, who was Burgomaster in 1546, belonged to the opposite party. It is very doubtful whether this Hans, whose anti-Protestant attitude we have just mentioned, is identical with the ancestors of the same name of the later Augsburg line of the family. For the last-mentioned Hans was a son of the Protestant Burgomaster, George Herwart, and his sons again participated to a quite prominent extent in the loans of the French Crown, with which, since that time, the fortunes of the house were involved in a wonderful manner.

In 1546 we hear for the first time that the Herwart, through the agency of Hans Kleberg, participated in a loan of the French Court raised in Lyons. But we do not know which members of the family they were. In 1553 Hans Paul and Hans Heinrich Herwart (the sons of Hans and grandsons of George) participated with 46,500 crowns in the great loan which the foreign merchants in Lyons had granted to the King of France. Of these two brothers Hans Paul, in 1576, after the failure of the house of the Manlich, became insolvent, and made over to his creditors amongst other things his claims on the French Court. The other brother continued the family in Augsburg, where it, however, never attained to a particularly prosperous condition.[3]

[1] *Antwerpener Schöffenbriefe*, 7th Nov., 1522, 6th Feb. and 15th Nov., 1524; Lille, B, 2301, 2315, 2320, 2351, 2357, 2361. *Antw. Stads-Protocollen ed. Pauwels*, I, 33.

[2] Thorsch, *Materialien z. Einer Geschichte der österr. Staatsschulden*, pp. 28, 34, 39, 40 ff.

[3] For the bankruptcy of Hans Paul Herwart cf. Hans Herwarth von Bittenfeld *in der Ztschr. d. histor. Vereins f. Schwaben*, IX, 147 ff. Cf. v. Stetten, *Gesch. d. augsb. Geschlechter*, and Seiferts, *Genealog. Tabellen*.

On the other hand, two other sons of the Burgomaster George, Ulrich and Jacob Herwart, settled completely in Lyons. Jacob died there young in 1572; while Ulrich, who had married a Welser, left descendants in France. Of these Daniel (born in1574, and married in Lyons in 1599) is worthy of mention, because his sons, Bartholomew and John Heinrich Herwart, played an important part under Louis XIV. This will occupy us later.[1]

Hieronymus Seiler. Sebastian Neidhart and His Heirs. Hieronymus Seiler is the stepson of Bartholomew Welser whom we already know of, who at first had been in the Welser Company and then with Alexius Grimel, a former agent of the same company, and had during 1536–45 carried on financial business in Antwerp in conjunction with the Florentine Gaspar Ducci. This company was international. They lent money to the Court of the Netherlands, but if they could utilize it better at Lyons and with the French Court. they did it in spite of the Emperor's prohibition. Political events only interested them so far as they had an influence on business and business profits. In 1544 the Seiler and their associates lent to the Netherlands Government 100,000 fl. at 16 per cent. per annum on the alum tax. But the business went over into other hands; and since soon after there was more to be made in Lyons than in Antwerp the company remitted from the last-mentioned place to the former large sums which should be lent to the King of France in the name of Seiler, because he was Swiss by birth and so a neutral, and belonged to a race particularly protected in France. The business with Lyons had to be carried on very cautiously and secretly, since the Emperor repeatedly had suspicious letters opened. Sebastian Neidhart also took a large share both in the Netherlands business of 1544 and in the operations conducted in Lyons in the following year. He was a son-in-law of that Christopher Herwart in Antwerp who has often been mentioned. As his heir he is mentioned in 1530 in connection with the imperial finance in the Netherlands. We then find him, too, in the Fugger balance sheet for 1536, in their large Spanish financial transactions, and in the ledgers of the Haug for 1541–7 as having, together with the Haug and the Fugger, a still larger interest in the loans granted by these companies to King Ferdinand. Also, in 1546, he had lent the Fugger the considerable sum of 14,570 pounds Flemish at $2\frac{1}{4}$ per cent. per quarter.

Sebastian Neidhart was an international financier. That especially came out in the war of Schmalkalden. At that time the Protestants

---

[1] What follows is chiefly drawn from the documents in the Augsburg Staats-archives. For the lawsuit against Neidhart, Seiler, Ducci and Partners see Augsburger Chroniclers (e.g. die Chronik 1548–63 im Augsb. Stadtarchiv, Schätze 10a). Also *Sentences du conseil de Brabant* in the Brussels Archives.

suspected him and had his letters opened. But, at the same time, in conjunction with Seiler, Grimel, and some other South Germans, as well as with the Florentine Simon Pecori, he established a trading company in Lyons which was managed by Pecori. In Antwerp this company again came into connection with Gaspar Ducci and carried on a flourishing arbitrage business between Antwerp and Lyons.

In August, 1546, just at the time when his letters were being opened by the Schmalkaldians Neidhart writes from Augsburg to Seiler, who was then in Antwerp, 'I should have no objection to lending half (of the company's capital) to the King of France.' Seiler agreed; Grimel recommended that the sum should be lent to the merchants in Lyons, which was safer. But he was outvoted, and Pecori did, in fact, on behalf of the firm, participate in October, 1546, in a loan to the French Court with 20,000 kronen at 4 per cent. per quarter = 16 per cent. per annum. The King then used this money to support the German Protestants.

In the following years this traffic was continued and gradually became of larger and larger dimensions. The company remitted and drew bills of exchange continually between Antwerp and Lyons. When money was abundant they borrowed and sent it where it got the highest rate. Soon individual partners, especially the two Florentines, tried to produce an artificial tightness of money in Lyons. Neidhart advised against this at first because it was dangerous and fundamentally 'an ungodly business, by which wealthy people must be undone, so that I think when this business is finished I will never go into a similar one, because it is *cargo conscientiæ*.' But he also wanted to get as high a rate of interest as possible, and finally himself gave advice how to make money still tighter. He feared, however, that as soon as Bartholomew Welser and his stepson, Hans Paul Herwart, got wind of the affair they would operate powerfully against it. In 1549–50 the company had lent to the King of France more than 100,000 kronen, the greater part of which belonged to Sebastian Neidhart.

The Court of Brussels had long suspected the dealings of the company and had, it appears, received a direct denunciation from Antwerp, where Ducci was generally hated, and at the beginning of the year 1550 had seized a number of letters of the company with remittances for Lyons. Since their contents were suspicious Seiler, Grimel and Ducci were imprisoned; after some months, however, they were set at liberty on heavy bail. The accusation was of usury and monopoly. In the reasons alleged it was stated that the accused had attempted to force the Antwerp Bourse so that the monetary position should be regulated as they wished. The Procurator-General demanded: against Seiler and Grimel, confiscation of all their goods and perpetual banishment from the Emperor's territories; for Ducci, the death penalty, and, if necessary, at first examination under torture. But, finally, the case dragged on till the end of 1551 – Grimel and Seiler were condemned to pay a fine of 60,000, and Ducci one of 20,000 Carolus gulden, and to pay the costs. So the punishment of the two Germans was materially heavier than that of the Florentine, who possessed powerful patrons in Brussels.[1]

Since this nothing more is told of Hieronymus Seiler. On the other hand, Michel Seiler, a relative, perhaps his son, represented the Welser in Lyons from 1553 to 1580, and personally participated in the loans of the French Court. Grimel tried to rehabilitate himself by serving the Netherlands Government as money broker; yet he appears to have had little luck with it and vanishes completely after 1552. Ducci's part, too, was played out with the long case.

Neidhart, who, it appears, was also imprisoned for a short time, must have died soon after. He left behind him four sons – Carl, Christopher, Paul, and Matthew. In 1553 Christopher Neidhart was the person who, next to the Florentine house Salviati, took the largest share in the great loan which the King of France had raised in Lyons. On the list his amount is 124,450 crowns, and, in addition, Gabriel Neidhart is on the list for 20,900 crowns.

Finally, we possess a very interesting ledger of Neidhart's heirs for the period 1559–70, from which it appears that the heirs carried on the banking business on a large scale, but finally were ruined by it. In 1564 the claim on the French Court had risen to 627,780 livres. It is true that up to 1567 20,000 livres were paid off. But the repayments ceased, and in 1570 the claim amounted to 496,583 livres, or 269,882 Rhenish florins. After that no more was ever got in. The firm then had a claim of 120,132 fl. against the King of Portugal, which likewise remained unpaid. This claim, too, was a very old standing one. Further, Neidhart's heirs participated in the advances which the German merchants in Lyons granted to the Cardinal of Lorraine and the Duke of Guise, the arch enemies of the Huguenots, in order, through their mediation, to obtain reimbursement of their claims on the French Court. But this did not happen, and the Guise gave just as little heed to repaying their own debt. Money was also lent to the Infante Don Carlos of Spain on inadequate security of jewels; the money should have been repaid in 1567, but was not, and since the Prince came to a tragic end the next year the debt was still outstanding in 1570. It was the same with a debt of the Duke of Florence, which dated from the year 1553. In short, the total assets of Neidhart's heirs, which at the end of 1570 were computed at 494,335 fl., consisted almost entirely of barren outstanding debts.[2]

---

[1] According to his actual documents. The Augsburg Chronicler gives a different account.

[2] The ledger is in the Augsburg Archives.

The Neidhart were closely connected with the Manlich by business and family ties. Carl Neidhart was the son-in-law and partner of the older Melchior Manlich. When the Manlich failed in 1574 it was all over with the Neidharts, and the family in Augsburg became extinct with Carl's sons in 1625.

The Manlich. The Manlich of Augsburg are mentioned as important traders in goods in the business correspondence of the Tucher for 1526–8, and in truth they at that time were people of some consequence both in Lyons and Antwerp. Until the fall of their house they remained whole-sale merchants proper, and just before the catastrophe they carried on from Marseilles – where they had set up a factory – an unusually important direct trade by sea to the Levant with their own ships. This had been done by no other German trading house. But like almost all the other merchants of Augsburg they could not resist the temptation of taking part in the business of lending to princes, which brought them down.

In 1543 Mathias Manlich, in Antwerp, in conjunction with the Paumgartner and the Haug, lent King Ferdinand 60,000 fl., and the Netherland Government in bonds of the Receivers General a sum which is not specified. During the years 1543–62, Melchior Manlich had a share in the Haugs.[1]

In 1553 Mathias Manlich lent the Fugger 14,000 £ fl.; two years afterwards he took a lease of the copper output from Neusohl in Hungary and granted King Ferdinand a new loan of 97,750 fl. In 1559 we also find Manlich financing Ferdinand. But their ruin was not due to this, but rather to their share in the French financial transactions. How this participation came about and how large it was cannot, unfortunately, be ascertained from the material available. But how large it must have been appears from the fact that in 1564–7 Oswald Seng, the Manlich agent in Lyons, managed the syndicate which represented the interests of the South German creditors of the French Court. And in November, 1573, when the house was on the verge of bankruptcy, Adam Hartlieb, who then for a short time had been in the service of Melchior Manlich the elder, rode to Lyons with Carl Neidhart, Melchior's son-in-law and partner, to rescue there what was to be rescued. Shortly before the Manlich, in Marseilles at any rate, enjoyed the best credit. But at the end of 1573, or the beginning of the next year, the catastrophe arrived. That in the Netherlands the Gueux had taken away 50,000 fl. worth of pepper helped to accelerate the crash. The liabilities of the house are

---

[1] Cf. for the following: Oberleitner, *Archiv, für Kunde österr, Gesch.-Quellen*, XXII, p. 101; Thorsch, l.c. p. 44; v. Stetten, *Geschichte von Augsburg*, I, 602, 608; Hans Ulrich Kraffts, *Denkwürdigkeiten, bearb. v. A. Cohn;* Hans Hartliebs Tagebuch (MS. of the Hartlieb family).

L

given on the one hand as 70,000 fl., but, on the other, and more probably as 307,554 fl. Their Levant agent, Hans Ulrich Krafft, confident
of the solvency of the house, guaranteed their extensive obligations,
with the result that he spent three years in a debtor's prison, of which
he composed a detailed and very attractive account.

The Adler. The Adler of Augsburg appear early in the history of
South German financial business, but they also vanish again betimes.
In 1507 the Venetian Quirini numbers them with the Fugger, Welser,
Hochstetter, Gossembrot, Paumgartner and Herwart as the seven great
trading companies of Augsburg, which at that time lent the Emperor
Maximilian 150,000 fl. on the security of landed property.[1] In 1522 we
come across Philipp Adler in Antwerp, where he conducted for the
Netherlands Government an exchange business with South Germany,
which, it must be admitted, was not a very important one. In 1530 the
Emperor borrowed 18,000 kronen from him in Antwerp, in respect of
which 20,160 kronen was repaid in Antwerp after half a year, which
means that this transaction cost the Emperor 24 per cent. for exchange
difference and interest. The sum was got in in Antwerp through Jacob
Welser. After this we do not hear anything about the Adler.

The Rem. The Rem in Augsburg had no conspicuous or independent
significance in the dealings in capital of the sixteenth century. As agents
of the Welser and Hochstetter, they served these great trading houses
truly in their business, but then quarrelled with them and left them.
Thereupon, in 1518, the brothers Lucas and Andreas Rem established a
business of their own which then often participated in the great financial
transactions of the Fugger. Also, in 1522, they paid to Franz Sickingen
for the Emperor an advance which after six months they received back
from the Netherlands Government. This would scarcely have been a
sufficient reason for a particular mention of them here, but the Rem
family were fond of writing. A cousin of the two brothers just mentioned composed a chronicle of Augsburg, and Lucas Rem kept a diary
which is justly used as an important source for the history of civilization. Here all that is important is the statement – to which we are indebted to Lucas Rem – of the profits of his company. This shows rates
of profit varying from $2\frac{1}{4}$ per cent. to $14\frac{1}{2}$ per cent., or an average profit
of $8\frac{1}{2}$ per cent. per annum over $21\frac{1}{2}$ years, which is by no means a high
rate of interest for a trading house of that time. When Lucas Rem died
in 1541 his share in the capital amounted to 57,000 fl. His son of the
same name succeeded in almost six months (reckoned from the time
Rem joined the Welser Company) in losing the money earned by his
father in twenty years of hard work.

[1] Albéri, *Relaz. d. Ambasc. Venet.*, XIV, 28; also Lille, *Chambre des Comptes*, B,
2301, 2363; Lanz, *Correspondenz*, I, 405.

Lucas Rem the younger was one of those who as early as 1546 remitted money from Antwerp to Lyons in order to lend it to the French Court there. He then participated more and more in this finance business of Lyons. Thus in 1558 he put in 63,000 livres all at once. That was fatal to him. He was one of the numerous Augsburg merchants who had to suspend payment in 1562, and he died soon after.

The Haug and their Relatives. This Augsburg house, considerable in itself, is important for us owing to the circumstance that we possess the chief books of the company for a period of more than thirty years, and from them can follow out very well the business activity of the firm, and in particular how they got more and more involved in big financial business and how the trade in goods fell into the background.[1]

On 1st September, 1531, Anton Haug the elder, Hans Langnauer and Ulrich Link, with some partners of secondary importance, signed articles of partnership for six years, and also took into partnership a number of their employés. The total capital amounted to 90,815 fl.; the number of partners was seventeen. The firm had agents in Antwerp, Venice, Cologne, Nuremberg, Ulm, and Schwatz in Tyrol. They obtained spices, silks and cotton from Venice, copper and silver from Schwatz, spices and English cloth from Antwerp. In Ulm and Augsburg they wove wool into fustian and sent it for the main part to Antwerp. But they carried on pure loan business as well with King Ferdinand, in which they partly operated alone, partly in conjunction with the Fugger and the Herwart.

When two years had elapsed the company with 90,815 fl. had gained no less than 85,461 fl. – that is, 47 per cent. per annum. Because of this heavy profit 20,000 fl. were put to reserve, and after withdrawing 10,000 fl. a capital of 144,000 fl. was carried forward.

On the 25th August, 1533, the assets in round figures were 410,000 fl. Of these 92,000 fl. represented the financial transactions with the Austrian Court. The rest consisted in the main of goods, documents representing goods, and cash. In Augsburg the assets amounted to 111,000 fl.; in Antwerp, 86,000 fl.; in Cologne, where the silks were mainly sold, 25,000 fl.; in Venice, 16,000 fl.; and 60,000 fl. were employed in the Schwatz business, and so on.

The liabilities consisted of 235,000 fl. in eighty-nine items, of which the most considerable belonged to the wives and children of some relations and friends.

We have no information for the years 1533–5. But these years must have been extraordinarily favourable for the business, for the capital with which in 1535 they entered into a new partnership amounted to 340,000 fl., although meanwhile many partners had retired. Allowing

---

[1] The ledgers are in the Augsburg Archives.

for the shares of these, the capital must have trebled from 1533 to 1535. It is given as 90,815 fl. in 1531 and 340,010 fl. in 1535. But after this brilliant development a period of stagnation followed. In the eight years 1535–43 there was only a total profit of 82,744 fl., which makes about 3 per cent. per annum. During this period the business in goods was continued, a new factory established in Lyons; on the other hand, one at Cologne was given up.

In the balance sheet for 1543 the increase (probably a recent one) of the Antwerp financial business becomes prominent. In this way almost 30,000 £ fl. (= 140,000 fl.) were invested; but, on the other hand, the sums of this kind outstanding in Germany only totalled 55,000 fl., and thus were considerably lower than in 1533. At that time the firm had had no financial transactions in Lyons.

Meantime, Hans Langnauer had died; his capital for the most part remained in the business as a deposit-carrying interest. Melchior Man-lich and a younger Hans Langnauer entered the firm, but both brought in little, so that the capital of the company was diminished by about 90,000 fl. and was carried on as only 295,067 fl. for the new partnership.

The next two years were again very favourable. With 295,067 fl. there was a profit of 94,928 fl., that is 16 per cent. per annum. 'But after this time the course of all business was anxious and heavy, and one must be apprehensive of waste' – it was shortly before the war of Schmal-kalden – so 6,023 fl. were put to reserve.

The claims from the Antwerp financial business amounted in 1545 to 40,000 £ fl. (= 180,000 fl.), so they were about £10,000 higher than in 1543; on the other hand, the German financial engagements had de-clined to 46,000 fl.

The two years 1545–7 brought in good profits; on 356,000 fl. there was a profit of 98,000 fl., or about 14 per cent. per annum. The next two years were still better; in them on 365,000 fl. a profit of 124,000 fl. was attained, i.e. 17 per cent. per annum.

The German 'Court contracts' fell off in this period, while the claims arising out of Antwerp financial transactions increased up to 1549 to 53,600 £ fl. (= 230,000 fl.). But, as well as this, in 1547 there was in addition a claim of 36,000 crowns on the French Court, which up to 1549 increased by compound interest to 40,000 crowns or 60,000 fl.

In 1549 the total capital was diminished by 200,000 fl., and went back to about the position of the year 1535. The firm's name then was 'Ulrich Link, Anton Haug and Relatives.' But this great reduction of capital was not due to any mistrust for the future of the business, but appar-ently arose from the desire of the partners not to let too much capital share in the profits, especially the shares of the deceased partners in the capital. These were at once received again as deposits at interest. Since this time the capital of the company diminished more and more, while the deposits of the former partners increase more and more.

In particular, after the balance sheet of 1553, Ulrich Link and Anton and Lienhard Haug went out of the firm. After that their capital carried interest at $7\frac{1}{2}$ per cent. In 1555 Hans Pimel retired, so that only eight partners remained. This number sank to four in 1560, which presumably was due to the increasing distaste for business of the more cautious elements. The partners who remained plunged into more enormous and world-wide undertakings, which were directly forced on them by the enormous quantity of deposits at high interest at their disposal. The profits were very good during this period. But if we reflect how small the capital was compared to the turnover, the average profit does not appear to be remarkably high.

The average yearly profit was:

	Per cent.
1549–51	12
1551–53	$11\frac{1}{2}$
1553–55	11
1555–57	$10\frac{1}{2}$
1557–60	40
1560–61	$10\frac{1}{2}$

The real solid trading went more and more into the background. The chief activities of the firm were directed to money transactions and particularly in carrying on the copper mining works at Schwatz and the sale of the copper produced.

According to the balance sheet of 31st December, 1561, there was:

	Florins
Locked up in mines, houses and barren debts	200,000
Lent to the Emperor	212,000
Stocks in hand, chiefly copper	157,000
Divers debtors	219,000
Cash in hand	122,000
	fl. 910,000

Against this their own capital (including the profits for 1560–61) was	268,000
Borrowed capital	642,000
	fl. 910,000

A very critical position for a business to be in. Now, at the end of 1562, Melchior Manlich retired from the business, leaving only three partners – David Haug, Hans Langnauer, and Melchior Link. The capital will also have become smaller, but unfortunately this cannot be established since no more balance sheets are available. On the other hand, we know that for the claim on the Emperor they had been given a charge on the produce of the Hungarian copper, and this gave the company almost the same control of the copper trade as that which the Fugger possessed earlier. It appears they were led on to establish an undertaking far beyond their strength for the improvement of English mining.

At that time English mining was still a very small affair, and in the main limited to working very ancient (prehistoric) tin and lead mines. The Germans, on the other hand, were the foremost miners of the world, and had developed the technique of mining to a high state. South German capital had especially, since the middle of the fifteenth century, co-operated prominently in this. So the English Kings since Henry VIII tried to interest German capitalists and miners in the mineral riches of their land. Like so many other industrial and political measures of the Tudors they first came to maturity under Queen Elizabeth. In 1564 a large company for prospecting for and winning minerals in England was promoted by the firm of David Haug, Hans Laugnauer and Relatives. In this the highest English statesmen and officials took shares. Dealings between the English Government and the Augsburg merchants were mainly in the hands of some new partners in the firm. Of the twenty-four shares the Haug firm took eleven; Elizabeth's minister, Cecil, two; Lord Leicester, two; and so on. At first they operated copper mines at Keswick and lead mines at Colbeck. The undertaking was far beyond the powers of the Haug and does not appear to have made a profit so long as they had an interest in it. We can here only state the result. In 1574 the Haug had to suspend payment.

Jakob Herbrot. Jakob Herbrot earned a position for himself in the Augsburg trading world. He was a well-known opponent of the Emperor Charles, and of the great Catholic patrician houses of Augsburg. He was the only one who used his resources directly in the service of his political and religious convictions.[1]

In 1520 he began business with 1,200 fl., and in the course of the following twenty-five years acquired so much property that in the war of Schmalkalden he could assist the Evangelicals with considerable sums of money. As head of the merchants guild, he was the recognized leader of the party of decidedly Evangelical views, who had their strongest support in the guilds. He became Burgomaster and drew on himself the hatred of the Catholic patricians, who had been robbed of their influence by him, and to such an extent that this later accelerated

[1] Heckerinin *Der Ztschr. d. histor. Vereins für Schwaben*, Bd. I.

his ruin. However, the real cause was the same as in the case of so many other Augsburg merchants – excessive credit. Jakob Herbrot had made considerable loans to the Emperor Ferdinand and the King of Poland, and to do this had himself borrowed largely. When, then, in 1562 there arose a general mistrust of the Augsburg trading community, there was also a 'run' of the Herbrot's creditors. The Emperor Ferdinand instructed Melchior Ilsung, the Governor of Swabia, to borrow 30,000 fl. in Augsburg to help the man who had got into difficulties chiefly through the advances he had granted to the Emperor. But as soon as it leaked out that the money was meant for the hated Democrats 'the counting houses and the Perlach' (the Bourse) would not give anything. Jakob Herbrot had to suspend payment and died in a debtors' prison in 1564.

The Tucher. In contrast to the condition of business at Augsburg, that at Nuremberg on the whole kept clear of financial business proper until the time of the war of Schmalkalden, although, as we have already seen, individual Nurembergers entered into the financial service of the Emperor Maximilian and some others, as we shall see later, attained to great importance and riches as financiers in Lyons and Antwerp. They soon divested themselves of their Nuremberg origin and became French and Netherlanders. Of the large traders properly settled in Nuremberg, it was only the branch there of the Welser which in early times carried on large financial transactions, especially in conjunction with the Fugger. They, however, until the war of Schmalkalden, kept within the limits of the usual prudence of merchants of Nuremberg. It was only when just before the war that the French Court, through Hans Kleberg, whom we shall get to know later, knew how to make use of the South German merchants who frequented Lyons, that the Nurembergers, too, began to turn from trade to finance. They were mostly Protestants, or at any rate not unconditionally attached to the Emperor. Only one of the great Nuremberg trading houses – the Tucher – kept off from the loans to the great Powers which gave a high rate of interest, but were very risky.

The two generations of the Tucher who come under our consideration here exhibit the best types of sturdy and solid German wholesale traders, whom we know of in the sixteenth century. Anton Tucher (1457–1524), the chief Burgomaster ('Losunger') of Nuremberg since 1505, a remarkable man, who was highly regarded by the Elector Frederick the Wise of Saxony ('he praised him above all the burghers of the Empire'), carried on in conjunction with his cousins, Hans and Martin, a considerable trade, chiefly with Lyons. His son, Lienhard Tucher (1524–68), with his cousin Lorenz, continued and considerably extended the business, especially by establishing a factory at Antwerp, so that the firm had establishments at the two financial centres of the world at that time. By means of the factories they carried on a very considerable trade in goods. But when in 1545 Hans Kleberg, like most of the other South German merchants who frequented Lyons, wished to persuade the Tucher to participate in that loan to the French Court, Lienhard Tucher wrote to his agent at Lyons that he and his cousin Lorenz had resolved not to involve themselves in such business with great 'Heads.' Lienhard Tucher again and again enjoined this principle on his junior partners and agents, and remained proof against all attempts. Thus he brought it about that his business suffered only a comparatively small loss through the great credit crisis of the years 1557–62. Lienhard Tucher, too, like his father, was for many years first 'Losunger' of Nuremberg, and in addition a conspicuously sturdy merchant of wide outlook, whose wise business principles deserve to serve as a model. In this soundness he affords a very characteristic contrast to Lazarus Tucher, a distant collateral relative, whose bold and fortunate financial dealings we shall get to know of later. Lazarus Tucher had no close business relations with the Nuremberg firm.[1]

The Imhof. The Imhof, too, remained longer than the other big trading houses of Nuremberg in the ways of solid trade, but they had no fundamental objection to financial business. During the period we are considering here, the large trade of the Imhof with Italy, France, and the Netherlands was mainly conducted by Endres Imhof under the firm name of Endres Imhof and Brothers. Endres Imhof played a conspicuous part in the public life of Nuremberg. He had a seat on the Council for fifty-six years, and in 1565 succeeded Lienhard Tucher in the office of first 'Losunger.' As a business man he exhibits a combination of the qualities of Lienhard Tucher and the majority of the other South German merchants. When in 1545, as a result of Hans Kleberg's power of persuasion, these began for the first time on a large scale to pour their money in the bottomless cask of French finance, the Imhof as well as the Tucher held back, so that Kleberg noted both houses as 'too extremely careful.' But later on the Imhof ceased to draw back, and participated to an increasing extent in the profitable financial businesses of the Bourses of Antwerp and Lyons. Endres Imhof, however, was at least sufficiently prudent after each account to withdraw his share of the profits from the incalculable risk of this business. In 1544 his share in the capital of the company was 15,000 fl.; in 1548 it sank to 12,000 fl.; and after 1550 remained at 14,000 fl.; while the very high profits were partly entirely taken out of the business and partly left in it as deposits at 5 per cent.

[1] Cf. Ehrenberg, *Hans Kleberg, 'der gute Deutsche'* (*Mitth. d. Vereins f. Gesch. d. Stadt Nürnberg*). Nuremberg, 1893, p. 24 ff.

The profits, from 1544 to 1560 (excluding the years 1554–6), average 18⅚ per cent. per annum.

For the years 1560–4 we do not know the profits, but we know them again for the years 1564–70, in which they were 77 per cent. in all, or 12⅚ per cent. per annum. In 1570 Endres Imhof retired from the partnership and left his capital of 42,100 fl. in the business only as a deposit bearing 5 per cent. In his lifetime he repeatedly made over large sums of capital to his sons.

Concerning the participation of the Imhof in the big international finance we possess some very interesting instructions, given in 1549 by the company to Paul Behaim, their Antwerp agent. It enables us to see how the Imhof at that time invested their funds. We will here give the chief contents:

The firm of Endres Imhof and Brothers, in conjunction with an associated firm of the family, Sebastian and Hieronymus Imhof (the last of whom had settled in Augsburg, where he founded a branch of the family which still flourishes), under the name of Bartholomew Welsers Company, lent to the Court of Brussels £6,615 1s. 6 gr., of which £4,410 1s. belonged to Endres Imhof and Brothers. This share in the 'Court paper' they now wished to have for themselves, and to dissolve the association with their relatives. They wished to 'have lying at the Court' the sum which was just falling due. But since the agent was not acquainted with the financial agent of the Court of Brussels, he was directed to request the Antwerp agent of the Welser to extend the repayment of the money of the Imhof, as far as possible. 'As to price and conditions, we should be content with the terms the Welser make for themselves, but we hope that the Court will not give less than 5 per cent. (for 2 fairs = half a year), since more could easily be got if, e.g., the Emperor or the King of England wished to get ready money from the Bourse. But if you cannot get the Welser to promise that they will prolong our money, then get into touch with Kaltinhofer and Poschinger (two South German financiers who had settled in Antwerp and whom we shall get to know) and notify them that if they wish to deal with the Court this quarter day, you are willing to employ 25,000–30,000 Carolus gulden on behalf of your principals. If you do business with them you must satisfy yourselves beforehand that the Welser will pay us; for if they do not, and you had promised a sum to the others, then we should have too much in one place. If you lend out the money through Kaltenhofer or Poschinger then we should like to have the promissory notes in our own hands; but if that is not possible we should be content to get from them a sufficient bond.'

The firm also possessed bonds of the town of Antwerp for £7,875, but only £2,100 belonged to them, while the rest was the share of the other

Imhofs and the above-mentioned Poschinger. These had then fallen
due: 'Our £2,100 and £1,900 more we would willingly once more prolong
at the highest possible rate of interest for another six months on such
bonds under the great seal of the town of Antwerp and under the conditions of which you have a copy. If much ready money is withdrawn
from the Bourse, or if sundry people should come together to make
money tight (Strettezza), money will be dearer this quarter and the
town of Antwerp will give more than 5 per cent. (for half a year); otherwise we should be content with that. And no matter whether money is
tight or plentiful the town of Antwerp we think will in any case pay
as much as good firms in the Bourse (dita di bursha). We should then
like them as much, and prefer them to dita di bursha. But if they pay
¼ or ½ per cent. less than these and you can do business with the firm
which Bair (the former agent of the Imhof in Antwerp) have told you
of, then take the money away from the city and give it them.'

We see from this how zealously the Imhof thought of the most profitable way to employ their capital, but that, all the same, they did not
forget caution. This was, in any case, the chief service of Endres Imhof
himself. For, as we see from their correspondence, the junior partner
pressed vigorously for a greater participation in the French loans.
Endres only slowly gave way to this pressure.

In 1552 the firm first embarked in the business of bonds of the Netherlands Receivers General; however, the total was not very considerable.
The next step was that in 1553 some individual members of the family
took a conspicuous part in the French Crown loans: Sebastian Imhof
with 14,100 livres; Lienhard Imhof in Augsburg with 5,000 livres; and
Michael Imhof with 12,000 livres. But the chief firm seems at that time
still to have preserved its customary restraint towards these French
loans. It is true that just at this time it had already taken in hand a
financial transaction on a large scale somewhat closer.

In the years 1553–4, the town of Nuremberg needed uncommonly
large sums of money for the war against their mortal enemy, the Margrave Albrecht (Alcibiades) of Brandenburg Kulmbach. When this war
was over the town began to extend and enlarge their fortifications, and
in particular to build the colossal towers in the wall which to-day yet
excite our astonishment. This likewise cost a great deal of money for
years. Particularly in the war with the Margrave very large sums had
to be made liquid in great haste. The old way of selling annuities on the
town was insufficient; the town had to follow the example of the great
princes and take up floating loans from merchants.

At first Endres Imhof formed a consortium to which, as well as his
firm, Sebastian and Hieronymus Imhof and the Augsburg Welser belonged. This consortium advanced to the town of Nuremberg the large

sums it was in need of at 12 per cent., and borrowed again at a lower rate of interest at Frankfurt am Main, Antwerp, and other places.

At first it was a matter of about 110,000 fl., of which the Welser brought in 60,00 fl. and the Imhof 50,000 fl. But soon further sums were added. In the autumn of 1553, owing to the large withdrawals of money by the consortium, money was tight in Antwerp. The importance of the Antwerp Bourse for dealing in capital cannot perhaps be shown more clearly than by the fact that Paul Behaim, since he no longer acted for the Imhof, begged their Antwerp agent to let him participate in the loans of his native town in Antwerp. The Imhof, too, sent their agent, Paul Behaim, to Frankfurt am Main; but he for the most part did himself borrow the money, but employed the services of the brokers, amongst whom a conspicuous part was played by 'the modest Jew Joseph, at the sign of the Golden Swan.' This is the only time that a Jew is mentioned in the large financial transactions of the sixteenth century, and it is certainly characteristic that it happened at Frankfurt am Main, which was then a comparatively insignificant place for international dealings in capital. Just because of this the Jews there from old times had kept a part of their importance in finance, while they were never mentioned in the great bourses of the world. Joseph the Jew procured the money for the Imhof chiefly in large sums. For example, the most considerable of these at the Easter Fair of 1554 was one of 16,400 fl., lent by an abbot. For then everywhere – and this again shows how ancient this traffic is – the clergy took part frequently. The rate of interest at that time was 5–6 per cent. The Jew got 1 per cent. commission and a yearly stipend as well. When he wanted to get out of it some other little incidental profits, he was rapped on the knuckles; nevertheless, Paul Behaim had orders to deal with him mildly, since he was still needed. The turnover of the Imhof in this way amounted to 100,000 fl. at many Frankfurt Fairs, and their turnover at Antwerp must at least have been as large. So far they only served the financial needs of the town of Nuremberg. The town at that time was trying to get money at any price, and the Imhof, who immediately had become the bankers of the Council, instructed their agents to take up all that was offered to them. This, however, changed when the war against the Margrave was over.

Heretofore the town of Nuremberg was in the habit of paying only 5 per cent. on their loans, which they effected by the usual way of selling annuities. For this reason they found it very painful that they had to pay 12 per cent. on the loans raised from the Imhof, and as soon as the most pressing need for money was over they tried to reduce this high rate of interest. Certainly the town had to leave outstanding at 12 per cent. that great loan of 110,000 fl. in which the Welser had participated with 60,000 fl., since with money so tight as it was then it was not so easy to find anybody who had such a large sum to lend them at a cheaper rate. But for the new sums lent to them they were not willing, after 1555, to give more than 10 per cent. Only in the case of specially large sums they declared themselves ready to pay 10–12 per cent. As the need diminished, the rate of interest had to be reduced. Thus, in 1558 it fell to 8 per cent.; in 1561 to 6 per cent.; and in 1565 to 5 per cent.: at a time when the mightiest princes could scarcely get money on any terms.

Through these great affairs which Endres Imhof undertook for his native town, and apparently without any considerable profit for himself, he must have completely lost his former repugnance to pure finance. For after this time his firm took part in this, both in Lyons and Antwerp, to the largest extent: notes of the Court of Brussels, bonds of the Receivers General, bonds of the town of Antwerp, and particularly of the French Crown, were with large speculations in pepper, saffron, and alum, the subjects on which the business correspondence of the Imhof, in the years 1555–62, chiefly turns. But the credit of the house remained excellent; in these years it was even better than that of the Fugger. If in 1553 Anton Fugger had obtained a small loan from Endres Imhof, Hans Jakob Fugger in 1556 got one from him of 10,000 fl., which, till 1561, was repaid by instalments. Even in the frightful crisis which in 1562 shattered the industrial position of the South German towns, the Imhof remained to all appearance unharmed. But they suffered frightful losses, and their inward strength was broken. In the French loans alone they lost 50,000 livres (the associated firm of Sebastian and Hieronymus Imhof 30,000 more); and they remained with 32,000 Carolus gulden unpaid on Netherlands Receivers General bonds.

Endres Imhof died in 1579 at the age of eighty-seven, after he had completely retired from business for nine years.

Other South German Trading Houses. There are many other South German business houses of which all we know is that they took a more or less prominent part in large financial transactions; yet our knowledge of the part they took is so incomplete, and it was in the main, too, only sporadic, that we here only give a summary account of them.

In 1522 the brothers Pimel paid for the Emperor to Franz von Sickingen a sum which was repaid in Antwerp with 19,200 Carolus gulden. They made advances to King Ferdinand of 56,000 fl. in 1527, of 45,000 fl. in conjunction with the Herwart in 1528, and of 18,000 fl. again by themselves in 1530. In the following year in Antwerp the Netherlands Government paid them 15,000 crowns on their bills, against which they on their side had made payments in Germany. Then in 1541 we come across them with the Fugger supplying money to the Court of Vienna;

and in 1560 Sir Thomas Gresham in Antwerp took up from them a loan for the English Crown. They are not mentioned after this.[1]

The Rehlinger of Augsburg were one of the trading houses who were definitely on the Protestant side in the war of Schmalkalden. Since they had a factory in Lyons the league wished to make use of them as intermediaries to procure the French subsidies there. In 1555 Christopher Rehlinger sent King Ferdinand 74,400 fl.; in the same year Hieronymus Rehlinger the elder lent the English Crown a sum that is not stated, and also sold them saltpetre, £1,560; he, too, participated with 5,000 livres in their Antwerp loan. Then their names vanished from the annals of finance.[2]

The Kraffter of Augsburg are only mentioned once, in 1551, in connection with the financial affairs of the Court of Vienna. In 1562 and 1563 they suspended payment, and their liabilities are given as 19,600 fl.[3]

The Roth of Ulm were regarded in the war of Schmalkalden as undoubted adherents of the Evangelical Party. Yet they are not mentioned in connection with the French financial transactions, but they were in 1541, 1544 and 1549, in connection with those of King Ferdinand.[4]

As early as 1546 the Zangmeister in Augsburg participated keenly in the French loans. In 1553 they appear as next to the Neidharts as the largest subscribers with 99,400 crowns. In 1562 they had to announce to their creditors at the Town Hall of Augsburg, 'that they without sufficient thought embarked in multifarious and highly important transactions in bills of exchange, but they had chiefly wrought their own destruction by locking up their money behind the Crown of France, since a large sum of money for some years had been outstanding there without producing interest, which they themselves had had to borrow at a high rate of interest.'

They offered to make over to their creditors their business with all the stock and book debts, and in case of necessity to pay for their evil deeds with their 'body and life.' This is the last we hear of this trading company.[5]

For a time the Ligsalz and the Fleckhamer – two Munich firms who, nevertheless, had their main business in Augsburg and Antwerp – must have played a conspicuous part. In 1526 Karl Ligsalz was mentioned in

---

[1] Lille, *Chambre des Comptes*, B. 2301, 2363. Thorsch, pp. 26, 28, 32, 34. Kervyn de Lettenhove, *Rélat. polit.* II, 430.

[2] *Augsburger Stadtarchiv, Litteralien,* 1546; Thorsch, p. 42. Turnbull, *Calendar Queen Mary.* No. 751. Kervyn, I, 174, II, 240.

[3] Thorsch, p. 41. There are some documents as to his bankruptcy in the Augsburg Archives.

[4] Thorsch, pp. 34, 40, 42.

[5] Augsburger Stadtarchiv. and Germanisches Museum.

Antwerp; but not till 1531 does Sebastian Ligsalz appear as taking a part, and not on a very considerable scale, in the business of bills of exchange between the Court of Brussels and Germany. In 1546 Ludwig Ligsalz, in Antwerp, had lent the Fugger 6,544 £ fl. at interest. In 1549 Endres Ligsalz, in conjunction with the Haug, participated in the loans of the city of Antwerp; in 1554 and 1558 in those of the English Crown; and in the latter year also in the French loans. In the period 1553–8 the Fleckhamer are many times mentioned in connection with the same financial transaction. In 1559 they borrowed largely on the Antwerp Bourse at 10 per cent., and were even considered solvent in the following year, but, like the Ligsalz, they failed soon afterwards.[1]

Two Strassburg business companies, the two largest there, the Prechter and the Ingold, are mentioned in the period 1543–58 in Antwerp, and particularly in Lyons, as often taking part in large financial transactions. Between 1560–72 the Ingold were declared insolvent. What happened to the Prechter we are not told.[2]

Finally, we may mention some Nuremberg houses who began to carry on financial transactions after the war of Schmalkalden. Among these are, in the first place, the Pömer, the Furtenbach and many others who helped King Ferdinand in the years 1547–53. Later the Furtenbach transferred their main business to Genoa and participated in the Spanish loans. They are, for example, mentioned in 1630 as creditors of the Fugger in Spain. But for the rest these Nuremberg families are not mentioned later in connection with financial business. It is otherwise with the Harsdörfer, the Fütterer, the Ebner, the firms of Ambrosy Bosch, Hans and Augustin Furnberger, of Caspar and Christopher Fischer, Hans Scheuffelin, and many others. They were involved in the French loans and seem to have been exhausted by the great losses they suffered from them.

The Great South German Financiers in Antwerp and Lyons. As we have already seen, the South German merchants from early times came into connection with Antwerp and Lyons, the two financial centres of the world of the sixteenth century, and contributed a great deal to their rapid rise. It was no small number of South German merchants who, in their young days as agents or on their own account, arrived in the great foci of a quite new trading life, where the money that they eagerly sought for seemed to be lying in the streets.

They then permanently remained there, and according to their luck and skill attained their end or again went under. Amongst these, for

---

[1] Lille, B. 2363. Fugger-Archiv, Bilanz von 1546. Haugsche Handlungs-bücher. Germanisches Museum. Turnbull, *Calendar, Queen Mary*, No. 111, 751, 843–4. Kervyn, I, 326. II, 240–1, 520.

[2] Lille, B. 2436. Ehrenberg, *Hans Kleberg*, p. 34. Augsburg. Stadtarchiv. and German. Museum.

instance, was that George Meuting who for a short time played a prominent part in Antwerp, but early vanished again. About the same time in Antwerp we come across the Conrad Imhof who, in 1503, bought a house in the Vlamincstrate and is mentioned as owner of a large house 'opt Clapdorp' in 1527. His daughter Anna married Jaspar Pruys, a Fleming. The family appears to have subsisted in Antwerp for a long time.[1] Many of the Fugger's agents remained on in Antwerp after they had become independent. Examples are: Bernhard Stecher, whose descendants are later repeatedly mentioned in Antwerp; Matthias Oertel; and Wolff Haller, of whom we are about to speak.

Some individuals from among these offshoots of South German merchant families in Antwerp come into prominence as financiers and speculators of the first rank. They are some of the most interesting phenomena of their time, and it is surprising that historians have not long ago turned their attention to them to a much larger extent than they have done. We want to make up for this neglect.

Wolff Haller von Hallerstein. Three generations of the Nuremberg family of Haller were in the service of the Hapsburgs. Wolff Haller zum Ziegelstein – the father of the man who will chiefly occupy us – was a counsellor of Maximilian and his Hauskämmerer (Chamberlain) at Innsbruck. In his grant of a coat of arms on 1st May, 1510, the Emperor declared that at the Court and elsewhere he had been 'useful, true and diligent in important offices, and during wars and serious states of affairs had served him well with his appreciable service,' and had been knighted on the battlefield by the Emperor. His brother Bartholomew was also an Imperial counsellor. They belonged to the South German patricians, of whom Maximilian availed himself in a way we already sufficiently know.[2]

Wolff Haller zum Ziegelstein had a son, who also was named Wolff. He is the man whom we have already got to know as the agent of the Fugger at Antwerp. He is first mentioned in this capacity in 1519. In the previous chapter we saw him earlier and by the orders of the Fugger must have performed real services to Charles, the then King of Spain. In 1526 he expressed his gratitude for 'his excellent services for a long time past, namely, first in this our Kingdom of Spain, when we first took possession of it (1517), then in our election as King of the Romans (1519), on our coronation as King of the Romans (1520); also in our journeys through the Kingdom of England (1522), and in our wars with France (1521–6). He furthered our military affairs in Italy and Burgundy, and in our great and difficult dealings in manifold ways has done

[1] *Antw. Schöffenbriefe,* and *Bulletin de la Propriété,* 1888, p. 23.
[2] From a codex in Museum at Brussels, Alt Herkomen, Stand und Wesen der Haller von Hallerstein.

conspicuous work with his body and by lending his property; daily, too, here [he has served us] in our Kingdom of Spain and our Imperial Court.' The Emperor then took him into his council and service and granted him exceptional privileges.

Wolff Haller had given up his Nuremberg citizenship. In spite of this, on the 29th June, 1526, the Emperor appointed him Mayor ('Schult-heisser') of Nuremberg for life, and in the document drawn up for the purpose he is quite unusually described as 'our Counsellor from his youth up.' Three years later he married in Antwerp a daughter of Cornelius von der Logenhagen, the Warden of the Mint there of the reigning prince.[1] In 1530 he is again represented in a not very impor-tant financial transaction of the Netherlands Government as representa-tive of the Fugger; in 1531 as representative of the Paumgartner; and, on the other hand, in 1531 as Treasurer of the Queen Maria, Stadtholden of the Netherlands, and as 'Chevalier.' But this did not prevent his having just then taken a vigorous part, apparently as banker, in the financial affairs of the Court of Brussels.[2]

In the family history composed in the lifetime of Wolff Haller the second, he is described as 'Wolff Haller von Hallerstein, Knight, Coun-sellor to his Roman and Imperial Majesty and steward to the Queen Maria of Hungary.' How highly she thought of him is shown by the fact that she stood godmother to his first child, with the Duchess of Milan, the Countess of Egmont, the Countess of Zollern, and other ladies of the highest aristocracy. He died in Brussels in 1559.

In the next generation there again was a Wolff Haller von Hallerstein, who is mentioned as Keeper of the Privy Purse (Pfennigmeister) of the Emperor in his financial affairs; and in 1557 he was appointed by King Philipp II to be Netherlands War Commissioner at a salary of 400 thalers.[3] It seems that in this office he was the successor of his uncle, Ruprecht or Robert Haller von Hallerstein, a son of Bartholomew Haller zum Ziegelstein. This Ruprecht had also settled in Antwerp; there he married a daughter of Lazarus Tucher and died Netherlands War Commissary. The family then continued on in the Netherlands.

In these Haller we must perceive the successors of those South German patricians who entered the financial service of the Emperor Maximilian. Only these had chiefly served the Emperor in Tyrol, while the later Haller transferred the theatre of their industrial activity to Antwerp, which put them on quite a different pedestal. But it seems that even there they always remained officials and courtiers rather than

---

[1] *Antwerpener Schöffenbücher*, 5/9, 1524.

[2] Lille, *Chambre des Comptes*, B. 2357 and 2363. Brussels, *Chambre des Comptes*, No. 28096.

[3] Kreisarchiv Nürnberg: *Manuale der Herren Eltern*, 1551. Wednesday after Christmas. Royal Archives. Brussels, Urk. v. 5/2, 1557.

bankers and merchants. If this is so they form a contrast to the remarkable man whom we must now get to know.

Lazarus Tucher. Lazarus Tucher was a contemporary of Wolff Haller von Hallerstein (both were born in 1492). Outwardly the course of life of these two men exhibit many similar features, but when regarded more closely the essential differences come to light.

Lazarus Tucher did not spring from that widespread Nuremberg family of Tucher who took such an important position both in public life and in the business of their native town. Three generations earlier this 'Hans line' had separated from the 'Endres line' to which Lazarus belonged. Berthold Tucher, the father of Lazarus, went to Eisleben, where he ran smelting works and a copper refinery. At first he made a good living out of it, but later he had 'to suffer many adversities and sorrows'; but it is not clear what these were. He died at Eisleben in 1519.[1]

Berthold Tucker had no less than twenty-two children. In addition to Lazarus we hear of: Erasmus, who traded with his uncle to Geneva, settled there and died in 1525; Endres, who in 1512, aged fourteen, came to the Netherlands, travelled for the Herwart to Portugal and 'the newly-discovered islands' (he justified the highest hopes, but he too died young): Bartholomew, Hans and Franz – all three similarly went to the Netherlands to try their luck there. The first two seems to have got on tolerably well, while Franz, as we shall see later, came to grief. We observe in this how strongly the young South Germans of that time were attracted to foreign parts.

Lazarus Tucher was the eldest of the brothers we have mentioned. He studied three years in Leipzig, but then went to the Netherlands, and, as the family chronicler informs us, 'sought the fortune which he got rather in old age than in youth.' In 1518 (23rd August) we come across him in the Antwerp Sheriff's books as 'Lazarus Tucher, merchant from Nuremberg, now living at Doernich (Tournay).' At that time he gave a full power of attorney to a merchant named Wolfgang Bucher, who came from Leipzig, to get in his book debts, sue, etc. In Tournay he, in 1520, married Jacobina Cocquiel, daughter of the respected merchant Nicolas Cocquiel, some of whose sons removed to Antwerp and there acquired a considerable position in the trading world.[2]

Lazarus Tucher, too, was only temporarily domiciled in Tournay. Antwerp was the proper field of his activity. He is first mentioned there in 1519.[3] On 17th June, 1519, Jan de Fontayne, a merchant from Tournay, made over to him a house in the Predikeerenstrate; but a year

---

[1] Genealogy of the Tucher family, Brit. Mus. Add. MSS, No. 19475.

[2] P. A. du Chastel, *Notices généalogiques Tournaisiennes*, 1, 535 ff.

[3] *Christof Scheuerls Briefbuch*, published by Soden and Knaake, II, 93. Also The Antwerpener Schöffenbücher.

later he transferred it again to Jan Berthout, a merchant from Atrecht. On 6th February, 1524, the Herwart's agent made over to him another house in the same street, which he resold on the same day. So at that time he appears to have been speculating in real property. His chief business till 1528, however, is of a completely modern type. He was broker, agent and speculator in some great articles of speculation like pepper and woad. Thus he comes before us in the Tucher business correspondence of the year 1526.

At that time the Antwerp agent of his Nuremberg cousin asked him if the Government had the design of putting a new tax on kinds of money in circulation. Lazarus Tucher said yes, and then had a long conversation with the agent. Just at the end he used an expression by means of which he apparently wanted the agent and his principal to 'bear' woad, of which they had bought a large quantity as a speculation. The agent informs his house of this and adds, 'I do not know whether he is in earnest or joking. He has often played such tricks and is often himself broker, buyer and seller all together.'

Soon afterwards: 'Lazarus Tucher has almost all the pepper in his hands, if one goes to some one who has it to sell, he refers one to Lazarus Tucher. For he is both seller and broker together. I have more than once said to him in a friendly way that he might think of me if anything should come to his hands. All the time he professes himself very ready to do this, and that if he could serve you and anything should come to his hands, you should have the preference. But I put no reliance on him; for I well know that he must be submissive to the Hochstetter, Manlich and Bartholomew Welser.'

In 1528 Lazarus Tucher first began his financial transactions. We learnt to know accurately the occasion in which this first occurred, when we spoke of the fall of the Hochstetter. He built his fortunes on the ruins of this mighty house. In that great financial transaction of the year 1528, in which he used his ability unscrupulously, he not only acquired a great deal of money and raised his credit in the business world, which always judges by results, but in particular he knew how to impress the Netherlands Government and to get into such good favour with them that afterwards, for a long space of time, he remained their most important financial agent.

We have already heard what an agent of the Tucher reported about the business position of Lazarus Tucher shortly after the events of 1528, which we have related. Here we may quote from these letters a few more passages relating to the inwardness of his business methods and his private life. At that time a young Tucher was to be apprenticed to a merchant at Antwerp. The agent advised against choosing Lazarus Tucher: 'With him he will have to consider for himself what he ought to learn. For he [Lazarus Tucher] pays no attention, is seldom at home, and has not eaten ten meals at home in the course of a year. Hieronymus Tucher (of the main branch of the house) keeps the books, his son-in-law (presumably Charles Cocquiel) is cashier: he looks after both of them.'

In 1529 Lazarus Tucher bought the house of Marcus van Kerken (at the corner of the present Rue de l'Empereur and Rue de l'Ammann) for 1,540 £ fl. He wanted to pay at once in cash. But the vendor, in accordance with the Antwerp custom, only wished to have a third or a quarter in cash and to leave the rest at interest until his children came of age.[1] Lazarus Tucher's son sold this again, and kept till his death a house he bought in 1534, which similarly was situated in the present Rue Ammann. In addition, he owned an estate called Gallifort near Antwerp.

Lazarus Tucher, in 1529, as successor of Pieter van der Straten, as well as additional to Gerard Stercke, was the chief agent of the Brussels Court for the great loans which they were always raising on the Antwerp Bourse. Since 1531 he maintained for ten years the first position in this department of business; he had then to give it over to the Florentine, Gaspar Ducci. Yet till 1552 he had many business relations with the Government. In particular, he knew how to utilize the capital of the South German merchants for the monetary needs of the Netherlands Court, which again, by this means, served the policy of the Emperor. Up to 1529 only individuals of the largest South German houses had participated in these profitable but risky financial transactions. After that they were more and more drawn in, which, as we saw, finally resulted in the ruin of many of the first families. The critical period of this traffic did not begin till Lazarus Tucher had ceased his business activities. But, in any case, he had contributed much to lead the South German trading community on to the fatal path of unsafe business. The details of the loans which Lazarus Tucher took up for the Court of Brussels we shall get to know later.

He also did financial business with the city of Antwerp and the King of Portugal, but first and foremost with the English Crown. The latter transaction we must here follow out in somewhat greater detail, since they enable us to get to know somewhat better the character and business principles of Lazarus Tucher. He was among the first of the Antwerp financiers who lent money to the English Crown. Already, by 1549, a loan of 167,218 Carolus gulden, which Tucher presumably had lent to King Edward VI shortly after he ascended the throne, was due for repayment.

---

[1] *Tucherscher Handlungsbrief vom* 29th June, 1529, and Thys, *Bull. de la Propriété,* 1889, p. 31.

William Dansell, the English financial agent at Antwerp at that time, was instructed to obtain a prolongation of the loan at 12 per cent.; but Tucher would not agree. Dansell then had to borrow the money to pay him from Erasmus Schetz, another important merchant of Antwerp. Only when this had been accomplished Tucher professed himself ready to make a fresh advance, but refused to co-operate in the export of coin to England, which was forbidden by law. Nevertheless, a loan of 150,000 Carolus gulden took place. Yet Dansell, on account of the way in which the money was conveyed to him, had to endure many reproaches from the Government, which over his head got into direct connection with Lazarus Tucher about a further loan. Tucher was willing to grant it at 12 per cent., but he would only pay in goods and be paid back in cash, while the English Government conversely wanted to receive cash and pay in goods. This appears to have rendered the business abortive.[1]

When, then, in 1552, Thomas Gresham was appointed financial agent to the English Crown in Antwerp, he immediately got into touch with Lazarus Tucher, who lent 10,000 £ fl. (= 60,000 Carolus gulden) at 14 per cent. In April, 1553, Gresham wrote home that his friend Lazarus Tucher would again advance to the King 200,000 Carolus gulden, which was to be considered a very satisfactory thing since the Emperor had to pay 16 per cent. But it seems that the business did not come off, since King Edward became dangerously ill and died some months afterwards. His successor, Mary, withdrew her confidence from Gresham and sent Christopher Dauntsey to Antwerp, where, by his clumsiness, he severely damaged the credit of the English Crown. At the beginning of November, 1553, he borrowed from Lazarus Tucher 100,000 Carolus gulden at 13 per cent. for a year. Tucher further promised to deliver a further 100,000 within a week, so far as his friends in Germany would not have made other dispositions of the money.

In England people were displeased with this settlement, because the rate of interest was considered too high. So Gresham was sent off to Antwerp in all haste, with instructions to borrow 50,000 pounds (= 300,000 Carolus gulden) at 11 per cent., or the highest 12 per cent. Immediately after his arrival Gresham tried to cancel this unprofitable business with Lazarus Tucher. It proved to be yet more unfavourable for the English Crown, because Tucher declared that he would not pay till the end of November, but that interest should run from the beginning of the month, which raised the rate to 14 per cent. This damaged the credit of the English Crown so much that Gresham at first did not dare to negotiate about a new loan. Full of vexation he wrote home that

---

[1] *Acts of the Privy Council*, II, 310. Turnbull, *Calendar, Edward VI*, Nos. 139, 142, 146, 148, 150, 153, 155, 161, 162, 164, 172, 184.

before Dauntsey's arrival people had obtained money at 12, or even at 10 per cent., and the merchants had been glad of it. If, on the other hand, Tucher's contract was carried out, it would be difficult to get anything under 13–14 per cent. But Lazarus wanted his pound of flesh.[1]

On the 26th November Gresham wrote to the Privy Council: 'This daye Lazzerus Tucher came unto me upon the Bourse, and asked "whether I had any answere whether his bargayne should take place or not." I said to him that I could only marvell that Dauntsey had offered such a rate of interest and that he should have required it. His answer was that "a had concludyd a bargaine, and that a looked to have his bargin kept; for that a knew that the Counsell had wrytten to the Fuggers for money" . . . Further a dyd declare unto me that at the fyrst a concludyd with Mr. Daunsey but for i c m floryns; and that aftyrwards, the said Daunsey came unto him, and requyred and prayed him to furnishe hym with i c m more: which a showed me that a had it not of his own, but was fayn to take it uppe upon his own credit, to doo the Queene service. Which (here writing) was small profitt to the Queene, but to *his own* profitt. For that he tooke it uppe aftyr x *per cento*, and woll make the Queene pay xiii. . . . But according as I have written you, if this bargain doo take place of Tucher's, you maye not looke to have any monny upon interest under xiij upon the hundred; by the reason this matter is so spread abroad, and advices given throughout all Cristendom.'

The last observation was entirely true. Thus, for example, Matthias Oertel, the Fugger agent, at once brought this affair to the knowledge of his masters, and Anton Fugger answered that 13 per cent. was certainly a high rate if the news was true. And in the following year a report of a Venetian Ambassador contains the information that the English Crown was accustomed to borrow money at over 14 per cent. at Antwerp, and that at the moment the Queen owed more than a million.[2]

Gresham now sought to satisfy the obstinate man. He wrote to the Council: 'This Lazzerus Tucher is a very extreme man, and very openmouthed. As also, according as I have wrytten you, a hathe dyvers partners in the bargayne; and considering the letter that your Lordeshipes have written him, wherein you [ac] knowledge Danssey to be her Highness' servant, he doth now ground himself not a littill upon that word.' In short, the business had to stand, with the result that when Gresham, according to his instructions, wished to borrow more money, he was asked for 15 per cent., and when he offered 10–11 per cent. the

[1] Turnbull, *Calendar, Edward VI*, No. 653; *Queen Mary*, Nos. 69, 73, 74, 77, 83, 85, 89, 98 ff. Burgon, *Life and Times of Sir Thomas Gresham*, I, 128–38. Flanders Correspondence, State Papers Office.

[2] Brown, *Calendar V*, 551.

merchants asked him indignantly if he thought they did not know that Lazarus Tucher had got 13 per cent. for eleven months, and whether their money was not as good as his.

But in spite of this Gresham remained on friendly terms with Tucher. In 1558 he advised his Government to honour him like certain others of the foremost financiers with a beautiful golden chain. When two years afterwards in Antwerp a monk preached very disrespectfully against Queen Elizabeth and for it was threatened by the English merchants he begged Lazarus Tucher to obtain the Queen's forgiveness through Gresham. Also Tucher repeatedly lent money to the English Crown – in 1558 11,000 £ fl. at 14 per cent., and further sums in the same year; in 1560 again 26,666⅔ £. Even the heirs of Lazarus Tucher had in 1564 to claim some thousands of pounds from Queen Elizabeth. Gresham, who at that time was extremely short of money, was in serious danger of having to go to a debtors' prison for this trifle. He only escaped this fate by quickly getting sureties.[1]

We possess letters from the last years of Lazarus Tucher which he addressed to Lienard Tucher, his cousin, of the Nuremberg main branch, who is already known to us. It was in 1561. The great credit crisis which irrevocably destroyed the prosperity of the South German business community had already broken out. The two old men, so dissimilar from every point of view, exchanged their experiences and business principles. Lazarus Tucher chiefly complained of his brother Franz. He had lived badly and had been beguiled by Wolff Poschinger (a financial agent of South German origin who will occupy us later) to take bonds of the Netherlands Receivers General. Lazarus, who knew well how unsafe this paper was, helped his brother in 1555 to divest himself of them again. But Franz Tucher did not give up his light-minded business habits, and had to suspend payment in 1560 or 1561, whereupon Lazarus satisfied the creditors.

So then Lazarus asseverated that as, thank God, he needed no more, he would have nothing more to do with a high rate of interest, which usually was accompanied with great risk, but chiefly would aim at security to bequeath to his descendants what God had bestowed on him through his work. Except a small amount of bonds of the Receivers General he had outstanding only a claim of 40,000 ducats on the King of Portugal; yet, according to the latest news, affairs in India were again quiet, so that he hoped in the course of time to get out without loss. 'And in truth you will find that next to the English, which is small, this Portuguese debt will be paid before those of all the other potentates. I wish from my heart that anyone who is involved with the Kings of Spain

[1] Burgon, I, 200, 260. Turnbull, *Calendar, Queen Mary*, No. 755. Kewyn de Lettenhore, *Rélat. polit.* I, 316, 326; II, 240–1; III, 609 ff.

and France should not have a harder bed to lie on than you or I. At times it is not possible to avoid serving the great. I, in particular, as an old Courtier, as I two days ago have had to lend my gracious master, the Prince of Orange, at his repeated pressing solicitation, 15,000 fl. for his marriage with the daughter of Duke Maurice. I desire now neither much nor little interest, in order in this way to obtain more easily the repayment of the capital. But I would rather have been free from it altogether. For my efforts now are directed to get away from all Potentates and Lords and to put out my money so that I can have it back again when I want it, as the present hard times, my age and my infirmities require it. I strive now more than I did before to obtain a quiet time for the rest of my life, and I, especially in summer, live at my house Gallifort, where I am seldom without good company.' If only all the South German bankers had acted like Lazarus Tucher in his old age it would have been better for them and the welfare of Germany.

Two years later Lazarus Tucher died. During the great days of the Antwerp Bourse he was unquestionably one of the most conspicuous and interesting phenomena which then attracted the notice of the whole world. He was a type of business man of such a modern character that history must consider him as one of the fathers of modern Stock Exchange methods. Although the Emperor made him a counsellor, and although he was highly regarded at the Court of Brussels and by many other princes, yet, in contrast to Wolff Haller von Hallerstein, he remained his whole lifelong primarily a man of business. His descendants became extinct at the beginning of the eighteenth century, but only after they had intermarried with many of the foremost noble families of the Netherlands.

Other Antwerp Financiers of South German Origin. Wolff Poschinger appears to have been a feeble copy of Lazarus Tucher. Unfortunately, we know little about him.[1] He is first mentioned in Antwerp in 1532, and since he then was aged twenty-eight he cannot have carried on business on his own account very much earlier. In 1549–55 he is several times mentioned as financial agent of the Court of Brussels, and one of those through whom the South German trading houses conducted their investments of capital in Antwerp. He died in 1558. His son of the same name is mentioned in 1560 in connection with similar transactions, while a daughter married Paul Tucher (a nephew of Lazarus) and brought to him her father's fine house in the Rue Haute.

A similar, only probably a less conspicuous, part was played in Ant-

---

[1] Also written: Boschinger, Puschinger, Putschinger. Cf. German. Museum, Dehalm Corresp. 1549, June; Tuchersches Familien-Archiv, *Brief von Lazarus Tucher*, 1561, 14/3; Haugsches Handlungsbuch v. 1549; Brüsseler Staatsarchiv, *Chambre des Comptes*, No. 23470.

werp about 1543–9 by a man called Kaltenhofer, who from his name
may have been a South German, but possibly a Netherlander – especially as his Christian name was Eustache.[1]

Hans Kleberg, 'the good German' of Lyons. We now come to a man
who, next to Lazarus Tucher, is unquestionably to be regarded as the
most remarkable figure in the large circle of German financiers of the
sixteenth century.[2] Hans Kleberg came from a bourgeois Nuremberg
family, Scheuhenpflug, a member of which many generations before had
fled from the town after an unusually scandalous bankruptcy. Hans
Kleberg's father appears then to have adopted a new name. His son
was early active in the trading house of the Imhof, and especially in
Lyons, where he presumably some time before 1525 established a business of his own, which he soon brought into a flourishing condition. At
the same time he remained in friendly relations with the Imhof. We
know further that by 1521 he had become a citizen of the town of Berne,
so that as a Swiss he could, without molestation, carry on his affairs in
Germany and France during the wars then breaking out between
Charles V and Francis I. Many other South German merchants did the
same. But Kleberg did more; he performed political and financial services for the French Government. In 1524 he is accused of having denounced to the authorities at Lyons two men who had letters on them to
the Imperial commanding officers in Spain, so that they were arrested
and imprisoned. In 1526 we come across him at the French Court. In
1527 the town of Berne dunned Francis I to pay a claim of Kleberg's for
18,187 gold crowns which was in arrear. This was the first really big
financial transaction which the King concluded with a German merchant. It is particularly interesting, in the communication of Berne
Town Council, to find the extraordinary free language which immediately recalls the letter written some years earlier with the same purpose
by Jakob Fugger to Charles V. The Council goes so far as to threaten
that if he is not paid Kleberg will call high personages to his assistance!

In 1528, after many years of vain efforts, Kleberg succeeded in bringing home as his wife Felicitas, the daughter of Willibald Pirkheimer, a
patrician of Nuremberg. But the marriage turned out unfortunate.
Kleberg had to promise before the marriage that he would settle in
Nuremberg. But he could not keep his promise because his business
affairs required that he should permanently be in Lyons. But his wife
refused to follow him there. His father-in-law, Willibald Pirkheimer,
took the side of his daughter, and tried unsuccessfully to prevent the
Council from absolving Kleberg from his duties as a citizen. Whereupon

---

[1] Lille, B. 2436. German. Museum, Behaim Corresp. 1549, June.

[2] From Ehrenberg, *Hans Kleberg, 'der gute Deutsche'* (*Mitth. d. Ver. f. Gesch. d. Stadt Nürnberg*, 1893).

Felicitas got ill and died in 1530, after a long illness. This caused Pirkheimer, who all along had been set against Kleberg, to make the monstrous accusation that his daughter had been poisoned by her husband. We possess, however, the statement of impartial persons, from which we learn with certainty that Pirkheimer's complaints were at least immeasurably exaggerated.

In general, Kleberg was much hated by the good families of Nuremberg. Kleberg was proud, perhaps, of his money, as the spiteful Pirkheimer thought, but certainly also of his great gifts, by the help of which he had become, not merely rich, but also much looked up to in Lyons. The great charitableness which he displayed there earned for him the name of 'the good German.' In Berne and Geneva, too, he equally enjoyed general esteem. But the members of the great Nuremberg families with whom he had daily intercourse in business and commerce did not cease to regard him with aversion. They did not forgive one of their despised plebeians for rising above their heads, and Kleberg, who in Lyons showed himself as a homely man, averse from all external marks of respect, turned his pride to his countrymen. The man who did a kindness to an opponent in Geneva and added, 'I will be his servant and friend whether he likes it or not,' never forgot till the end of his life the injuries of his countrymen.

In the last period of Kleberg's life we have more information about his business activities. In 1536 he had obtained French naturalization from the King; then in 1543 was appointed 'Valet de Chambre Ordinaire du roi' – a title which, in any case, shows that he had been of real service to the King. He at once brought several seignorial properties, in respect of which the King permitted him to exercise jurisdiction. By this Kleberg had become a member of the French nobility, as so is repeatedly described as 'noble homme.' Certainly the services by means of which he had climbed to this height were of an essentially financial kind, for the tale that he rescued the King's life at the battle of Pavia is unquestionably a legend.

Kleberg at Lyons achieved what Lazarus Tucher succeeded in doing at Antwerp. He succeeded in utilizing the capital of the South German merchants for the abundant loans to the King. Probably this first occurred in 1543, but especially in 1545. Then the first South German houses which had branches in Lyons were induced by Kleberg and the high rate of interest promised by the King of France to participate with 50,000 crowns in the loan raised at Lyons. As well as promises, energetic threats must certainly have been used at that time to produce this result. Kleberg played with his fellow countrymen like a cat with a mouse. At times he was useful to them and said 'he would leave his body and goods with the Germans.' Then, again, when a new higher tax was imposed on them he declared 'He could help them with fifty words, but he wouldn't do so,' and they then came together to beg for his help, he treated them hardly, complained of their ingratitude and asked 'whether they did not at home regard him as a needlemaker or a coppersmith?' And even added that 'He wished to be a Frenchman here and not to assist Germans any more, unless they should also be useful to him.'

On this basis an understanding was arrived at. The South German merchants fell into the trap, and Kleberg had, in addition, got the personal satisfaction that the proud families of Nuremberg had to humble themselves before him. Only the Tucher and the Imhof kept away from the French loans.

We cannot here tell all which more recent researches have brought to light about this remarkable man. We will only touch on a few particularly interesting facts.

When the war of Schmalkalden broke out the Evangelicals at first thought of Kleberg, in order by his agency to procure in Lyons the monetary resources they were pressingly in need of. To this end Jakob Sturm travelled from Strasburg to Lyons, but to his consternation he found Kleberg seriously ill and had to go off again without having effected his object.

Soon after Hans Kleberg died, leaving behind him a great fortune, which his heirs seem to have lost again in a short time, in spite of the fact that Kleberg personally had lent only a little money to the King, so that at his death his fortune consisted for the most part of cash, and in spite of the fact that his widow (Kleberg had married again in Lyons) had invested it in real estate in accordance with the provisions of his will.

There stands in Lyons an old statue which has been renewed in the nineteenth century. Immemorial tradition alleges that it had been erected by the people of Lyons to the 'good German.' Whether the 'rockman,' as the statue is popularly called from its rocky surroundings, was in fact originally dedicated to Kleberg (as is the case since the renovation in 1849), the materials we have at present do not enable us to determine. But it is sure that the 'good German' lived on in the remembrance of the people, and meanwhile that tradition may be considered as worthy of credence until it is conclusively disproved.

An accurate analysis of the characteristics of Kleberg, so far as the unfortunately limited material allows us, reveals that in almost all points this remarkable man had a double nature. It is characteristic that his good qualities as a whole are turned towards foreign parts, while regarded from his native land the Janus head of Kleberg exhibits only hostile, distorted features.

Later Lyonese Financiers of South German Origin. Hans Kleberg has only a few friends among the Germans at Lyons. As such are mentioned: Christopher Ebner from Nuremberg, Christopher Freihamer from Augsburg, Jäcob Jäger and George Weikman from Ulm. The first three were the only German witnesses present when Kleberg's will was drawn up, and they are remembered in it. After Kleberg's death George Weikman with some other German merchants were considered by the Schmalkaldian League for making arrangements for procuring money for the League at Lyons. All of them took part in the loans to the King of France – Weikman and Freihamer in considerable amounts. Also they all permanently remained in Lyons. We know that Christopher Ebner died there in 1559. But apparently none of them took a leading part in the relations of the South German merchants to the French Crown and its financial affairs. It is only more than a decade after Kleberg's death that some moving spirits arose among the South German merchants carrying on business in Lyons: they are George Obrecht and Israel Minckel, both of Strasburg.

George Obrecht is mentioned in 1544 in the Tucher business letters from Lyons. At that time there was a threat of taking away the safe conduct from the German merchants there in order to make them accommodating for the loans of the French Crown. Obrecht was sent by the Germans to Paris to obtain the continuance of the safe conduct. But he was unsuccessful; he rather made the affair worse into the bargain by his indiscreet handling of it. Finally Kleberg, who himself very likely had done an ill turn to the German, again smoothed things out. In 1555 we again find Obrecht in Paris, whence he communicates to the Nuremberg Council information about the stay of the Margrave Albrecht Alcibiades.[1] He no doubt had had something to do at the French Court. After 1556 he and his countryman Israel Minckel appear as recognized leaders of the South Germans in their financial relations with the French Crown. Minckel, who, in spite of his fore name, was not a Jew, is mentioned in 1561 as Master of the Mint and a member of the old Corporation of Companions of the Mint.[2] He was also a man whose calling – as the Mint was then organized – was very near that of a banker. Obrecht, meanwhile, probably had traded at home and did not get into touch with financial affairs until he had come to Lyons.

The details of the big affairs which Obrecht and Minckel carried on in the years 1556–64 for the South German merchants with the French Crown we shall get to know later, and shall then see how tragically these

---

[1] Behaim Correspondence in German. Museum. Cf. Brown, *Calendar VI*, 764; Clerjon, *Histoire de Lyon*, VI, 10; *Lettres de Catherine de Médicis*, ed. de la Ferrière, I, 285, 349, also section, 2, chap. 2.

[2] Hanauer, I, 148.

affairs ended. The two men by their activities inflicted unspeakable harm on the well-being of the South German towns. For the immense sums that then migrated to France were for the most part never repaid. We are told nothing of the further fate of Obrecht and Minckel. At any rate, their part was played out with the year 1565.

At this time Lyons was in rapid decay, from which it did not recover till much later, when the wars of religion were over. Yet many merchants kept on their businesses there during the confusion. Among these were those relatives of the old patrician family Herwart, who we already know had settled in Lyons. Our recital of the South German financiers will end with these, the last, who are demonstrably offshoots of this family.

We know that two of the sons of the Augsburg Burgomaster George Herwart died in Lyons, and that one of them left descendants there. We have also indicated that two grandsons of this Ulrich Herwart later played a prominent part. They are the brothers Bartholomew and Johann Heinrich Herwart.[1]

These two brothers, of whom Bartholomew was manifestly the most important, were born at Lyons in 1606 and 1609; and since their father was born there they can no longer be considered as Germans. We came across them first in 1632, the year in which Gustavus Adolphus died. At that time they were closely attached to Bernhard of Weimar and supplied him with money which enabled him to take Alsace in 1638. When Bernhard died in the following year they supplied the money which was necessary to induce his army to enter into the service of the French.

In the following year they appear to have transferred their main business to Paris, and after that only to have kept on a branch in Lyons. Mazarin, in 1643, recognized their great services to the French state. In 1644 their advances made it possible for the King to make the most of the victory of Freiberg and take Phillipsburg. The King rewarded this by appointing Bartholomew Herwart Intendant of Finance. In 1649, when the Treasury was so exhausted that they could not pay the troops of Turenne's army which threatened to declare itself for the Fronde, Herwart, by paying up the arrears of pay, succeeded in alienating the troops from the celebrated commander. Mazarin, in the presence of the King and the Court, announced that 'Herwart has rescued France and preserved the crown for the King. This service shall never be forgotten.'

By the above-mentioned and other similar loans in the following year, the Herwart handed over 2½ million livres in all, which were by no

---

[1] Cf. the interesting article of Freiherr Hans Herwarth von Bittenfeld in *der Ztschr. d. histor. Ver. f. Schwaben*, I, 184 ff., and Depping, Un banquier protestant en France au XVII siècle, (*Revue historique*, X, 285 ff., XI, 63 ff.).

means sure to be paid back. Bartholomew risked his life in the repeated negotiations with the seditious troops. For all these services he was appointed Controller-General of Finance in 1657, and after that was directly under the Surintendant Fouquet, to whom he personally advanced large sums of money.

Like many financiers of the sixteenth and seventeenth centuries these Herwarts were both state officials and bankers, which naturally was more useful than state finance from the point of view of business results. Bartholomew's character, too, does not appear to have been one of the best. Later, his friend Fouquet accused him of having, in conjunction with Colbert, brought about his (Fouquet's) fall. Colbert himself, too, thought very little of Herwart, and only used him so long as he needed him, namely, till 1665, when he combined Herwart's office with his own.

Bartholomew Herwart died in 1676. He was an intimate friend of La Fontaine, who spent his last years in his house. Finally, it is noteworthy that he used his high position in the financial administration to introduce many Huguenots into it, where they made themselves so useful that after the revocation of the Edict of Nantes Colbert saw them depart with a heavy heart. Herwart's descendants then emigrated to England.

The chief importance of the two Herwarts lies in the fact that they were the last offshoots of the South German financial magnates of the sixteenth century. When Colbert nationalized French finances the only field still remaining for the international princes of finance was finally lost, about the time when the tragic remains of the Fugger money business were buried in Spain.

North German Capitalists. Apart from the people of the Netherlands proper it was only quite a small number of North Germans who took part to any considerable extent in the great international financial transactions of the sixteenth century, and among them there is scarcely one merchant to be found. On the other hand, we are astonished to notice for decades in the front ranks of the Antwerp capitalists the well-known names of prominent members of the Holstein nobility; above all, of the Rantzau, but also of the Brockdorff, Ahlefeld, and others.

The Rantzau at that time were one of the richest German noble families. Heinrich Rantzau, in his *Genealogia Ranzoviana* (which appeared anonymously in 1585), himself gives us information as to the wealth of his family, and adds: 'In our time one of the family has almost simultaneously lent many hundred thousand thaler to the Emperor Charles V, the Queen of England, the King of Denmark and the towns of Antwerp, Ghent, Lübeck, and Hamburg.' Heinrich Rantzau undoubtedly here refers to himself. But not only he, a great statesman, a

Maecenas and a learned man, and Stadtholder of Schleswig and Holstein, but his father Johann, the celebrated soldier, his cousin Moritz, the bold cavalry leader, and his father-in-law Franz von Halle aus Drakenburg und Rintelen – all of them had lent extraordinary large sums of money at Antwerp at high rates of interest. We only know a part of these Antwerp financial transactions, but that is sufficiently remarkable.

In 1550 Johann Rantzau, in conjunction with Franz von Halle, lent King Edward VI of England 70,246 Carolus gulden, which were repaid in the following year. In September, 1552, Franz von Halle is noted as a creditor of the English Crown for 185,560 gulden, and Johann Rantzau for 18,559 gulden. Apparently Franz von Halle had permanently taken up his quarters in Antwerp. At any rate, he is buried there.[1]

Then we hear for the first time again in 1563 that the English Government owed money to Moritz Rantzau and Paulus Brockdorff. They had the same representative in Antwerp, whose name we are unfortunately not told. Queen Elizabeth had sent Sir Thomas Gresham to Antwerp to obtain a prolongation of her debts which were falling due. Everybody agreed except the agent of Rantzau and Brockdorff. He demanded his money and threatened that if he did not get it he would exercise his right of holding Gresham and other English merchants as security and would arrest them. For the security of the city of London, which was given with the bonds of the English Crown, included the right to do this.[2]

In any case the Holsteiners did not make any loss on their English claims. But they did much worse with their claims against the town of Antwerp. How these arose the materials that we have do not make clear. We only hear that they chiefly served to pay the cost of the fortifications of Antwerp. They date from the 'sixties of the sixteenth century. Originally the rate of interest was 12 per cent. But in 1570 the town declared that it was not in a position to pay such a high rate, and asked that it should be reduced to 5 per cent. The Holstein creditors were very indignant. They were willing at the most to reduce the interest to 7 per cent. provided that the capital was paid off by seven yearly instalments in Hamburg. At last they agreed on 6 per cent., and payment off within seven years. The agreement was confirmed by the Finance Council of the Netherlands, but nevertheless was not kept. The interest was never paid, and ultimately a considerable part of the capital was lost.

Yet, comparatively speaking, the Stadtholder Heinrich Rantzau

---

[1] *Acts of the Privy Council*, III, 408. Nares, *Memoirs of Burghley*, p. 405.

[2] Burgon, *Life and Times of Sir Thomas Gresham*, II, 28, 38, 43. Kervyn, III, 241.

came off best. It is true that during his life he exerted himself in vain to get any payments. In 1581 he requested King Philipp II to allow him to attach the burghers of Antwerp and their goods. He repeated this request in 1585 in a letter to the Stadtholder Alexander of Parma and also threatened the town to take the law into his own hands. At the intercession of Parma he kept his patience longer. But in 1592 he wrote to the people of Antwerp: 'Not small is the sum which you owe me. For if the yearly interest unpaid had been capitalized, the sum exceeds a million Carolus gulden; and if some of your obligations stand in other people's names, yet they belong to me, my wife and my children.'

Through the mediation of the King of Denmark Rantzau at last obtained, at any rate, the promise that the town would use their utmost endeavours to recognize his claim. For it appears that they did not consider themselves unconditionally obliged to pay it because the debt was on account of the Government. At last, in 1596, they formally admitted at least 125,000 thaler of the claim. This was only arrived at through Rantzau's relations with Brussels. Yet he died two years later without having lived to receive the repayment. His heirs had to wait many years longer for it. It was not till 1606–16 that at any rate half of the 400,000 guldens (which they claimed inclusive of interest) was paid out to them. The remaining Holsteiners who were interested appear mostly to have got nothing. According to the settlement of 1570 their claims amounted in all to 117,000 thaler.

But that was by no means the whole. For from other sources we know of an admitted debt of that time of the town of Antwerp to Benedictus von Ahlefeld which amounted to 43,713 thaler. It appears that ultimately half of it was cleared up in 1600. We know that in 1597 the heirs of Moritz Rantzau demanded satisfaction both in the Netherlands and at the Court of Spain. But there is no trace of their having got it. Friedrich Brockdorff, Detlef von Ahlefeld and Melchior and Otto Rantzau appear to have taken the law into their own hands and imprisoned some Antwerpers who were travelling through Holstein. But it is not clear what they got from this.[1]

The town of Antwerp obtained loans from many other German nobles, in particular 400,000 thaler from Count Mansfeld. This was through the mediation of Gresham, who for this purpose sent his trusted servant Richard Clough to the Count, who had given his word to Queen Elizabeth. Further, a Herr von Holzfeld who had a claim of 21,767 fl. against the town, succeeded in being partly paid in 1570 by intercepting

---

[1] Cf. *Antw. Stadsprotocollen* ed. *Puuwels*, I, 341, 346 ff., 358 ff., 370, 386, 422 ff., bis 458, in Hambg. Commerzbibliothek 'Copybook of Jürgen Poorter, a clerk of Frau Barbara Rantzau, widow of Moritz Rantzau; von Bertheau in *d. Ztschr. d. Ges. f. Schleswig-Host.-Lauenbg. Geschichte*, XXII (1892), 277 ff.

some Antwerp merchants on their way to Frankfurt am Main. In the following year it is mentioned that the town made some repayments to Duke Adolf von Holstein. And in 1572 the town had to defend itself in the Imperial Chamber (at Wetzlar) against a claim of Count Johann zu Wiedt for 42,000 fl. But it is not certain that the last-mentioned claims really were concerned with loans transactions.[1]

Finally we must here shortly allude to a North German noble or patrician family, the Bodeck, who were induced to carry on financial business through the fact that their kinsmen settled in Antwerp and acquired a large fortune there. They came from Prussia, and belonged to families of Knights of the Order who had conquered this land. Johann von Bodeck lived from 1454 to 1521 in Thorn. His son Bonaventuro went over to the Augsburg confession and settled in Antwerp, where he had dwelt at least as early as 1554. In 1564 he stood security to the town of Antwerp for the Hansa Town in respect of the interest in a claim of 40,000 fl. which Antwerp had against them.[2] When the disorders broke out in Antwerp he migrated to Frankfurt am Main, and died there in 1591.

[1] Cf. Burgon, I, 337 ff.; Kervyn de Lettenhove, *Rélat. dipl. des Pays-Bas. et l'Angleterre*, II, 270–526.

[2] *Antw. Stadsprotocollen ed. Pauwels*, I, 181.

CHAPTER 3

THE FLORENTINES AND THE OTHER TUSCAN FINANCIERS

I

⌊THE FLORENTINES

GENERAL Considerations. The fact that the Florentines played the chief part in the history of the Renaissance has never yet been satisfactorily explained. Venice and Genoa were also rich cities, and no one can dispute the many-sidedness of Venetian enterprise. If therefore the importance of Venice, not to speak of Genoa, is not to be compared with that of Florence, one fact which has not yet been observed in this connection was largely responsible for this. The chief strength of the Venetians and Genoese during the Middle Ages lay in industry and trade in commodities, while the Florentines since the thirteenth century had gained their riches chiefly as bankers, and this had brought them important connections in the Courts and high places of almost the whole of Europe; and since their trade required little work from the individual it had left them plenty of leisure for higher interests. These facts gave a powerful stimulus to their already highly developed capacity for culture and to their ambitions. Moreover, since their state was so small, that at any rate while it had no port, they could only play a leading part in the world through their money, many of the nobler spirits among them threw themselves with extraordinary passion into the cult of art and science. They managed to combine a munificent liberality in these directions and a mode of life of the greatest elegance with a certain distinguished simplicity – a fact well brought out by one of their best historians, Varchi.[1] Among the great financiers of the sixteenth century, the Florentines are the only ones whose chief branch of business in the Middle Ages was dealing in large international bills and other credit transactions. When economic changes at the close of the Middle Ages forced into the background the commerce and industry of Florence as in the case of the other Italian cities, the Florentines had to turn their inherited faculty for finance to greater account than ever; and the greatly increased demand for credit offered them abundant opportunity for its exercise. Until late into the second half of the fifteenth century the Medici and the families connected with them, the Portinari, Sassetti, Tornabuoni, Guidetti and so on played the leading part among Florentine bankers, though their aim in the

---

[1] Varchi, *Stor. fiorent. lib.* 9: 'Il vitto de' Fiorentini è semplice e parco, ma con maravigliosa e incredibile mondizia e pulitezza.' Cf. also Reumont, *Gesch. der Stadt Rom*, III b, 49.

case of the Medici at any rate was no longer money, but political power. Lorenzo the Magnificent no longer carried on trade as an end in itself. His agents turned this to account by furthering their own interests at his expense, so that the business fell into a dangerous disorder. Other families then came to the front, among them those who had been at enmity with the Medici and therefore had been banished and deprived of political power, and who therefore aimed at getting fresh strength and influence through financial dealings abroad. The course of events restricted their field of operations, but it remained large enough for experienced business men by means of intensive cultivation to continue to reap a rich profit for a long time.

There were five principal regions where the Florentines during the last centuries of the Middle Ages had developed their business as merchants and bankers on a large scale. These were the Levant, Italy, France, the Low Countries, and England.

The Levant was taken from them by the forward movement of the the Turks, but chiefly by the change in the direction of the world's trade. Their efforts to make good its loss by bringing in Spain and Portugal were not successful.[1] They were able to keep their hold longer over the other regions, but the struggle of the Medici for supremacy in the Republic had as a consequence an ever-growing connection between Florentine business and political interests and those of the French Crown. This fact forced them on to the side of the Valois in the world struggle between the Valois and the Hapsburgs. Finally the Republic was overthrown by the Medici backed by the Hapsburgs, and this drove all their opponents and those who had not yet come to terms with the new state of affairs into the French camp. This development was fostered by the rise of new powers in the Low Countries, Italy and England, who finally drove out the Florentines. In France, on the other hand, these either, like the Fugger, never found a firm foothold, or, like the Genoese, were gradually forced out by Florentines, or finally, like the South German Protestants, came to grief over their own business.

It came about therefore that of all their business fields, the Florentines retained only France, which, however, continued for a long time to yield them rich and growing profits.

The Florentines in Rome and Naples. Lists dating from about 1470 of the Florentine branches in the different countries have come down to us.[2] These show that at this time there were thirty-two banks in Florence itself, and that among them the chief part in large international finance was played by the firms of Pier Francesco e Lorenzo de Medici e

---

[1] Cf. Heyd, *Geschichte des Levantehandels*, II, 523 ff.

[2] From the Chronicle of Benedetto Dei and a Ms. in Münchener Hof- und Staatsbibliothek (Ital. MSS. No. 160).

Compagni and Jacopo de Pazzi e Sue Nipoti. The most important centres of Florentine banking in Italy, apart from Florence itself, were Rome and Naples. In Rome at least ten Florentines had important business, and forty persons are named as entrusted with the charge of them. There were about the same number of Florentines staying in the Kingdom of Naples.[1]

In Rome there was little wholesale trade proper, but banking business flourished on an extraordinary scale, for it was fed both by the world-wide financial system of the Papal Curia and by the streams of foreigners who came to Rome in the years of Jubilee and the other feasts of the Church. The connection is notorious between these financial trans-actions and the distribution of high ecclesiastical office and prefer-ment. It came about, therefore, that in one period the Florentines played the first part also in the College of Cardinals and generally speak-ing in the whole organization of the Curia.

Among them the Medici had been since the beginning of the fifteenth century the chief bankers of the Curia, an influential and profitable position which they had managed to retain under a succession of Popes. Only when Lorenzo il Magnifico fell out with Pope Sixtus IV the Pope transferred his financial business to Francesco de' Pazzi, an action which materially helped to inflame the enmity of the two great families. The attempt of the Pazzi two years later to overthrow the Medici led to their own downfall. This again provoked the war between the Floren-tines on the one side and the Pope and King Fernando I of Naples on the other, a war which did considerable damage to Florentine business in both markets. Under the next Pope, Innocent VIII, Lorenzo de' Medici regained his former position. The business connection between the Medici and the Curia ceased on the death of both these men, and other Tuscan bankers came to the front, notably the Sienese Agostino Chigi and the Florentine Bindo Altoviti, the friend of Rafael, Michael Angelo and Benvenuto Cellini. The Altoviti had branches in France, the Netherlands, and England. We know, however, very little about their business.[2]

The highest ecclesiastical interests were intimately connected with the finances of the Florentines. Rome became the scene where an un-paralleled splendour was united with an extreme corruption. It was this combination which first struck in Luther's reverent soul the note which afterwards resounded so powerfully when he saw the conse-quences of the same system on German soil.

Among the Florentines settled in Naples the Strozzi at this time held

---

[1] Reumont, *Gesch. d. Stadt. Rom*, III a, 441 ff., III b, 398 ff.; B. Brown, *Calendar II*, 176; *Marino Sanuto Diarii*, XVI, 27, 1513.

[2] Reumont, l.c. *Passerini, Genealogia della famiglia Altoviti*, p. 51 ff., 54 ff.

the chief place. Filippo Strozzi the elder, one of the most noted and favourite members of this gifted family, was banished from Florence and settled about the middle of the fifteenth century in Naples. There he gained a large fortune by business with the King Ferrante, who was always in need of money, and with the similarly situated nobility of the country. In Rome, Naples and Florence there was then no place where money could be more safely deposited than in Strozzi's bank. No interest was paid on such deposits, which could, however, be employed with caution in active credit operations. Filippo's assistants were chiefly members of his own family, as at his table in Naples he was able to count more than eighteen Strozzi. He was the founder of the fortunes of this branch of the family.[1] Recalled from exile, he spent the end of his life in Florence. The Medici honoured, and at times even employed him, but did not cease to regard him with suspicion. He built the magnificent Palazzo degli Strozzi, and died in 1491. We shall have more to say later of his son, the famous Filippo Strozzi, and his grandson, the no less famous French maréchal.

In the first quarter of the sixteenth century the Florentines were still the chief financiers both in Rome and Naples. The Genoese, the Fugger and the Welser ran them closer and closer, but the Florentines still kept the lead. It was only taken from them by the Genoese after the sack of Rome and the changes which ensued on the political scene.

The Final Period of the Medici in the Netherlands and England. The Florentine branches in Bruges and London had from early days been closely connected. As late as 1470 Benedetto Dei says of them: 'They rule these lands, having in their hands the lease of the trade in wool and alum and all the other State revenues, and from thence they do business in exchange with every market in the world, but chiefly with Rome, whereby they make great gains.' This statement is rather boastful, but we have evidence from other sources as to the continued predominance at this time of the Florentine financiers both in England and the Netherlands.

At first the Medici played far the most important part in the case of both countries. Their chief representatives were Tommaso Portinari and Tommaso Guidetti. In 1462 they are mentioned as representatives of the firm Lorenzo and Giuliano Medici, and by 1468 they must have lent large sums both to the King of England and the Duke of Burgundy.[2] The business they transacted in the following years with both princes was, however, more important still. According to Philippe de Commines,

---

[1] Cf. Reumont, *Beitr. z. ital. Gesch.*, V, 223 ff.

[2] Pagnini, *Della Decima*, III, 171; Buser, *Die Beziehungen der Medicäers zu Frankreich*, 437; Olivier, *De la Marche*, quoted in Dupont, *Mémoires de Comynes*, II, 337.

who was well informed on this point, in the year 1471 Charles the Bold of Burgundy lent Edward IV of England 50,000 crowns to enable him to return and regain his kingdom, which he succeeded in doing. Tommaso Portinari gave security to the Duke for the 50,000 crowns and soon after for 80,000 crowns more. Guidetti lent to the King similar sums on several occasions during the struggle for supremacy; and Edward when he had overcome his opponents rewarded him by the grant of valuable trade privileges. The Medici meanwhile had great trouble in getting their money back again.[1] The other business which Tommaso Portinari did for them in Bruges turned out even worse.

Tommaso Portinari held a very distinguished position at the Burgundian Court. This may have made him incautious in granting credit to the warlike Charles the Bold and his daughter Maria, who was the wife of Maximilian I, the worst payer of all princely debtors. His masters did not, however, fare so badly as the Florentine trading companies Da Rabatta and Dei Campie in Bruges, who after Maria's death in 1482 were ruined as the result of the advances they had made to her. The Medici did, however, lose large sums, and as a result apparently, in 1485, Lorenzo gave up the branch in Bruges [2] and discharged Tommaso Portinari. Portinari thereupon entered the Netherlands service altogether and continued to play a large part in finance, though he was also employed in diplomatic missions.

At this time the Burgundian Hapsburg Court was so deeply in debt that a large part of the famous Crown jewels had to be pawned. An inventory of the year 1489 puts their value at 801,000 fl.[3]

Jewels estimated at the values given below were held in pawn by the following persons:

100,000 fl. by Christoforo Nigsoni of Genoa.

100,000 fl. by Tommaso Portinari ⎫
36,000 fl. by Antonio Gualterotti ⎬ all of Florence.
12,000 fl. by Antonio Frescobaldi ⎭

Others again were held by merchants living in Bruges.

Tommaso had a costly lily richly set with gems, which 'riche fleur de liz' was called by the Italians il Riccho Fiordalisio di Borgogna. It weighed 19 lb. The money lent upon it was to be repaid from the Flemish customs on English wool, the Tonlieu of Gravelinghen which Portinari had leased in 1485. As this failed to materialize, the jewel

[1] *Mémoires de Philippe de Comynes*, ed. Dupont, I, 257, II, 337; Kervyn de Lettenhove, *Lettres et négociations de Philippe de Comines*, I, 66; Rymer, *Foedera*, XII, 7 (1475, 6/6).

[2] Gino Capponi, *Geschichte d. florent. Republik*, translated by Dütschke, II, 129; Reumont, *Lorenzo de' Medici il Magnifico*, 2nd ed., II, 302.

[3] *Jahrbuch d. kunsthistor. Sammlungen des österr. Kaiserhauses*, Vienna, 1883. Urk., p. xxv.

found its way to Florence, and after the death of Tommaso Portinari was first taken over by his nephews Folcho and Benedetto and then by the firm Girolamo Frescobaldi e Compagni as Portinari's representatives in Bruges. In 1498 it came into the hands of Alemanno and Jacopo Salviati who deposited it in the Spedale di Santa Maria Nuova in Florence. Two years later it was handed over to Antonio by Pier Gualterotti and had not been redemeed by 1502.[1]

Folcho Portinari, one of Tommaso's nephews whom we have already mentioned, had in 1494 a claim of 3,800 £ Fl. against the city of Bruges, and in 1498 the Frescobaldi took a lease in his name of the Flemish customs on English wool which had been leased to his uncle.[2]

Tommaso Portinari also did signal service to King Henry VII of England. Later his sons Francesco and Guido settled altogether in England, where they were treated with special favour by the King. In 1554 a Portinari is mentioned who had served Henry VIII and Edward VI as a military engineer for fortifications.[3]

The last of the Medici mentioned in the Netherlands was Raffaele, who was a partner in the Gualterotti firm from 1513 to 1522, but was also a Knight of St. James and Imperial Chamberlain. The Guidetti also are very often mentioned at this time in connection with finance, but the first place had already been taken by other Florentine houses, especially the Frescobaldi and the Gualterotti.

The Frescobaldi and the Gualterotti. At the time when the Medici had ceased to count in the business world and the Fugger had not yet attained their predominant position, the Frescobaldi and the Gualterotti were the foremost financial powers in Europe, but not for long. Their importance rested entirely on their business in the Netherlands and England. There is scarcely any mention of it in Florence in 1470, when they still had no banks there; while Girolamo Frescobaldi, then twenty-six, was carrying on business in Bruges. He is mentioned in Bruges down to 1515, but before that date had a branch in Antwerp. Here he bought a piece of land and it gradually became the centre of gravity of the business. The Gualterotti, who are first named in 1489, did the same. In 1518 they had branches both in Bruges and Antwerp. Antwerp had been their centre since 1504 for the pepper import from Lisbon, organized on a joint basis, and they had shared in the expeditions of German and Italian business houses to the East

---

[1] Pagnini, *Della Decimi*, III, 294; Gachard, *Rapports sur les archives de Lille*, p. 69 ff.; Archives de Lille, *chambre des comptes*, B. 2152, 2160, 2163; Ulmann, *Kaiser Maximilian I*, 845 ff. (Brit. Mus. Add. Charters 1262, Brewer, *Calendar IV*, No. 6227 ff.)

[2] Gilliodts van Severen, *Invent. des Archives de Bruges*, VI, 386; Gachard, *Rapport sur les Archives de Lille*, p. 70.

[3] Brewer, *Calendar I*, 5434; *IV*, 2171. Turnbull, *Calendar, Queen Mary*, No. 196.

Indies.[1] Pure finance, however, occupied them more and more. Here Girolamo Frescobaldi and Filippo Gualterotti were the traders, but we meet many other names.

We have seen that in 1489 the Frescobaldi and the Gualterotti had lent large sums to the Burgundian Court, and that these had remained outstanding many years. Girolamo, or, as he was mostly called in the Netherlands and England, Jerôme Frescobaldi, had in 1494 a claim on the city of Bruges for 5,800 £ Fl., the largest claim of any individual with the exception of the agent of the King of Portugal.

In 1498, as we have seen, the Frescobaldi, representing Folcho Portinari, leased the Gravelinghen customs. From this time onwards they were in constant relations with the Netherlands finance administration; but the amounts of the transactions were usually small.[2] The Frescobaldi's business with the English Government began soon after the accession of Henry VIII, who lent large sums from the treasure accumulated by his father to Florentine merchants in order to develop their trade with England. The Frescobaldi as well as Guido Portinari and Giovanni Cavalcanti were among these favoured Florentines. They in their turn furnished the King with munitions and commodities and managed his payments abroad.[3]

In the beginning of 1516 the Frescobaldi enjoyed the confidence of the English Crown to such an extent that the King employed them to act as his agents in paying large subsidies to the Emperor Maximilian, though Bernhard Stecher, the Fugger's Antwerp agent, had previously pointed out to the English agents that the Frescobaldi were hardly in a position to carry out the transaction. This in fact turned out to be the case. The Florentines were unable to convey the money in time to Northern Italy, where the Emperor and his army then were; and Maximilian, as we have seen, was therefore forced to make an inglorious retreat. The Frescobaldi were accused of having been bribed by France. The King and Wolsey were extremely angry, while every one else believed that their delay had been due to secret instructions from the English King. In reality they had neither the means nor business connections in South Germany sufficient for such a transaction. Finally they had to borrow from the Fugger under the guarantee of the English Ambassador the sum of 60,000 fl. in order to relieve the Emperor's most pressing needs.[4] The inner weakness of the firm which became evident at this juncture led to its downfall two years later. The Frescobaldi

---

[1] Heyd, *Geschichte d. Levantehandels*, II, 523 ff. (French edition. II, 530 ff.).

[2] Lille, B. 2173, 2177, 2210, 2224, etc.

[3] Brewer, *Calendar I*, 022–9, 1413, 3410, 3496, 4068, etc.; Brown, *Calendar II*, 585.

[4] Cf. Brewer, II, Nos. 1384, 1475, 1736, 1792, 1816, 1928, 1937, 1968, 2023, 2034, 2153, 2113, 2166, 2230. Brown, II, 722, 730.

and the Cavallari from Lucca, who were closely connected with them in business, owed King Henry VIII the sum – enormous for those days – of £60,000, part of which was to be repaid in alum and salpetre, while the rest was to be kept at the King's disposal at any time. In the year 1517 a new agreement was concluded between the King and his debtors under which the debt was to be repaid in yearly instalments. In the following year, however, they were unable to pay the instalment.[1] Either from this cause or because the Frescobaldi had lost their credit for other reasons, the firm went bankrupt in May and June, 1518. Their Antwerp property had to be put up to auction and a composition was made with their creditors. In 1532 among the arrears due to the English Crown the claims on Filippo Frescobaldi and Antonio Cavallari were regarded as hopeless, and the Fugger too in 1527 wrote off their claim on Lionardo Frescobaldi e Fratelli as a bad debt. The total liabilities in 1518 were estimated at 300,000 ducats.[2]

In June, 1518, when the fall of the house was already inevitable, Cardinal Campeggio besought Wolsey to shield the Frescobaldi. The fact that a composition was reached shows that Wolsey did so. When, however, Leonardo Frescobaldi died, about 1529, Wolsey transferred the Frescobaldi's acknowledgments of indebtedness to third parties, who tried to obtain payment from the surviving members of the young Francesco, Leonardo's brother then asked Wolsey to continue the protection which had helped his father and brother.[3] Whether this request was granted we do not know. The Italian writer Bandello, who on his travels stayed in London, tells a tale of Francesco which if true – and Bandello is fairly reliable in such stories of his own time – sheds a friendly light on his further history.

According to this story Francesco, after living a long time in London, had returned to Florence.[4] Here he befriended a young Englishman who on his travels came to Florence in need of help. This was Cromwell, Wolsey's secretary and eventual successor. Frescobaldi meanwhile had been ruined and had nothing but a few doubtful arrears, among them 15,000 ducats in England. In order to collect these he went to London, where Cromwell, recognizing him in the street, took him home and gave him friendly entertainment. Cromwell helped him to make good his claims and offered him a large sum to found a new bank. Frescobaldi, however, wanted quiet and went back to Florence, where he died.

The house of Gualterotti lasted rather longer. It is mentioned in the Netherlands financial transactions till 1519, when they held a share of

---

[1] Brewer, Nos. 2953, 4004. Nos. 3098, 3141, 3491. Brown, II, 443.
[2] Marino Sanuto, *Diarii*, XXV, 427.
[3] Brewer, *Calendar IV*, 5974–5.
[4] Brewer, No. 2953 (No. 5974–5).

55,000 fl. in the large loans which Charles raised for his election as Emperor. They, however, probably lost heavily over the Frescobaldi, with whom they had business connections, or else political conditions told against their business in Antwerp. Anyhow, after the death of Filippo Gualterotti, who was the soul of his business, his son Francesco resolved to wind it up. He employed for this purpose Benedetto Gualterotti, who continued to be spoken of in Antwerp till 1529.[1]

End of the Florentines' Financial Transactions in the Netherlands and England. With the Gualterotti the last Florentine banking house of importance disappeared from the Netherlands. Gaspar Ducci, though mostly called a Florentine, really came from Pistoja, and in any case did not belong to the firms we are now discussing.

There were, however, even in later times, a considerable number of Florentine merchants in Antwerp, and they in 1546 were even granted a new privilege. Even those among them who, like Cavalcanti, were of some importance in England, were of very little account in Antwerp business.[2] The chief reason for this is probably that the business situation of the Florentine banking houses was increasingly embarrassed by their connection with the policy and finances of the French Crown. Here we have the counterpart of the relations of the Fugger and the Genoese in regard to Lyons. The financiers who had thrown in their lot with one of the parties contending for the mastery in Europe, could no longer hold out in the chief financial centre of the opposite party.

The development in England was quite different. Here Giovanni, Bernardo, and later Tommaso Cavalcanti, throughout the reign of Henry VIII held the first place in finance after the Bonvisi of Lucca. Tommaso Cavalcanti in 1544 was a chief creditor of the King, who for some years then had been unable to lend broadcast in his early manner and was forced to get more and more into debt. In order to do this he made use at first of the Italian merchants resident in London. Shortly before his death, however, the English Government learnt that they could borrow to better advantage in Antwerp, and this became the regular method under Henry's successors. The services of the Florentines were therefore no longer necessary. Tommaso Cavalcanti was, however, still in business in London in 1556, but he had no further connections with the finances of the Crown. The last remnants of their trade in England was soon taken from the Florentines by the English merchants. The descendants of the old Florentine merchant families still spoken of in England under Elizabeth had taken to other professions.[3]

[1] Cf. Lille, B. 2177, 2210, 2218, 2224, 2286; Gachard, *Rapports sur les Archives de Lille*, p. 70; *Antwerpener Schöffenbriefe*, 1525, 27/7.
[2] Priv. of 1546 in the *Liste des Édits de Charles V*, p. 295.
[3] Cf. Brewer, *Calendar I*, Nos. 1089, 3425, 3466, 3496, 3746, 5030 u. s. f.; Green, *Calendar Add.*, 1547–65, p. 436.

The Florentines in France. The Florentines' connection with France had lasted for some centuries before the opening of our present period. In early times it had been entirely an economic connection. The Florentines, in their capacity as merchants and bankers, had acquired great wealth in France, but at the same time had often done important service to the country and the Crown. Under Cosimo de' Medici the Elder, his son Piero and his grandson Lorenzo, the connection gained political importance, at first on the side of the Medici, to whom the French King's favour was important for their political ends. Since their opponents also sought this favour, the rivalry so developed only served to make Florentine policy dependent on France and to give the French the casting vote in Italian affairs.[1]

We shall see in detail later with what energy and success Louis XI and his successors strove to attract and keep at Lyons the international markets, which since the decay of the Champagne fairs had been held at Geneva, and which were of the greatest importance for the whole of Southern Europe. Their aim was chiefly the Florentine merchants. It is doubtful, however, whether Louis XI meant to entangle the Florentines in their relations with France to such an extent that they would never be able to free themselves. In any case, throughout his long reign he never tried to use his growing influence over the Florentines for his own political ends. His dislike for foreign wars is given as the explanation for this omission. In view of what is known of his character it is certain that Louis XI would not have taken such pains with the Florentines without some definite purpose. He must at least have wanted to put their trade and their capital as freely as possible at the disposal of France. This purpose was attained. It was not the military adventures of Charles VIII and his successors in Italy that brought lasting advantage to the French Crown, but the large increase of economic relations which had followed from the Lyons fairs.

In 1462 the King had pronounced his ban on the visits to the Geneva fairs, and in 1463 he transferred their privileges to Lyons. Immediately the Florentine merchants, who had previously done business in large numbers in Geneva, transferred their factories to Lyons. A factory of the Medici is mentioned there in 1464; and their first chief representative was Francesco Nori. The King at first does not seem to have done business with them on a large scale. A coolness moreover soon arose between Louis XI and the Medici, whom he accused of having advanced large sums to the King of England and the Duke of Burgundy for the war against France through their branches in London and Bruges. He accused Francesco Nori of having supported his enemies. On the discharge or recall of Nori, the coolness ceased. Even after this it appears

[1] Cf. Buser, *Die Beziehungen der Medicäer zu Frankreich,* pp. 33, 105 ff.

that the political and monetary interests of the Medici were often at odds, until the political interests finally won the day.[1]

About 1470 there were two Medici banks in Lyons. The chief bank ('e grandissimo,' according to Benedetto Dei) was that of Lorenzo e Giuliano Medici, Francesco Sassetti e Compagnia. Their chief agent was then Lionetto de Rossi, who gave his master Lorenzo de Medici even greater cause for discontentment than Tommaso Portinari. It is said that he managed so badly that the bank was several times on the verge of bankruptcy, and in 1481 Lorenzo insisted on the winding up of the Lyons factory. Lionetto de Rossi was, however, only recalled and the Medici business in France took a turn for the better under the steady hand of Cosimo Sassetti.[2]

The second Medici bank in Lyons belonged to the Pier Francesco branch of the family. It sent money to Florence and also carried on a trade in cloth.

There were also banks of the Pazzi, Capponi, Corsini, and Ghini Portinari and Company. About 1470 the Florentines already had in Lyons a consulate and their own church. There were besides large numbers of Florentine bankers and merchants in Avignon, Montpellier, Marseilles, and Aigues-Mortes.[3]

Important as Florentine interests in France already were, they were greatly increased by the fact that every one of the many revolutions in Florence ended with the banishment of many of the adherents of the defeated party and a great number found their way to Lyons. This happened in 1466, 1478, 1494, 1512, 1527, and after the fall of the Republic in 1530. This and the intermarriage of two daughters of the Medici with French Kings (1533 and 1600) made the number of Florentines settled in France, and until the middle of the sixteenth century especially in Lyons, so great that people could speak of 'a French Tuscany.' In order to get a clear idea of the importance of the Florentines in the French state, we only have to remember the two Strozzi, who were commanders by land and sea of the Duke of Luynes, the all-powerful minister of Louis XIII, an offshoot of the Florentine Alberti, of the Maréchal d'Ancre (Concini), the favourite of Marie de Médicis, of the Duc de Retz, Maréchal de France and High Chamberlain under Charles IX and Henry III, and his brother the Cardinal Gondi.[4] These

---

[1] Buser, pp. 119, 141, 156, 165 ff. Vaesen et Charavay, *Lettres de Louis XI*, vol. III, 43 ff., 251; Pagnini, *Della Decima*, II, 50.

[2] Buser, pp. 248, 294; Reumont, *Lorenzo de' Medici il Magnifico*, II, 301 ff.; Gingins, *Dépêches des ambassadeurs milanais*, II, 309; Kervyn de Lettenhove, *Lettres et négociations de Philippe de Commines*, I, 214, II, 83 ; Molini, *Documenti di storia italiana*, I, 13 ff.

[3] MS. of Benedetto Dei quoted in *Pagnini*, II, 304, cf. II, 50.

[4] As in L'Hermite de Solier, *La Toscane Française* (Paris, 1661).

brilliant figures are not, however, our chief interest. The people we deal with are men whose work made less stir, but left far deeper marks in the French state than that of the warriors and statesmen we have mentioned.

The Period 1494–1512. At the death of Lorenzo il Magnifico, in 1492, the direction of public affairs in Florence passed into the hands of his son Piero. The Duke of Milan, Lodovico Moro, was then trying to summon the French to Italy in order with their help to obtain supremacy in the peninsula. Piero de Medici accordingly found himself in a situation with which he could not cope. He refused to lend money to the French King Charles VIII, who was bent on trying his luck in Italy. The King accordingly borrowed the necessary money for his expedition from the Genoese under the Duke of Milan and banished the agents of the Medici from France.[1]

In Lyons it was feared that the other Florentines would also be banished, and this measure was actually threatened in order still further to excite the rage of the people of Florence against Piero de Medici and so by his fall to obtain support for the great French expedition. This two-edged measure was, however, not put into force. As the Florentine envoys then staying in France said in their letters to Piero, the Province Lyonnais would have lost a third of its revenues at the going of the Florentines.

The French King's anger was, however, only directed against the main branch of the Medici, whose business in France thus came to a sudden end. The other branch of the Medici, that of Pier Francesco, which was at enmity with the others, received special marks of favour from the King.

In November, 1494, Piero de Medici was driven from Florence. Amid general rejoicing King Charles made a state entry into the city and concluded a treaty with the Republic which secured to Florentine citizens the privilege of trading in his kingdom with the same rights as his own subjects. In return Florence promised to pay the King 120,000 gulden. These two clauses of the treaty, though hitherto they have excited little attention, are more important than those which relate to the cession of Pisa and other cities to the Florentines. They are specially notable for the fact that they were not broken.

The first to betray the Medici in this crisis and thus to seize the slipping reins of government was Piero Capponi. In all probability he had conspired to this end with the King, during the long months when he stayed with him as Florentine envoy during the preparations for the Italian expedition. On the fall of the Medici, when Charles was in their palace negotiating with Capponi about the treaty, he wished to impose

---

[1] Desjardins, *Négociations diplomat. de la France avec la Toscane,* I, 313, 408.

hard conditions on the Republic. Capponi is said to have torn up the draft treaty and to have replied to the King's angry exclamation, 'We will have the trumpets sounded,' 'We will ring our bells,' whereupon better terms were granted. This account of the proceedings cannot be accurate. We get a better glimpse into the play of the interacting forces when we notice that the Florentine war indemnity was paid either wholly or in part through the agency of the Capponi in Lyons; and that as late as 1498 the Capponi acted as agents for the letters between the Florentine Signoria and their envoys in France.[1]

The period of thirty-six years which followed, the final period of Florence as a free city, is filled with the struggles of the democracy, which sided mainly with the French and the Medici party which favoured or opposed the French in accordance with their own ends. There had then arisen the influential group of the Optimates, who supported the Medici and hoped to form a plutocratic government with their help.

In the first half of the period (1494–1512) democracy ruled, from 1502 onwards under the Gonfaloniere Piero Soderini. It might be thought that in these years there would have been constant and close economic and political connections between Florence and the French Crown. This, however, does not appear to have been so. There were many political disputes, especially about Pisa, which the French, contrary to their engagement, did not hand over to Florence. The King on his side made repeated demands on the Republic for money, which were either granted unwillingly or often not at all. The Republic did not wish to destroy its chances with the Emperor, and tried as far as possible to remain neutral, thus incurring the charge from the French side of favouring the policy of the Emperor.

In these circumstances it is not to be wondered at that so little is heard of financial transactions between Florentine merchants established in Lyons and the French Crown. This may be partly due to lack of information, but Machiavelli, who visited France three times at this period as the envoy of Florence, would surely not have passed it over in silence if the merchants of his country had then been very important to the French Crown.

After his third embassy (1510) he gives a detailed account of French finances, and especially of the extraordinary financial measures. He, however, says nothing as to floating debts raised from the Florentines.[2] On the other hand, we know that the Florentines living in the Netherlands, especially the Frescobaldi and Gualterotti, had frequent money

---

[1] Desjardins, I, 605; II, 20.
[2] Cf. Ritratti, *Delle Cose di Francia.*

dealings at this time both with the Emperor and the Netherlands Government, which was closely allied to him both dynastically and politically. It appears therefore that the Florentines were then not very dependent on the French Crown in an economic sense. The fact is noteworthy that the Florentines who played the chief part in Antwerp belonged to other families than those who had their chief business in Lyons and that the trade of the latter no doubt extended still further in this period, and thus increased the community of interests between France and Florence.

Jacopo Salviati and Filippo Strozzi, 1512–27. In 1512 the Medici returned to Florence and the political relations with France became distinctly cooler. In the following year a Medici became Pope as Leo X and Florentine policy became entirely dependent on that of the Papal Curia, which was swayed by other motives than the monetary interests of the Florentine merchants. These nevertheless now became important politically. They were incarnated in the persons of the Pope's brother-in-law and trusted adviser, Jacopo Salviati, and in Filippo Strozzi, the son of that Filippo Strozzi 'the Elder' who had made his fortune in Naples. He, like Jacopo Salviati, had married a Medici and had been nominated by the Pope as Depositario of his revenues. These men were undoubtedly the two most distinguished citizens of Florence. As leaders of the Optimates they had helped largely in restoring the Medici and were now their chief supporters. Above all, they were both at the head of large banks which had branches both in Rome and Lyons. Our sources unfortunately do not enable us to follow out in detail the connection of all these relations; they leave no doubt, however, that such a connection must have existed.

In 1515 Francis I came to the French throne and immediately embarked on the expedition to Italy which resulted in the victory of Marignano and the conquest of Milan. Pope Leo was long undecided which party to choose, and we hear that his reflections at this time turned on the business interests of the Florentines in France.[1] Nevertheless he maintained the alliance with Spain and only went over to the French side after Marignano, hoping by so doing to ensure the supremacy of his family.

At this time we again hear of large financial transactions between the Florentine merchants in Lyons and the French Crown. In contrast to his predecessor Louis XII, Francis I was a prodigal prince, splendour loving and open-handed. His coronation cost enormous sums, more than the first expedition to Italy. The customary extraordinary forced loans from his subjects now proved totally insufficient. Loans had to be

---

[1] Gino Capponi, *Geschichte d. florent. Republik.* German trans. by Hans Dütschke, II, 291.

raised from the Florentines in Lyons on the security of future revenues. In the beginning of 1516 he owed them apparently 300,000 écus, which fell due but could not be repaid, and the Lyons Fair settling days had accordingly to be extended. The loan, however, still remained unpaid, as the royal finances were entirely exhausted. Nevertheless in April more money was raised for an expedition to Italy, which, however, did not come off. This was done by pledging the salt tax to some Florentines. At this time the Salviati had the largest business house in Lyons. The Pope used all his power to further their interest even in regard to the French King. When in 1518 Francis was planning a crusade against the Turks, for which the Pope had granted money, he wished that this money should be deposited in the Salviati's bank in Lyons, but the King did not agree.[1]

Jacopo Salviati stayed in Rome, and was therefore able to keep a good watch over his financial interests. Filippo Strozzi, on the other hand, returned to Florence, where Lorenzo Medici honoured him, but kept him as far as possible from state affairs. Only when Giulio Medici, who was Filippo Strozzi's brother-in-law and most intimate friend, became the most important man in the state, Filippo obtained great influence and began to neglect his business. After Pope Leo's death he was sent to Rome in 1521 and found the affairs of his bank in great disorder. His credit had been gravely affected by bad management and a large failure in Naples. He managed, however, to put things straight again and to maintain the honour of his house. Pope Adrian VI made him Treasurer of the Curia, and under Clement VII he went even farther. With him he was on a very confidential footing and served him in a most liberal manner without commercial calculation, for he was far too ambitious and restless to be able, like Jacopo Salviati, to combine his monetary interests with his political aims. Both men succeeded, however, in getting their sons into the College of Cardinals. We shall soon see that in the Italian wars of the French King the Florentines must have transacted a large amount of financial business for him; but their economic dependence on the French Crown only developed very gradually. In the election of the King of the Romans in 1519 they did nothing for Francis, while the Gualterotti, as we know, shared in the loans by which the House of Hapsburg secured the election.

In 1521 the King ordered all the property of the Florentines in Paris, Lyons and Bordeaux to be seized. Everything was inventoried and a watch was set on the houses. This, it was said, had come about because the Florentine bankers had betrayed the war preparations by their letters to Flanders and other countries of the Empire. Moreover, they

---

[1] Canestrini, *Négoc. dipl. de la France avec la Toscane*, II, 761, 765, 770. Brewer, *Calendar II*, No. 1393. Marino Sanuto, *Diarii*, XXII, 167; XXVI, 259, 303.

had promised the King a loan of 100,000 écus, but afterwards had lent this money to the Emperor in return for a charge on the revenues of Naples. In the following year the Emperor complained that the Florentines, who had been unwilling to advance him on good security 20,000 ducats, had now engaged troops for the French King without asking for security.[1] We see therefore that the Florentines were still wavering. It needed events of a different order entirely to destroy the neutrality of Florentine capital.

The Period 1527–30. The sack of Rome by the Emperor's troops in 1527 brought heavy loss to the Florentines who lived or had factories in that city. This catastrophe, however, was only a beginning of a series which affected their trade yet more adversely. The next of these events was the second expulsion of the Medici from Florence. The group of Optimates who were specially influential in the last years of the Republic contained many different elements. Their chief common characteristic was that they aimed at a government of the distinguished and rich. These aims naturally did not appeal to the people. The Optimates therefore sided with the Medici and the Medici with them. Their relationship was, however, quite peculiar. The Medici made use of the leaders of the Optimates with their distingusihed kinsman Pope Clement VII, and they also helped them in business; but they tried to keep these dubious friends as far as possible out of Florentine politics. The Optimates' most respected leader, Jacopo Salviati, was kept by the Pope constantly busy in Rome, and Clement was not displeased that he as well as the other great Florentine bankers should incur popular hatred in the Papal State on account of the financial transactions which they undertook in the service of the Curia. Further, when, in 1527, the Pope, either from imprudence or stinginess, had disbanded his troops so that he was overcome practically without resistance by the Imperial forces, he had the report spread that Jacopo Salviati was to blame for this. It was only on his deathbed that the Pope withdrew this false charge which had made Salviati hated throughout Italy. In 1526 the Pope had been besieged in St. Angelo by Colonna, instigated by Hugo di Moncado, an emissary of the Emperor, and had been forced to come to an agreement with Moncado. He had then handed over Filippo Strozzi as a hostage and had neglected to ransom him. Strozzi, however, was released by Moncado in order to turn Florence away from the Medici. He, however, returned to the Pope, and waited a year for the moment for taking revenge and achieving his party's end.[2]

---

[1] *Journal d'un bourgeois de Paris sous le règne de François I*, ed. Lalanne, p. 103. Bergenroth, *Calendar II*, 407.

[2] Cf. Varchi, *Stor. Fior.* Lib. II, Filippo Strozzi's biography by his brother Lorenzo and Machiavelli's letters to Guicciardini.

After the sack of Rome he hurried with his wife to Florence, bringing the first certain news of the great catastrophe. Helped by his wife and another leader of the Optimates, Niccolo Capponi (whose father Piero Capponi had been the chief actor in the expulsion of the Medici in 1494), Filippo Strozzi managed to get the Medici out of the city under his protection, and thus remained on good terms with them. This rendered him suspect to the people, who anyway hated the Optimates. Niccolo Capponi, however, still retained the confidence of the majority and was chosen Gonfaloniere. Even he, however, in spite of his undoubted honesty, was the subject of violent attacks.

In 1528, after his wife's death, Strozzi left Florence for Lyons, giving business there as his reason. There he occupied himself with study and had dealings only with the Florentines in Lyons, with whom he made himself very popular. On one occasion, during a famine when the rich Florentines were threatened by the people, Strozzi organized the defence, arming all men capable of bearing arms and so saving the city from the looting which threatened it.

Meanwhile Niccolo Capponi was deprived of his office as Gonfaloniere, tried and only just escaped being sentenced. The attempt to bring in a government of Optimates thus utterly failed, and for a while the Democrats ruled once more. But their days, too, were numbered. In the summer of 1529 Charles V came to an agreement with the Pope which brought the Emperor the grant of the profitable Cruzada and other ecclesiastical sources of income. The price of this agreement was the Republic of Florence.

At this time the Venetian envoy Suriano gives us the following account of the Florentines' business: 'The Crown of France owes private persons in Florence 600,000 ducats. In Rome the Florentines have spent 350,000 ducats on buying offices. They suffered great losses at the sack of Rome. Formerly Florence alone made a profit of 8,000 ducats a week from goods delivered to Rome, but now only 1,000 ducats or a little more, since intercourse with Rome has been forbidden for fear they should again come to depend on the Pope. Trade in commodities with Naples has been destroyed by the war; the export of silks and brocades to France has likewise been destroyed by the war and the secession of Genoa to the Emperor's side. Trade with Flanders has been stopped by the closing of the Venetian territory. These barriers are, however, circumvented, and in spite of all these losses and hindrances the Florentines are still extremely rich. Eight or ten families have about 100,000 ducats apiece. Tomasso Guadagni is said to have 400,000 ducats, though most of it is in France; Ruberto Degli Albizzi about 250,000, Pier Salviati 200,000; the Bartolini, Antinori, Soderini, Strozzi, and others, each more than 100,000. More than eighty families have between 50,000 and 100,000, and the number with property worth less than 50,000 ducats cannot be counted.'[1]

Among the families here named as the richest, the Salviati and the Strozzi at any rate belonged to the party of the Optimates. The Florentine historian Varchi also calls Pier Salviati very rich, and says that he was one of those who lived in the grand style, not like merchants, but like nobles. The Guadagni, the Albizzi, as well as the Salviati, had apparently made most of their money in France. The firm of Tommaso Guadagni e Compagni is mentioned in Lyons in 1508, and Ruberto Albizzi in 1523, both in unimportant financial dealings with the French Crown.[2] Salviati's transactions, however, were more important, and here we must pause for a moment.

In June, 1528, Clerk, the English envoy in Paris, was trying to defend himself against Wolsey, who charged him with having used Piero Spino as an agent for a payment to the French King though he knew him to be in the service of the Genoese Antonio Vivaldi and on the side of the Emperor. Clerk answered: 'And as for this man, he is a Florentyn, on that hath contynuyd and folowyd the Frenche Courte many yerys, and on that hath made and makith contynually all the great exchanges that hath ben by th King for his affayres of Italy, whither th Frenche King hath not always sent redy monay, as your Grace can right well considre if he wer imperyall, the Frenche King and other of the Counsaill here wold not use hym, and trust hym with ther monay, as they have don and dayly doo.' . . .[3]

This Piero Spino or Spina was apparently an important person in connection with the French King's financial dealings. Like Lazarus Tucher, Gaspar Ducci and Hans Kleberg, he was half financial agent and half banker. He is mentioned in 1524, just before the battle of Pavia. He was then sent by King Francis in order to look after a convoy of munitions to Cardinal Salviati, a son of Jacopo Salviati, and at this time Papal legate in Lombardy. At the beginning of 1527 Pope Clement VII was, as we know, in a critical position and besought the French King for help. After long hesitation it was decided to give Piero Spino 10,000 scudi to be sent to Lyons, where with the 20,000 scudi already there, they were to be given to the Salviati for transmission to Italy. In February, 1529, it is reported that the Salviati undertook for the King a payment to Italy of 30,000 scudi.[4] A Tucher business letter of 1532 mentions Leonardo Spino as the Salviati's agent in Lyons.

[1] Albéri, Rélat. d. Ambasc. Venet., Ser. II, vol. V, p. 420 ff.

[2] Pagnini, Della Decima, I, 129; Tardif, Monuments historiques, No. 2957.

[3] Brewer, Calendar, No. 4390 ; full text in State Papers, Henry VIII, vol. VII, p. 83.

[4] Canestrini, Négoc. dipl. II, 808, 887, 1049.

This all seems to show that the Spini had close business connections with the Salviati and that Piero was probably their representative at the French Court.

To return for a moment to the Venetian envoy's report in 1529. Even supposing its figures are not quite accurate, it shows at least that the large Florentine bankers in the year 1529 had invested a considerable part of their property in France and chiefly in the towns of the French Crown. This was when the agreement between the Emperor and the Pope had already sealed the doom of the Republic. In vain Florence besought the French King for help: he gave nothing but empty promises. As he had deserted Genoa, so now in the peace of Cambrai he abandoned Florence. He never even sent help in money to any considerable extent. He had just ransomed his sons from the Emperor for the enormous sum of 1,200,000 crowns and had nothing to spare for Florence. The Republican Florentines in Lyons entreated him to pay at least a part of his debts to them as they fell due, but he only sent 30,000 scudi to Italy through the Salviati in 1529. When in the year following it was proposed to repay the same amount, this proposal was forbidden by the Papal legate, who appealed to the Treaty of Cambrai.[1]

A few of these Republicans in Lyons, among them Ruberto degli Albizzi, succeeded in getting together another 20,000 ducats. Those who shared their views in England and the Netherlands also collected a little money – not much, for the Florentines in those countries were now neither numerous nor specially rich – and moreover they did not all favour the Republic. The Florentines in Venice gave nothing, in spite of frequent entreaties. Few too of the Optimates came to the help of the Republic in its extremity. The Consul of the Florentines in London, a Carducci, obtained money from King Henry VIII, but as he went bankrupt immediately the King lost more than 50,000 ducats. All help was, however, vain; the Republic was lost.

It is not our business to inquire into the importance of this event in the history of Italy. It is important for us to ascertain the effect on Florentine business of the loss of their freedom and the final supremacy in Italy which the House of Austria obtained after its long struggle with France.

The Florentines now put their business and their capital almost exclusively at the disposal of the French Crown, which had so long deserted their cause.

In Rome and Naples the Florentine bankers were soon completely driven out by the Genoese; in the Netherlands by the Genoese and the

[1] Canestrini, II, 1003 ff., 1049. Gayangos, *Calendar IV*, 1, pp. 375, 522, 691. Varchi, ed. *Arbib.* II, 323, 361 ff. Brewer, *Calendar IV*, 6774.

South Germans; in England by the English merchants. They had never played a prominent part in finance in Spain. Their finances in France developed in consequence all the more vigorously.[1]

An important fact, which has hitherto escaped the notice of historians, is that the victory of the House of Austria drove Genoese capital into the Imperial Spanish camp, while it made Florentine capital entirely French.

No doubt political and economic forces combined to produce this development. The political causes were decisive, but they again had economic roots. If the greater part of the rich Florentine families sympathized with the French, this was because their monetary interests bound them to France. They could not free themselves; the community of interests between them and the French Crown became closer and closer. Many of them hated the Medici; and when banishments on a large scale began once more, the Florentine colony in Lyons became a hotbed of conspiracy against the new Tuscan dynasty. Many left their country of their own free will, because there was no opening for their energies. Political confusion and speculation meant ruin. Anyone who could not make terms with the new order had to try his luck abroad. No place offered such favourable conditions to the Florentines as France, where they were welcomed at the Court with open arms; for the enemies of the Medici were enemies of the Emperor. These refugees from Florence therefore for a long time cherished the hope of driving out the Medici by means of French help. There were several attempts, though the refugees had to help themselves almost entirely. The French Court made all possible use of them, learnt from them all it could and accepted their good money very joyfully, but never again involved itself in Italian adventures. The marriages of the daughters of the Medici with French princes made no difference, as they were not important for French foreign policy. Both before and afterwards Tuscany under Hapsburg protection counted among the enemies of France.

The Strozzi after 1530. Capponi had died just before the fall of the Republic. The other leaders of the Optimates, Jacopo Salviati and Filippo Strozzi, directly afterwards tried to realize the aim of their party, the creation of an oligarchy under the leadership of the Medici. Pope Clement, however, was now aiming at an absolute monarchy, and in this plan he made skilful use of the leaders of the Optimates, so that all the popular hatred fell to their share. When they had done their part and Alessandro de' Medici was Duke of Florence, he soon rid himself of such questionable adherents. Filippo Strozzi, who had played the chief rôle in the comedy the Pope had arranged, was accused of having wished

---

[1] For Rome, cf. Reumont, *Geschichte der Stadt Rom*, III b, 449 ff., 583; for Naples, Rocco, *De' banchi di Napoli*, p. 3 ff.

to poison the Duke, and though he established his innocence he thought it better to go to Rome.

Here Strozzi came to an arrangement with the Curia, but he could only get his claims recognized by renouncing many years of accrued interest. When, in 1533, the Pope had betrothed the youthful Catherine de' Medici to Prince Henry of France, he asked Filippo Strozzi to escort the bride to Marseilles. He wished to utilize the Strozzi's credit in order to pacify the French Court on the subject of Catherine's dowry. Filippo accepted this task and promised to pay over the dowry of 130,000 scudi within a year. At the wish of the Pope, who was anxious to get him out of Italy, he remained, though much against his will, for six months longer as Papal legate at the French Court, where he made himself much loved by the King.

Meanwhile Filippo's son Piero was imprisoned in Florence on a false charge. His father complained in vain both to the Pope and Alessandro, and it was only after a long interval that Piero regained his liberty. He thereupon set out for France, and meeting his father in Lyons, he told him that the Duke had obviously decided not to suffer the Strozzi to remain in Florence any longer.

This was in 1534, when the Pope was very ill. Filippo Strozzi found himself, at the French King's wish, on the journey to Rome, where it was intended that he should further French interests in the case of the election of a new pope. This journey met Filippo's wishes all the better because there were still arrears of 60,000 scudi outstanding on Catherine's dowry. When he reached Rome the Pope was already dead.

As we know, the Florentines, and more especially the Strozzi, were hated by the Roman populace as the directors of the Papal finance. At the time we speak of, the people thought that they had a special reason for this hatred. The Strozzi in Rome had promised to provide the Eternal City with corn from Sicily at an agreed price. The Viceroy of Naples had, however, forbidden the export of the wheat, so that the Strozzi's agents had had to import it from distant countries – Brittany, and even Flanders – a thing which very rarely happened. Some cargoes, moreover, were lost by shipwreck, and others arrived behind time. There was a famine in Rome, and the people in their anger tried to destroy the Strozzi's house.

This was the state of things which Filippo Strozzi found on his return to Rome. He took it greatly to heart; and when he noticed that his credit was suffering, he made over the Roman business to two Cardinals on terms very unfavourable to himself. The new Pope, Paul III, demanded the return of the ecclesiastical revenues and other valuable objects pledged to Strozzi on account of the arrears of Catherine de' Medici's dowry. Filippo was clever enough to accede to this demand, and the Pope thereupon recognized his predecessor's engagements, so that Strozzi once again only lost the interest.

Meanwhile he tried to liquidate his property in Florence. This, however, did not succeed as he had hoped, for the property was valued at over half a million. Nevertheless he did not return to Florence and his relations with the Duke Alessandro became steadily more unfriendly. Filippo joined the movement of the banished Republicans and accused the Duke of having tried to have him assassinated.

The Florentine Republicans now (1535) for a short time pinned their faith to the Emperor, but soon saw that nothing was to be expected from him. He protected Alessandro in spite of all his crimes, and finally gave him his daughter in marriage. The banished Florentines were thus thrown once more entirely on the French side. The Cardinal du Bellay, then French ambassador in Rome, was nevertheless nervous lest these negotiations with the Emperor should succeed and warned Strozzi not to take part in them. In order to exert still greater pressure the King had Filippo's agent in Lyons, Gian Francesco Bini, imprisoned on account of the 30,000 scudi still owing on Catherine de' Medici's dowry, and this in spite of the fact that the King had for a long time himself been owing Bini a larger sum. This incident, however, seems to have been cleared up when the Florentine negotiations with the Emperor broke down.

The renewed outbreak of war between the Emperor and France once more awakened the hopes of the Florentine exiles. King Francis, they thought, would go to Italy with a large army to set Florence free. They accordingly contributed to the cost of the French armament with advances of money. The agents of Filippo Strozzi in Lyons advanced 15,000 écus, although their master could not as yet be counted among the avowed enemies of the Medici.

When the news of Filippo's shares in the French war loans was brought – in an exaggerated form – to the Emperor, he caused Strozzi's property in Naples and Sicily to be confiscated. Strozzi now feared that the same thing would happen in other parts of the Empire, where he had money owing to him, and he was in fact forbidden under a heavy penalty to have financial dealings with the French Court. He accordingly sent his son Piero in all haste to Lyons to get the transaction annulled. This, however, was not necessary as no further steps were taken against the Strozzi. The sending of Piero, however, in itself turned out very badly for his father, because King Francis caused the young man to take part in the war in Piedmont against the Imperial forces, and even made him a commander. His father, much incensed, tried in vain to turn him from his decision, and as he no longer felt safe in Rome, went to Venice.

The Emperor had hitherto refused to yield to the pressure of the Duke of Florence and have him proscribed, but he now gave him up. Hereupon Filippo and his sons Piero and Ruberto, together with many of their friends, were declared rebels, and all the goods of the Strozzi in Florence were confiscated. Filippo now had his employees in Venice and Lyons informed that if they wished they could leave his service, since it was forbidden to serve rebels. They all, however, declared that they would not leave him, so that Filippo's commercial interests did not suffer.

He now lived quietly under the protection of the Signoria of Venice and occupied himself chiefly in study, till one night Lorenzo di Pier Francesco de' Medici came to him and told him that he had just assassinated the Duke Alessandro. This was the signal for Strozzi to begin open war against the dominion of the Medici. Under the advice of the French envoy in Venice he joined the Cardinals Salviati and Ridolfi, who had both been among the chief opponents of the murdered Duke. A coup was prepared against Florence. Cosimo de' Medici was, however, at once chosen Duke, and the Emperor sent troops to Florence which were more than a match for their opponents. They accordingly wished to give up the game. The French, however, now interfered, promising to support them with money to hire troops. Here the prime mover was the Cardinal de Tournon, the Governor of the Province Lyonnais. Strozzi, however, answered that the favourable moment was past, and the opposing party were now too powerful. Moreover, he had never been repaid the 15,000 scudi which he had lent the Cardinal on the King's account some months before in Lyons for the war in Piedmont. Evidently the King wanted to make war at Strozzi's expense. The French envoy in Venice hereupon declared that the King would give 20,000 scudi if the Florentine exiles would do the same. The exiles, however, would not agree and sent Bartolomeo Cavalcanti to the King to inform him as to the state of the case and to tell him that the undertaking could not be carried out unless he granted 100,000 scudi.

Meanwhile the French King had sent Filippo 15,000 scudi and urged him to free his country with this exiguous sum. Piero was also working in the same direction. He had hired troops which he could not keep together without a war and he wanted to earn laurels. Filippo, however, stood his ground. He laid stress on the fact that the undertaking had no hope of success, and declared that it was for princes and republics to keep up armies and not for private people. Hereupon his own son and the other exiles accused him of putting his own profit before his country. The French advanced no more money, so that Piero had to disband his troops, and went to Rome. At last, against his better judgment, Filippo gave in so as to avoid the hatred of his friends and kinsmen. He paid 20,000 scudi, and said that he would make further contributions if the exiles did the same. The enterprise failed. Filippo was taken prisoner, and in all probability secretly murdered. The victorious Duke meanwhile spread the report that he had killed himself after writing on the wall of his cell in his own blood the words, 'Exoriare aliquis.' (May some (avenger) arise.) We have seen what matter-of-fact considerations played a decisive part even in Filippo Strozzi's last venture, and it is on this account that we have treated it in detail. The sad end of the man called with many others the 'richest man in Italy' made a deep impression on his contemporaries.

Two of his sons took military service under the French – Piero became Maréchal, Leo, the Prior of Capua, an admiral. They both remained bitter enemies of the Medici. The fact that their service was chiefly military did not, however, prevent them from giving the attentions to finance which was demanded by its importance in war. In 1546 the Schmalkaldian League sent Jacob Sturm of Strassburg to France to negotiate with the King about a treaty and the grant of subsidies. Sturm got into touch with the Maréchal Strozzi, who offered to put the sums paid by the King to himself at the disposition of the League on security without interest. Strozzi on this occasion showed great technical knowledge of finance. The same thing is reported of him again in 1557.[1]

Two other members of another branch of the family, Giulio and Lorenzo Strozzi, settled in Lyons after the great revolution of 1530. They founded a banking house, which participated in the loans of the French Crown as early as 1536–7. In 1576 the firm was called Alfonso e Lorenzo Strozzi. They then used the Genoese bill fairs, but their domicile was certainly Lyons. On the other hand Lorenzo Strozzi, who is mentioned as a financier under Henry III, had already moved to Paris.

Other Developments of Florentine Business in France until the Death of Henry II, 1559. Our sources do not enable us to follow in detail the relations of the different Florentine businesses to the French Crown in the century following the fall of the Republic and we must content ourselves with a general sketch.

In the first period, which extends to the financial crisis of 1557 and the death of Henry II, the firms we already know, the Salviati Capponi, Albizzi, Guadagni and Strozzi, still play the chief part. Their financial relations with the French Crown were first managed by the Cardinal de Tournon, Governor of the Province Lyonnais. In June, 1537, he was granted powers to give security on the royal revenues for the sums lent to the King by Tommaso Guadagni, heir of Tommaso the Elder and also

[1] Sturm's Report in Augsbg. Stadtarchive. Brown, *Calendar VI*, 904.

of Olivieri Guadagni. In August this process was repeated and in April, 1538, the Guadagni and the Delbene, a family which had just begun to come forward, shared in the lease of the salt tax effected through the Cardinal. In 1543 Albizzo Delbene, together with Tommaso Certini (?) took a lease of the alum import for ten years, and Albizzo's brother Alberto Delbene was sent in 1548 by the King to the Pope to promise him 350,000 scudi of subsidy, in case of an attack from the Emperor, though in fact no such attack was thought of. In 1559 Albizzo Delbene still belonged to the Florentines who followed the French Court.[1]

In 1545 the firm Averardo Salviati e Compagni in Lyons secretly tried to induce South German merchants to share in the loans of the French Crown and were also in touch with Antwerp for the same purpose. These attempts, as we have seen, were successful. We have a list from the year 1553 giving the shares of the Florentine business houses in the French loans. They amount to a total of 523,075 écus, not so much as the South Germans and Swiss with 720,925 écus, but nevertheless a large sum, which in the next few years increased greatly. The Salviati in 1553 advanced a further sum of 99,325 écus to the King.[2]

This was the period of the Sienese war. Pier Strozzi as a French Maréchal defended the Republic of Siena, threatened by the Duke of Florence, Cosimo, and the Spaniards. The money he used to pay his troops was produced in great part – like the leadership of the undertaking – by the Florentine exiles. Siena fell in 1555, but the war nevertheless continued and the Florentines in Lyons tried to spur King Henry II to fresh efforts.

In 1556, Bindo Altoviti concluded in the name of the Florentine exiles a loan with the King's representatives. This amounted to 300,000 écus, at 16 per cent., and Altoviti made himself personally liable for its repayment. In August of the same year the King through the Maréchal Strozzi once again borrowed 300,000 écus in Lyons at 16 per cent. interest. Of this amount 120,000 écus was obtained from the Florentines, in whose name Albizzo Delbene acted for the Guadagni; and 180,000 écus from the South Germans under Israel Minckel and Georg Obrecht. The whole sum was forwarded to Venice by the firm Lorenzo Capponi e Tommaso Rinuccini, which then managed the Guadagnis' business in Lyons, and it was used to pay the Pope's subsidies. The loans grew at an enormous rate. The Maréchal Strozzi was dissatisfied with these transactions. At the beginning of 1557 he stated that these loans

---

[1] *Actes de François I*, vol. III, 9055, 9252-3, 9956; IV, 13255. Desjardins, Canestrini, *Négoc. diplomat*, III, 232, 398.

[2] Seiler Correspondence in Augsbg. St.-A.; Behaim Papers in German. Museum; Bibl. Coste in Lyon, No. 6933.

cost the King 23 per cent., i.e. 16 per cent. for interest, 4 per cent. on loss on the bill transactions with Venice, and 3 per cent. on account of the depreciation of the currency.[1]

A few months later came the inevitable crash and the French Crown stopped payment. This was followed in 1559 by the peace of Cateau Cambresis, which made an end of the political hopes of the Florentine exiles; and a few months later by the death of Henry II, which was equally final for their loans. In vain Leonardo Spino put in claims on behalf of the Florentine creditors of the Crown, chiefly the Capponi Albizzi and Salviati. Many efforts were made to come to a composition. The Florentines must, however, have lost the greater part of their money, as we can prove to have been the case, with the South Germans.[2] Of the rich Florentine families which had a leading position in Lyons at this time, the Guadagni and the Albizzi immediately disappear from the ranks of financiers. The firm Pietro Salviati e Compagni appears once more in 1563 in the business papers of the Welser and is not mentioned again. We meet Madame Delbene in financial dealings in 1582, and the Capponi bank was in existence in Lyons as late as 1594. These firms had, however, ceased to play a prominent part in finance: they had given place, either voluntarily or of necessity, to others among their own compatriots.

The Time of Charles IX and Henry III. The chief feature which distinguishes this period from the preceding one is the transfer of the chief centre of Florentine finance from Lyons to Paris. In the last stage it ceased altogether at Lyons. In 1575 there were only a few Florentine houses still left there; in 1592 the Capponi alone remained, and two years later their firm was taken over by the Zametti of Lucca.

The first Florentines, who under Charles IX, or rather under the Regency of Catherine de' Medici, again dared to have financial dealings with the Crown, were Orazio Rucellai and Lodovico Diaceto. The first had left Florence as an opponent of the Medici, and the second had fled on account of a murder. Both had then acquired property in Lyons. When the Huguenot rising of 1562 was put down in Lyons, the lease of the Lyons Douane was transferred to Diaceto. The Douane was an institution very dangerous to the fairs, and Diaceto so greatly damaged trade by his exactions that the city, which had previously held the customs itself, did everything to recover them. Though it offered as much as Diaceto, he was preferred, because a favourite of Catherine's was his sleeping partner. The lease of the domains in Picardy was then transferred to him, in spite of the opposition of the people. By this time he himself was then numbered among the favourites of the King and the Queen Mother – a position he owed chiefly to his liberality and the

---

[1] R. Brown, *Calendar VI*, 314, 330, 587, 649, 904.
[2] Desjardins, l.c. III, 400; Albéri, *Relaz d. Ambasc. Venet.*, VIII, 424.

splendour of his appearance. The King nominated him Court Chamberlain. He then moved to Paris, where he built a splendid palace, spending 150,000 écus on its decoration. In order to enter the ranks of the French nobility and to marry one of their daughters, he bought Château-Vilain, which carried the title of Count, for 400,000 francs. He gained the means for this style of living by further financial dealings, which he continued during the reign of Henry III until the great investigation which was brought against the financiers in 1584. He then disappears from the scene. Henry IV remitted to his widow the sums which her husband was still owing on the lease of the Lyons customs, presumably after the strict accounting which followed the inquiry of 1584.[1]

It was also during the rising of the Huguenots in 1562 that Orazio Rucellai came into relations with the Crown, which was then without credit and had tried in vain to raise money in Antwerp. Rucellai's bank in Lyons came to the rescue and received the Crown jewels in pawn. This business connection seems to have lasted. Orazio is not mentioned in our authorities till Henry III. In 1581 he had taken the lease of the Gabelle, the notorious tax on salt. He demanded a reduction in the rent on the ground that he was suffering great loss through frauds. He was able to obtain this reduction because Monsieur d'O, the Surintendant des Finance, and the Chancellor Chiverny themselves were interested in the lease. Rucellai belonged to the King's Conseil, and even in the great inquiry of 1584 he remained at first untouched. Later it was extended to him, but he seems to have got off scot-free. Next year, in any case, he was still mentioned as making advances to the French Crown. A fresh inquiry in the year 1588 into the abuses which had taken place during the lease of the Gabelle in the years 1578–88 was originally directed chiefly at Orazio Rucellai, of whom we hear nothing further in finance. He had at this time already returned to Florence and he reappeared at the French Court at the opening of the inquiry, not to make money, but to negotiate the marriage of the Archduke Ferdinand (with whom he was now in high favour) with a French princess. He brought this affair to a successful conclusion, and this silenced the attacks on his previous financial administration. He remained from this time onwards in Paris, where he died rich and respected in 1605.[2] The next Florentine, who came to the front as a financier under Henry III, was Girolamo Gondi, who, however, was only a collateral of the French main line of this family. Antonio, the ancestor of the French Gondi, had emigrated to France in 1527, where he later had a dis-

[1] Clerjon, *Histoire de Lyon*, VI, 13 ff. Picot, *Histoire des Etats Généraux*, III, 32. Desjardins, l.c. IV, 189, 205, 510, 533. Ammirato, *Fam. nob. Fiorent.*, pp. 18, 137. Tardif, *Monum. histor.* No. 3512.

[2] Desjardins, III, 493; IV, 359, 433, 538 ff. Picot, III, 117, 199 ff. *Archives curieuses de l'histoire de France*, Ser. I, XVII, p. 51 ff.

tinguished position at the Court of Henry II, having been already ennobled. His sons were: Albert Duc de Retz, Pair de France, Maréchal
and Generalissimo of the French Army, Lord Chamberlain under
Charles IX and Henry III, Gouverneur de la Provence, etc., and Pierre
Cardinal Gondi, Archbishop of Paris, President of the Conseil d'Etat
under Charles IX, Henry III and Henry IV. Albert's descendants intermarried with the oldest French nobility. It has been pointed out that
the Magdalena Gondi, who in 1455 married Giovanni Salviati and was
the ancestress of Cosimo de' Medici, first Duke of Florence, was through
Cosimo's granddaughter Maria de' Medici also the ancestress of the
French Kings from Louis XIII and of the last reigning Stuarts.
Girolamo Gondi belonged, however, to another branch. He was in any
case not a protégé of his distinguished cousins, but of the Cardinal
Birague, an Italian who had a share in his business, as the Duke of
Retz had in those of Vidiville, the first Frenchman who managed to
penetrate the circle of the great financiers hitherto in practice, excluding
Italians. Girolamo Gondi is mentioned under Henry IV as late as 1599.
The Archduke Ferdinand I of Tuscany had since 1593, and perhaps
earlier, advanced large sums to the Kings through the agency and in the
name of Gondi. They amounted in all to 1,298,955 écus, and were an
important help to Henry in his struggle for the Crown. Nevertheless
the King, when the victory was won, on Sully's advice withdrew from
Gondi and the other old 'Partisans' the revenues they had leased, so that
even the Archduke, in spite of repeated warnings, had a claim of 517,989
écus outstanding in 1619.[1]

With Girolamo Gondi the last member of the old Florentine families
disappeared from French finance.

In the case of the Italians who did this business down to the time of
Colbert it is often impossible to determine where they were born. In the
case of a few of the most distinguished we know that they did not come
from Florence. For a long time the inhabitants of some other Tuscan
cities followed in the footsteps of the Florentines. To these we must now
turn our attention.

II

OTHER TUSCAN FINANCIAL MAGNATES

Agostino Chigi of Siena. The Sienese were the first of the Italians to carry
on financial business beyond the Alps. During the thirteenth century they
had travelled to England and the Northern Kingdoms as papal collectors.
At the Champagne fairs they played a chief part; they then were more

---

[1] Brown, *Calendar VII*, 430. Desjardins, IV, 420, 438, 492, 494, 533. *Arrêts du
Conseil d'Etat de Henri IV*, t. I, Nos. 2260, 2866, 3122, 4236, 5581. Reumont,
Geschichte Toskana's, I, 337, 342, 388, 399. Sully, *Oeconomies Royales*, III, 68.
Pezey, *Histoire de la maison de Gondi*.

important than the Florentines, who did not, until the fourteenth century, thrust them into the background, where they remained. In Bruges they no longer were called a separate 'Nation.' Yet towards the end of the fifteenth century they had an Indian summer of their prosperity.

For then the Spanocchi of Siena were among the most important bankers in Rome and Naples, and Agostino Chigi 'il magnifico,' who for a long time had close business relations with them, was in 1494–1520 accounted the richest merchant in Rome, or even of all Italy. Certainly the Italians were very generous with such superlatives. Undoubtedly Agostino Chigi was very rich. He left in money and personal property at least 150,000 ducats, as well as important real estate. His contemporaries estimated his income to be 70,000 ducats, yet he was not a financial magnate of international importance.

He played a great part at the papal Curia. At first he was only one of that considerable number of merchants who were designated 'mercatores Romanam Curiam Sequentes.' But under Pope Alexander II he had repeatedly supplied the pressing needs of the Eternal City for wheat to the satisfaction of the Pope, who gave him preferential treatment in other matters. So he took a lease of the duties and taxes of the Curia, the Roman and Neapolitan salt works, and especially the large papal alum works at Tolfa. He also had important financial transactions with Alexander VI, Julius II, and Leo X. Under Julius II he had almost the position of a finance minister. Charles VIII of France, on his way through Rome to Naples in 1494, borrowed of him. In 1511 and 1519 he helped the Republic of Venice with considerable sums on the security of jewels.[1]

Even larger than his capital was his credit, which he was extremely skilful in increasing. Some envious rivals once organized a 'run' on his bank. But he had foreseen this, and not merely at once paid out what was demanded, but he asked each one in a friendly way whether he would like gold or silver and in what form. Another time he exhibited a lot of small sacks filled with grain and implied that they were full of gold. By such arts he is supposed to have increased his credit so much that at the Sultan's Court he was called the great Christian merchant. There, as well as in the west, he was specially known through his extensive dealing in alum. In 1508 he got the lease of the Netherlands monopoly for importing alum at a rent of £85,000. But he appears to have kept aloof from financial business proper outside of Italy. He became known as a great patron of art. He helped almost all the foremost artists of the time who were then in Rome by giving them commissions and in other ways.

His heirs very soon lost the greater part of his riches. The advances they made to the Popes Adrian and Clement were not repaid. Pope

[1] G. Cugnoni, *Agostino Chigi il Magnifico*, Rom. 1878–1883. Also Reumont, *Geschichte Roms*, IIIa, 441, IIIb, 398 ff.; Albéri, *Relaz. d. Ambasc. Venet.*, V4, p. 431.

Clement in 1526, by means of Andrea Doria, took them away from the Castle of Port Hercole in Etruria which Agostino Chigi had bought from the republic of Siena. The sack of Rome in 1527 increased their losses. The lease of the alum works got into the hands of the Genoese, who then began to dominate papal finance.

Gaspar Ducci of Pistoja. The man with whom we have now to deal had a yet more peculiar position than Agostino Chigi. He rises before our eyes like a meteor and vanishes again quickly, without our knowing whence and whither. Gaspar Ducci [1] is first mentioned in 1517 as the Antwerp representative of the Lucca firm of Jacopo Arnolfirci, Niccolo Nobili & Co. He bought for them English woollens of John Gresham, the representative of Richard Gresham. In the same year he appears as representative of Bartolomeo Gondecini. He was then one of those half brokers, half agents, and held a position like that of the English broker of to-day. He is so mentioned in 1531 and 1532. Then he was already much involved in lawsuits, as later his relative the well-known Gillebert van Schoonabeke in a petition to the Antwerp magistrate complains that Ducci had always been a ill-conditioned intriguer and quarrelsome fellow, who could not live in peace with anyone. [2] In the 'thirties Ducci appears to have begun to act as an intermediary in financial affairs. In this way he get into relations with Alexius Grimel, the Antwerp agent of the Welser, Bartholomew Welser and the latter's son-in-law Hieronymus Seiler. But his connection with the house of Welser broke off in a bitter dispute in which the Welser appears to have come off worst. Hieronymus Seiler had much to put up with from his father-in-law on account of this. But since this time Ducci was generally feared on the Antwerp Bourse, and his desire for business and his pride increased more and more. He kept up his connection with Seiler and Grimel, who had left the Welser firm. We have already narrated the various kinds of new complications which came out of this.

Not unjustly was Ducci pointed out as the originator of all these questionable excesses and abuses which brought financial business on the Antwerp Bourse into bad repute and had then already ruined many well-to-do merchants. An occurrence in 1540 caused a great sensation. In this year Ducci had contrived a monopoly (not further specified, presumably an artificial tightness of money, such as he unquestionably produced later) to ruin the agent of the King of Portugal, who in fact got into sore straits. The affair came to the ears of the city authorities, who forbade Ducci to go to the Bourse for three years. He

---

[1] His name is also spelt Casper, Gaspar oder Jasper Douche, Douchy, Duchy, Dozzi, Duci, Tutzy, and so on.

[2] Cf. Génard, *Un procès célèbre au XVIe siècle* in the *Compte-Rendu de la Commissions d'histoire* 4, Ser. XV, 307 ff., and papers to the Seiler-Neidhart-Grimel suit in the Augsburg archives.

did not, however, have to endure this penalty to the full, for in 1542 he had business relations with the Brussels Court. There he could not have carried on without going on change.

In 1542 he was the general collector of the fees for the letters of safe conduct issued by the Netherlands Government for exceptional permission to trade with France. Ducci used the short time during which he collected these fees to remit large sums of money on his own account by Hieronymus Seiler to Lyons, where they probably were lent to the King of France as was the case later. The affair was discovered and the money confiscated. Since the Welser had a share in it, Seiler did not disclose his principals and Ducci, who then was also suspected, only paid a small part of the loss, and Seiler had to bear the greater part himself.

Before this Ducci had got into high favour with the Emperor of the Netherlands Court by obtaining for them on the Antwerp Bourse in a number of separate sums loans on bonds of the Receivers General of not less than one million Carolus gulden at 12 per cent. – a comparatively cheap rate. Certainly he got an extra $\frac{1}{2}$ per cent. for 30,000 Carolus gulden, and 1 per cent. for a further 300,000 since he had to raise the former a month and the latter six weeks before paying it out. But all the same it was a considerable service that he thus performed. In addition he contributed 20,000 Carolus gulden to the non-interest-bearing loan made by the merchants for the defence of the country. This was the highest amount paid by an individual.[1]

By these means he succeeded in thrusting Lazarus Tucher from his position of chief financial agent of the Netherlands Government. Ducci acted as intermediary in by far the greatest part of the Government loans in Antwerp during 1542 to 1549. Undeniably he served the Government well, for the rate of interest sank first to 11 per cent. and then to 10 per cent., and later he obtained small amounts at 9 per cent. Only temporarily in 1544 the rate rose to 16 per cent. In 1543 Ducci further recommended the introduction of a new export tax of 10 per cent., which he then farmed himself. The tax brought in considerable sums, but increased the hatred of the merchants of Antwerp against the man who invented it. The same result followed when in 1544 he outbid the former farmers of the alum import and in conjunction with Sebastian Neidhart, Alexius Grimel and their associates took over the lease against an advance of 100,000 fl.

In such circumstances it is not surprising that he was as well thought of in Brussels as he was badly in Antwerp. He was made an Imperial Counsellor, he bought the beautiful estate of Hoboken near Antwerp, and married into a most respected Netherlands family. But his conflicts in Antwerp increased continually. He was accused of having

[1] Lille, B. 2430, 2436 and others.

slandered to the Regent two rivals, Francisco Juliani and Francisco de Baros, and caused them to be punished, that he had even had an attack made on Baros' life by hired bravos, so that Baros had to leave Antwerp. Then it is said he boasted that he had procured the condemnation of Baros by means of bribery and so mocked at the Court. Further, he had instigated men of bad repute to seize with pikes and halberds the house of Marie van der Werwe, a lady of one of the foremost families of Antwerp. He always had 15 to 20 bravos in his pay, which made the streets unsafe. This was so well known that even the little children ran behind Ducci's creatures, to whom he gave instructions to kill one, to mutilate another, to give a box on the ears to a third. In short, he assumed a right of punishing and at the same time boasted that he could do what he liked without any expectation of punishment himself. This unheard-of behaviour aroused general popular indignation, and Gillebert van Schoonabeke (the great Antwerp builder with whom Ducci, although related to him by marriage, had quarrelled, at the beginning of 1545) became the popular mouthpiece in the address to the magistrate we have already mentioned.

Schoonabeke was then keeper of the public scales. A dispute which at first was of no importance arose between him and Ducci as to the method of weighing alum. Other matters embittered the dispute, and one day as he left the Bourse Schoonabeke was attacked by two of Ducci's men with naked weapons. He thought that he would certainly have been killed if his servant had not thrown himself between. After that he only dared go out with an armed guard. The Ducci had threatened him with such a beating that he would have to keep to his bed for four months. He had even recently sent him an insulting message through Lazarus Tucher, who wished to compose the quarrel, that he still had in the town the servants who had made the attack and that Schoonabeke had better look out.

The complainants did not merely call Ducci a notorious seeker of the quarrels, but also 'a Florentine who plays the hypocrite well, but neither forgives nor forgets till death,' a hater of God and men, enemy of all good, liar, intriguer, and in short the worst fellow in the world.

But all these complaints were fruitless. In spite of being summoned five times Ducci did not appear before the Town Criminal Court (Vierschaere) and finally obtained an Imperial prohibition. Since the Court had meanwhile banished from the town the people who had been set on by the Italian, Ducci accused the magistrate of having done this out of enmity for him, and a new quarrel arose.

How much Ducci was looked up to in Court circles after all these scandals which attracted great attention is shown by the fact that the foremost members of the Netherlands nobility, such as Philippe de Croy, the Duke of Arschot, Maximilian d'Egmont, Count von Buren, and many others, were entertained by him.[1]

In business too Ducci's position was as important as it was peculiar and many sided. First he was the most important financial agent of the Emperor and the Netherlands Government in Antwerp, secondly he carried on an extensive business as a capital broker on the Antwerp Bourse, thirdly he acted as agent in large financial transactions for foreign business houses, with whom he corresponded directly, and fourthly he was a banker on his own account and director of financial syndicates. The importance of his activities can be gathered from the fact that, for instance, at the end of 1546, the Fugger had a claim against him for 43,200 pounds Flemish (= 259,200 Carolus gulden). On the other hand, at need he lent them equally large sums, and from other South German firms. In 1545 he is represented as owing the Haugs 12,600 pounds Flemish, while later the Fugger turned out to be the real debtors.

In addition to these many-sided businesses there was another, as interesting as it was dubious, which finally proved fatal for Ducci. He carried on a large arbitrage business with Lyons. We have already described the technique of this. The transactions were made on the joint account of Sebastian Neidhart, Alexius Grimel, Gaspar Ducci, and Simon Pecori; but Ducci was the soul of the business. Anyhow, he instructed his partners in the art of making money tight. The conscientious scruples of the German partners were quite foreign to him. According to them he was just as avaricious, high and mighty, ungrateful and untrustworthy, as the whole population of Antwerp thought him. Ducci's part in the whole affair was in every way very suspicious. At the beginning of 1545 Stephen Vaughan, an English agent, wrote from Antwerp to Henry VIII that Ducci had been summoned to the King of France to get him money, and he was pro-French like all the Italian merchants in Antwerp. The latter statement is palpably wrong, and Ducci was only pro-French so far as his monetary interests were concerned. He did not begin to be a traitor in this year, if he sent money to Lyons which there would be lent to the French Crown. For during all this period there was outwardly peace between the Emperor and France. But it was going far for the privileged financial agent of the Court of Brussels, an Imperial Counsellor, not to find it incompatible with his position to give assistance to the Emperor's bitterest enemies. Yet in 1550 the whole company were only officially condemned for usury and monopoly. We have already described the course of the proceedings and how, although Ducci in the end got off better than his companions in fortune whom he had led astray, yet his part as a financier was over.

Of his later life all we know is that what he had so often done to

[1] Gairdner, *Cal.*, vol. XX, 875.

others befell him. He was treacherously wounded. Soon after he must have lost his fortune, for in 1560 he made over all his rights on the Lordship of Hoboken to Melchior Schetz. Guicciardini, who in the 'sixties wrote his excellent book on the Netherlands containing full details of the merchants and bankers of Antwerp, does not say a syllable about Ducci. Other sources only say that he died about 1577.

The Bonvisi of Lucca. The merchants of Lucca were among the first of the Italians who crossed the Alps for the purposes of trade. By the thirteenth century they are frequently mentioned as merchants and bankers in England as well as at the fairs of Champagne, and unlike the Sienese they managed later to retain a respectable share in this business. At Bruges they formed a separate 'Nation,' at the Geneva fairs they played a prominant part, and they understood how to maintain their position at Antwerp and Lyons in the sixteenth century. In finance, where the Florentines, Genoese or South Germans worked with the full force of their large capital, the merchants of Lucca certainly fell into the background. But their cautious neutrality made it possible for them, even at the time when Europe both politically and industrially was divided into two hostile camps, to keep in with both. In England they repeatedly attained the lead, and later on in France too, when the Florentines there had more or less retired from business. In Antwerp they outlived most of the other Italian trading houses. This seems chiefly to be due to a wise moderation in acquiring and serving. The Bonvisi in particular were typical from this point of view. Unquestionably during the whole of the sixteenth century theirs was by far the most important of the Lucca trading houses.

By 1505 the Bonvisi are mentioned in England. For decades they were among the Italian merchants who paid interest on large sums of money to Henry VIII, till towards the end of his reign the position was reversed and they on their side granted him substantial loans. Next to Lorenzo it was Antonio Bonvisi who was highly regarded under Henry VIII. He helped the advance of science, was a true friend of Sir Thomas More and Cardinal Pole, and an opponent of the Reformation. When after Henry VIII's death the Reformation took a very decisive course in England, Antonio Bonvisi went back to Antwerp. There in 1555 Sir Thomas Gresham had financial transactions with him for the English Crown. In the same year the friendly spirit and straightforwardness which he exhibited in this business was praised in contrast with Gresham's avarice and stinginess. The financial relations of the Bonvisi with the English Crown continued until the reign of Elizabeth.[1]

[1] Brown, *Calendar*, I, 345; VI, 255. Brewer, *Calendar*, II, No. 1364; III, No. 54; IV, No. 2212; V, p. 1715; Green, *Calendar*, Add. 1547–65, p. 436. *Acts of the Privy Council*, I, 395, 479–80. Turnbull, *Calendar, Queen Mary*, p. 197, 199, 212–13, 367, 371.

They were among the first Italians to settle in Antwerp, where in connection with cloth and silk businesses we find mentioned in 1517 Martino, in 1529 Martino and Ludovico Bonvisi (the latter also in 1542), in 1521-6 the firm of Niccolo Bonvisi & Co., which had Bernardo Cenami as partner and chief representative. Apparently they kept clear of monetary transactions with the Emperor and the Brussels Court. So they did not lose their credit in the great crises of 1557 and 1575. On the contrary, in 1579, when Antwerp had lost most of its importance, they are described by an agent of the Fugger as one of the trading houses remaining there which had by far the best credit, the Fugger naturally excepted.[1] During the whole of the sixteenth century the Bonvisi were established in Lyons. Here they participated prominently in the financial business of the French Crown. But all we know for certain is that Antonio and the heirs of Ludovico Bonvisi had a claim against Henry II of 39,925 écus in 1553 and 121,023 écus in 1557.

At last only the branch in Lyons remained. There in 1629 the firm failed with liabilities of 700,000 écus. But the cause of this catastrophe does not appear. The date points to a connection with Spanish finances, in which in fact the firm at last appear to have taken a part.[2]

Other Merchants from Lucca. Apart from the Bonvisi and the Cavallari who were associated with the Florentine house of Frescobaldi and disappeared soon after its fall, there is only one other Lucca merchant to be mentioned in connection with England. This was Acerdo Velutelli, who played an important part during 1570 to 1576 as a retainer of the Earl of Sussex and representative of the Florentines established in France and the merchants from Lucca and Genoa in Antwerp. But he is not mentioned any more. He and the Genoese Horatio Pallavicino were the last Italians employed to any considerable extent in the financial affairs of the English Crown. After the Bonvisi the Cenami were presumably the largest Lucca business house.[3] In 1553 their collapse was announced in Antwerp, where Bernardo Cenami is mentioned in 1521 as representative of the Bonvisi and Bartolomeo Cenami founded his own firm. But after this the family was prominent in Lyons. In 1553 Bernardo Cenami with his compatriots the Bernardini had a claim of 27,725 écus against the French Court. Unquestionably the firm then remained in connection with the French financial adminis-

---

[1] Sanuto, *Diarii*, XXIII, 563. Cf. Guicciardini, *Descritt. d. Paesi Bassi*, ed.n. 1581, p. 127, *Antwerpener Schöffenbriefe and Fugger Correspondence*. Thys, *Histor. d. straten v. Antwerpen*, 2 ed. p. 502 ff.

[2] Brown, *Culendar*, III, 177. Rubys, *Histoire de Lyon*, p. 458; Behaim, Correspondence in German. Museum and Fugger Correspondence.

[3] *Correspond. dipl. de la Mothe Fénélon*, IV, 117; V, 148; VI, 9, 425. Kervyn de Lettenhove, *Négoc. Dipl. des Pays-Bas et de l'Angleterre*, VIII, 175.

tration, but they are not mentioned as having a foremost position till after 1586, especially during the period 1593–7. In these years a Cenami with Gondi Zametti and others, was one of the most important tax-farmers and 'Partisans' in France. Cenami and Zametti often operated together, apparently also frequently for the Grand Duke of Tuscany, who, relapsing into the business of his forbears, lent large sums to Henry IV. But when Henry was secure on the throne, Sully thrust aside Cenami with the other old 'Partisans.' [1]

This makes it all the more remarkable that the family reappeared again under Mazarin. They were favoured by him and the Queen Mother Maria de Medici. When, after the death of Louis XIII, Mazarin ruled France quite alone, a Cenami was, after Herwart, the most important Court banker, and, what comes almost to the same thing, Mazarin's private banker. It is expressly mentioned that he lived in Lyons. Mazarin had deposited large sums with him which were confiscated at the time of the Fronde. Before 1653 Cenami went bankrupt, and Mazarin lost 413,000 livres. He is not mentioned any more.

The Arnolfini, another Lucca family, were represented in Antwerp in 1517 by Gaspar Ducci. In 1525 they bought a house of the Frescobaldi, and in 1579 they were one of the few trading houses of note which still remained in Antwerp. For many decades the firm was called Bonaventura Michaeli, Jeronimo Arnolfini and Companions, later (1556–79), the heirs of Bonaventura Michaeli and Jeronimo Arnolfini. Their financial business in Antwerp was unimportant. But the Arnolfini in Lyons and their firm undoubtedly in 1553 in Lyons took up 17,675 écus in the French Crown loan. They are mentioned in Lyons in 1576; we do not know their further fortunes. [2] Other families of Lucca like the Balbani and the Deodati only occasionally engaged in finance. Yet in the case of the Balbani there is the same development as in the Bonvisi and Cenami. For a long time Giovanni Balbani was highly respected and carried on in conjunction with the Diodati a large sugar refinery in Antwerp, where the firm failed in 1566. It appears to have been re-established, but after that the Balbani were no longer of importance in Antwerp, but they are mentioned in Lyons in 1590. They were then entrusted with the care of the carriage of letters and dispatches of the Spanish Crown between Spain on the one hand and Flanders and Italy on the other, and they complained that the post was opened by the

---

[1] *Arrêts du Conseil d'Etat de Henri IV*, t. I, Nos. 51, 402, 490, 504, 1482, 1744, 2186, 2351, 2549, 2685, 2942, 3039, 3109, 3329–30, 3428, 3497. *Oeconomies royales* de Sully (Coll. Petitot, III, 11, 68; VII, 159).

[2] *Corresp. dipl. de la Mothe Fénélon*, IV, 117; V, 148; VI, 9, 425. Kervyn de Lettenhove, *Négoc. dipl. des Pays-Bas et de l'Angleterre*, VIII, 175. Velutelli wird schon.

French Government, which had a special office in Lyons for this purpose.[1]

Under Henry III and Henry IV Sardini of Lucca is named as a great 'Partisan,' but he was not so important as Diaceto, Rucellai, Gondi, Cenami, and Zametti.[2]

Zametti, the most important financier of Henry IV, also came from Lucca. In 1594 he acquired the bank of the Capponi, the last Florentine house in Lyons, and after that had uncommonly large loan transactions with the King, who had by then established his position. The largest of these was one of 700,000 écus in 1598. Zametti was often associated with Cenami, but often worked without him. Zametti was of low origin, but his descendants played no insignificant part in France. For instance, one of his sons was Bishop of Langres.[3]

The Affaitadi of Cremora. The Affaitadi of Cremona are among the first Italians who tried to take part in the direct trade between Lisbon and the East Indies. Giovanni Francisco Affaitado was already in 1501–3 of some importance in Lisbon.[4] When they were debarred from the direct trade with the East Indies the Affaitadi were again among the first to conduct large contracts for spices with the King of Portugal so as to secure for themselves at second hand this profitable monopoly. For this purpose they had an important factory in Antwerp, which from about 1525 was managed by Tommaso degli Affaitadi. His sons Giovanni Carlo and Giovanni Baptista became highly looked up to. The former was called Chevalier, Seigneur de Ghistelles (he purchased this latter in 1545); Baptista was even 'Count.' About the middle of the century they were the chief shareholders in a large syndicate that bought from the King of Portugal the whole cargo of spices of his East Indian fleet, and paid him large advances in respect of it.[5] During the period 1542–58 the Affaitadi are frequently mentioned as creditors of the town of Antwerp, the English Crown and King Philip. They also appear for a time to have had a share in the lease of the Netherlands alum monopoly. But these engagements were never very

[1] Kervyn de Lettenhove, l.c. IV, 353. Péricaud, *Notes et documents p. servir à l'histoire de Lyon sous le règne de Henry III*, p. 16. Cf. also Thys, *Histor. d. straten v. Antw.* passim.

[2] *Journal de l'Estoile* (Coll. Petitot), I, 102, 313. *Arrêts du Conseil d'Etat de Henri IV*, t. I, No. 42 ff. bis No. 4654.

[3] *Arrêts du Conseil d'Etat de Henri IV*, t. I, Nos. 690, 2572, 3329, 3428, 4254, 4483, 4633, 4990, 5121, 5258, 5328. *Oeconomies royales* de Sully, II, 208; III, 89, 103, 191, 205 u. s. f. Cf. *Mémoires of l'Etoile and Bassompierre.*

[4] Cf. the French later edn. of Heyd, *Geschichte des Levantehandels*, II, 512–14, 526, 551.

[5] *Handlungsbücher der Affaitadi im Königl.* Staatsarchive at Brussels; Lille, B. 2516; *Antw. Stadsprotokollen* ed. Pauwels, I, 33. *Bulletins de la Propriété* (Antw.) 1887, p. 15; Green, *Calendar*, Add. 1547–65, p. 436; Fugger-Archiv 2, 5, 12.

important, and in 1575 it is expressly stated in one of the Fugger commercial letters that the Affaitadi had nothing to do with the Spanish Crown. But all the same they got into difficulties two years later and had to ask their creditors for a moratorium of six years in which to discharge their liabilities. This is the last we hear of them.

The Last Italian Financiers in France. In 1584 when the French Gabelles were going to be farmed out, two syndicates,the first Parisian and the second Italian, Ramelti of Turin, who for some years had been active in French financial business, negotiated on behalf of the Italians. He offered to pay out the claims of the former lessees of whom Gondi was the most prominent, amounting to 800,000 écus. The Florentine envoy who reports this adds that he will get the bargain, since the French could not produce such a large sum. In fact the loan was transferred to the Ramelti's syndicate, partly through the influence of the Duke of Epernon.[1] But the observations were just. For under Henry III Vidiville is the only person with a French name in the foremost ranks of the 'Partisans.' Two more – Le Grand and De l'Argenterie – are added in the first years of Henry IV. Under Sully this development progressed further; meanwhile Sully tried to rob the 'Partisans' of their power by wise economy. Under Louis XIII so long as Concini, the Maréchal d'Ancre, bore sway and then again under Mazarin the Italians, protected by Marie de Medici, obtained new influences. And, what had never happened before, Mazarin handed over the direction of the finances to an Italian, Jean Particelli, Sieur d'Emery. In addition to Cenami and Herwart, several Italians, Vanelli, Cantarini and Serantoni (we do not know what towns they came from), acted as chief bankers for the Crown and Mazarin. But numerous Frenchmen are mentioned as Partisans. They were mostly of low origin, in particular Court lackeys. They associated together and worked in the main with the money of private people to whom they paid interest.[2]

The popular hatred of the Italian favourites, which in Catherine de Medici's time had repeatedly led to outbreaks, broke out under Marie de Medici in 1617 and caused the fall of the Maréchal d'Ancre. Then it in 1648 greatly strengthened the Fronde against Mazarin, since which time Italian names entirely disappear from French finance. This is rather earlier than the last offshoot of the South German financial magnates, Herwart, who lasted on till the early days of Colbert. There did not remain much more for Colbert to do in nationalizing French financial administration. The French who replaced the Italians inherited both their technique and the hatred of the populace, who gained nothing from having driven out the old masters of finance.

[1] Desjardins, IV, 507 ff. and cf. IV, 420, 494.
[2] Moreau, *Choix des Mazarinades*, I, 113; *Défense de Fouquet* passim.

BOOK II

THE INTERNATIONAL BOURSES OF THE SIXTEENTH CENTURY

CHAPTER 1
ANTWERP

THE Rise of Antwerp. Antwerp is one of the many cities whose favourable situation for world trade was only fully exploited at a late stage. Since the beginning of the fourteenth century it had been a market of some importance with two fairs a year, attended by merchants from England, Italy, and the Hansa towns, but the city grew very slowly till the middle of the fifteenth century. There was a great trade in commodities between the Mediterranean cities, which controlled the Levantine commerce, and the whole of Northern Europe, where the German Hansa towns monopolized the trade. This trade in commodities, together with the international dealings in bills and money, was concentrated in Bruges. The transfer of the centre from Bruges to Antwerp was brought about by a combination of political, economic, and other causes and occupied nearly a century. The first great movement of foreign merchants from Bruges to Antwerp took place in 1442, and even in 1533 Bruges had not quite lost its international importance.[1]

The silting up of the Zwin which hindered the loading and unloading of sea-going ships in Sluys, the port of Bruges, might perhaps have been got over, but this was prevented by the long and sanguinary disturbances of which Flanders was the theatre after 1482. These made it impossible for foreign merchants to stay in Bruges, while the rulers did all they could for Antwerp, which was already favoured by nature, in order to punish the rebellious population of Bruges.[2]

Before this time the English, whose already great privileges were largely extended in 1446, had raised their trade in cloth to be one of the most important branches of Antwerp's business. Now, on the discovery of the sea route to the East Indies, the agent of the King of Portugal introduced the spice trade, which soon gave a distinctive character to the Antwerp trade, and an ever increasing number of Portuguese, Spaniards, South Germans and Italians settled permanently there, whereas before they had only visited the fairs.[3]

[1] Papebrochius, *Annales Antwerp*, 1, 414; Gilliodts van Severen, *Compte-rendu de la Commission d'histoire*, Ser. 4, vol. 7, pp. 216, 233, 272.

[2] Schanz, *Engl. Handelspolitik gegen Ende des Mittelalters*, I. 8 ff. Guicciardini, *Descritt. di tutti i Paesi Bassi*, 1567, p. 84. Bertijn, *Chronyck der Stadt Antwerpen*, ed. 1879, pp. 49, 52; Verachter, *Inventaire des Chartes d'Anvers*, Nos. 580, 581.

[3] The merchants of Nuremberg received privileges for Brabant also in 1432, 1433, and 1468. Antwerp is mentioned in that of 1433, in that of 1468 only Ghent, Bruges and Ypres. The first South German visitors to Antwerp are mentioned in 1477. Cf. also Ghillany, *Geschichte d. Seofahrere Ritter Martin Behaim*, pp. 24, 102, 104. The Florentines moved from Bruges to Antwerp 1512–18, the Genoese mainly after 1522. The Portuguese agent is first mentioned in Antwerp 1494. Guicciardini, *Descritt. d. Paesi Bassi*, edition of 1581, p. 126,

Now, in the course of four decades Antwerp developed into a trading centre such as the world has never seen before or since; for never since has there been a market which concentrated to such a degree the trade of all the important commercial nations of the world. An English memorandum of 1564 says that the men of Antwerp had 'eaten out of their trade' the merchants of the other towns. This is quite correct if instead of the men we put the city of Antwerp, for the market attracted to itself the trade of the other markets, and their merchants settled in Antwerp to obtain the extraordinary advantages offered them there. The natives, on the other hand, were only of secondary importance. They had comparatively little commerce on their own account, as a Venetian envoy remarked in 1525, but occupied themselves with subsidiary trades. They helped the foreigners by acting as brokers, agents for warehouses, later also as bankers, agents, etc. Wholesale trade proper was, both in Bruges and Antwerp, chiefly in the hands of foreigners.[1]

What now were the extraordinary advantages of Antwerp? What was there specially to distinguish it from Bruges?

The Importance of Antwerp in General. Antwerp took the place of Bruges as the metropolis of the trade of Northern Europe, but even a superficial view shows important differences between the commerce of the two cities. Among the foreign merchants trading at Antwerp some nations were much less strongly represented there than at Bruges: for instance, the Venetians whose rôle in the world's trade was now played out; then, the Florentines, who kept away from political reasons; the 'Osterlings,' at any rate the merchants of the Baltic, who in part suffered the same fate as the Venetians, and in part from an early date were connected with Amsterdam, already in the sixteenth century more important for the Baltic corn trade than Antwerp. Antwerp was accordingly all the more frequented by inhabitants of the North German North Sea cities and those of the North of the Low Countries. The chief influx, however, consisted of merchants from Portugal, Spain, England, and South Germany.

The English now first betook themselves to active trading and Antwerp served as far their most important staple. Spaniards and Portuguese were brought in shoals by their large colonial undertakings. The alteration of the centre of commercial gravity which told against the Venetian and Baltic merchants made the North Germans visit Antwerp in great numbers. They had previously dealt chiefly with Venice, but had played only a small part at Bruges. In Antwerp, on the other hand, thanks to the amount of the capital they held and their enterprising spirit, they kept the chief place for many decades. A similar development can be traced in the case of the Genoese.

---

[1] Sloane MSS. 818. Albèri, *Relaz. d. Ambasc. Venet.*, IV, 22.

If we penetrate a little farther, we note that the foreign merchants dealing in Antwerp represented a far greater proportion of their countrymen than in Bruges. Here we think of the important development which has led to the system of dealing on commission. In the Middle Ages the merchant at first travelled in person and then, since the Crusades, he had sent his agent. Now, in Antwerp we meet, not only agents representing different business houses, but also an innovation, foreign merchants permanently settled in Antwerp who had a business connection with a whole group of their fellow-countrymen. We find the same thing occurring in the Netherlands also. It is rather astonishing to find in Antwerp in the early sixteenth century the quite modern type of the English broker, both broker and commission agent, which has only just began to be usual in Germany in quite recent times.[1]

In order to show the scale of the business done by foreigners in Antwerp as compared with Bruges, we have only to turn our attention to the two great branches of the Antwerp trade, East Indian products and English cloth. In earlier times the East India trade had branched out from the Levant into many different channels; now for the greater part it flowed in one stream to Lisbon and thence to Antwerp, for the King of Portugal sold the cargoes as a whole to large rich syndicates who obtained a monopoly and took care that, in order to keep up prices, the whole trade should be concentrated in Antwerp.[2] For the same reasons the English managed their cloth trade in the same way. For this reason too most other commodities were concentrated in Antwerp and their quantities were correspondingly increased, e.g. we note that South German fustian, an important article in the world's trade, was only now produced in a wholesale capitalist manner for export; or, to take another example, Hungarian copper, for which Venice had formerly been the chief market, had since the beginning of the sixteenth century been sent in large quantities to Antwerp and thence exported to the rest of the world.

This tendency to progressive concentration was, however, chiefly manifested by the fact that the bourses of the different nations which had existed in Bruges were in Antwerp united with the international

[1] For the Genoese Desimoni e Belgrano *in den Atti d. soc. ligure,* vol. V, 460 ff., for the Portugese the Antwerp Jury rolls: Statutes of the Adventurers Company for the English, Cologne histor. Archives for the German Hansa.

[2] Wheeler, *Treatise of commerce* (1601), p 36: 'The Portingall – like a good simple man, he sailed every yeare full hungerly about 3 parts of the earth almost for spices; when he had brought them home, the great rich purses of the Antwerpians, subjects of the king of Spain, ingrossed them all into their own hands, yea oftentimes gave money for them before hand, making thereof a plaine Monopoly.' For English cloth, cf. Ehrenberg, *Hamburg und England im Zeitalter der Königin Elisabeth*, p. 27 ff.

bourse, a point to which we shall return. The best answer to the questions as to why the world trade was concentrated in Antwerp is given by a memorandum drawn up at the beginning of Philip II's reign by the foreign merchants in Antwerp as a determined protest against the proposed nomination of sworn insurance brokers. 'No one can dispute, they say, that the libertys granted to the merchants is the cause of the prosperity of this city.'[1]

The trade in Bruges had been free compared with the restrictions prevalent in other cities in the Middle Ages, but in comparison with the absolute freedom enjoyed by the foreign merchants in Antwerp Bruges seems mediæval. For instance, in Bruges the brokers were a monopolist corporation, but in Antwerp they were free. In Bruges only sworn money changers could engage professionally in money changing or giro bank business. In Antwerp, on the other hand, the Charter of 1306 granted this right to all burghers, and in the city's prime there were practically no restrictions on the trade in money, precious metals and bills. Clearing-house business was carried on by book transactions without ready money. The hotel and lodging-house trade, which was extraordinarily important to the foreign traders in the Netherlands, was in Bruges, but not in Antwerp, the subject of many stringent regulations on the part of the authorities. The trade restrictions which remained in Antwerp originated almost entirely with the foreign merchants. Both the ruler and the city magistracy tried to give trade all the freedom possible.

Foreign merchants had as much liberty as those of the country and no one of the foreign nations was more highly privileged than the rest. Accordingly the divisions which had existed in Bruges between different sections of the population fell into abeyance, at any rate in so far as they had originated in jealously guarded rights and provileges. Only the English, who had had a considerable trade in Antwerp's early period, kept a somewhat special position. The other nations were distinguished by their appearance, language and customs; but in other respects they formed one merchant class with identical rights, duties and interests.

The absence of trade restrictions in Antwerp had one very important consequence. It altered the significance of the fairs.

Fairs and Bourse in Antwerp. In the fifteenth century Antwerp had two fairs, the Whitsuntide fair in the spring and the St. Bavon's fair, vulgarly the Bamas or Pamas fair (the French St. Remy) in the autumn. There were in addition two other fairs whichwere held till the 'forties of the sixteenth century, in Bergen-op-Zoom, though they had then rather fallen into decay and were transferred to Antwerp. These were

---

[1] *Bulletin de la Société de Géographie d'Anvers,* p. 215.

the Cold market at Christmas and the Easter market which originally
began at Candlemas.[1]

The two old Antwerp fairs in the early spring and the early autumn
were what the English merchants used chiefly for their cloth trade.
The cloth fleets came in at these times and on their arrival the English
held their 'show days.' It was very seldom that they visited the other
fairs.[2] There was no important change in these arrangements while the
English dealt in Antwerp, and even afterwards, for they were determined by national conditions on which the English wool season as well
as the shipping season depended. When, however, the English cloth
trade ceased to be the determining factor in Antwerp, and the other
foreign merchants transferred themselves in a body from Bruges to
Antwerp, the firm structure of the old fairs was broken down. In 1484
the Bruges Office of the Hansa towns complained that in Antwerp the
men of Brabant held a new staple with all sorts of goods and booths
the whole year through not only at market times. Two years later it
was said that the people of Antwerp had begun a new market with the
English and now wanted to do business out of season.[3] As far as the
English were concerned, the alteration was not followed up. The importance of fair time in the Middle Ages consisted in the temporary
suspension of the restrictions on the trade of foreign merchants which
took place at these times. In Antwerp, since trade was free all the year
round, the fairs lost much of their importance.

The other reason which had made fairs necessary in mediæval times
also became obsolete. Trade had grown till it was sufficient to keep up
a regular market all the year round. Another important alteration is
closely connected with this growth of trade. Many commodities were
now made in standard types which served as a basis of trade, and others
were only dealt in from samples. In both cases the goods were not seen
before the transaction was concluded. The result was the conversion of
Antwerp from a fair centre to a bourse centre.

Bruges also had its 'Burse,' the first that bore the name. This, however, was not a bourse in the modern sense that is a meeting place for all
merchants, it was the meeting of the Italians who had their consular
houses in the Bourse Square. Each of the other nations had a separate
assembly. The Bruges Bourse was chiefly used for dealing in money and
bills; the trade in commodities was carried on either in the large 'Halles'
or in the houses and warehouses where the goods were stored.[4]

[1] Cf. *Vaughan's Report to Cromwell*, 1534; and Brewer, *Calendar*, vol. VII, 575.
For later times Guicciardini, *Descritt. d. Paesi Bassi* (1567), p 83
[2] Schanz, *Engl. Handelspolitik gegen Ende des Mittelalters*, I, 12.
[3] *Hanserecesse* ed. Schäfer, I, 399, II, 25.
[4] Cf. Ehrenberg on brokers, lodging-house keepers and the Bourse in Bruges
from the thirteenth to the sixteenth century. *Ztschr. f. Handelsrecht*, vol. XXX.

In Antwerp in the second half of the fifteenth century there was a merchants' bourse. When the trade boom began, apparently in 1460, the Antwerp City Council set it up close to the Great Market in the English or Wool Street, where the English had their pack houses; this was also close to the port, the public weighing place and the money changers' banks. This was done for the express purpose of furthering trade.[1]

An institution of this kind, set up by the authorities for a certain purpose, was an important innovation. It is still more important that the Antwerp Bourse was meant from the first for all trading in Antwerp. This is proved by the inscription on the splendid new bourse erected in 1531: 'In usum negotiatorum cujuscunque nationis ac linguæ.' The English alone, at any rate in later times, had a special bourse; and this, as Guicciardini remarks, gave rise to a remarkable division of business, not according to nations, but according to transactions.[2]

'The merchants,' Guicciardini says, 'go morning and evening at a certain time to the Bourse of the English. There they do business with the help of brokers of every language, who are there in great numbers, chiefly as to the buying or selling of commodities of every kind. Then they go to the new Bourse, where in the same way they deal chiefly in bills and money loans (depositi).'

We need not inquire here whether all dealing in commodities in Antwerp when of a bourse-like character took place on the English Bourse. It is sufficient to establish the fact that all nations when they had bourse business to transact had to visit one of the two bourses. Within the new bourse the different nations fell into divisions, as also happened later on in Amsterdam. The Antwerp bourse was the first international or world bourse in the full sense of the word. A contemporary poet, Daniel Rogiers, describes the business in the new bourse: 'A confused sound of all languages was heard there, and one saw a parti-coloured medley of all possible styles of dress; in short, the Antwerp Bourse seemed a small world wherein all parts of the great world were united.'

Generally speaking, Antwerp in the sixteenth century must even to the outward eye have been an incomparable city. The splendid luxury, often united with fine artistic feeling of a number of merchants who came together from every quarter of the globe, made much money, and

---

[1] Verachter, No. 704. Thys, *Histor. der Straten von Antwerpen*, 2nd Ed., 1893, p. 92 ff.

[2] *Descritt. d. Paesi Bassi Ausg.*, v. 1581, p. 171. Mertens en Torfs (*Geschied. v. Antw.*, IV, 188); Henne (*Règne de Charles Quint en Belgique*, V, 319). Schanz (*Engl. Handelspolitik*, I, 14) puts the creation of the English Exchange in 1515, while Guicciardini (Ed. v. 1581, p. 102) and Thys (2. Ausg. p. 86) put it as 1550 (Schanz, II, 231).

in the manner of the time, and especially the population among whom they lived, lost no opportunity of making display and joyful celebrations – all this made a life such as the world has never again seen.[1]

The four fairs at Antwerp continued, but lost most of their importance for business in commodities properly speaking, with the exception of the English cloth trade. The payments of the fair which had been an appendage became the matter of chief importance. This is clearly proved by the fact that in the case of the two fairs at Bergen-op-Zoom only the payments were moved to Antwerp, the fairs themselves remained in Bergen, though no business was done there. The fair payments were to begin on the 31st October, or the 31st January, on the 1st May and on the 1st August, and to last ten days in each case. Later these developed into four quarter days:

10th February for the Christmas market.
10th May for the Easter market.
10th August for the Whitsuntide market.
10th November for the Bamas market.

Finally these quarter days were often prolonged, if fiscal necessity made it desirable. In this case it was a question of quarter days for the entire business in bills and loans, whether for private or public ends. The payments for commodities were made separately a month later. Apart from the payments at fair time money was usually scarce and dear; and far the largest part of the gigantic dealings in capital in Antwerp was accordingly transacted at the quarter days. This was not carried out as in Lyons by clearing-house methods, but by assignment from hand to hand – a still more imperfect form of clearing-house business which gave rise to many lawsuits.[2]

Speculation in Antwerp. We cannot here enter into the technique of the Antwerp trade. In order, however, to understand what follows it is necessary to show how extremely speculative was the trade in the chief articles, East Indian spices. Among these pepper was the most important and the most risky. The pepper trade was a prerogative of the King of Portugal, who sold the cargoes of the East Indian fleets to large syndicates who thereby obtained a monopoly at second hand. They often bought the cargoes while still at sea, gave the King of Portugal, who always needed money, large advances, and repaid themselves by charging a high price. They were able to regulate the price in their own interest in Antwerp, where the bulk was disposed of, at any rate till the arrival of the new fleet from the East, which then set the price.

[1] Kervyn de Lettenhove, *Rélat. polit des Puys Bas et de l'Angleterre*, II, 596 ff., 611.
[2] Cf. speech of the Venetian Senator Contarini in 1584, quoted in Lattes, *Libertà delle Banche a Venezia*, p. 121, *die Coutumes de la ville d'Anvers*, II, 522 ff., and the Imperial Edicts of 1537 and 1539 in the *Placc. v. Brabant*, I, 511, 513, 515.

These two factors, the interest of the large syndicates and the amount of the new imports, determined the price of pepper on the Antwerp Bourse. Both were incalculable, as were all the other contributory conditions, of which war and peace were the most important. The course of prices was often therefore very 'jumpy' and speculation had an hitherto unparalleled opportunity. This was made the more important by the fact that the price of pepper determined most of the market by acting as a barometer for the temper of the bourse.[1] The conditions of the business in many other commodities were analogous, e.g. the importation of alum was a prerogative of the Netherlands Government, which farmed it out to syndicates of merchants. Other branches were treated at times as practical monopolies, which were then broken down, giving rise to extravagant fluctuations, e.g. the copper trade.

All this contributed to make dealing in commodities in Antwerp a risky business for anyone who was not able to follow the market from hour to hour and even for those who did so. Of the abundant evidence on this head we will confine ourselves to the commercial reports sent in the years 1543 and 1544 by Christopher Kurz, a Nuremberg man, to the Tucher firm, by whom he does not seem to have been directly employed.

At this time astrological prognostications flourished in the Netherlands ; these were prophecies of every kind which were reproduced in print. Christopher Kurz had puzzled out an astrological system by which he said he could foretell prices. He praised his invention to the Tuchers, mixing sober business statements with fantastic combinations in a way that seems absurd to us, but which probably at the time gave quite a different impression. Kurz writes in one of his first letters that Lienhard Tucher, whom we know as a much respected and able merchant prince, had shown himself disposed towards his proposals (though 'after many appeals and requests'). Lienhard Tucher made marginal notes on the reports Kurz sent which prove that he read them carefully and did not fail to observe the prognostications.[2]

Kurz started from the unimpeachable statement that 'trade in spices needs great foresight.' He said that he had found a system for foretelling a fortnight in advance the prices of pepper, ginger, and saffron. 'I sought it three years, but until this year found it not. I think God hath given it to me. I have observed it for the space of a year. Yet will I not boast myself of it, till I myself have observed it for yet a time longer with mine own eyes and have traced it out. Yet I doubt not, it is

[1] Tucher business correspondence, 1529–46, ledgers of the Affaitadi in the Brussels Archives (1548–51 and 1556–8).
[2] *Tucher Family Archives*, III, 11. For Netherlands 'Prognosticatien,' cf. Knuttel, Pamfletten, Nos. 86, 91–4.

well founded; if it be not, I shall know ere a half year be out. In the same manner I have known how to show for the matter as touching cinnamon, nutmegs and cloves from one market to another. But as I have always seen you wary about committing yourselves with such goods, I have forgot some pieces of this experiment, as I write not of all those which I have. Still should I hear that ye would hazard with spice dealing, there shall be no lack of such. But ye must be diligent to frequent the places where such are bought and sold, as Venetia – and wonder seized me wherefore you use not Frankfort which lieth near to your hand. For there is not only good gain oftentimes to be made with spices, but likewise with bills can one hap on many a good chance. As ye have often noted in my writings to you how great an alteration is there here day by day in bills on Germany, Venice, or Lyons, so that in the space of eight, ten, fourteen or twenty days with other folks' money, a man may make a profit of 1, 2, 3, 4, 5, or more per cent., with such there is here each day great business on the Bourse. On these also have I my experiment so that I may foretell not only from week to week the Strettezza and Largezza (tightness or ease in money), but also for each day and whether it shall be before or after midday. I have, however, nigh forgot this again, since I have found you so reluctant.' Then he speaks once more of saffron. Lienhard Tucher had written that he might perhaps act on Kurz's advice as to this commodity: 'So bethink you that the sale lies with you and buy in with all heat at Lyons. Truly, Honourable Sir, from such motions of the mind you must learn wherefore I speak my judgment in part. So soon as ye see how much hath from this year and how much remaineth over, and that now such wares be driven so high in every place that they, according to the store of them, cannot come higher, what course have you then to buy as you, I wot well would be fain to do? But this is naught for the upper influences so blind the natural reason with affections or desires.' Here he adds a long reasoned statement as to the best times for buying saffron.

Kurz writes that he always rose before four and was surrounded 'with work as a man in the ocean with water, for our astrologers aforetime have written much, but little with reason; wherefore I trust not their doctrine, but seek mine own rules, and when I have them I search in the histories whether it hath fallen out right or wrong.' He took up political prophecy and gradually became an astrologer by profession and of great repute. Among other things he prophesied that the Papacy would be extinct in from 40 to 60 years' time. He could not foretell the fate of the city of Nuremberg till he was told the date when the first stone was laid 'for where no root is, there can nothing grow.'

As to the Infante Philip, later Philip II, Lienhard Tucher sent him

Q

exact details as to his birthday, when Kurz began to cast his horoscope. The result was sad, but practically the exact reverse of actual facts. The only thing that came out right was 'that he wasteth himself with his wars and therefore always becometh poorer.' Kurz regretted 'that the Prognostication fell out so ill; other astrologers would perhaps have thrown a cloak over it; but as there is nothing but sickness and povertie and so much of ill luck that I would not fain be Philip. Should the Empire have such an Emperor, which I believe not if man have complained over Ferdinand, they shall yet shriek forth complaints over Philip. Why should I write much in Summa? A worse Nativity hath not come to one this year past. Cloves (he continues, in the same breath) will be profitable and it could do no damage to make trial with eight or ten small sacks.'

We have here the beginning of modern speculation in commodities clearly recognizable though mixed with strange mediæval whimsies. Lazarus Tucher, whose dealings we know, was in his early days a great speculator in the present-day sense. Christopher Kurz is only a caricature of the type and reminiscent of many phenomena which may be met with in the bourses of our own day.

First of all it must be clearly stated that a large part of the dealing in commodities in Antwerp was so risky that prophecies of this kind as to the future course of business could obtain credence even with merchants of the first rank like Lienhard Tucher. We need not attend further to Kurz's statement that his system was already used in many business houses in Antwerp.

The speculative colouring which dealing in commodities assumed injured it in the eyes of many solid merchants, while the poor development of the technical side of speculation had the same effect on the less solid. The arrangements had not yet been invented which made it possible later to speculate in commodities without the complicated information, trouble and expense of actual trade.

There is a very important opinion of fourteen Paris jurists in 1530 as to whether the forms of business then practised in Antwerp were allowed by canon law.[1] It is based on data supplied by Spanish merchants resident in Antwerp. It is stated that many of the richest firms no longer like dealing in commodities unless all the merchants were unanimous in believing that there was a good prospect of profit. Otherwise they preferred to refrain mainly for three reasons:

---

[1] Escritto que los dottores de Paris embiaron a los señores de la nacion española residentes en la ville de Emberes sobre ciertas deudas que les embiaron a preguntar assy de cambios y fianças como de otras cosas, segun que por el dicho escritto parece, el qual saco de latin el muy r^{do} señor Dottor Alvaro Moscoso (MSS. d. Münich. Bibl. Hisp. 30).

(1) It was so troublesome to export or import commodities, to warehouse and resell them, a process needing investigation of the buyer's credit, while the number of sound firms dealing in commodities was declining.

(2) It was too risky, for they feared to lose their capital or get it 'frozen.'

(3) Finally, it did not offer so good nor so sure a profit as dealing in money and bills. They therefore engaged increasingly in the latter.

A few decades later Lodovico Guicciardini, a man of good economic sense, who in other respects was full of enthusiasm for the greatness of Antwerp's trade, confessed that the dealings in money at Antwerp were now a public danger. 'Formerly the nobles, if they had ready money, were wont to invest it in real estate, which gave employment to many persons and provided the country with necessaries. The merchants employed capital of this kind in their regular trade whereby they adjusted want and superfluity between the various countries, gave employment to many and increased the revenues of princes and states. Nowadays, on the other hand, a part of the nobles and the merchants (the former, secretly through the agency of others, and the latter openly in order to avoid the trouble and risk of a regular profession) employ all their available capital in dealing in money, the large and sure profits of which are a great bait. Hence the soil remains untilled, trade in commodities is neglected, there is often increase of prices, the poor are fleeced by the rich, and finally even the rich go bankrupt.'

We know that in the main this picture is a true one. The merchant class of the mediæval centres mostly turned their energies to dealing in money. The people who were their successors, the Spaniards and Portuguese, did not know how to profit by this chance. They borrowed the capital necessary for world trade from the former and had to give back to them the lion's share of the profits. The trading nations of modern times, the English and the Dutch, had not yet laid hands on the heritage of the Mediterranean cities. Guicciardini's pessimistic view of his own times is easily understood.

The Beginnings of Premium Business. In the year 1541, perhaps before and certainly often later, the Netherlands Government forbade 'Contrats de gageures et d'assurances des changes.' We learn what this was from an interesting tract of the Licentiate Christoval de Villalon printed in Valladolid in the year 1542.[1] 'Of late in Flanders a horrible thing hath arisen, a kind of cruel tyranny which the merchants there

---

[1] *Provechoso tratado de cambios y contrataciones de mercaderes,* cap. XV. Verachter, Invent. No. 1542, *Coutumes de la ville d'Anvers,* II, 401 ff.; IV. 9. Belgrano in *Giornale ligustico,* II, 255. Bensa, *Il contratto di assicurazione nel medio evo,* p. 125, 178 passim. (Scommesse di promozione di Cardinali, di Sede Vacante.) Marino Sanuto, *Diarii,* XVI, 27. Brown, *Calendar,* II, 176; V, 296, *Codice d. Tosc. Legislaz.*

have invented among themselves. They wager among themselves on the rate of exchange in the Spanish fairs at Antwerp. They call these wagers parturas according to the former manner of winning money at a birth (parto) when a man wagers whether the child shall be a boy or a girl. In Castile this business is called apuestas, wagers. One wagers that the exchange rate shall be at 2 per cent. premium or discount, another at 3 per cent., etc. They promise each other to pay the difference in accordance with the result. This sort of wager seems to me to be like Marine Insurance business. If they are loyally undertaken and discharged, there is nought to be said against them. But there are many ruinous tricks practised therein. For dealing of this kind is only common in merchants who, holding much capital, perhaps draw a bill of 200,000 or 300,000 ducats in Flanders or Spain and conclude on one of these wagers, whereby one leaves the other free which of the two transactions he will carry out. By their great capital and their tricks they can arrange that in any case they have profit. This is a great sin.' We shall see later in detail what the merchants did. It is easy to see that here we have the beginnings of the present premium business. Unquestionably it was also used in dealing in commodities. We find in 1591 in Hamburg, which took its modern commercial technique from Antwerp and Amsterdam, that there is a form of business where one party wagers that in six weeks wheat will sink below a certain price. At the beginning of the seventeenth century the purchase op conditie, op weddinge, à condition ou gageure had already become usual both in Rouen and Amsterdam in commodity dealing. In many cases it had sprung from the original system of wagers.[1] The fact that the premium business originated for bill business was natural, since it was always of a more speculative nature than dealing in commodities.

Traffic in Bills at Antwerp. The Paris opinion of 1530 describes the Ricorsa bill in two documents between Antwerp and the Spanish fairs as the most usual kind of bill business. In this form it was not merely a veiled loan transaction, but was rather a speculation since two bill transactions had to be concluded which were separated both in time and place, the one in Antwerp, the other in Spain. There was, however, as well the Ricorsa bill in one document, which was purely a veiled loan. The first kind, however, was much commoner, and those who wished to defend it against the doctrine of usury could point to the fact that money was as often lost as won over it.

The speculative nature of the bill transactions is shown by many

---

[1] Van Damme, *Manière la plus industrieuse à tenir livres*, etc., Rouen, 1606. Henry Waningen, *Trésor de tenir livres de compte à l'Italienne*, Amsterdam, 1648. Van Neulighem, *Boeckhouden* Amsterdam, 1630. Macynes, *Lex Mercatoria*, London, 1622, p. 144.

sayings of the merchants. Christopher Kurz we have already quoted. In 1550 the Imhofs sent to Antwerp a new agent, who wrote to his predecessor, 'If a man see profit before his eyes, he must undertake nothing with arbitrio unless he have orders, it turns itself about three times.'

Arbitrage in bills, which had been much carried on in Antwerp since about 1540, contained three elements: (i) the wish to make money on the difference between the prices of bills in different places, (ii) speculation on their fluctuations, (iii) the wish to obtain the highest possible interest. Sometimes the one element was more prominent, sometimes the other, but in most cases they were all inextricably mixed, e.g. Paul Behaim writes that he wants to remit money to Frankfort-on-Main and to draw on Venice; but since money has become more liquid, nothing is to be got out of such arbitrio. The order to borrow money on Nuremberg and to lend it out again profitably in Antwerp could not be carried out, as no solvent borrowers could be found. If money were to be had in bills on Venice at $72\frac{1}{4}$ gr. per ducat, he would try to lend it out in Antwerp at 4 per cent. for four months (= 12 per cent. per annum) which would mean getting $75\frac{1}{8}$ gr. for the ducat. Hence a bill could be drawn from Venice on Antwerp and get a profit of $1\frac{1}{2}$–2 per cent. without having to tie up one's own money in the transaction. This example will be enough to show how bill arbitrage was carried on in Antwerp.

There were attempts to force the market to create artificial tightness or ease (strettezza or largezza), as we have seen in the case of Gaspar Ducci and the syndicate he formed. This had its chief office in Antwerp; but his attempts to rig the market were chiefly at Lyons, and its devices were exercised first in one market and then in another, borrowing money in Antwerp to lend it out again in Lyons or *vice versa*. It was thus possible to reduce the risk of bill arbitrage, or even at moments to establish a virtual monopoly.

These excrescences discredited the whole Antwerp bill business. The arithmetician Jan Impyn writes in 1543: 'As to bills, the common people here knows very little. People fall foul of the merchants and yet wot not what a bill is. Men hold the merchants for usurers and sharper than Jews, whereas they should be praised; for without bills there can in no more trade than sea-going without water. Yet of course bills, like all else in the world, can be mishandled.'

The merchants defended the Ricorsa bill and arbitrage on the ground of the necessity of adjusting tightness and ease in the different markets, but strict canonists did not allow this. Even Guicciardini blamed these excrescences, though he defended bill business in general.[1] No attempt

[1] Jan Ympyn Christoffels, *Nieuwe instructie ende bewys der looffelycker consten des rekenboecks*, Antwerp, 1543; Guicciardini, *Descritt. d. Paesi Bassi*, ed. of 1581, p. 171.

ever seems to have been made in Antwerp to fix official average rates for bills in Antwerp as was done in Lyons. This no doubt depended on the fact that in Antwerp the bill business was not as in Lyons concentrated at the close of the fairs, but was distributed throughout the year, and the daily amount of the business was too large for such attempts. The Paris opinion of 1530 says, however: The price at which the merchants do business they call the bourse price (precio de la bolsa); for no one sets the price for himself, but only the Bourse association (commidad de la bolsa).

It is interesting to note that the bourse is here called in its first beginnings an association, and is given the name by theorists who thought of other corporations as bourses. Actually, however, the Antwerp Bourse price was only the market price in the sense of the German commercial code, i.e. an actual price, not an average price fixed by any official body. These bill prices were communicated in the merchants' letters or in special leaflets, the origin of which is uncertain, but it was probably first in Antwerp.

Antwerp Deposit Business. The bourse 'depositum,' a name which is a cloak for a loan, is not mentioned at Antwerp till comparatively late. Among theorists well versed in the Antwerp business, the author of the Paris opinion of 1530 makes no mention of the Deposito: Villalon, writing only thirteen years later, mentions it only as a bill from one fair to the next, as it had existed from quite early times; but Saravia Della Calle, writing only a little later, mentions 'deposito' at interest and condemns it as a form of concealed loan. The usual form is first described by Guicciardini, who says: 'Here it is now called Deposito in order to cloak with a fine word the ugliness of the act – the loan of a sum of money for a certain time at a fixed price and interest, e.g. according to the permit granted by the Emperor Charles V, confirmed by his son King Philip, at an annual rate of 12 per cent. This rate was granted to merchants in bad times in order to avoid worse evil. . . . Such transactions would be actually useful, if people would be content with reasonable interest. This, however, is not the case, and the deposit business has assumed an arbitrary and unbearable shape.'

What Guicciardini describes here is the undisguised loan, which has no similarity with the bank deposit we know. The so-called 'Deposito' in Antwerp was as old-established as the bourse business itself, but it had previously borne another name, and in the business community, e.g. in the correspondence between the South German merchants and their agents the new expression came into use very slowly. They spoke of 'money' or 'money at interest' which was worth 2 per cent. or 3 per cent. from one fair to another. The older designation 'finance' is used as equivalent to deposito, and if a distinction is to be drawn between the commercial and the fiscal loan Ditta di Borsa is spoken of. In 1549 the Imhofs write to their Antwerp agent: 'We hold the city of Antwerp will pay as much interest as Dita di Burcha. At the same price we like the city better.'

The interest rate for the Deposito was the Antwerp market rate as determined by the frequent fluctuations of the money market. The 'fixed time' which Guicciardini mentions was usually one fair, less often two, rarely three or four. A fair, as we know, was on the average a quarter. The time of the fair payments was, however, often altered, so that a fair often meant more or less than a quarter.

In commercial loans on the bourse, the interest was usually 2 per cent. or 3 per cent. a fair, i.e. 8 per cent. to 12 per cent. per annum; sometimes the interest was as low as 1¾ a fair (7 per cent. per annum). We do not hear that it ever rose above 3 per cent. Only when some individual firm was in difficulties, it had to agree to far higher rates. Even the Fugger were so situated in 1563, when they borrowed 300,000 crowns from Juan de Curiel della Torre. The nominal rate was only 10 per cent., but since the Fugger had to take in payment Spanish State rentes at par, though they stood only at 50 per cent., the actual rate was a little under 30 per cent. The 300,000 fl. which the Schetz had to borrow in severe embarrassment from the Genoese in 1572 were just as dear. These loans, however, cannot be called regular bourse loans. There was unexampled tightness in 1562–3 and 1572, but we know that in 1563 the Fugger owed large sums to other people in Antwerp at 8 per cent. to 10 per cent.

Conditions were quite different for the princes' loans and sometimes with those of the cities. These were not, properly speaking, deposit business, and are hardly ever so called. We will return to this point, but must first discuss the form of the acknowledgment of indebtedness in deposit business.

In the correspondence of the South German business houses there is the most often mention of 'letters,' e.g. 'On good dittas and German letters 2½ per cent. is paid. Everybody at this time is looking for a Fugger letter.' The expressions dittas and letters are often used as equivalent. It is not stated whether the 'letters' were bonds or bills (Schuld or Wechsel Briefe). Both forms were actually used in deposit business in Antwerp, the bond being a bearer bond, and the bill a bill with one signature. Of these the former, which was used also in credit dealing in commodities, was the commoner. These bonds could be sold and pledged without cession or giro, and if lost they could be paid off after public proclamation. An imperial order of 1537 declared them formally binding like bills. It was henceforward sufficient to make them valid that the drawer had put his signature or trade mark on them. Bearer bonds accordingly offered all the advantages of the bill exclusive of the greater facility for being turned into ready money, which the bill obtained towards the end of the sixteenth century through the giro at the Genoese bill fairs.[1]

General Sketch of Antwerp Finance Dealings. Originally all loans at interest were called 'finance' in Antwerp, but later this term was reserved for loans concluded with princes, provinces, or cities. In this sense, a distinction was drawn between 'finance,' i.e. fiscal money dealings and commercial transactions, bills, and deposito. The original meaning was retained, however, in the Netherlands finance accounts. There we find a standing heading entitled 'Deniers Prins (Pris) à Fraict et Finance,' the fact that interest was payable was expressly contrasted with 'Empruncts or Prests sans Fraict ne Finance.'

The different kinds of loans concluded on the Antwerp Bourse were as follows:

(1) *Bonds of the Court of the Netherlands*, i.e. loans of the Netherlands Government, of which there were many varieties. They bore the personal undertaking of the Emperor, or later the Spanish King, as ruler or his Governor, whether man or woman, and were charged upon certain definite revenues, or were under the guarantee of high state officials or individual cities, especially the city of Antwerp.

(2) Private bonds of the highest officials or dignatories of the Netherlands on the Government account. We shall come across cases when this was the Government's only means of raising money.

(3) Bonds of the Provincial Diets of the Netherlands, especially the states of Brabant on account of the Government for taxes (aides) already granted to it, but not yet collected.

(4) Bonds of the individual Netherlands cities, partly on their own account, but chiefly for the Government. Those of the city of Antwerp were the most popular. Next those of the 'Seven Cities of Flanders' either together or separately, those of Antwerp, Malines, etc.

(5) *Bonds of the Netherlands Receivers General.* We have already mentioned these important papers. They were private bonds of the Rentmeister, i.e. General Tax Receivers of the different Netherlands provinces on Government account. Originally they were only given to the creditors for greater security in addition to the Government bonds. Then the latter were omitted. As, however, the creditors were often discontented with the Receivers' bonds by themselves, they were given Court bonds in many different towns, which stated the special revenues from which the Receivers General were to pay the debt and

---

[1] Verachter, Invent. No. 711; Place. v. Brabant, I, 509, 511, 515, Register in Bulletin des Archives d'Anvers, vol. I.

promised not to apply these revenues in any other way. In many cases, however, the Receivers General were the principal debtors, and the ruler, in spite of his promises, did not feel bound to step in should they fail to pay. Hence the creditors obtained no payments for the enormous quantities of these bonds. Fine examples of them engrossed on parchment can still be found in the archives of the South German patrician families.

(6) For completeness' sake, it must be added that large bourse firms often issued loans on account of the Netherlands Government, charging 1 per cent. to 2 per cent. for their del credere. In this case it was not the bonds of the Government but of the issuing house that were dealt with on the bourse. Accordingly these did not constitute a public finance transaction.

(7) Bonds of the English Crown, regularly under the guarantee of all Privy Councillors and the City of London, and on occasions under that of the Merchant Adventurers who had their staple in Antwerp.

(8) Bonds of the King of Portugal, whose Antwerp agent was in most cases personally liable.

In these bonds, the princes always promised repayment 'in verbo regio' 'de bonne foy, en parolle d'empereur et roy'; the cities engaged all their burghers with their property 'conjunctim sive insolidum'; interest was granted in form only as a special concession (in remuneratione laborum suorum ex nostra mera liberalitate et favore donavimus –) in order to avoid the laws against usury; and the interest was often reckoned in the capital of the debt. There is still much that might be said as to these formalities and they were certainly important in law. Their economic significance, however, was small, as the creditor was not secured by the more or less binding form of the bond, but by the certainty that the debtors could and would pay.

Economically speaking, little importance attached to the bearer clause inserted in all Netherlands bonds and in no others, not even those of foreign princes. The latter on occasion were transferred as easily as the former. This was specially applicable to the Netherlands bonds of the Receivers and those of the King of Portugal. Even those provided with the Bearer clause seem like the rest to have required special transfer if assigned. As a rule neither the Netherlands Receivers General nor the city of Antwerp nor the other public debtors lent their bonds and seals for small amounts. Anyone who wished to invest small sums in bonds had to apply to a large bourse firm, who did the business under their own name and made out to the person who paid them the money a declaration of trust (revers) which set out his share in the original bond and promised not to part with it before the part creditor was fully satisfied. For example, the Fugger in 1556 formed great syndicates for taking over large lots of the Netherlands bonds of the Receivers General. If, however, there was any question of dividing up the bonds in which many persons were interested, great difficulties arose.

Many examples will show us how extremely complicated the business became through the system of numerous guarantees which mutually propped one another up. Most princes' loans bore interest higher than the market rate, so that merchants often borrowed money at 2–3 per cent. at one fair and lent it to a princely borrower at 4 per cent. In times of financial stress the difference was often 12 per cent. a year and more, but the risk was more than correspondingly increased. The city of Antwerp, on the other hand, did not usually pay much more than the market rate. When in 1557 the Kings of France and Spain ceased payment the bonds of the city of Antwerp were still in good repute, and Antwerp could still borrow large sums at the same interest as the best bourse firms. At last, however, towards the end of 1561 people began to mistrust Antwerp, withdrew their money and lent it to the Diet of Brabant. Finally, however, even this was no longer solvent.

Views as to the goodness of the different securities were very different at different times. Thus for a long time the bonds of the Receivers General were regarded with distrust, while later even the largest amounts of these were easily disposed of. Finally they proved entirely worthless. Lazarus Tucher, who had a good judgment in such matters, still held in 1561 that the Portuguese loans were the best next to the English, although at that time no interest had been paid on them for years and they continued to pay nothing, while a composition was effected in the case of the French and Spanish Crown loans. The bonds of the English Crown, the only loans of this class which in fact proved safe, were often entirely discredited. Bourse opinions were just as misleading then as they are now. The bourse's reactions to political news also have altered very little in the last three hundred years.

Financial Agents of the Netherlands Court and the Crown Agents in Antwerp. It happened on occasions that the financial counsellors of the Netherlands came in person to Antwerp to raise loans. This, however, was a symptom of financial difficulties and was therefore damaging. The Brussels Court for the most part used a broker or merchant as agent for its Antwerp loans, and the other governments had always to do the same.

We have already learnt to know the financial agents of the Brussels Court as a body. This office was filled from 1516 to 1523, and on occasions until 1531 by Pieter van der Straten; he was followed from 1528 to 1531 by Gerard Stercke and the well-known Lazarus Tucher (1529–41); then Gaspar Ducci (1542–50); finally, after 1552, Gaspar Schetz. In the intervals other merchants again held a similar position, Jorys Meuting,

Thomas Muller, Jan Mois, and Gilles Sorbrucque. They served the Government as agents on behalf of others and as bankers on their own account. Besides this they occupied certain official posts and had the title of Imperial Counsellor. Their work as financial agents was not legally defined; it was not an office, but an occupation. It was, therefore, distinct from that of the established agents. For a long time only the King of Portugal had an established agent in Antwerp. He sold pepper and other spices from the East Indies – a trade of which the King had a monopoly, and bought copper, munitions of war, shipbuilding materials, and other commodities. This gave rise to advances on an increasing scale and finally to pure loans. The first of the Portuguese agents was Diego Fernandez, who is spoken of in Bruges about 1490, but by 1494 had begun to stay at times in Antwerp. Others were: about 1500, Alonso Martini; 1503, Thomas (?) Lopez; about 1511, Albert (?) Lopez; 1514–21, Jean Brandon, who honoured and protected Albrecht Dürer when he stayed in Antwerp. His successor was Ruy (Rodrigo) Fernandez (d'Almada) who held the position for some time, perhaps till 1543, the year when there is first mention of João Rabello, who was still acting in 1548. After 1556 we come across Francesco Pesoa, whom Guicciardini mentions in this position in 1667, by which time its importance had sunk considerably. When the correspondents of the South German firms speak of 'the agent' it is usually the King of Portugal's agent that they mean.

The English Crown had from early times many connections with Antwerp, which was far the most important centre for English foreign trade. Henry VIII's political agents, Spinelli, Knight, Pace, etc., often stayed in Antwerp, where they had relations not only with the English merchants, but with those of other nations, collected news and negotiated on many occasions about money. For a long time, however, their dealings were not about loans, but large money payments to be conveyed to the Emperor. The first agent proper of the English Crown was Stephan Vaughan, a merchant from London, a member of the Adventurers Company, who stood in relations in 1557 with Cromwell, not yet a Minister. Later he was often employed by the Government to collect news in the Netherlands, to buy war materials and conduct negotiations about trade policy.[1] He did not borrow in Antwerp till 1545. His successor two years later was William Dansell, who did much the same work as Vaughan till 1551, not, however, to the satisfaction of the English Government, which recalled him in disgrace. Both Vaughan and Dansell were also Governors of the Adventurers in Antwerp.[2]

[1] Brewer, *Calendar*, IV, 3053. Cf. Burgon, *Gresham*, I, 57 ff. Schanz, *Engl. Handelspolitik*, I, 77.

[2] Burgon, I, 63–5. Turnbull, *Calendar*, *Edw. VI*, No. 33 ff.

At the beginning of 1552 Dansell's place was taken by Thomas Gresham, also a London merchant and member of the Adventurers Company, who, like his father, uncle, and brother, had often had dealings with the English Crown. His services, not only to the Crown from 1552 onwards, but also to the whole of England, so far exceed those of other financial agents and established agents that we must give him a section to himself. First, however, we will say a few words as to the agents of the Governments of Spain and the Netherlands. One of these was Gaspar Schetz, who after Ducci's fall was financial agent of the Brussels Court. In the year 1552, when Gresham took up the parallel appointment for the English Crown, Schetz was entitled 'Facteur des finances de l'empereur,' which none of his predecessors had been. Three years later he was nominated by King Philip II of Spain as his permanent agent in Antwerp. From the instructions then given him we see that he received a fixed annual salary, together with a commission on his business and allowances for any journeys. So far as we know none of the other royal factors had a position so closely analogous to that of an official. Yet Gaspar Schetz had large monetary transactions on his own account with the Government he represented as well as with other Governments. The King of Portugal's agent was even interested in the great pepper contracts which he concluded with merchants in Antwerp on account of his King. If we consider essentials rather than the form, Thomas Gresham was the agent who served his royal employer the best and the most faithfully.

The last of the princely agents, Juan Lopez Gallo, was entrusted in 1559 with the management of the Spanish finance business proper, while Gaspar Schetz kept those of the Netherlands. We have already seen that his actions were not above reproach.

In 1567 Guicciardini, enumerating the agents resident in Antwerp in his time, called them all 'huomini qualificatissimi,' an understandable description as he was close friends with some of them and had reasons to shield the others. He tells us that the Spanish and Portuguese agents since the bankruptcy of their Kings did no more business for them. There was subsequently no real change in this situation.

Sir Thomas Gresham. It is clear from what has been already said why this is the place to describe the work of this remarkable man. He did not belong to the financiers 'Geldleute,' with whom he did constant business in Antwerp, but was originally one large commodity merchant, a 'Merchant Adventurer,' who was employed by three rulers on account of his outstanding qualities and the high position he enjoyed in the business world as Crown agent in Antwerp. In this capacity, that of 'royal merchant,' as he was also called, he is one of the most important figures in the sixteenth century and the history of England. His importance, however, mainly took its rise from Antwerp.[1]

Gresham's first task was to raise loans in Antwerp for the English Government. The English merchants were not yet able to satisfy by themselves the Government's demand for credit, while the foreigners dealing in England had mostly, on the initiative of their native competitors, been slowly harried home to their own countries. In any case they would not have been able to provide the large sums which the English Crown had to borrow since the end of the reign of Henry VIII. This could only be done by means of the great Antwerp money market. In 1566 Gresham could boast that since he took up his post fourteen years before he had obtained 1,840,000 £ Fl. for the English Crown and had repaid it nearly all. The loans were concluded in the usual way for one or two fairs and on maturity had to be either repaid or prolonged. Before Gresham's advent, extension had always been an expensive business, as his predecessors had as a usual thing bought jewels and commodities of all kinds at high prices from the creditors, thereby making the real interest much higher than the nominal rate agreed on. Gresham soon abolished this practice. More important still, however, was the improvement he effected in the credit of the English Crown. Soon after the death of Edward VI, Gresham boasted that he had raised the credit of the King so greatly that he would have been able to borrow any sum he liked in Antwerp, 'wherefore his enemies began to fear him, for hitherto his power had not been known.'

Allowing for some exaggeration it is certain that under Gresham the credit of the English Crown was far better than that of the other princes who borrowed in Antwerp. This was specially true of the period since the accession of Elizabeth. Under Mary, Gresham had at first been removed, but was recalled when the Queen's credit had been damaged by the stupidity of another agent. During Mary's lifetime, however, Gresham was unable to carry out his own wise financial plans, so that the credit of the Crown underwent some temporary setbacks. He was able nevertheless to establish it again, thanks to his unrivalled knowledge of the Antwerp Bourse and the large financiers, of whom many – including the Schetz – were his intimate friends.

Gresham treated the financial dealings of the English Government as they should be treated – that is to say, as commercial business, with discretion, caution, and honesty. This was the secret of his success. From the first he insisted that all obligations must be punctually ful-

[1] Based on Burgon, Turnbull and Kervyn de Lettenhove, *Acts of the Privy Council.* Cf. also Ehrenberg, *Hamburg und England im Zeitalter der Königin Elisabeth,* p. 50 ff.

filled. If necessary he pledged his own credit. He always kept himself exactly informed as to the state of the money market. He knew how to rivet the money and bill brokers to his interest; and as early as 1553 he wrote home, 'No bourse passes wherein I am not furnished with a statement of all monies borrowed on that day.' On Mary's death he hastened to Antwerp to assure the Queen's creditors that all her obligations would be promptly discharged according to her dying injunction to her successor.

Finally, when the outbreak of rebellion in the Netherlands had thrown the Antwerp money market into confusion, Gresham felt that the moment had come for making England independent of foreign countries, not only as to trade, but also in credit. On the 14th August, 1569, he wrote to Sir William Cecil: [1]

'. . . I would wissh that the Q. Majestie in this time shuld not use any *strangers but her own* subiectes wherebie he and all other *princes maie se what a prince of powr she ys*. And bie this meanes there is no dowbt but that her highnes shall cause the Duke of Alva to know him self and to make what end with that low Countreys as Her Majestie will her self what brute soever is here spredde abrode to the contrary. Sir, seing I am entrid so farre with youe for the credit of the Q. majestie beyond the seas wherein I have travailed this 20 yeres and bie experience in *using oure owne merchanntes* I found gret honnor to the prince as also *gret profit* to the merchanntes and to the whole Realme whatsoever our merchanntes saye to the contrarye for when our prince ought owr own meane merchanntes 60 or 80 (thousands pounds) (Mti) then they knew them selves and were daily reddie and sure as good chere as stranngers did whiche Syr I would wissh again in this time of extremity to be usid for that I know our merchanntes be able to do yt. . . .'

This was true, but at first Gresham had difficulties in obtaining large sums from the English merchants, and they often complained of the harsh treatment of them. Gradually, however, they came to appreciate such an opportunity for capital investments; and since Antwerp was no longer available, after a longish and uncomfortable period of transition the moment arrived when the English Government could satisfy their extraordinary credit requirements at home. Gresham introduced this great change and actively supported it; he was also one of the first to press for the abolition of the State ban on interest. Before this, however, he had done other, perhaps even more important, services. In the early days of his appointment he had managed by skilful manipulation to influence the rate for bills on London in favour of England and the Crown loans. Afterwards he directed all his energies to improving the

[1] Brit. Mus. Lansd. MSS. 12, fol. 16.

English trade balance and the value of sterling. He achieved these ends chiefly by two acts which needed long and careful preparation, the destruction of the trade of the German Hansa towns with England and the coinage reform of 1560. In his reports to the English Government he laid down the principles which finally regulated the currency of the European States in the new epoch. He acquired his exact knowledge of currency and bills through his business in Antwerp. We need not prove this here, and the fact by no means detracts from Gresham's merits. His merits consisted in the application of the principles and expert knowledge of the business world to the affairs of a great monarchy.

He remained all his life an exact and successful merchant, as well as a patriot and a true servant of his rulers – a rare phenomenon among the merchants and financiers of the sixteenth century, who seldom managed to combine both sets of qualities.

Gresham owned a house in Antwerp in the Lange Nieuwstraat, but London was his home and the chief seat of his extensive business. He crossed the sea repeatedly on the Crown business, without in all cases getting a recompense in proportion to his trouble and deserts. His travelling allowances were only 20*s.* a day, and he often had trouble in getting the promises of compensation for his services fulfilled. Yet there is no doubt that his post as Royal Agent was a source of profit. He died one of the richest men of his day, after giving London an Exchange on the pattern of the one at Antwerp and founding a college called by his own name. He left his widow an annual income of £2,388, so large for the sixteenth century as to excite doubts as to its correctness. It must, however, be regarded as authentic.[1]

Gresham was also frequently employed on political missions in the Netherlands, and in the critical times of the Netherlands rebellion he provided England with materials for war, risking life and property in evading the prohibitive laws of the Netherlands. For many years he conducted the extensive news service of the English Government in the Netherlands, and it was in the first instance due to him that Queen Elizabeth and her statesmen were better informed as to everything that went on in Europe than any other Government. Gresham's remarkable double position comes out here, for the news which sent to his Government originated chiefly in the commercial world. He was thus able to exploit for his country on every side the advantages of the world bourse.

Chronicle of the Antwerp Finances up to 1542. Up to 1510 or thereabouts the merchants who could lend capital in the Netherlands had their agencies in Bruges. In the year 1510 there first appear in the

[1] Burgon, II, 490.

Loans of the Netherlands Government.

Date of Loan.	Amount in £ Artois at 40 Gr. Fl.	Date of Repayment.	Interest per cent. per annum.	Lender.	Remarks.
1509.10.3	10,500	1509.1.9 } 1510.1.3 }	11½	Antonio de Vaille, Antwerp	For restoration of the dykes, and pay of the garrisons in Guelders.
1509.10.3	10,500				
1510.20.6	15,900	1511.Dec.	7½	Same	Payment of soldiery in Guelders.
1510.28.6	1,000	1510.Oct.	24	Giacomo Doria, Antwerp.	
1510.1.10	16,000	1511.31.3	13¼	Fil. Gualterotti, Bruges.	
1511.20.5	20,000	1512.1.3	6¼	Various Antwerp merchants	On the request of the Regent for the Emperor.
1511.Whitsuntide	3,600	1512.15.1	10	Jeron. Frescobaldi	
1511.15.7	14,500	1512.Dec. }	15	Fil. Gualterotti, Bruges, and the Agent of Christ. Herwart, Antwerp	War in Guelders.
1511.15.7	14,500	1512.June }			
1512.September ?	100,000	?	?	Diego de Haro, Antwerp.	
1512. ?	10,000	?	?		
1.1	7,000	1512.31.8	8½	Fil. Gualterotti, Bruges.	
25.1	8,000	1512.14.8	12½	Various merchants in Bruges.	

Netherlands finance accounts payments to the Fugger on bills drawn in Augsburg and repayments of advances made by the Spaniard Antonio de Vaille, who, like the Fugger, was already settled in Antwerp. The loan business which then grew up in Antwerp had for long a very irregular character. The loans were not concluded from fair to fair; other and usually larger terms were fixed by agreement – half a year or even more. Moreover, the loans were not yet very considerable. There were enormous fluctuations in the rate of interest. As yet there was no trace of a market rate as far as these loans were concerned. The latter gives further details for the years 1509 to 1512.

On the 29th January, 1512, the city of Antwerp, at the most urgent request of the Queen Regent and the financial connections, borrowed from certain unnamed German merchants 20,000 £ on the Government account to pay the German mercenaries. These merchants were to obtain repayment for themselves from the Aides of Brabant already granted. This loan cost 2,400 £ for five months and ten days = 27 per cent. The broker also received 100 £.

On the other hand, there were at this time loans which bore no interest.

In 1515, Prince Charles, afterwards Charles V, was declared of age, on the promise of 140,000 £ Fl. to his needy grandfather Maximilian. He then entered in state into Antwerp, already declared in this year by one of the English envoys to be 'one of the flowers of the world.' He prepared to make the journey to his Spanish kingdom. He was in great need of money both for this journey and the payment of the 140,000 £ to the Emperor, and also because his grandfather on his mother's side, King Ferdinand of Aragon, had bequeathed him a great load of debt. Large sums accordingly had to be borrowed in Antwerp, amounting in all to 166,000 £. The greater part of this sum had to be prolonged on maturity in 1516. For this year we can state in tabular form the money borrowed in Antwerp by the Netherlands Government.

Besides the increase in the size of the loans we note that the fairs have begun to be used as terms. The sums borrowed in the second half of the year were meant for the war in Friesland, which made necessary even larger loans in the following year.

At the beginning of 1517 the city of Antwerp, in order to meet the costs of the war, tried to sell annuities repayable within three years from the Aides of the province of Brabant. All efforts failed, however, to attract buyers on tolerable conditions. Accordingly in February, 1517, a sum of 45,000 £ was borrowed under the guarantee of the city of Antwerp from Antwerp merchants, the Government paying the cost. The interest amounted to 5,000 £ to the St. Remy fair, or 19 per cent.

Loans of the Netherlands Government in Antwerp in 1516.

Date of Loan.	Amount of Loan in £ Artois at 40 Gr. Fl.	Date of Repayment.	Interest per cent. per annum.	Lender.	Remarks.
1516.1.3	14,000	1516.16.9 }	20	Different Antwerp merchants	Brokerage to the broker Pieter v. d. Straten. The city of Antwerp guaranteed 60,000 £ fl. and the Seigneurs de l'Ordre et du Conseil Privé, et du Conseil des Finances and other officials the rest.
1516.3.3	16,000	15.9 }			
1516.Easter	92,700	1516.St. Remy	15½	,,	
1516.Easter	10,000	1516.St. John's Day	31½	,,	
1.5	11,000	1516.Candlemas	17	,,	
1516.St. John's Day	27,000	1517.St. John's Day	11	The Fugger	Guarantee of the city of Antwerp.
1516.Sept.	16,800	1517.St. John's Day	13½	The Genoese merchants in the Netherlands	,,
1516.1.10	30,000	1517.1.2	40?	Antwerp merchants	
1516.Christmas	100,000	1517.St. Remy	14¾	Pieter van der Straten	Guarantee of the city of Antwerp.

per annum. Moreover, the loan of 27,000 £ from the Fugger which matured at the Whitsuntide fair was prolonged, together with interest then amounting to 3,000 £, till Christmas, 1518, and a further sum of 42,000 £ was borrowed from the Fugger at a cost of 7,000 £ in interest. We need not calculate the rate here.

At the St. Remy fair in 1517 60,000 £ of the maturing debts could not be met. The city of Antwerp, high State officials and nobles had given their guarantee. In order, therefore, as is expressly stated in the finance accounts, 'to keep his word and protect the honour of the lords and gentlemen and their credit, and that of the city of Antwerp,' King Charles ordered the prolongation of the remainder till the Easter fair, 1518, at a cost of 10 per cent. for the half-year. The total amount paid in interest on such loans in the year 1517 was 34,441 £ at 40 gr. = 5,760 L fl. In January, 1518, bands of discharged soldiers, eight or nine thousand strong, threatened to invade the Netherlands to plunder ('pour piller et menger les subgects'). Cavalry of the standing army (compagnies des gens de guerre à cheval des ordonnances du roy) were summoned to drive away the unbidden guests. Since, however, these regular troops could not leave their garrisons without having their quarters paid for, it was necessary to give them six weeks' pay. Since, however, the State Treasury was empty on 15th February 11,000 L had to be borrowed in Antwerp till the following Easter fair at a cost of 486 £ 10s. 6pf., or about 18 per cent.

On the 15th July in the same year the Court of Brussels, in order to give their months' pay to the garrisons of the province of Friesland, which was as yet unpacified, borrowed 38,000 £ in Antwerp from the Fugger, a debt for which a Receiver General of Revenue for the first time made himself personally liable. The loan cost only 4,000 £ for thirteen months, not quite 10 per cent., supposing the facts are correctly stated. At the autumn fair in the same year a sum of 41,000 £ was borrowed on Receivers General bonds till Easter, 1519. This operation cost 4,000 £ or about 20 per cent. inclusive of the brokerage to Pieter van der Straten, who also raised 107,600 £ at 15½ per cent. The total spent in this year on interest was 22,602 £ at 40 gr. = 3,767 £ fl.

Among the loans of the years 1519, 1520 and 1521 we note the following:

	Per cent. per annum
13,000 L from 14.8.1519 to Christmas at	16
24,000 L from Sep. 1519–Easter 1520 at	15
26,000 L from May 1519–Easter 1520 at	7
22,800 L from June 1520–Candlemas 1521 at	12
28,000 L from June 1520–Candlemas 1521 at	10
72,000 L from Aug. 1520–Christmas 1521 at	13

		Per cent. per annum
$\left.\begin{array}{l}50,000 \text{ L} \\ 32,636 \text{ L}\end{array}\right\}$ from Sep. 1520–Easter 1521 at		$15\frac{1}{2}$
71,539 L from Dec. 1520–Whit-Sunday 1521 at		$16\frac{1}{4}$
30,000 L from May 1521 to St. Remy 1521 at		17
23,200 L from 1.7.1521 to Candlemas 1522 at		$21\frac{1}{2}$
20,000 L from 1.10.1521 to 15.1.1522 at		$27\frac{1}{2}$
$\left.\begin{array}{l}125,000 \text{ L} \\ 40,000 \text{ L}\end{array}\right\}$ from Oct. 1521 to Easter 1522 at		16–18

In addition considerable sums in brokerage were paid to Pieter v. d. Straten and to Bernhard Stecher, the Fugger's agent. There is as yet no question of a market rate of interest for these loans.

The year 1522 is specially interesting for us. Early in the year money had to be raised at any price for the Emperor, who was in the greatest possible straits for money. In February 100,000 £ was raised in the following way. The Spaniards Francesco de Vaille and Francesco de Moxica, in association with certain other firms, lent this sum in Antwerp and were to receive in return 52,500 ducats in Spain. The loan was granted 'sans frais ne finance,' but the interest was included in the exchange rate for his ducats. There was some nervousness, however, lest the 52,500 ducats in Spain should not be paid. To meet this emergency on the request of the merchants, two nobles of high rank, Heinrich Graf von Nassau and Anton Lalaing, Graf von Hoochstraten, who was head of the Netherlands finances, pledged themselves personally to pay the equivalent in Antwerp at the September fair in 1522. This operation cost 7,494 £.

For another claim De Vaille and Moxica were referred to Naples. Since, however, this bond was not honoured ways and means had to be found to meet it in Antwerp.

In April a further sum of 64,000 £ was required in haste. Pieter v. d. Straten advanced this in his own name, receiving in return four bonds of 16,000 £ apiece: the first issued by Jean Seigneur de Berghes, the second by Count Floris Egmont, the third by Adolf of Burgundy Seigneur de Bevres, and the fourth from Philippe de Croy, Marquis d'Arschot., This sum of 64,000 £ was also to be repaid at the September fair. The real lenders were as we shall see the Herwart of Augsburg. Several other loans were raised. At the end of April, or the beginning of May, the Emperor needed at once another sum of 140,000 £ for his projected journey to England and for other purposes. He accordingly summoned the Conseil Privé and the Conseil des Finances in order to consider how to raise the money. There was no lack of proposals. The domains were to be pledged; or life annuities or perpetual annuities to be sold; the

Aides could be anticipated on floating loans. Objections were advanced against all these financial expedients. Perpetual annuities were difficult to redeem, life annuities very costly; floating loans from merchants still more so (these including brokerage cost 18 per cent., 20 per cent., or 22 per cent. per annum). Pledged domains usually remained in the hands of the lenders; the cities which formerly had advanced money on Aides already granted were now overloaded with debts and their credit had gone. Finally, as time pressed, the Emperor sent the Counts of Nassau and Bergen twice in great haste to Antwerp, and through the agency of the Magistrate the following agreement was arranged. Certain merchants declared their readiness to pay the Emperor at once 70,000 £ in return for the three years' rent for the lease of the Customs of Antwerp and Zeeland, amounting to 117,000 £ (39,000 £ per annum). The city of Antwerp had to guarantee the payment of the 117,000 £ to the merchants, and were on the other hand released from their obligation to pay to the Archbishop of Mainz and the Count Palatine 18,000 fl. a year on the Emperor's account. The customs above mentioned had been pledged for this amount. This last act was obviously illegal, but then the whole transaction was highly extortionate. When the imperial envoy reported in Brussels, it was remarked at once that the merchants would get their capital back in less than two years. Nevertheless the agreement had to be sanctioned. The merchants nominally

paid in cash to the Emperor	117,000 £
and received at once in interest	47,000 £
and therefore they paid actually only	70,000 £

For this they received 39,000 £ a year for three years, i.e. an interest of more than 30 per cent. per annum on £70,000. In fact, however, the transaction was not finished on these lines. The Genoese Tommaso Bombelli brought about another arrangement whereby the merchants received back their 70,000 £, together with 15,666 £ interest for one year, 22½ per cent., still a very high rate. The Emperor wanted to give Bombelli 1,000 £ for his service, but he refused 'because he had not succeeded in inducing the merchants to forgo the interest for the first year.' This unparalleled action shows how such extortionate transactions were regarded by respectable merchants.

Since the transaction we have described brought in only 70,000 £, instead of 140,000 £, a further 72,000 £ had to be raised by other means. The Emperor accordingly in June owed the merchants at least 300,000 £ to 400,000 £ at the time when he wished to travel direct from England to Spain in order to put down the last rebellions of the Comuneros. Then occurred one of those moments of acute financial embarrassment which we have already mentioned. There was no money to equip the ships which were to convey the Emperor, or to pay the soldiers who were to conduct him to Spain. Only Erasmus Schetz, after great efforts on the part of Count Hoochstraten, lent 10,000 £ on the security of a goblet of the Emperor and several gold chains belonging to the Countess. The other merchants excused themselves on the ground 'that there was no money on the bourse, that trade was at a standstill on account of the disorders,' and so forth. Finally, however, the Count succeeded in getting 20,000 £ till the autumn fair, paying 4,339 £ interest, or 52 per cent. per annum.

At the autumn fair several large loans matured, including the 100,000 £ of Francesco de Vaille and his associates. The Queen Regent was then in Antwerp, and since the creditors pressed for payment, a grand esclandre was feared. Means were at last found, but the new loans raised to pay off the old again cost on an average 21 per cent. per annum. On the different loans it varied between 13 per cent. and 27 per cent., without counting the brokerage to Pieter van der Straten. The interest paid in this year on floating loans was 82,000 £.

The financial situation, however, was at bottom a favourable one. All the same in the year following 18–24 per cent. interest had to be paid for the prolongation of the floating loans, and when an attempt was made to pay off the 64,000 £ due to the Herwart by selling annuities no one was found to buy them and the loan had to be prolonged. At the end of 1523 the floating debt amounted to about half a million.[1] The greater part of this, however, was paid off by the end of the year following, and in 1526 it was entirely disposed of. The Government had completely got the better of the merchants, as we see from the following story. The amount due to the Herwart, 64,000 £, was to be repaid in October, 1524. Actually the repayment took place in instalments in the course of the following year. The Herwart naturally demanded interest for this delay, only 12 per cent., however. This request was not granted, and after long negotiations they had to be content with 9½ per cent.

The course of a few years witnessed enormous fluctuations in the general level of interest.

The whole organization of business in Antwerp was still very imperfect in 1526, as we see from the following statement by an agent of the Tucher:

'I will endeavour to learn when the four markets here and in Bergen begin. I have asked many men and no where have had a sure answer. Men say they begin at various times. The last Pamas market begins

<hr />

[1] Brussels Archives, *Chambre des Comptes*, No. 120, fol. 202 ff.

after Our Lady's Birthday in August and the payment for the same on
the 23rd October.'

Antwerp at this time was not yet a money market of great international importance. We possess an English memorandum, drawn up in
1564, which deals with this point as follows: 'What nations or merchants
were wont formerly to lend out money in order to serve the princes and
states in their wars and other necessities? The German merchants were
the greatest and some Italians. Who now lends the most money? The
merchants of Antwerp and other merchants in the Low Countries. It is
not much more than thirty years since in Antwerp there were not above
two or three merchants who lent money at interest, and these from their
own resources could advance barely 20,000 £ fl. or 80,000 thaler.
Now, on the other hand, there are thirty or forty great merchants who
could lend 300,000 £ without hurt to their other business.'

This testimony is to be received with caution. The English memorandum wished to magnify the rise of Antwerp, which it attributed to
English trade. It is moreover not clear whether the designation 'merchants of Antwerp' covers those whose chief business was there or those
who had a factory there. In the first case the Fugger, Welser, Herwart,
de Vaille, Gualterotti, etc., were not to be regarded as Antwerp merchants; in the other it would be wrong to say that in 1530 in Antwerp
only two or three merchants could lend large sums of money. The real
state of affairs was that the Netherlands Government could then on
occasion borrow considerable sums from the foreign merchants trading
in Antwerp. The largest sum, however, in the period treated hitherto
did not exceed 500,000 £ Art. at 40 gr., or 357,000 fl. Rh. There was no
change either in the next few years. On the other hand, in 1527 the
Fugger alone had claims on the Hapsburg brothers amounting to three
times this amount, and only a small part of this originated in Antwerp.
Only the King of Portugal, besides the Netherlands Government, owed
the Antwerp merchants large sums. These, however, were not pure
financial transactions, but advances on pepper sales, purchases of
copper or credit, etc. That Antwerp in the first quarter of the sixteenth
century was not an important money market is shown above all by the
high rate and violent fluctuations of the interest which the Netherlands
Government had to pay in that market. These were almost the same as
those which, except in certain isolated cases, the Fugger, Welser and
other South German houses charged their royal creditors on the
Augsburg loans.

In 1526 and 1527 there was nothing doing in the Antwerp money
market; but in the following years business began to revive. In 1528
there was only one important transaction, the loan of 200,000 £ from
the Hochstetter. In this case the Government had to take in payment

quicksilver and cinnamon, commodities which were then purchased by Lazarus Tucher at a loss to the Government of 74,000 £. The financial officials regarded this as a very huge loss, but since no other interest was paid and the loss distributed over five years, it was tantamount to interest at 18 per cent., and in reality things might have been worse. The usual rates of interest in 1528, 1529 and 1530 fluctuated between 14 per cent. and 22 per cent., the upper limit being nearer the average. The largest transaction in these years was a loan of 218,812 £ concluded in November, 1529, for seven months at the rate of 20 per cent. per annum in order to meet bills drawn by the Fornari and other Genoese merchants on the Netherlands finance administration. Next most important was a loan of 125,000 £ contracted in August, 1529, to meet the bills of the Fugger, Welser, and Herwart. This cost 21½ per cent. per annum, in spite of the personal guarantee of the highest finance officials; also, after a quarter, 74,000 £ of it had to be prolonged, which cost a further 17¾ per cent. This, however, was a small matter compared with the enormous loans which the Fugger at this time granted to the Emperor and his brother.

The following examples will show the extreme complexity of the transactions of the Netherlands Government at this time. In 1527 the Emperor had to make a payment of 45,000 £ to the Bishop of Utrecht. A bond of the Hochstetter for 30,000 £ payable in 1529 was given in payment. The Hochstetter, who did not pay over any ready money, were given a guarantee by the city of Antwerp, which in turn received a guarantee from Count Hoochstraten, the chief of the Netherlands finances. He promised the Bishop of Utrecht, should the Hochstetter fail to pay, to do so himself, and received in his turn undertakings from the Emperor that he would be compensated for any payments he might have to make under his guarantees. The Hochstetter, as we know, got into difficulties and transferred the guarantee of the city of Antwerp to Diego Mendez in Antwerp. They became bankrupt shortly afterwards, and the Bishop of Utrecht applied in the first instance to Count Hoochstraten, while at the same time Diego Mendez applied to the city of Antwerp, which in turn had recourse on the unfortunate Count, now in danger of having to pay twice over. He accordingly seized the remainder of the Hochstetter's claim still due on the loan of 200,000 L. This claim, however, which amounted to 170,000 £, had been handed over by the Hochstetter on the eve of their bankruptcy to the Fugger. This gave rise to new lawsuits; finally, however, Wolff Haller undertook to redeem for 6,000 £ one of the Count Hochstraten's bonds, while the other had already been met.

The following statement shows the sums shown in the Netherlands finance accounts under the heading 'Deniers pris à frais et finance' during the years 1521 to 1530. They contain chiefly interest and brokerage for the floating loans, their losses on bill transactions and instalments of repayments. They therefore give a fair picture of the Netherlands finances at this period. The livres are at 40 gr. Flemish.

1521	62,263 £	1526	1,092 £
1522	112,195 ,,	1527	1,623 ,,
1523	18,569 ,,	1528	93,688 ,,
1524	5,679 ,,	1529	92,151 ,,
1525	10,864 ,,	1530	57,079 ,,

This makes a total of 455,000 L for ten years or an average of 45,500 L. a year. During this period the total revenues of the Netherlands Government averaged 1,440,000 L a year and the Aides (the direct taxes granted by the Diets) alone averaged a million L at 40 gr. From this must be subtracted, however, the considerable grants of reductions and remissions of taxation amounting on an average to 250,000 L a year. Taking this into account the Netherlands Government rejoiced in an average yearly income of 1,200,000 L, against which the 45,500 L for the floating debt charge was a mere trifle. The financial situation of the Netherlands was extraordinarily favourable, and yet it could not always borrow even at 20 per cent. and over.[1]

Further, in the year 1531, the Emperor undertook enormous repayments of his old and new debts in the Netherlands from the extraordinary receipts under the Peace of Cambrai and from the Aides of the same year; the city of Antwerp alone received nearly half a million L Art. at 40 gr. On the other hand, during the same year he had to take up large floating loans at 12 per cent. to 21 per cent. interest; and Stephen Vaughan, who for some time had done all sorts of business for the English Government in Antwerp, was never tired of reporting how short of money the Emperor was.[2] He borrowed largely in Augsburg at this time, as we have seen, promising repayment in Antwerp, losing 18,375 L or 215,250 L, owing to the adverse exchange. Even his contemporaries wondered why, in spite of the increasing stream of gold and silver from America flowing into his treasury, the Emperor always had recourse to short-term loans at high rates.[3]

The following decade saw little change in these conditions; but there is an unmistakable, though slow, reduction in the rate of interest. In 1535 and 1536 it fluctuated between 13 per cent. and 20 per cent. Most

[1] In Brussels Archives (Papiers d'Etat et de l'Audience, No. 873): Revenues et dépenses d. Charles V, 1520–30.

[2] Gairdner, *Calendar*, V, No. 246; *State Papers, Henry VIII*, vol. VII, 301.

[3] Brewer, *Calendar*, VII, No. 440 (1534),

large loans, however, only cost 13 per cent. to 15 per cent., though the demand for money was increasing and the market was tight.[1]

In February, 1535, when there was fear of a French invasion, a sum of 250,000 L, partly for six months and partly for a year, was borrowed from Lazarus Tucher at 14 per cent. under the guarantee of the Queen Regent, the Knights of the Golden Fleece, and high officials. The loan was not met on maturity – (it was not in fact paid till 1542) – and the rate of interest rose accordingly to 18 per cent. to 20 per cent., but not beyond this; it then gradually sank, and in 1539 fluctuated between 10 per cent. and 13 per cent., and in 1541, the demand for money having increased, between 12 per cent. and 16 per cent. In the last-mentioned year the rate of interest is usually stated in the finance accounts, while hitherto only the amount paid had been entered. At this time 3 per cent. to 4 per cent. was usually paid from one fair time to the next on the Court loans. Lazarus Tucher, Dismes de Ferrere, and Gilles de Sorbrucque lent money on these terms, the largest amount being 197,000 L. The total interest paid in 1541 was 96,516 L, not higher than in many of the preceding years. It was only in 1542 that this limit was considerably exceeded.

The Period from 1542 *to* 1551. There is no better illustration of the financial situation of the Netherlands Government at this period than the following figures from the *Comptes de la Récette Générale.*

	Receipts.	Expenditure.
1540	1,040,795 £	928,855 £
1541	1,051,017 „	976,075 „
1542	1,986,294 „	2,631,200 „
1543	3,376,437 „	3,674,531 „

While, therefore, the years 1540 and 1541 together showed a surplus of almost 200,000 L, the two years following had a deficit of nearly a million, in spite of the inclusion in the receipts of large loans and other extraordinary receipts. This change for the worse is due entirely to the war with France, which cost in the Netherlands alone 1½ million pounds (at 40 gr.) and in 1543 2 million. As a result the Brussels Court's financial transactions in Antwerp greatly increased in scope under the skilful management of Gaspar Ducci, while the rate of interest at first fell because the supply of capital exceeded the demand.

Guicciardini takes 1542 as the beginning of a new and important period in the history of Antwerp. The danger of war had caused the building of new fortifications, and the city had at the same time been extended and had become such a well-secured place that 'many men

[1] Lanz, *Correspondenz Carls V*, t. 658, 665. For 1537, *ibid.* II, 673, 677.

from the country and other districts streamed in to dwell there.' [1]
Guicciardini seems perhaps to exaggerate the importance of this cause of
Antwerp's development.

In 1542 an arrangement was made as to several large advances of
Lazarus Tucher, who did not come off particularly well under it. In
1535 and 1536 he had lent 368,825 L, and for six years no interest had
been paid, nor had the promised repayments been carried out. He now
received his capital and only 52,731 L for interest over the whole period,
equivalent to not more than $2\frac{1}{2}$ per cent. per annum. For small advances
in 1538 and 1539 he obtained as much as 13 per cent. to 16 per cent.

The first loans for which Gaspar Ducci acted as agent were concluded
at Candlemas, 1542, at 11 per cent. to 12 per cent., in order to repay
the maturing bonds of the Receivers General at 12 per cent. He received in return as security new bonds of the same kind, which he resold
to merchants and other holders of capital. At the subsequent fairs he
raised in the same way still larger sums for the war expenses. In the
course of the year he borrowed about a million pounds (at 40 gr.),
almost all at 12 per cent. per annum.

In August, 1542, when a French invasion was feared, a subscription
was opened on the Antwerp Bourse for a voluntary loan without interest, which yielded the sum of 209,800 £. This was repaid next year
by the sale of annuities and in other ways, and another voluntary loan
was made, 200,000 £ being contributed by the city of Antwerp and
104,000 £ by private individuals. This, however, was not a financial
transaction, but a contribution from patriotic or other motives to the
defence of the country.

In 1543 Gaspar Ducci raised 1,200,000 L, Lazarus Tucher 200,000 L,
and Eustace Kaltenhofer 120,000 L, of which a part remained unsettled
for not quite the whole year. As the interest paid amounted to 102,200
L at 12 per cent., the amount of the debt throughout the year averaged
850,000 L, an hitherto unprecedented burden of floating debt.

The city of Antwerp also raised in this year extraordinarily large
amounts for the building of the new fortifications and the enlargement
of the bounds of the city. [2]

In the year 1544 the loans continued; the supply of money was shorter
and the rate higher. We can see this process best in the business letters
of Hieronymus Seiler. As late as the Pamas fair in 1543 12 per cent.
was paid on the prolonged bonds of the Receivers General; but by the
end of January, 1544, the rate had risen to 14 per cent. At the beginning
of February, the letters say, 'I am glad that thou thinkest the Bonds of

---

[1] *Descritt. d. Paesi Bassi*, ed. 1581, p. 127.

[2] *Descritt. d. Paesi Bassi*, ed. 1581, pp. 95, 127. *Stadtsprotokollen*, ed. Pauwels,
I, 33.

the Receivers General will bring a good deal of ready money on the Bourse this quarter day.'

The rate asked now began to be 8 per cent. till the Whitsun fair, i.e. for six months. 'Should peace come there would be money enough at 5 per cent. (the half year).' The scarcity of money was partly due to the fact that the Receivers General had paid no interest for several fairs.

In May and June the rate for the Court loans was usually 16 per cent., and this continued in the months following. We have a certificate of the Netherlands finance administration for the 26th August, 1544, which states that on the sums borrowed for the Emperor in Antwerp the rates are ordinary interest (frait ordinaire) 12 per cent. per annum, extraordinary (par forme de gratuyté) a further 1 per cent. per fair, a total accordingly of 16 per cent. per annum. The reason for this increase of the rates is stated to be the extraordinarily large sums raised, not only for the Emperor, but for the King of England. Nicolas Nicolai, the Receiver General of Brabant, at the Whitsun quarter day had been unable to meet the obligation of 360,000 L he had assumed, from the Aide of 400,000 L which the Diet had already granted. The Diet had to issue its own bonds for capital and interest. Finding the interest too high however, the Finance Administration issued this Certificate and the Diet accordingly granted interest at 16 per cent. and repayment at the Christmas market, 1545.[1]

We are never told the amount of the loans borrowed in Antwerp for King Henry VIII by his agent Stephen Vaughan; but we know that in 1545 the King owed the Fugger in Antwerp 152,180 pounds Flemish, or 913,080 L of 40 gr. on a single transaction. The Netherlands Government had never dealt on this scale in Antwerp.[2]

The Antwerp debt of the King of Portugal at the end of 1543 is estimated by his agent João Rabello at two million Cruzadi or Portuguese ducats, an incredible amount even allowing for the fact that a great part of this was merely payments in advance for pepper contracts. The chronicler adds that the agents had reckoned such a high rate of interest that the King's debt doubled in four years. This is quite probable, for the agent had himself paid 12 per cent. to 16 per cent. per annum, or rather 3 per cent. to 4 per cent. per fair. If he charged the King $4\frac{1}{2}$ per cent. $= 18$ per cent. this would double the capital in four years at compound interest.[3]

The Haug of Augsburg had the following claims outstanding in Antwerp in 1545:

[1] Brussels, *Chambres de Comptes*, No. 110.
[2] Rymer, *Foedera*, ed. 1704, XV, 101.
[3] Sousa, *Annaes de el rei Dom João III*, ed. Herculano, p. 408 ff.

8,648.4.2 L	City of Antwerp.
3,150 L	King of Portugal.
13,929.6.3 L	Bonds of the Receivers General.
12,600 L	Gaspar Ducci, interest in Fugger loan.
1,646.5 L	Various.

This amounts to a total of 39,973.15.5 L Fl., or in round numbers 240,000 L of 40 gr.

The Fugger had the following claims outstanding in Antwerp in 1546:

21,746.13 L	City of Antwerp.
30,739.11.8 L	Brussels Court.
6,000 L	King of Portugal.
83,900 L	King of England.
44,000 L	Gaspar Ducci, interest on bonds of Receivers General.

These sums amount to 186,386.4.8 L Fl., or in round figures 1,118,000 L of 40 gr. This gives some idea of the sums which the South German merchants taken by themselves invested in Antwerp. Some of this money of course was borrowed in Antwerp. For instance, the Fugger borrowed as follows:

14,570.12.6 L	from Pamas fair, 1546, to Christmas fair, 1547, at $2\frac{1}{4}$ per cent. ($= 9$ per cent. per annum), from Sebastian Neidhart.
12,600 L	from Pamas fair till Easter fair, at 5 per cent. ($= 10$ per cent. per annum), from Barth. Welser & Co.
4,090 L	from Pamas till Christmas fair, at $2\frac{1}{4}$ per cent. ($= 9$ per cent. per annum), from Anton Haug and kinsmen.
6,544 L	from Pamas till Christmas fair, at $2\frac{1}{4}$ per cent., from Ludwig Ligsalz.
6,201 L	for two fairs, at $4\frac{1}{2}$ per cent. ($= 9$ per cent. per annum), from Count van Dale.
8,170 L	for one fair at $2\frac{1}{8}$ per cent. ($= 8\frac{1}{2}$ per cent. per annum), from Geronimo Diodati.
2,385 L	for one fair, at $2\frac{1}{4}$ per cent., from Erasmus Schetz.

And so forth, making a total for 35 entries of 110,234 L Fl. or 661,404 L at 40 gr.

This money cost the Fugger on an average 8 per cent. to 10 per cent. per annum, while on their side they received 12 per cent. on the bonds of the Receivers General, 13 per cent. on the debt of the English King, $13\frac{1}{2}$ per cent. on that of the Brussels Court, and 11 per cent. on that of the King of Portugal.

It appears that the Fugger regarded the interest paid by the King of England as high, for they asked their agent not to tell Ducci how high it was. The bonds of the Receivers General fell into discredit at the

Pamas fair, partly because no interest was paid and partly on account of the onset of the war of Schmalkalden. No one would have them and money generally was easy. Even now, however, the Government borrowed through Ducci large amounts at 11 per cent. to 13 per cent.

The next few years up to and including 1551 saw little change in these conditions. The princes continued to borrow largely, but on the whole the interest showed a downward tendency. In 1549, however, William Dansell, the English Crown agent, borrowed at 13 per cent., and said he could raise another 100,000 L Fl. at 14 per cent.[1] He said emphatically that this was not excessive as the Emperor paid 15 per cent. to 18 per cent. This, however, was incorrect, for we see from the Netherlands Finance Accounts that the Government only paid 10 per cent., and even 9 per cent. on small amounts which were offered to it.

This is confirmed by the interesting instructions given in June, 1549, by the Imhofs in Nuremberg to their Antwerp agent. All this shows how intensely at this period the South German business houses wished to invest their capital in financial transactions, and that they were quite content with 10 per cent. per annum.

Dansell was a clumsy agent, and the interest he paid for what he borrowed on the Crown account in Antwerp was therefore unduly high. The Privy Council knew better and recommended him not to pay more than 12 per cent. Lazarus Tucher in fact declared his readiness to lend 22,500 L Fl. at this rate, but the agent was to take payment in kind, a losing game. On loans in money he was asked to pay 13 per cent. as before, and he offered 12½ per cent. without success. The unfavourable treatment accorded to the English Crown by the Antwerp financiers had become such a settled habit that Gresham had the greatest trouble in getting better conditions by his skilful management of the market.[2]

The higher interest paid at this time by the French and English Kings naturally made it harder for the Emperor to get the money he required. The Government accordingly tried to carry out in all stringency the long-standing prohibition on the export of specie, e.g. Lazarus Tucher, who was the most intimately acquainted with the Brussels Court, refused decidedly to help the English agent to export ready money. Dansell succeeded, however, in secretly sending away large sums at his own risk. The merchants' preference for paying him in kind was, however, stimulated by the prohibition. Gaspar Ducci, less scrupulous than Lazarus Tucher, carried on exchange dealings with Lyons, whereby he managed to create artificial tightness of the market, sometimes in Lyons

---

[1] Turnbull, *Calendar, Edward VI*, No. 137.
[2] Turnbull, l.c. Nos. 139, 142, 146, 148, 150, 153, 155, 161, 162, 164, 172, 184, 193, 198–9, 207.

and sometimes in Antwerp, in order to get more for his money in either market. This arrangement, however, came to grief in the end.

The development of the Antwerp money market after 1522 unquestionably owes much to Ducci, who succeeded by his sly and daring financial expedients in attracting money from all sides. To a far greater degree than Lazarus Tucher he is the first representative of a class of financier which has become increasing familiar.

Already at this time in the Antwerp money market small syndicates had begun to be formed. We know already the Ducci-Seiler-Neidhart–Grimel-Pecori syndicate. This, however, was, properly speaking, a commercial undertaking: what we mean here is something different. The Fugger had for a long time past granted other business houses an interest in their financial undertakings. This system was further developed in the period 1542–51. The Fugger granted the Haug an interest, and the Haug did the same to yet other merchants, e.g. in 1549 the Haug had outstanding in Antwerp:

4,503 L lent to the Receiver General, Jan van Roden. Wolff
       Poschinger was interested in this and also in:
2,500 L claim against the Receiver General Jan Partnol.
20,400 L lent to the city of Antwerp.
14,489 L lent to the Queen Regent.
       The Ligsalz were interested in both these last loans.

As the Imhof then wished to invest money, their Antwerp agent applied to Ducci, Poschinger, Kaltenhofer, the Welser, etc.

Perhaps it would be more accurate not to speak of syndicates in all these cases. A syndicate was frequently formed, but still more frequently the interest only came about because there were no divided bonds in round numbers, so that in a financial operation in which several persons were interested only the largest holder held the bond and then issued declarations of trust to the rest. Generally speaking, there were seldom such large syndicates in Antwerp as in Lyons; for there all financial dealings were concentrated on the loans of the French Crown, while in Antwerp the business was distributed among many different kinds of loans.

Though at this period the merchants and other capitalists began to crowd into the finance business, yet so far not to an excessive or unhealthy extent. Foresight and caution still prevailed in many quarters, and many groups still remained without the dangerous inclination to participate in finance, while certain of the greatest business houses, notably the Fugger, had the intention of withdrawing from this business. Many firms of the second rank, however, had of late made much money with little trouble in financial dealings, and these took good care that this inclination reached an ever widening circle, as soon as new calls of an extraordinary sort were made in the money market.

The Period from 1551 *to* 1557. The state of the Netherlands finances was again quite satisfactory by 1551. There was no extraordinary expenditure and the floating debts were either repaid or shortly to be so. The budget showed a surplus of 173,500 L (at 40 gr.), available for fortifications, arrears of soldiers' pay, etc. The outbreak of the war with France and the rebellion of the Elector Maurice of Saxony altered all this.

In the Pamas fair of 1551, the quarter day of which fell in November, 445,900 L of the bonds of the Receivers General fell due for payment. The sums destined for this purpose had, however, to be used for the war, and another 554,000 L had to be borrowed, so that Gaspar Schetz, who was now financial agent of the Brussels Court, had to borrow in all a million pounds (at 40 gr.) or Carolus gulden. He resold bonds of the Receivers General at 12 per cent. and so was able to satisfy the most pressing needs. Money was, however, so tight during the fair that Alexius Grimel, who had also promised the Government 300,000 L, was unable to keep his word. With great trouble he got together 246,228 L, obtaining 128,000 L from the Affaitadi, 70,000 L from Martin Lopez, 30,000 L from Christopher Welser, etc. Grimel had to give the Government bonds on these firms, since ready money was unobtainable. The rate, however, did not rise above 12 per cent. per annum.

At the Easter fair, 1552, a loan of 255,000 Carolus gulden at 12 per cent. was borrowed from the Fugger through Gaspar Schetz. On the other hand, Thomas Gresham, the newly appointed agent of the English Crown, in February, 1552, had to pay Lazarus Tucher 14 per cent. on a loan of 14,000 L Fl. (= 84,000 Carolus gulden). He must have borrowed other money in addition, for in April he repaid the Fugger 77,500 L Fl. (= 465,000 Carolus gulden), and in the whole period from 1st March to 27th July 106,300 L (= 637,800 Carolus gulden), none of which he brought with him from England. A debt of 44,000 L owing to the Fugger and one of 12,000 L to the Schetz, a total of 56,000 L Fl. (= 336,000 Carolus gulden), had to be prolonged at 14 per cent. till the pay day of the Whitsun fair in August.[1]

Meanwhile the Netherlands Government was also forced to pay higher rates; but even at 13 per cent. and 14 per cent. it could only raise small amounts in May. At the beginning of April the Queen Regent had entreated the Emperor to send from Spain some of the rich supply of American silver which had just arrived there. The permission was given, but the Government had no money to equip the fleet which was to fetch the silver. The city of Antwerp now came forward. It bor-

[1] Burgon, I, 80 ff.

rowed the necessary sums, mostly at 13 per cent. or 14 per cent., from
the merchants, who themselves wished to import large sums by means of
the fleet, and were therefore some of them disposed to assist at low
interest. One of them, Joos van den Steene, even advanced 50,000
Carolus gulden without interest. The arrival of the fleet was delayed,
however, and in the autumn market little money was to be had for 14
per cent.[1] The Netherlands Government accordingly, in 1552, only paid
in interest 141,300 Carolus gulden and this mostly on loans contracted
outside Antwerp, chiefly by the Emperor in South Germany. This was
less than had been paid in 1542. In this year the Government had the
extraordinary demand for money chiefly by selling annuities. In 1551
about 23,000 Carolus gulden worth of annuities on the provinces of
Flanders, Brabant, Holland, etc., at 4–6 per cent. were sold and a capital
of about 310,000 fl. was raised.

In 1552, on the other hand, the sales were :

for war expenditure   94,600 fl. annuities at 8 per cent. to 10 per cent.
for repayment of float-
   ing debt   79,000 fl.   ,,   ,, 6 per cent.

amounting to a total 173,600 fl.

a yield in capital of $2\frac{1}{2}$ million Carolus gulden.[2] These sales of annuities,
however, had nothing to do with the financial transactions of the
Government on the Antwerp Bourse, as is testified by the difference in
the rates. In the sale of annuities, the personal credit of the Emperor,
the Queen Regent and the Netherlands Receivers General did not come
in, while it was the decisive factor in the Antwerp dealings. This personal credit was then at a low ebb, a circumstance largely attributable
to the Emperor's ill-starred policy and also the ruinous system of
financial management introduced by Erasso.

The Antwerp money market could easily have let the Government
have the money, as it proved by its treatment of the English Crown,
whose new agent had contrived by his skilful and honest management
greatly to improve his King's credit.[3] Gresham had endeavoured at the
Whitsun fair to induce the Fugger and the Schetz to consent to a further
prolongation of their claims, which amounted to 56,000 L Fl. He was
unsuccessful in this and went home to report to the Government. He
was ordered to resume his efforts and in particular to tell the Fugger that
the King would gladly have paid his debt on maturity, 'but in this
troublesome time of the world, it behoved his Majesty to so consider

[1] Brussels, *Chambres des Comptes*, No. 23469 and 23470.
[2] Brussels, *Chambres des Comptes*, No. 434.
[3] Burgon, I, 86 ff.

S

his estates that for divers great and weighty considerations, his Majesty otherwise is moved to employ the same money which was prepared for their payment. And therefore his Majesty doubted not that the said Fulkers will be content to think this consideration reasonable and not forget the benefits and good bargains that they had had of the King's Majesty, with good and true payments at all times made, and assure themselves that were it not for weighty causes, his Majesty would not at this time defer any such payment. Wherein his Majesty the rather hopeth of this contentation, for that Antonio Fulker himself, being herein conferred with by his Majesty's Ambassador with the Emperor, seemed ready to gratify his Majesty, not only in this matter, but also a greater.'

Gresham was but little edified by this commission. On his return to Antwerp on the 20th August, the day when the claims of the Fugger and the Schetz should have been met, he wrote to the Duke of Northumberland, who then had the greatest influence on the King's Council: 'For that yt shall be no small grief unto me, that in my tyme, being his Majesty's agent, anny merchant strangers shulld be forssid to forbear their monny against their willes; wyche matter from hensforthe must be otherwayse foreseen, or else in the end the disonnestye of this matter shall hereafter be wholly layde upon my necke, yff any thinge shuld chance of your Grace, or my Lord of Pendbrocke, otherwise than well; for we be all mortal. To be playne with your Grace in this matter according to my bowndyd dewtye, veryly if there be not some other ways takynne for the payment of his Majesty's detts, but to force men from tyme to tyme to prolong yt, I say to you the end thereof shall neyther be honnorable nor profitable to his Highness. In consideracyone whereof, if there be none other ways takynne forthwith, this ys to most humbly besche your Grace that I may be dischargyd of this offyce of Agentshipe. For otherwise I see in the end I shall reserve shame and discredit thereby, to my utter undoing forever: wyche ys the smallest matter of all, so that the King's Majesty's honour and creditt be not spotted therebye, and specially in a strange country; whereas at this present his credit is better than the Emperor's. For now the Emperor geveth xvi per cent., and yet no monny to be gotten.'

Gresham had raised some of the money with which he had paid some of the King's debts in his own name and credit, for otherwise he could not have obtained it. He had, moreover, begun to break the habit introduced by his predecessors of taking in payment at each prolongation of the debt jewels or other goods at exaggerated prices. He now proposed a new method of raising the King's credit and paying the royal debts.

He proposed that the Government should put at his disposal in London the sum of 1,200 £ a week; that he should daily sell bills for 200 £ on London, using the proceeds for the payment of the King's debts. He hoped by this means to make the exchange more favourable to England. The plan was sanctioned, but was shortly afterwards abandoned by the Government. Gresham, however, succeeded in attaining his object by other methods.

We cannot pursue this subject in detail here; it is sufficient to say that before King Edward's death, in 1553, Gresham had paid all the Crown debts and raised the exchange of sterling from 16 Sch. to 22 Sch. He had in this way relieved the Treasury of an annual burden of interest amounting to 40,000 £, converted an export into an import in the case of money, and so greatly improved the King's credit that he could obtain any money he wanted. We have already reported his boast as to this service and its political effects.

Gresham had a tendency to exaggerated self-praise. Thus he reports that on the 12th April, 1553, his friend Lazarus Tucher had offered to advance the King 200,000 fl. at 12 per cent., at which Gresham was the more rejoiced as the Emperor had to pay 16 per cent.[1] Now, on the same day the Emperor had sold to the Fugger 30,00 fl. of perpetual annuities on the provinces of Brabant and Flanders in return for a capital payment of 300,000 fl.; the rate was, therefore, 10 per cent. It is possible, however, that bonds of the Receivers General and other loans on the bourse may have cost as much as 16 per cent. When, however, Gresham writes four days later that the 100,000 ducats lent to the Emperor on the 14th would not last a month, and that he had neither money nor credit, his statements were exaggerated. At the end of 1553 the Fugger alone had claims on the Emperor on bonds of the Receivers General amounting to 92,528 £ fl., or about 555,000 Carolus gulden, the interest being usually 14 per cent., but sometimes 12 per cent. The Fugger at this time borrowed money at 10 per cent. and lent it out again at 12 per cent. to 14 per cent.

The fact remains, however, that the Emperor's credit was much injured by the methods of Erasso and his associates, while that of the English Crown improved through Gresham's skilled operating. Gresham's merits were clearly shown when on Edward's death Mary had him removed and replaced by Christopher Dauntsey, whose clumsy dealings with Lazarus Tucher soon did great damage to the credit of the English Crown. Dauntsey borrowed 200,000 Carolus gulden from Tucher at 13 per cent., which became 14 per cent. owing to the conditions of payment, while the market rate was only 10 per cent. (November, 1553), and Lazarus Tucher had obtained the money himself at this rate. Gresham, recalled in haste to Antwerp, was justified in writing to the Privy Council.

---

[1] Turnbull, *Calendar, Edward VI*, Nos. 653 and 655.

We have a letter from Anton Fugger to his Antwerp agent Matthew
Oertel written a few weeks after Gresham's report. Anton Fugger expresses astonishment that the English Queen was again wanting to
borrow at 13 per cent.: 'it is a great interest, if it be so.'

Gresham reported soon after that the tightness of the money market
was not solely due to Dauntsey's relatively unimportant transactions,
but was also due to the South German cities borrowing all the money
they could raise at 12 per cent., e.g. the city of Nuremberg did so
through the Imhof, for the war against the Margrave Albrecht Alcibiades of Brandenburg, both in Antwerp and elsewhere.

In December, 1553, Gresham was ordered to raise in all haste
100,000 £ at 12 per cent. at most. He could not do this, and had to
report that there were indeed two persons ready to advance sums of
40,000–50,000 Carolus gulden, but they were shameless enough 'to ask
15 per cent. He had offered 10 per cent. to 11 per cent., but had been
indignantly asked whether he thought that they did not know of the
affair with Lazarus Tucher and whether their money was not as good as
his. The financiers had agreed among themselves not to lend under 13
per cent. Only Art van Dale and Christopher Pruen had offered 16,000
at 6 per cent. for six months, but at that time he had no authority
to borrow for a shorter period than a year. Meanwhile he had received
the authority, but the Emperor's borrowing had made money tighter.

' . . . This Bourse of Antwerp is strange – one day there is plenty of
money and the next none – because there are so many good takers and
deliverers, that if one will not, another will. Fugger and Jasper Schetz
are bare of money, and no good can be done with them at present, as
the Emperor owes about 300,000 l. . . .'[1]

There are several contradictions here, to be attributed to a misunderstanding. Gresham could not give as a reason for the sudden fluctuations
in the supply of money the presence of so many sound borrowers and
lenders. Their presence would make the supply more constant. It was not
because, but in spite of this fact the supply fluctuated at this disturbed
time, and this must have seemed 'strange' to one who knew the Antwerp
market as Gresham did. Gresham wrote soon after that he would not
rest till the credit of the English Crown was as good as in the last days of
King Edward. Shortly after he had to borrow 120,000 Carolus fl. at 13
per cent. from the Schetz, the Ligsalz, and the Fleckhamer; but early
in January he was able to get 50,000 fl. from the Diodati at 12 per cent.

It is interesting that at first Gresham had difficulty in getting from
the merchants the sums they had promised, because the Queen's promissory notes still bore the late King's seal. Gresham had accordingly
to add his own signature to the bond for the money advanced by the

[1] Turnbull, *Calendar, Queen Mary*, No. 104.

Ligsalz, and had to promise to produce either a promissory note provided with the Queen's seal or else a certificate signed by the Queen and the Privy Council to confirm the legality of the old seal. This difficulty raised by the German merchants was removed, when the Italians declined to pay over their advance on account of a rumoured rebellion in England. This also prevented Gresham from obtaining money elsewhere; and it was only on the news of the suppression of the rebellion that the Queen's credit rose again. At the time of Gresham's departure from Antwerp at the end of February, 1554, it had not entirely recovered from the shock it had received six months before. Some months later Mary married Philip of Spain. This event, even before it actually took place, notably affected the money market and the financial transactions of the English Crown and the Emperor.

The Antwerp money market, as we have seen, had at this time become increasingly dependent on the import of Spanish-American silver. Most large financiers, especially the South Germans and the Genoese, were so deeply engaged in Spain that they would take on no further business unless by this means they could get some of their Spanish holdings in the form of ready money. The Spanish people pursued with fanatical hatred those who sent money out of the country, and the Emperor had to bear in mind this temper, which was a chief reason of the great rebellion of the Comuneros. The financial policy initiated since the time of the Schmalkaldian League by the help of his Spanish secretary Erasso was chiefly directed to prevent Spanish finances from being overstrained for the benefit of other countries. Since the days of Villach, however, this end had proved unattainable, and claims on the 'Indian gold and silver' were the favourite method for the repayment of the Emperor's loans. Under these circumstances the ban on the export of money was untenable, and we know that since 1552 very large sums had been sent both by the Government and the merchants from Spain to the Netherlands and Italy. On the betrothal of the English Queen to the Spanish Heir Apparent, the finances of both countries were to a certain extent pooled, with the result that the English Crown was allowed to draw ready money from Spain.

Already in January, 1554, this had been suggested to Gresham by the Genoese, who hoped in this way to reduce their Spanish holdings. The arrangement was, however, only concluded in May, immediately before the marriage. We know that the Fugger were also interested in the affair as well as the Genoese, and that Gresham travelled to Spain to fetch the money.[1] He found there indescribable tightness of money and his measures resulted in the immediate bankruptcy of one of the oldest banking firms in Seville. 'I fere,' he wrote, 'that I shall be the occasione

[1] Cf. Burgon, I, 149 ff.; Turnbull, *Queen Mary*, Nos. 135, 205 ff.

that they should play all bank-rowte.' If such were the plight of Spain, what could Antwerp expect from it ? How was money to be raised for the war with France which broke out again in 1555?

In March of that year, the French King concluded in Lyons a loan on so large a scale that it was known as 'Le Grand Parti.' This was a great threat to the Emperor, already weary both of war and Government. His credit was, however, insufficient even to secure the prolongation of the maturing debts – 500,000 ducats' worth of these were due at the Easter fair, and the merchants would only consent to their prolongation on condition that King Philip, then only King of England, should add his signature to the promissory notes and would promise to have payment made, not in Spain as was originally arranged, but in Antwerp. If the statement is correct that the ducat was here taken at 80 gr. Flemish, while in ordinary exchange it was only worth 60 gr., the Emperor had indeed to pay heavily for the prolongation of these bills.[1]

There was at this time great tightness at Antwerp; even at 3 per cent. a quarter there was no money to be had on 'deposito.' There was a rumour of the impending arrival of a fleet from Seville and the Canary Isles, which was to bring specie, but little credence was given to this. Erasso arrived in April, but though he now acted for the English King in his negotiations with the merchants for a loan, he only succeeded in getting 300,000 crowns in return for pledging the Netherlands customs on alum. Nothing was to be got without special security.

In the following months there were several other loans of about the same amount; in June 300,000 crowns for the daily expenses of the Court, which for weeks had been without ready money to the indignation of all the purveyors. It appears that this loan cost over 25 per cent., and a previous loan not less. The merchants said that all the revenues were pledged till 1557. The pooling of the Spanish Netherlands finances with the English injured the English without benefiting the rest.[2]

In August Erasso came once again to Antwerp. The Imperial troops were in pressing need of money, but nowhere loans could be raised, and the payment had to be compulsorily deferred for a month. Meanwhile the hope was that a fleet would arrive from Spain with specie. The market rate stood at about 12 per cent. The English Crown owed in Antwerp, apart from the King's personal debts, 148,256 L Fl. 38,000 L of this amount was paid at the Pamas fair by Gresham, who compelled the English merchants to advance this amount in Antwerp against repayment in London. In the prevailing scarcity of money the merchants took this very hard. Gresham managed, however, to bring about a momentary improvement in the English exchange, and the credit of

---

[1] R. Brown, *Calendar*, VI, p. 26.
[2] Brown, VI, pp. 48, 99, 107.

the English Crown. The payment of 38,000 L of debt was regarded as a
'Royal payment' and reported everywhere.[1] Gresham applied the process which he had thus tried several times afterwards. But he had once
more to borrow large sums from the foreign merchants at 14 per cent.
The Queen in the autumn of 1556 resorted to the old expedient of a
forced loan at home and obtained a considerable sum at the cost of
a large increase of unpopularity.[2]

Meanwhile Charles had abdicated in favour of his son, who came in
for a crushing load of debt and a war with France which continued to
become more intense. Philip succeeded in the two first years of his reign
in raising the enormous sums necessary for the war and the payment of
the interest on the old debts, but only by overburdening his countries
and overstraining his credit on a scale such as the world had never seen.

It is quite impossible to give a complete picture of the far-fetched
methods of Philip's financial policy in these years. We shall deal with
it later, meanwhile we only give some data in reference to financial
transactions in Antwerp.

The Netherlands finance administration, which in 1552 spent only
141,300 L of 40 gr. for interest and other expenditure in connection
with the floating debt, had to pay on this account:

In 1554	285,982 L
In 1555	424,765 L
In 1556	1,357,287 L

In view of this gigantic increase in the floating debt it is all the more
remarkable that the average rate of interest did not rise, but throughout
this period varied between 12 per cent. and 14 per cent. It is stated,
however, that the King had to pay as much as 24 per cent. in Antwerp.[3]

In this instance, however, special transactions were in question,
e.g. Asientos for Spain, where the money famine had reached its peak.
The merchants, who could not withdraw their large holdings from Spain,
tried to avoid increasing them; and if the King forced them to provide
new advances for Spain they repaid themselves for the risk by correspondingly high exchange rates. In his extremity the King had on
occasions to consent to take goods in payment at exaggerated prices, a
proceeding which would result in an interest rate of 23 per cent. to 24
per cent. In the same month, however, when such a transaction is
reported (April, 1556) the Fugger in Antwerp took over $1\frac{1}{4}$ million of
Carolus gulden worth of bonds of the Receivers General which paid
interest at 12 per cent.

[1] Turnbull, No. 429–30; Brown, VI, 213; Burgon, I, 182 ff.
[2] Brown, VI, 588, 623, 1057; Burgon, I, 192; Turnbull, No. 474.
[3] Turnbull, *Calendar*, VI, 421; Albéri, *Relaz.*, VIII, 297.

As we have said, everybody was affected by the credit boom, and every one wanted to share in financial operations which promised such profits for so little trouble. Even the great business houses like the Fugger, in spite of their experience and their serious desire to withdraw from risky business, gave way to the general tendency and thereby greatly strengthened it.

It was only in the spring of 1557 that the Antwerp Bourse, which had seemed an inexhaustible source, at any rate as far as direct loans were concerned, first failed the Government. The city of Antwerp, however, which was then in reality a financial agency of the Government, at whose disposal the city's credit had to be put without reserve, managed to borrow large sums on the bourse at 12 per cent. to 13 per cent.; for the city's bonds were generally considered a good investment and the market rate in general was only 11 per cent. to 11½ per cent.

Anton Fugger himself wrote to his Antwerp agent: 'I have learnt that the Christmas payment is to be prolonged till Easter, and that the city of Antwerp will thus help itself out; since one can do no otherwise and there is no harm in it, I must let it be.' This shows how little the true relation between the Netherlands Government and the city of Antwerp was evident even to the greatest financier of his time, in his old age. The city at any rate proved the more solvent of the two. The Government ceased payment in August, 1557; but the city continued to pay, though only because its credit then still continued good, and only sank very gradually. In point of fact the city was already at this time overburdened by the debt which it had contracted in the service of the Government.

It is impossible even to give a rough estimate of the number of millions of floating debt, whether direct or indirect, on which the Netherlands Government had to pay interest in Antwerp. The total amount of financial transactions concluded on the Antwerp Bourse in the course of a year was estimated in 1557 by a Venetian envoy at 40 million ducats or crowns.[1] This figure is, however, only meant to give a rough idea of the importance which Antwerp had attained as a money market.

Thirty or forty years earlier floating loans of the Netherlands Government amounting to 100,000 to 200,000 Carolus gulden had been sufficient to drive up the rate of interest from 13 per cent. to 27 per cent., even though the Government was easily in a position to repay their borrowing very soon. Now the Antwerp Bourse lent not to the Netherlands Government alone, but to the Governments of Spain, England and Portugal also, year in and year out, many millions which these Governments could never repay. Yet the interest never rose much over 13 per cent. This is the effect of stock exchange methods even in their infancy on the management of credit.

[1] Albéri, *Relaz.*, VIII, 290.

THE Rise of Lyons. The rise of Lyons was to a far greater extent than the rise of the International Bourse at Antwerp, the conscious and carefully tended creation of the rulers of the country. After the old fairs of Champagne had fallen into disuse in the first half of the fourteenth century, France was without a trading centre of international importance. Geneva, meanwhile, had become important with its fairs, and, thanks to the peace and freedom enjoyed by foreign merchants there, that city was for long relatively as important a trade centre for Italy, France and South Germany as Bruges was for traffic with the Northern European peoples and those of the Mediterranean. Notably, it is stated by various authorities that the Geneva fairs were specially important to the Florentines' trade in money and precious metals.[1]

As early as 1419–20 and 1443–44 the King of France, Charles VII (in 1419–20 still Dauphin), had tried to attract the Geneva fairs to Lyons by the grant of large privileges, especially the decontrol of the trade in money and precious metals, rigidly controlled everywhere else in France. The attempt was unsuccessful, though the King confirmed the privileges in 1445, 1454, 1457 and 1461. At last, Louis XI was more successful. On the 20th October, 1462, he forbade all merchants to visit the Geneva fairs, and was able to induce their natural protector, the Duke of Savoy, to join in this prohibition, as he was on bad terms with Geneva. The Duke bitterly repented this later, as the decline of the fair thus engineered did him great damage.[2]

The year 1463 was the real date of the birth of the Lyons fairs, which rose very rapidly after that time. The King gave them all the privileges of the Geneva fairs. For several decades, indeed, the two were rivals; but in spite of all the efforts of Geneva, soon abetted by the Duke of Savoy, large international business tended increasingly to go to Lyons, both for trade in commodities and more especially for dealing in money.

Louis XI was one of the earliest of mercantilist politicians. The chief economic reason advanced by him in his *Ordonnance* of 20th October, 1462, against the Geneva fairs was the fact 'that French gold and silver are daily exported thither.' This was perfectly true. The Florentine

---

[1] For decay of the Champagne fairs see Bourquelot, *Etudes sur les Foires de Champagne* (Mém. de l'Acad. des. Inscript. et Belles Lettres, 2 sér. t. 5), vol. II, 301 ff., esp. Coustumes des foires (l.c. II, 367); Höhlbaum, *Hans. Urk.-Buch*, III, 455; Lefevre, *Les finances de la Champagne*, p. 38; Borel, *Les foires de Genève au 15 siècle*, 1892, p. 8). For Florentines in Geneva cf. Borel, l.c. p. 106 ff., 134 ff. and passim.

[2] Borel, l.c., pp. 13 and onwards. Péricaud, *Notes el Documents pour servir à l'histoire de Lyon*, s.a. 1485. A Genoese Chronicle, *Histor. patr. mon. Scriptores*, I, 627.

money changers in particular did a feverish trade through Geneva in French and other coins. They took the coins of full weight home with them and had them recoined, putting the light coins again into circulation. The gold of Salzburg and the silver of Tyrol brought by South German merchants in great masses to Geneva reached the Italian mints without touching France.

It had already been realized that it was a great advantage for a prince if there was a large trade in monetary capital in his dominions. In 1470, when the city of Geneva appealed to the Duke of Savoy to support its efforts to restore the fairs, it was represented that if the Duke needed 100,000 or 200,000 gulden, he could easily raise them in Geneva in three or four days at fair time, while, as things were, he had to have recourse to Lyons, which was both troublesome and risky. If the fairs were brought back to Geneva, money would flow in from all sides; if they were held out of the country, they drew the money with them, and nothing remained in the country except a little customs on goods in transit. Moreover, when in 1485 two of the Lyons fairs were temporarily transferred to Bourges, the city of Lyons supported its appeal for their return with the same reasons.[1]

Undoubtedly this was a chief reason of the steady support which Louis XI and his successors gave to the Lyons fairs. For example, a special commercial Court of Justice, the first in France, was introduced for the fairs, and those who failed to recognize its jurisdiction were severely dealt with. Finally, in 1538, exemption from taxation was granted to foreigners, especially those from Florence and Lucca who did not marry in Lyons and acquire land there. This connection is still more plainly evident in 1550, when the King increased the privileges of the fairs 'on account of the profit which he derived daily from the great dealings in money transacted at the fairs in Lyons.'[2]

The Importance of Lyons in general. The expectations of the French Crown in regard to the Lyons fairs were more than fulfilled. Even if the trade in commodities could not compare with that of Antwerp, it was yet in the traffic between France, on the one side, and South Germany on the other, sufficiently ample and many sided.[3] The creation of the fairs rendered Lyons vastly more important for the French Crown. What Lyons meant for the Crown, either in a political, military or financial sense, in the century from 1463 to 1562 cannot be rated too highly.

[1] Galiffe, *Matériaux pour l'historie de Génève*, I, 382; Péricaud, l.c.

[2] Cf. *Privilèges des Foires de Lyon* (1649); Vaesen, *La Jurisdiction Commerciale à Lyon sous l'Ancien Régime* (Mém. de la Soc. Litt. de Lyon, 1877). *Lettres de Louis XI*, ed. Vaesen et Charavay, II, 203, *Actes de François I*, t. III, 10560, 10695, 10723; IV, 13020, 13790; Rubys, *Histoire de Lyon*, p. 376.

[3] Nicolay, *Descript. de la ville de Lyon* (1573), publ. by la Soc. de Topogr. histor. de Lyon, 1881, p. 159 ff.

Lyons became above all the centre of the large and delicate web of political relations between France and Italy. It became the focus of the news service for all Europe. In Lyons the Swiss Cantons, without whose troops France could not carry on her wars, received their payments. Lyons was the great recruiting ground for the French Kings' warlike expeditions into Italy. Often these Kings themselves lived in Lyons, the second capital of France. Lyons also was the channel through which the greatest influences of the Florentine renaissance reached France.

The chief root of all these effects was not in the trade in goods, but in the traffic in money and bills. All the French Kings since Louis XI had directed their efforts to the increase of this traffic. On this account they granted Lyons unlimited freedom of exchange, including re-exchange and lending at interest which were elsewhere prohibited. Only the English, as hereditary enemies, were excluded from this permission. Bill business with Rome was also forbidden: a restriction attributable to the complaints of Parliament as to the export of money on account of the Papal Curia. All exchange transactions settled at Lyons were subject to the strict exchange law, and for the fairs every form of currency was granted free circulation.[1]

These measures succeeded so greatly in increasing the traffic in money and bills that Andrea Navagero could say in 1528: 'In the four fairs at Lyons an infinite number of payments are made on every side, so that they form the basis of the circulation of the whole of Italy and a large part of Spain and the Netherlands. Herein lies their use for merchants.'[2]

We should add that this was also the immediate cause of the advantage which the French Crown derived from the fairs. Large masses of liquid capital, for the time being free, were attracted to Lyons, so that the French Crown could capture an increasing quantity of these by offering higher interest. When this habit was once established, it served as a bait for other capital lying idle outside Lyons and which was producing less interest than the French loans.

The great importance of Lyons for the finances of the French Crown was soon recognized by its opponents, as is shown by the fact that before 1513 the opponents of the French Crown had tried to induce the Papal Curia to take steps against the Lyons fairs. This is proved by a petition which the Emperor's envoys in Rome brought before the new Pope, Adrian VI, either at the end of 1522 or the beginning of 1523. The text

---

[1] Fair privileges of 1462, cap. 2, 6, 7, 8 (*Ordonnances des rois de France*, XV, 646). Cf. *Ordonnances*, XV, 204 ff.; Le Glay, *Histoire de Louis XI*, vol. I, 291 ff., 327 ff.; Picot, *Histoire des États Généraux*, I, 511 ff. Cf. *Journal des États Généraux de 1484 red. par Masselin*, p. 699; Monfalcon, *Histoire monumentale de Lyon*, I, 347; Péricaud, *Notes et documents*, a. 1485.

[2] *Relaz. d. Ambasc. Venet.*, ed. Tommaseo, I, 36.

of this interesting effort is as follows:[1] 'The Emperor says that both Pope Julius and latterly Pope Leo (1513–21) sanctioned the restoration of the fairs from Lyons to Geneva, where they were aforetime. The Cardinal Medici (later Clement VII) is perfectly informed on this point. The execution of this permission would be most advantageous both to His Holiness and to His Majesty. For if the trade of the merchants, who are for the most part subjects of the Church and the Emperor, is once more set free, this will diminish the strength of the King of France, as in that case that trade (at Lyons) ceases.'

The obstinate efforts of Charles V to stop the Lyons fairs resulted finally in the founding of the Genoese bill fairs – an important consequence.

Fairs and Bourse in Lyons. Lyons also had four fairs: the Foire d'Apparition des Rois in January, the Foire des Pâques in April, the Foire d'Aout in August, and the Foire des Toussaints in November. Each fair lasted fifteen days; only the South German merchants had a further fifteen days of liberty and the Swiss ten days. Generally speaking, the Lyons fairs kept their full mediæval significance longer than the Antwerp fairs; it was relatively late before they sank into mere quarter days; but for the Italians the money and bill transactions which followed the commodity fair had from early times been the principal thing. Except at fair-time money, even in Lyons, was hard to come by. In Lyons business in money and bills had a peculiar form based on the older institutions of the Champagne and Geneva fairs.[2]

The settling days of the fair had from the first formed a separate period longer than the fair itself. At the beginning this was two or three weeks; later fiscal reasons caused its undue prolongation as in Antwerp; finally, its length was fixed by municipal regulations at a month.

Before the merchants attended the fair they entered in their 'market book' (Italian *Scartafaccio*) all the payments due from or to them in the fair. At the beginning of the fair payments these books were compared with one another. In the case of every entry found correct the person from whom the payment was due made a mark which was taken as a binding recognition of the debt; later he had to sign his whole name. The bill – for, generally speaking, there was no question of anything but bills – was *accepted* in this way. If an item was not recognized, the owner of the book wrote by it 'S.P.' (*sous protest*).

After the acceptances of the old bills there followed the new business

---

[1] Gachard, *Correspondance de Charles V et d'Adrien VI*, Préface CV.

[2] Cf. Meder, *Handelbuch, Nürnberg*, 1558, Bl. 53; Nicolay, l.c. p. 150 ff. (1573); Péricaud, *Notes et documents*, s.a. 1576; Rubys, *Histoire de Lyon* (1604), p. 496; Roberts, *Merchants Map of Commerce* (1638), cap. 303.

with foreign markets, which originated either at the preceding fair or as the result of the acceptance, or otherwise. Here we meet for the first time a peculiar arrangement, the settlement of an official average price for each species of bill, the so-called Conto. This arrangement, the origin of which is not clear, is first mentioned by the Florentine cleric Buoninsegni.[1]

He distinguishes between real trade bills (*solo per commodo delle mercanzie*) and speculative or loan bills (*con oggetto di guadagno, per arte senza oggetto di mercatura*). At first he thinks only the first sort existed and thus the price fluctuated very little. This, however, had lately altered, and now most bills were purely speculative or loan bills. Abuses had crept in in this connection. Skilful operators had tried successfully to settle the price of bills arbitrarily, and they had accordingly formed syndicates and had artificially tightened the supply of money and so managed to get control of the price of bills. In order to obviate such practices and the consequent disputes as to the true and just price, the bill dealers had decided to fix average rates for bills as soon as bills began to be dealt in at each fair, so that foreign business connections could, if necessary, be referred to these rates.

The process is on the whole correctly stated here. At any rate, later, in other fairs, these were the reasons for the institution of the Conto. In Lyons this was done as follows: The bill dealers met on a certain day and formed a circle (*Faire la Ronde*); the Consul of the Florentines then asked the dealers of the different nations in turn what they thought the price ought to be. The answers were noted and the average taken. This was the official rate for bills, which was noted in the bulletins (*Lauf* or *Läufzetteln*; in Italian *Liste*) and sent abroad. The dealers themselves were naturally not bound by this, their business was left to free bargaining. Yet the Conto at the beginning had some meaning for the market itself, as previously many transactions had been concluded at the average rate which had not yet been settled. Later on the proceedings were altered in many particulars. The Prévôt des Marchands of Lyons took the place of the Florentine Consul, and the different rates were given in writing. The Conto remained in existence, as an empty form, up to the time of the French Revolution, but its practical importance had long departed.

The payment proper closed the fair. It was affected chiefly by *virement de parties, giro* or *scontro*, as follows: Two persons were commissioned to collect and compare (*scontriren*) all the fair books. They then cancelled the payments against one another, and only paid the balances

---

[1] *Trattato dei cambi*, 1573. Cf. e.g. Scaccia, § 1, Qu. 5, No. 53 ff., § 1, Qu. 7, Par. 2, Ampl. X, No. 101; De Turri, Qu. 1, No. 30 ff.; Roberts, *Merchants Map of Commerce*, 301; Rubys, p. 498; Peri, *Il negotiante*, I, c. 25.

in cash.[1] We note that one unit of account, the écu de marc or scudo de marcé, was taken as the basis of all payments, and that the actual payments were made in a special currency, originally a pure gold currency, but afterwards a mixed currency with a fixed relation between gold and silver, only dissolved at the end of the fair. The total result is a peculiar organization very modern in most of its chief features, the characteristic product of the Latin commercial genius. The fair payments at Lyons owe their form to the Florentines, a fact which is clearly shown by the development of the Lyons Bourse. The Bourse took its name from the business which was first and for long to the exclusion of all others transacted in it; it was la Place du Change, or simply le Change. It was a square near the Church of St. Eloi, near the single bridge which then linked the different quarters of the city on either side of the Saône. The bridge still bears the name of the Pont du Change and the square also retains its name. In 1389 it was called the Place de la Draperie, a name it kept for some time after the first institution of the fairs in 1419; at that time the square on the other side of the bridge before the church of St. Nizier was set apart for the money changers. The 'change' at St. Eloi is mentioned in 1489, and probably it had been there since 1462.[2]

The Consular house, the Loge of the Florentines, was here, and it was originally the scene of the characteristic acts of the Lyons, fair payments, the acceptances, the settlement of the average price and the clearing house operations. The historian de Rubys, writing in 1604, adds to his account of these proceedings the statement that the Florentines had introduced exchange dealing and therefore kept the lead in this form of business as well as in the fair payments. This is true, but if he means that it was introduced two hundred years before the fairs, this cannot refer to Lyons, but to France as a whole.[3]

When later the Florentines gradually disappeared from Lyons, the leading place in the fair payments fell to the head of the Lyons merchants, 'Prévôt des Marchands. The Place du Change was provided in the seventeenth century with a special Loge du Change, which since 1810 has been used as a Protestant Church.'[4]

The organization of the Lyons system of payments has been much admired, and was in fact a notable achievement for the times. The

[1] Speech of Venetian Senator Contarini in 1584 in Latte's *Libertà delle Banche a Venezia*, p. 121.

[2] Montfalcon, *Hist. Monum. de Lyon*, I, 452, 510. *Régistres Consulaires de Lyon*, 1416–23, ed. Guigne, I, 295. Clément, *Jacques Cœur et Charles VII*, t. II, 352.

[3] Rubys, *Histoire de Lyon*, p. 496. Péricaud, *Notes et documents* (Henri III), p. 90, and *Archives historiques et statistiques du departement du Rhône*, t. IX, 332.

[4] Péricaud, l.c. p. 5, 94; Clerjon, *Histoire de Lyon*, VI, 148. (*Arch. municip. de Lyon, Invent. gén*, XVI, 395 ff.). Cf. Vaesen *in d. Mém. de la Soc. litt. de Lyon*, 1877–8, p. 148.

Spaniards, however, had a still more highly developed system, and at a later time the Genoese equipped their fairs with a system of payments which far outshone that of the Lyons fair.

Dealing in Capital in Lyons. In Lyons, like Antwerp, loans were usually given the form of the deposits and the Ricorsa bill. The former was the more prevalent in the heyday of the Lyons fairs, though the Florentines still continued to use the Ricorsa as well. It was only after the bull which Pope Pius V issued against it in 1570 that the deposito was less often employed both at the Geneva fairs and at Lyons.[1]

There is nothing special to note about the Lyons deposito, and we will accordingly content ourselves with a few quotations from German commercial letters, e.g. Vincenz Pirkheimer, an agent of the Tucher's, wrote in 1531 from Lyons: 'At the last Easter fair a considerable sum of money was left on our hands, because there was no special use for it. There were no bills to be bought, which could have been resold on delivery, which else would have come to pass. There are enough good Dittas that lend money at 2–2½ per cent. till the next fair, but not enough good Dittas that want money.' Accordingly, he lent the money for two fairs to the treasurer of the Duke of Savoy on the pledge of jewels, or rather, he bought the jewels and 'of our grace we may let him redeem them at the appointed time.' This brought in interest at 16 per cent. Soon after he says: 'There is now no demand for money, and in exchange (au change, i.e. on the Bourse) there is not more than 2 per cent. a quarter.' This state of things continued, and in 1535 we hear, 'Money is not worth more than 1¾ to 2 per cent. in Banqua.'

These were all bourse deposits, but this expression is first used in 1559. At that time the French merchants complained that every one was now ceasing to deal in commodities in order to engage in bill and deposit business, i.e. to commit usury. This Nouvelle Façon de Dépôts, they said, enriched few and impoverished many.[2] Soon after we note the rate for deposits regularly stated at the end of the exchange bulletin.

The best account of the method of dealing with the Ricorsa bill at Lyons is drawn from the treatise on bills of the Florentine merchant Davanzati, who describes this business in the middle of the sixteenth century on the basis of his own practice in Lyons:[3] 'If thou (A) hast money in Florence and wilt have exchange in Lyons, because thou mayst have profit from the exchange back again, so give to me (B) who need money, 64 scudi in Florence, if that be the exchange rate; against

---

[1] Nicolay, *Description de la ville de Lyon* (1573 ed. 1881), p. 153. Cf. also Rubys, p. 289; Péricaud, *Notes et documents, Henri III*, p. 113.

[2] *Arch. municip. de Lyon H.H.* IX, p. 629; undated, but probably of the period 1552–3.

[3] *Custodi*, II, 58.

this I promise to have a mark of gold paid in Lyons to Tommaso Sertini (D). I give thee a bill on Salviati (C), thou sendest him to Tommaso (D) so that he may cash it and deal with the re-exchange. The letter wherein thou dost this is called the Advice or Spaccio. Tommaso (D) carried out thy orders. He pays thy mark of gold in Lyons to Piero (E) and receives from him a bill on Federigo in Florence (F) in accordance with which he (Federigo) has to pay thee (A) $65\frac{1}{2}$ scudi in so many days. Tommaso sends thee this re-exchange, and when it matures thou hast made $1\frac{1}{2}$ scudi. Herein, however, thou hast to run the risk of three failures, mine, Tommaso's and Piero's. Therefore must thou look with Argus eyes at the firm to whom thou shouldst give the bill, him to whom thou remittest it and him by whom this second man should have the re-exchange drawn. Wherefore those who are not in business are wont to give their money to a bank, which deals with the transaction for a double charge: 2 per cent. for the trouble and 2 per cent. for the delcredere for the quarter. The fees in Lyons (Consular fee, charges and brokerage) amount to $1\frac{1}{2}$ per cent. A man who does not employ the agency of a bank will, after deduction of the above fees, make on an average 8 per cent. If a banker is employed, his fees $1\frac{1}{3}$ per cent. are also to be deducted.'

These figures are, of course, only rough averages. In view of the violent fluctuations in the price of bills, the Ricorsa in two acts as practised in Lyons was often very risky. Conditions in Lyons were similar to those we have seen in Antwerp. Anyone playing for safety had to use the deposito, and anyone not satisfied with the rates paid by sound firms on the bourse (buone ditte) – mostly not more than 10 per cent. – could lend money to the Crown, which usually paid 16 per cent. This was the form of investment to which capital turned more and more.

The total of the Lyons traffic represented extraordinary sums at any rate for the period. Even in 1573, when Lyons had passed its zenith by more than ten years, Nicolay says: 'There is not a fair in Lyons, be it never so poorly provided, but what millions of gold are dealt in on the Bourse.' Even in 1638 the English merchant Roberts writes: 'I have seen that in such wise (by clearing-house methods) in one morning payments worth a million crowns are settled, without a pfennig of ready money changing hands.'

The Beginnings of the French Crown Loans in Lyons. There is no question of dealing in capital at Lyons before 1463. Even then, however, it is a long time before we hear of large borrowing by the French Crown from the merchants doing business at Lyons. Louis XI, throughout his reign, usually met his extraordinary financial requirements by raising forced loans without interest from his subjects. We hear only of small interest-bearing loans at Lyons, e.g. in 1467 the King's officials, in order to pay for war material, borrowed money at the Lyons fair 'à perte et interêts.' This was unwelcome, and the King ordered the immediate repayment of the loan.[1]

Louis XI did not carry on expensive foreign wars. His successor, Charles VIII, when in 1494 he was getting ready for his great expedition to Italy, had to borrow largely from the Genoese bank of the Sauli. This was done at their Lyons factory, for Philippe de Commines reports that the loan was ' de foire en foire,' and cost 14 per cent. for each four months.[2]

In the subsequent period the Florentines are mentioned on several occasions as lending money to the French Crown, always, however, in small amounts. Charles VIII did not require to take large loans at interest in Lyons because he had at his disposal a less costly source of money in the subsidies and contributions of the Italian princes and republics. His successor, Louis XII, was a careful manager. In 1512 he tried to raise a forced loan from the foreign merchants doing business in Lyons, but had to desist on their threatening to leave the city. He was more successful with new forced loans from his own subjects.[3]

It was only under the prodigal and warlike Francis I that the loans of the French Crown in Lyons reached the grand scale. We know that in 1516 the King owed the Florentines in Lyons 300,000 écus, and in 1529 600,000 ducats. About this time the 'Good German,' Hans Kleberg, began to have dealings with the French Government, and the whole development attracted great attention from the Hapsburgs, who tried from the first with great pertinacity to deprive the French Crown of the financial strength it derived from the Lyons fair.

A report of 1521 shows us the way the Crown managed its financial dealings in Lyons at this time: 'The King sent lately from his Parliament in Troyes the directors (Généraux) of his finances to Lyons, there to raise money for his requirements. They are returned and have borrowed at interest about 200,000 écus from the bankers and merchants of Lyons.'[4] In his bill transactions with Italy, which were mostly advances, the King at this time already employed a permanent agent, Pier Spino, who followed the Court; but in Lyons the Crown had then no permanent representative.

The French Finance Administration had now got over its dislike of loans at interest; but as we have seen the Florentines were not disposed to lend the King all he required for his swollen expenditure on war costs

---

[1] *Lettres de Louis XI*, t. III, p. 190.
[2] *Mémoires de Philippe de Comynes*, ed. Dupont, II, 292, 331.
[3] Vaesen in *Mém. de la Soc. litt. de Lyon*, 1877–8, p. 25; *Registres des délibérations du bureau de la ville de Paris*, t. I (1499–1526), p. 204.
[4] *Bibl. de l'Ecole des chartes*, XX, 372.

T

and personal luxury. What his thrifty mother gave him from time to time or the many loans of the Pope and different Italian states, all disappeared like drops on a hot stone. Down to 1522 the King's financial straits are described in the strongest terms; in spite of all his boasting he could never dream of keeping the promises with which he wished to buy the Roman Crown.[1]

At the crisis of his financial difficulties in 1522 the directors of finance, who had travelled to Lyons for the purpose, managed to raise a fairly large loan from the foreign merchants. The Strozzi contributed 31,000 écus, the Guadagni 22,000 écus, Hans Kleberg 17,087 écus, etc. This is perhaps the first loan which can be called a bourse loan. It was not, however, carried through without compulsion; at any rate, shortly before the property of the Florentines was confiscated at the order of the King; while immediately after the loan they were granted new privileges.[2] This same year, 1522, is to be considered the year which saw the beginning of the French funded debt.

The money famine was now somewhat abated; but the King did not keep his promises to the merchants, and this destroyed his credit. The historian Guicciardini, who must have known, gives as one of the causes of the slackness of the French war operations in 1526 that the King had lost his credit with the Lyons merchants and could get little or no loans.

This situation remained unchanged in the following years, and finally made the Peace of Cambrai necessary for the French. This peace entailed heavy financial obligations on France. The ransoms of the King's children amounted to 1,200,000 écus; the power of the dynasty and the loyalty and capacity to pay of French people were now strikingly illustrated, for the notables granted this enormous sum, which was then compulsorily assessed as a loan and paid without too much grumbling.[3]

In the period of peace which followed, only once is there any talk of a large Crown loan in Lyons, and it is not certain whether it was ever carried through. A Tucher agent reports in 1532 from Lyons that the King wanted to raise money there in order to send it to Switzerland and Germany, 'God wot why or whither.' We know from other sources that the King sent that year and in the following years considerable sums as subsidies to the German allies, and that he needed a great deal of money for the pay of the Swiss mercenaries; but we do not know whether he

[1] Brewer, *Calendar*, II, Nos. 253, 522, 626, 1393, 2349; Baumgarten, *Geschichte Karls V*, vol. II, pp. 38, 96. Cf. also Desjardins, II, 899, *Actes de François I*, No. 1910.

[2] *Actes de François I*, Nos. 1529, 1594 and 17485.

[3] *Journal d'un bourgeois de Paris sous le règne de François I*, ed. Lalanne; Gaillard, *Histoire de François I*; Brewer, *Calendar*, IV, Nos 789, 1072; *Coleccion de documentos ineditos*, vol. XIV, p. 254; *Actes de François I*, Nos. 4385, 4623, 5492, 6421 ff.

actually borrowed this money in Lyons. In any case, it was only after the outbreak of war in 1536 that the scale of the loans became very large.

The Work of the Cardinal de Tournon. The great French publicist Bodin in his famous work *Les Six Livres de la République,* published in 1577, in the part dealing with finance inveighs against interest-bearing loans, which he designates 'the Ruin of Princes and their Finances.' He then adds in regard to such loans: 'This financial expedient was introduced into France in the year 1543 by the Cardinal de Tournon, who was induced by certain Italians to represent to King Francis I that there was only one way of attracting money capital from all sides to France; for which purpose the bank must be formed at Lyons and money borrowed from every man at 8 per cent. interest. In reality, however, what the Cardinal wished was to find a safe and profitable investment for 100,000 écus which he had in his own coffers. His proposal was accepted, and the bank was opened. Every one invested money there – French, Germans, and Italians – so that at his death King Francis I owed the Bank of Lyons 500,000 écus.[1]

Three distinct springs of action are to be distinguished in this remarkable statement: first, the action of the Cardinal; secondly, the participation of the Italians; thirdly, the organized dealing in capital which resulted. Of these we will here discuss the first two.

In the first place, it is not true that interest-bearing Crown loans were introduced into France through the Cardinal de Tournon, but it is right to say that he largely extended their scope. This development dates, not from 1543, but from 1536, though in 1543 it took on a new character which Bodin describes correctly as to its general tendency, though with certain errors in detail. The Cardinal de Tournon was one of the most important French statesmen of the time. It was he who had carried through the negotiations in Madrid as to the ransom of the King taken prisoner at Pavia; and he had been employed on many other diplomatic missions, most recently in Italy. In 1536 he was governor of the Province Lyonnais. In this position, and perhaps even previously, he came into contact with the great Florentine bankers who had their headquarters in Lyons, the Strozzi, Guadagni, Capponi, etc. He managed to arouse in them the hope that the King of France would free Florence from the rule of the Medicis and so induced them to be willing to lend to the King.

When in 1536 the Emperor invaded the South of France, the Cardinal succeeded in obtaining large floating loans from the Florentine bankers, at first 30,000 livres and then again 40,000 livres at 3 per cent. per fair. The details are not clear, but the Cardinal's large share in the business is evident. At the request of the bankers he had to act as a co-

[1] Bodin, l.c. ed. of 1583, VI, 2.

signatory.[1] Still larger sums, however, were then raised, partly on compulsion and in part voluntarily through loans of the cities and the clergy. For the second time since the introduction of this method of raising money large annuity loans were contracted with the cities, to which the royal revenues were pledged in return. Since the loans were not repaid, the revenues remained in the possession of the cities. For example, in 1530 Paris lent 100,000 livres and Lyons 84,733 livres. The latter transaction was carried out by the Cardinal de Tournon, who also had charge of the lease of the salt tax for large parts of the country, a business in which he employed the Florentines.

As warlike operations ceased in 1537, the need for further extraordinary receipts ceased and did not reappear till the renewed outbreak of the war in 1542. Only in 1541, on the pretext of a coming attack from the Emperor, the King recruited troops in Germany and raised a loan from the bankers and merchants of Lyons, which seems to have had the character of a forced loan.[2]

We have a Venetian ambassador's report of the year 1542, dealing in detail with the French finances. The French King, it is said, if he were economical, could easily lay by a million crowns a year. It is added that this is not the case and that the 300,000 écus set apart for his *menus plaisirs* did not suffice. Items on the expenditure side are: Pensions, a million livres. Gifts, half a million. Extraordinary expenses, 400,000 livres, etc. The annuity debt begun in 1522 had accordingly considerably increased. The report distinguishes these funded annuity loans from the floating loans at interest. The ambassador says that on his departure the State Treasury was empty and 'people begin to think already of borrowing money at interest from the merchants, as I observed on my passing through Lyons.' The raising of floating loans at interest in Lyons was undoubtedly a regular financial expedient of the French Crown from 1542–3 onwards.

The Period from 1542 *to* 1547. We are indebted for our first exact information as to this period to the English envoy Paget, who was then staying in Lyons.[3] He writes that the King of France has no money and little credit, as many old debts are still unpaid. He states in contrast the large loans which the Emperor had raised in a short time in Antwerp, Augsburg and Genoa. 'Great efforts are made daily to obtain money. For while here in Lyons and in other markets people who have liquid

[1] Cf. Monfalcon, *Histoire monument. de Lyon*, II, 290; *Archive municipale de Lyon: Invent. générale*, VIII, p. 175 ff., Nos. 29, 157; XII, p. 42, No. 81; Péricaud, *Notes et documents*, s.a. 1537[38] 22/1; Fleury, *Histoire du Cardinal de Tournon*, p. 146; *Actes de François I*, Nos. 8661, 8730, 8812, 8824, 8867, 9291, etc., and Nos. 21123, 21186, 21290.

[2] Gayangos, *Calendar*, VI, 1, p. 381.

[3] Gairdner, *Cal.*, vol. XVII, Nos. 554 and 589.

capital, and also widows and orphans, are wont to invest their money in banks at 5–8 per cent., the King will now take all this and promises for this purpose 10 per cent. interest.'

The 10 per cent. refers only to natives, the King promised foreigners 16 per cent. Under such conditions he was able, in spite of his bad credit, to raise 400,000, of which

the Florentines advanced	200,000 francs
the Welser	50,000 ,,
the Lucca merchants	100,000 ,,
the French merchants	50,000 ,,

It is certain, however, that Cardinal de Tournon, who once more raised this loan for the King, must have exerted more or less heavy pressure on the merchants. The Welser declared later to the Emperor that they had had to lend the King 12,000 crowns in order to stay in the country, which otherwise they would not have been allowed to do; the money was sent from Antwerp to Lyons, in spite of the Emperor's prohibition. Gaspar Ducci and Hieronymus Seiler were also interested. The Seiler letters show that the Welser and the other merchants were attracted by the interest, which was unusually high for the period. It is indisputable, however, that compulsion was also exercised.[1]

In 1542 and 1543 further sums were borrowed in Lyons, but we have no details. We only know that Hans Kleberg, 'the good German,' was interested himself and brought in other German merchants. At the end of 1543, however, everything seems to have been repaid.[2]

The loans of the Crown so soon became habitual in Lyons that a commercial handbook appearing in Antwerp in 1543 states that the exchange rate in Lyons depends, amongst other things, on whether the King is borrowing much there or not.[3]

In the spring of 1544 safe conduct was withdrawn from the Germans in Lyons because they supported the Emperor. They were hard pressed and some even were imprisoned. The Tucher agent, who reports this, adds that the French Court knew well that the 'Germans in Augsburg had much money to lend to the King.' This they must have done, for they were soon well treated again, and in June the King paid their maturing claims, while those of the Florentines and Lucca merchants were prolonged. This year and the next the Cardinal de Tournon was the King's chief representative in all monetary transactions in Lyons.[4] In the year 1545 other agents became more prominent.

[1] *Actes de François I*, t. IV, Nos. 12636, 12642, 12646, 12651, 12742, 22570.
[2] Ehrenberg, *Hans Kleberg (Mitth. d. Ver. f. Gesch. d. Stadt Nürnberg*, VIII, 21); *Actes de François I*, t. IV, Nos. 13349, 13491, 13509.
[3] Jan Impyn, *Nieuwe instructie d. looffl. consten d. rekenboecks*, Antw. 1543, fol. 15.
[4] *Actes de François I*, t. IV, Nos. 14008, 14357, 14479.

A Tucher agent reports in 1545 that he had been approached on 'change by Hans Kleberg, who asked him to write to his masters in the following sense: An official often employed in the financial transactions of the French Crown, Martin de Troyes (also called Maître Martin or Sieur Martin), who owned a house in Lyons, had asked Kleberg to consult his friends as to whether they would lend the King a sum of money at Easter. Kleberg tried to bring out clearly the profitableness of the business, praising his security and the high rate of interest, he said that the best South German houses were ready to come in. He had already raised 40,000 écus and was ready to let the Tucher have a share also. He himself wished to invest largely. He had always carried through his with good repute and without talk. The profit in this business was 'godly and fitting.' [1] The Tucher did not, as we know, wish to undertake this kind of business, but the loan came about, the Germans advancing 50,000 écus and the Italians 100,000 écus, making a total of 340,000 francs.

Later the merchants became very nervous at the report that the King was mortally ill; if he should die a quite different government was expected. In short, 'Every man is heavie because the King is so sick and weakly.' The merchants accordingly desired that the Dauphin should act as co-signatory, and Kleberg acted as their representative in bringing his wish before the King. He immediately granted this request and declared solemnly that the 'gifts' which he had made or should make to Kleberg and the other foreign merchants, as compensation for the loans they had made to him, were to be regarded as valid bonds without the merchants needing to trouble themselves on that account.[2]

In Antwerp also propaganda for the French loans was carried on by the Florentines settled in Lyons, especially by the Salviati through the agency of Gaspar Ducci, and we know that this was not unsuccessful. In August of the same year further loans were concluded in Antwerp.

In December, 1545, it is reported that the King had paid back 300,000 écus, 'whereat the Germans who had lent him money were not pleased.' However, in January, 1546, he once more borrowed 300,000 fr., and in March Kleberg was again approached to prepare himself and the members of his syndicate for further advances; the King, it was said, would engage himself in what manner the Germans wished. In September Jakob Sturm came to Lyons from Strasburg, commissioned by the Schmalkaldian League, in order through Kleberg's agency to borrow money for the war against the Emperor. He found Kleberg on his death-bed and thereupon applied in his need to the King, who at first declared his readiness to repay the merchants the half million écus

[1] Ehrenberg, *Hans Kleberg*, p. 23 ff.   [2] *Ibid.*, p. 26.

which he then owed them in order to help the Schmalkaldians.
Finally, through the agency of Maréchal Strozzi the following arrangement was arrived at. The King paid 100,000 crowns to the Maréchal,
who paid the same amount to the merchants to whom the King owed
money. The merchants lent it to the Protestants, and the princes engaged themselves to the cities and the cities to the merchants. The
King said everything must be kept very secret because, is it happened,
he was at peace with the Emperor. According to another version, the
King himself borrowed money in Lyons and had it conveyed to the
Protestants. The rate for Crown loans was then 12 per cent. per annum.[1]
Shortly afterwards, however, the King again borrowed at 4 per cent. per
fair.

In October, 1546, Sebastian Neidhart and Hieronymus Seiler ordered
that half the capital of the company which they had formed, together
with Alexius Grimel and others, should be lent to the King of France.
Grimel thought that this would be expedient, if no other safe investment were forthcoming. Good firms in Lyons were ready to pay 3 per
cent. per fair; and it would be best to be content with this. A part of the
capital was, however, lent to the King. The Welser's representative in
the Emperor's camp wrote home in February, 1547, that, considering the
violent and deceitful policy which the Emperor's counsellors had entered
on, it was small wonder that so much money was now withdrawn from
the Netherlands Court and lent to the French Court, 'though mayhap
in time even that investment may be still less fortunate.' We know too
that the Haug in Augsburg at the Easter fair in 1547 lent the French
Crown 36,000 crowns at 4 per cent. per fair.

King Francis I died on 3rd March, 1547. Bodin asserts, and many
authorities have repeated after him, that at the time of his death the
King had in ready money, not only the half million écus which he owed
'the Bank of Lyons,' but 1,200,000 écus as well in the Treasury. Others,
on the other hand, say that there were only 800,000 écus.[2]

In June, 1547 – shortly after the King's death – an envoy of the
Emperor's at the French Court reports that 'The French ministers and
others have often said that the late King had left enough money in the
Louvre to pay an army for six months and that this money was not to
be touched. Nevertheless, 200,000 écus have been taken from it and put
in the hands of the Trésorier de l'Epargne, who had no money, or rather
who had to pay out 500,000 fr. Moreover, there was less money in the

[1] Augsbg. Stadtarchiv, *Litteralien und Sielersche Correspondenz.* Cf. Ehrenberg,
Kleberg, p. 31, and Kius, *D. Finanzwesen d. Ernestin. Hauses Sachsen im* 16
Jahrh, p. 78.

[2] Bodin, l.c. pp. 893, 896, 905. *Traicté des Finance de la France* (1581) *in den
Archives curieuses de l'histoire de France,* 1 ser. t. IX, p. 394. For what follows,
Revue historique, V, 118.

Louvre than had been reported – 500,000 or 600,000 écus at most. Money is still owing to the Lyons merchants, and it is considered important to pay them their interest in order to be able to have their help should occasion arise. The present King has recognized as King his predecessor's debts at the request of the merchants who sent a special representative to the Court for this purpose. In short, the finances are not so brilliant as is boasted.'

The tendency to represent the royal finances in too rosy a light was of long standing in the case of Francis I and his ministers and counsellors. Bodin, who handed down these boasts as truth, was influenced by the wish to represent the reign of Francis I as the golden age of French finance in contrast to the financial mismanagement which reached its climax for the sixteenth century in his own day. Though he could not deny that in Francis' last years the debts grew apace, he said that the money so obtained (at 12 per cent. or 16 per cent. a year) was used by him, together with his savings, to form a large State treasure. There is a grain of truth in this. In the last years of his reign in peace-time Francis had collected money in order to be better prepared than formerly in the event of war. There was, however, no question of such sums as those quoted by Bodin.

The case is similar to Bodin's other statement which we quoted at the beginning of the previous section. We now know that Cardinal de Touron initiated a new era for French Crown loans from 1542 onwards. Bodin gives as the true inwardness of this movement that the 'Bank of Lyons' was formed to attract money from all sides and that it succeeded in the attempt. Bodin used the same expression 'Bank of Lyons' previously elsewhere, while contemporary writers only speak in general terms of the introduction of banking through the Italians.[1] Bodin has often been interpreted as if he meant that a bank was created in Lyons in 1543. This is, however, an erroneous meaning for the phrase 'Établir la Banque à Lyon.' Apparently this was meant to designate all banking and bill business and not a definite public bank, which certainly did not then exist in Lyons.[2]

The following facts are well established. Since 1542 the Crown had been engaged in a conscious effort to attract monetary capital from all sides to Lyons in order to be able to employ it there for the Crown loans. This end was attained by giving high interest and by using as agents the Italian and German merchants and bankers trading in Lyons. The Cardinal de Tournon as prime mover had often to apply pressure to attain his end. Certain specially prominent merchants, the Salviati

---

[1] Cf. Bodin's *Responsio ad Paradoxa Malastretti,* and his *Discours sur les Causes de l'Extrême Cherté.*

[2] Cleirac, *Commerce des Lettres de Change* (1656).

and Hans Kleberg, had to undertake propaganda for the French loans, both in the market and outside. Capital was attracted by the high rates of interest and the punctuality with which the Crown had the sense to pay them, as well as by the manifest anxiety of the French Crown to meet the lenders' wishes. This was the more easily done as the Emperor's financiers at this time did their best by their violence and deceit to scare away capital. Bodin's statement that the innovation was due to the Italians is confirmed by the fact that at the same time in Antwerp Gaspar Ducci was trying to do the same thing for the Emperor and the Court of the Netherlands, though at Antwerp methods were uglier and propaganda less skilful than at Lyons. It is significant, however, that the English agent Stephen Vaughan reports from Antwerp in February, 1545, that the French King had summoned Gaspar Ducci in order to organize his loans on the Antwerp model. The aim was similar in both places and to a certain degree the methods and persons engaged in them were identical. Bodin's statement that Cardinal de Tournon was only consulting his private interest is a gross exaggeration, though, of course, it is probable that he managed to unite his own interests with those of the Crown.

The Period from 1547 *to* 1551. According to several independent authorities, at the time of his death King Francis I owed the merchants of Lyons at least half a million écus. This, however, was a trifle compared with what happened under Henry II, who was his father's equal in his delight in war and his superior in prodigality.

In December, 1547, there began to be talk of large new loans. In Lyons, floating loans were raised amounting to 300,000 or 400,000 ducats, and at the same time 10 per cent. annuities for 100,000 francs were sold, and the capital value of these, a million francs, was about equal to the amount raised in floating loans.[1]

In 1548 a Venetian envoy at the French Court reported to his superiors the following interesting project which was then under consideration: 'I have learnt that the King intends to open in his kingdom four banks, in Paris, Rouen, Toulouse, and Lyons. Anyone depositing money in them is to receive 8 per cent. and to receive bonds of the States General for capital and interest. If the King needs money he will use the deposits in the banks, which otherwise will be lent out at 11 per cent.'[2]

It is interesting to find such a scheme under consideration at the French Court, certainly on the advice of the Italians. It confirms our criticism of Bodin's statement. Still more important is the fresh light

---

[1] Desjardins-Canestrini, *Négoc. dipl. de la France avec la Toscane*, III, 219; Vührer, *Histoire de la Dette publique en France* (1886), I, 21.

[2] Desjardins, l.c. III, 221.

it throws on a little understood measure of the French Government in creating bourses in these cities then mentioned as the localities destined for the creation of banks.

In July, 1549, the King issued an edict declaring that the city of Toulouse had less trade than its good situation would warrant because, unlike Lyons, Antwerp, and other great commercial cities, it did not possess a place known as 'Change, estrade ou Bourse,' where the merchants assembled twice a day to do business: whereby the costly wares of foreign countries were attracted and home commodities were more easily converted into money. The citizens of Toulouse had brought all this to the notice of the King. He accordingly ordained the institution there of a Bourse Commune on the model of the Change of Lyons, and he granted all the same privileges enjoyed by the merchants of Lyons, especially the special commercial jurisdiction. In 1551 further regulations were issued, of which the following may be instanced: The habitués of the bourse might lend to one another at interest up to 15 per cent. without being liable to be punished as usurers. They were to use for bills amongst one another the strict shortened form which had been in use at the Champagne fairs and was still in use in Lyons; they were to exercise the calling of money changers or bankers without the necessity of a special concession.

Under similar conditions a bourse was founded in Rouen in 1556, in Paris in 1563, and in other French cities later. This action, and especially the general introduction of commercial jurisdiction in France, is generally ascribed to the Chancellor Michel l'Hôpital, who urged this step in a speech before the Paris Parliament in 1560. He was, however, certainly not concerned in the creation of the Bourses of Toulouse and Rouen, and the legal aspect of the matter in which he was chiefly interested did not at first become prominent. At first attention was concentrated on the bourse as an economic institution from which a marvellous increase in trade activity was expected. The Government wanted to try to do for other towns what had been so successfully done at Lyons, with the intention, it must primarily be supposed, of increasing the means of satisfying its own financial requirements. This aim remained unfulfilled and the banking scheme was not realized. Lyons remained for the time the only place where the Crown could borrow, and the method of borrowing remained at first much the same as before. The loans, however, increased in size with an ever widening circle of investors.

For example, in 1549 the only loan made to the King was that of 100,000 crowns from the well-known firm of Neidhart, Seiler and Company; the greatest part of this was held by Sebastian Neidhart. The following were also interested: Hieronymus Seiler, Matheus Pflaum,

Georg Muelich, and Wolffgang Langemantel, all of Augsburg. By September, 1550, the claims had grown to 123,214 crowns. The King paid in 1549 in Lyons 16 per cent., though the rate for commercial loans (deposito) was only 10 per cent. to 12 per cent. For the last time on this occasion some Genoese (Gianbattista and Benedetto Fornari) seem to have been interested in the French commercial transactions; this, however, was discovered and severely punished.[1]

The South German merchants were already eagerly on the look out for the French King's bonds with their high rate of interest, as is shown by a letter sent on 6th February, 1550, by Andreas Imhof in Venice to Paulus Behaim in Nuremberg. 'I hear that thou wert too late with the 1,000 crowns to lend to the King of France. A piece of good fortune has been slept away. If a good sum had been lent him at the beginning, it had already been received back twofold and his money could have been done without.' This refers to the reluctance of the old Endres Imhof, father of the writer and head of the Imhof business in regard to financial transactions of this kind. It would have been better if in this matter he had never given way to his sons and young kinsmen. Paulus Behaim was able to carry out his scheme of lending 1,000 crowns to the King of France in September, 1550. Willibald Imhof sent him the good news that he had been able to invest the sum under the name of the Cenami, who gave him $\frac{1}{4}$ per cent. on the capital. The business was done through an Italian broker. Imhof adds: 'I could not do better. Before I came those who wanted to take up the King's bonds were giving $1\frac{1}{4}$ per cent. But yesterday there was largezza (easy money) and they were not offering $\frac{1}{4}$ per cent. for a place with the King; but things change very quickly.' We hear for the first time of the King's bonds being at a discount and of fluctuations in price. In November Imhof writes: 'Had I tarried longer to invest thy money with the King I had failed altogether, for the King would have naught. If thou wilt, thou canst have thy money and $1\frac{1}{2}$ per cent. thereto, but on such terms no one will come out.'

The rate for the King's loans fell during 1550 to 3 per cent. per fair = 12 per cent. per annum. Even at this rate, however, capital flowed in. In October, 1550, we are told that the King's credit was excellent because he always paid the interest promptly. He owed the merchants $1\frac{1}{4}$ million ducats already, and money was sent daily from Antwerp to Lyons. A Florentine historian says of the year 1550: 'In order to rival the Emperor in his loans, the King set up a Monte in his kingdom, and borrowed from any who would lend. He paid the interest every four months and restored the capital on demand. Hence so much money came together from all sides that within six months the King

---

[1] Bonfadio, *Annali d. cose de Genovesi* (1528–50) *ed. Passchetti*, p. 191 ff.

owed over three million ducats, whereof more than 800,000 were said to
belong to the Florentine merchants.'[1]

This was an exaggeration; there are several obvious mistakes. The
state of things described only came to pass some years later. The
statement is important as a proof that the large loans of the French
Crown were gradually creating a new organization for dealing in capital
which excited universal interest and which had as yet no settled designation. Other steps were soon to follow.

The Period from 1551 *to* 1557. In February, 1551, it is stated that the
King was continuing to pay 3 per cent. per fair and would only pay 4
per cent. if war were renewed. In August it was thought that the King
might well pay 4 per cent. and would do so, if he were seriously pressed,
'but no man will; the Italians are content with 3 per cent.; yet there are
some who would gladly withdraw at a loss of 4 per cent.' Those persons
were well informed. In Italy fighting had already begun between the
Emperor's troops and the French. This was followed in September by a
definite breach and the end of the year saw the treaty between King
Henry II and the German Protestants, especially Maurice of Saxony.

In October, in view of the unfavourable course of the war, the Imhof
also wished to sell their claim on the King and were ready to lose·5 per
cent. Their representative was only able to get rid of 2,000 crowns at a
loss of 6½ per cent. Every one wanted to sell and soon no one would buy
even at 7–8 per cent. discount. A fortnight later the Imhof were ready
to sell at 8 per cent. below par; but even at 10–12 per cent. discount
buyers were not forthcoming. In November feeling improved a little;
small parcels of the King's bonds changed hands at 8½ per cent. discount. Willibald Imhof could not advise Paulus Behaim as to his holding, 'for the great lords have it all their own way.' His 1,000 crowns was
sold at a loss of 8–8½ per cent.

At the December settling day the King gave the money market a joyful surprise by repaying 200,000 crowns. This so greatly improved his
credit that he was able temporarily to reduce to 3 per cent. the interest
on his loans, which had risen to 4 per cent. per fair. Those who had sold
at a loss were very sorry for themselves. Paulus Behaim wished once
more to invest 1,000 crowns if 4 per cent. per fair were to be had.
Willibald Imhof answered in January, 1550, that the King was disposed
to pay 4 per cent. per fair to those who would not only extend their
loans but would lend 50 per cent. in addition. The temper of the market
had already gone round again, most people wishing to be relieved of
their holdings. Money was very plentiful. On good commercial paper

---

[1] Segni, *Istor. Fiorent. ed. Gargani*, p. 488. Cf. Turnbull, *Calendar, Edward VI*,
No. 248. Report 21 October, 1550: 'Large sums come daily from Antwerp to the
bank of Lyons.'

only 1¼ per cent. to 1½ per cent. per fair (5 per cent. to 6 per cent. per
annum) was paid. At the beginning of 1552 the market rate had once
more risen to 2¾ to 3 per cent. per fair (11 per cent. to 12 per cent.) as
the King was once more borrowing largely and paying 15 per cent. 'It is
a fine profit for him who can take it' was the opinion of an agent of the
Tucher in Lyons. This was the time when King Henry II, through his
treaty with the German Protestant princes, took Metz, Toul, and
Verdun. Unfortunately there is no doubt not only that this step was
put in his power by German dissensions, but also that German capital,
in spite of the increased stringency of the Emperor's prohibition, took
part in the loans which he then raised. Authentic information is lacking for the year 1552. For 1553, however, there is a complete statement
of the sums which the King owed the Lyons merchants at the Easter
payment.

The Germans according to this had claims amounting to 700,000
crowns or écus; 200,000 or more of this amount was, however, held by
the Swiss. The Florentines' holding amounted to more than half a
million; that of the Lucca merchants, Venetians and Portuguese, to more
than 200,000 crowns. The total amounts to 1,463,375 crowns, 'whereof
the interest or "Don," reckoned at 4 per cent. for each fair, amounts to
about 58,535 crowns.'

This is confirmed by a direct statement from Lyons in October, 1553,
which says that in addition to the half million gold which the King
owed at the last fair he borrowed 400,000 fr.[1] This information, unquestionably correct, shows that at the Easter fair, 1553, the King was
owing the merchants of Lyons about 1½ million crowns; that he was once
more paying 4 per cent. per fair; and that he went gaily on getting into
debt though there was an armistice between him and the Emperor. He
had, however, to defend Corsica, which he had lately taken, against the
Genoese, who were supported both by the Emperor and the Duke of
Florence. Pietro Strozzi was in command of the French troops. Soon
money was to be needed on a different scale.

About this time there began to be complaints in France also that dealing in commodities was declining, while trade in money and bills was
flourishing. This fact is specially striking in a protest made by the
French dealers in commodities against an agreement of the foreign
bankers in Lyons relative to the kinds of money to be taken in exchange
payments. The foreign bankers are here accused of coming to France
only for their own interest, in order to attract to themselves all the specie
in order to export it. The new-fangled deposit business, it is said –
'usury,' to call it by its other name – enriched only the few and ruined

[1] Turnbull, *Calendar, Queen Mary,* No. 57. The écus or crown was then worth
2⅓ livres tournois or francs.

solid dealing in commodities so that many commodity merchants now deal only in money. Dealing in exchange is stigmatized as barren. These complaints later on were echoed loudly elsewhere and had momentous consequences.[1]

We have little information as to 1554. We hear of a loan of 40,000 écus, which the King borrowed at the August fair at 4 per cent. per quarter. According to Bodin's account the Capponi, the Albizzi and the South German merchants must have lent still larger sums, for his dates are not wholly reliable. He says that the interest in each case was added to the capital. This, however, was only done later; in the period 1554 to 1557 the interest was paid each fair time at 4 per cent.[2]

Bodin adds the observation that King Henry meant to attract capital by paying higher interest than the Emperor and the King of England, but that by so doing he gradually undermined his credit, 'for the best economists and calculators judged that at the last he would be able to pay neither capital nor interest since the interest with compound interest amounted to 18 per cent. at least.'

This was quite true and we know that not only cautious merchants like Anton Tucher, but also the much less prescient Welser had expressed this opinion ten years before. In the actual period before us the financial situation of the French Crown was judged by most capitalists very optimistically.

The year 1555 is remarkable in the financial history of the sixteenth century for being the year of the 'Grand Parti.' Any prince's loan was then called Parti, or in Italian Partito ; the largest loan contracted by the French Crown in the sixteenth century was accordingly 'Le Grand Parti.' It was the great or common investment as contrasted with the later Partiti Particolari. It was formed by a combination of all floating loans hitherto raised by the French Crown in Lyons, together with new loans to the amount of a third of the former ones. This transaction was effected at the Easter fair in 1555, when the war over Siena between the Duke of Florence and the French under Maréchal Strozzi was nearing its conclusion, but a general outbreak of war with the Emperor was imminent.

At the Easter fair in 1555 the usual market rate was 3 per cent. a quarter or 12 per cent a year. Money could be easily obtained for this rate, while 2⅔ per cent. to 2¾ per cent. was often offered. The Consuls of the foreign 'Nations' in Lyons were then asked whether the 'Nations'

---

[1] *Remonstrances des marchans contre l'accord des banquiers (Lyon. Arch. municip. H.H.* IX, 629). This is undated, but is undoubtedly of the period 1551–6.

[2] Bodin, ed. 1583, p. 893. Cf. Lyon, Bibl. Coste MS. 6932 N. and Ebner. Archives Contocorrent of Georg Ebner in Lyons.

would grant the King a loan to the extent of a third of what he already owed them. He would then pay 16 per cent. on the whole, though some of the older debts only bore interest at 12 per cent. On 7th March an arrangement was effected on these lines. The King received a new advance from each creditor amounting to a third of his previous debt, and promised in return 4 per cent. on the whole at each fair, together with a sinking fund payment of 1 per cent., so that the debt would be repaid in 41 fairs.[1]

The precise amount of the King's floating debt at this time is not known, but two years earlier it had been $1\frac{1}{2}$ million crowns. If we assume an increase of only half a million in the years, which is certainly not too high, it would amount to 2 millions, or with the new third $2\frac{2}{3}$ million crowns, it may possibly have been more. From the side of financial technique the Grand Parti is interesting as being the first instance of a royal finance transaction with a sinking fund with compound interest. This innovation bears the stamp of its Italian origin, but was soon adopted by all arithmethicians in their textbooks and widely popularized.[2] Next it is important that on this occasion the principle of the public or subscription loan was first adopted in the case of a great monarchy. The mediæval Monti of the Italian republics were also public loans, and the Florentine chronicler calls the new kind of loans in the French Bourse Monte since the King borrowed from any that would lend. This had never happened before north of the Alps, as contemporaries clearly recognized.

Rubys says: 'The King made a financial affair in Lyons which was called "le grand parti" because this loan was open to all kinds of persons, all whosoever would lend to His Majesty. They paid in their money to the Receiver General of Lyons and received in return bonds. A special office was created for the payment of the interest and the instalments of repayment, the Receveur du don Gratuit, who received the whole amount each fair from the Financial Administration and distributed it among the persons concerned. God knows how greed for these excessive gains, disguised by designation of a "free gift" (don gratuit), lured men on. Every one ran to invest his money in "le grand parti", the very servants brought their savings. Women sold their ornaments and widows their annuities in order to take shares in "le Grand Parti". In short people ran for it as if to see a fire.'[3]

Bodin speaks elsewhere of the Princes and gentlemen who invested money 'à la Banque de Lyons' for not only the rich Swiss gentlemen and

---

[1] Sources: Delaim papers in German. Museum; Ebner family archives; Haug ledgers in the Augsburg Museum.

[2] Michel Coquet, *Livre d'arithmétique*, Anvers, 1573.

[3] Rubys, *Histoire de Lyon*, p. 378.

German and other princes took their share, but even the Pashas and merchants of Turkey invested under the names of their agents more than 500,000 écus.'

Now we see exactly what Bodin meant by the La Banque de Lyons – it was the Grand Parti, or as the South Germans called it the 'Gemeinsame Platz' in reference to the fact that the loan was open to all. It is also clear why the statements as to the introduction of this great innovation are so varied and inexact. What happened in 1555 was the amalgamation and increase of loans, some of which went back to 1551. The process we have described continued to widen its scope and perfect its organization. The Grand Parti is by no means the end of the process of development. This continued to gain in width rather than depth up to the time of the financial crisis of 1557. Other large loans were effected, but up to that moment there was no really important progress in the system itself. From this point onwards, however, a further development took place which renders the finances of Lyons an object of increasing interest to us.

For the year 1555 we have nothing but the receipt of Martin de Troyes, who had become the King's Receiver General in Lyons, for the sum of 99,325 écus, which had been advanced to the King in Lyons by Pietro Salviati and Company. The receipt is dated 7th October, 1555, and refers therefore to a transaction subsequent to the Grand Parti.[1]

The fugitive Florentines in Lyons were at this time trying to spur France on to fresh efforts against Duke Cosimo of Florence, who was in alliance with Spain. This movement was headed by the Strozzi and the Altoviti. We are told that on 12th January, 1556, the Florentines lent the King 400,000 crowns at 16 per cent., and wished to advance a further 200,000 without interest on condition that the King would use this money against Florence. On the 27th January we are told that Bindo Altoviti concluded with the King's representatives a loan contract in the name of the Florentine émigrés for the sum of 300,000 crowns at 16 per cent. The matter, however, remained unsettled as the bonds offered were found unsatisfactory.[2]

Towards the end of August Maréchal Strozzi arranged a further loan. The King paid over to Pope Paul IV 300,000 crowns of 'subsidies' through the Florentine bankers in Venice. They in their turn advanced 120,000 crowns, while the remainder, 180,000 crowns, was taken up by German merchants under the names of Israel Minckel and George Obrecht. The terms of the loan were that it was to be repaid in two yearly instalments and was to bear interest at 16 per cent. It actually cost the King over 20 per cent., since there was a loss of $6\frac{1}{2}$ per cent. in

[1] Bibl. Coste, Lyon MS. No. 6933.   [2] Brown, *Calendar*, VI, 314, 330.

the two years on the exchange on Venice, and moreover the interest was compound. The reason why the German merchants came in was, as we learn from Maréchal Strozzi that 'the Florentines would not bear the risk alone,' and the Germans were only too ready to take a part of it from them.[1] They were strangely optimistic about the state of the French provinces. There set in, at this time, a blind, senseless rush of fools who wanted to make money quickly – a phenomenon which has always since been a feature of epochs of that kind. It is probable that the Florentines did all they could to lure on the Germans.

When at the end of December Michel Imhof in Lyons wrote to Paulus Behaim in Nuremburg that through the Welser he had been able to 'place' 1,500 crowns for him with the King and had got a profit of 2 per cent. on the capital, i.e. bought at 98, Behaim was greatly pleased at this excellent piece of business, and Hans Imhof wrote from Antwerp that he had been glad to hear of it 'for the investment is safe and the interest good and has helped many a good fellow into the saddle.'

The business in which Behaim was interested was what the Germans called the Salz Partita (salt loan). On the 1st of November, 1556, a new loan was concluded, it is said, with George Obrecht, who was at the head of a large syndicate of Germans and Italians. The amount is put at 900,000 crowns and the interest once more at 16 per cent. On the 16th December a further loan of 300,000 crowns was concluded at the same rate.[2] If these facts are correct, the Germans only held a third of these loans, for according to the Ebner list Israel Minckel, George Obrecht, and Company lent the King at this time only 400,000 crowns, repayable within $5\frac{1}{2}$ years in quarterly instalments and bearing interest at 4 per cent. per fair. The loan was secured on the revenue from the salt tax (Gabelle) in Nantes, Tours and Bourges. Hence the name Salz Partita.

Though the payments of the interest and sinking fund at the subsequent fairs was very slow, the faith in the public in the French Crown's solvency remained for a time unshakeable. At the beginning of May, 1557, Michel Imhof wrote from Lyons that he had no anxiety on account of the French debt; he would be glad if the Imhof had lent the King in addition to their other loans half of their claim against the city of Antwerp. In the early fairs of 1557 money was extraordinarily plentiful. The market rate fell as low as $1\frac{1}{3}$ per cent. per fair $= 5\frac{1}{3}$ per annum. The King's Partito stood at 98–99 and at these rates there were people anxious to buy than to sell. The King knew well how to keep up this favourable temper. Reports were spread of coming financial reforms on a larger scale. When at the beginning of August, 1557, it became known that the King of Spain had ceased payment, King Henry assured the German merchants that they need have no fears on his

---

[1] Brown, VI, 904. [2] *Ibid.*, VI, 764, 869.

account: he would keep his promise, he knew what was due from a prince's honour. Hereupon the German merchants who a few days earlier had lent him 200,000 crowns advanced a further 300,000 crowns at 16 per cent.[1]

A short time afterwards the King, in conversation with a Venetian envoy, boasted that the Lyons merchants competed with each other in offers of money. They had lately lent him 600,000 crowns, of which 100,000 was without interest. 'To tell the truth,' he added, 'I am myself amazed at such openhandedness in such a situation. The German merchants too are no less ready to serve me than the others.' The situation here mentioned by the King was evidently that created by his defeat at St. Quentin ten days before. The blind confidence of the German merchants might well arouse wonder – Minckel Obrecht and Company lent, for one instance, 400,000 crowns to the King on the security of the Lyons customs, though these receipts were already pledged to the Florentines. Most curious of all, the interest on the loans was only 12 per cent.

Scarcely three months after making his solemn promise the King followed the Spanish example and ceased payment of the interest and sinking fund on the Lyons loan, which then amounted to about 5 million crowns. The price then fell to 85 per cent., but nevertheless Michel Imhof wrote on 26th November, 'We (the Imhof) are with thee (Behaim) in not wishing to sell out with loss, though things are setting not towards peace, but towards war. The King of France is not thus to be driven out and luck may soon turn again. God preserve us from loss.'

[1] Brown, VI, 1238, 1255.

CHAPTER 3

DEALINGS IN CAPITAL ON THE INTERNATIONAL
BOURSES OF THE SIXTEENTH CENTURY

External Development of Antwerp and Lyons. The development of the two international Bourses of the sixteenth century, in spite of many important common traits, shows certain decided differences. Both owe much in the first place to their favourable geographical situation, and secondly to the help of their respective rulers, who pushed their development by the grant of large privileges. While Lyons was almost entirely a product of this policy, in Antwerp the national development of trade counted for more. Bruges had played its part and could no longer compete with Antwerp for the fruits of the great discoveries overseas.

In the case of Lyons, on the other hand, the Geneva fairs would certainly have continued to prosper but for the interference of the French Crown, and the new discoveries had relatively little importance.

The French Kings recognized earlier than the Hapsburgs how enormously their power was increased by the possession of such a market. They made Lyons their financial arsenal. Accordingly Lyons had a less international character and was not a world Bourse of such predominance as Antwerp. Nevertheless, Lyons also took its stamp as far as business was concerned from foreigners, chiefly Florentine and South German merchants, while in the case of Antwerp there were also, besides these, Spaniards, Portuguese, English, Genoese, and (though these were less important) merchants from Northern Germany. In both cases these foreigners were attracted by the practically unlimited freedom of trade which distinguished the world bourses of the sixteenth century from the mediæval Bourses and fairs which were subject to more or less severe restrictions.

This freedom of trade resulted in the concentration in Antwerp and Lyons of most of the international trade of Europe and its colonies. Here again there is a distinction. What was concentrated in Antwerp was above all a trade in commodities, which was followed by a corresponding trade in bills and means of payments, which in turn produced trade in liquid money capital. In Lyons, on the other hand, the trade in bills was from the beginning the chief business, and it is probable that a real capital market developed from it earlier than in Antwerp. More of the details later: here we must first give a sketch of the process of development.

We have seen what forced European princes, more especially those who were aiming at world power, since the close of the Middle Ages to resort to ever-increasing loans. This had been so for some time before Antwerp and Lyons became of chief importance in regard to these loans.

In the twenties and thirties, and even to a certain extent in the forties, of the sixteenth century, the largest international financial transactions were carried out for the Emperor, at any rate, not in Antwerp, but in Augsburg and Genoa. Lyons attained a decisive influence in regard to the French Crown somewhat earlier. It is, however, striking that credit dealings with the Government in the case of both Bourses only became a regular thing and a really important branch of business from about 1542. The years 1551-2 saw the beginning of a new and important phase in this development. At this time Augsburg, Genoa, and Florence lost what had remained of their importance as centres of great international finance, which henceforward was entirely concentrated in the Capital Bourses. On both Bourses a credit boom set in which led in five years' time to the first large financial crisis. Another interval of five years brought events which led immediately to the ruin of both markets.

The short period of greatest prosperity in Antwerp and Lyons was the time when Turkish pashas invested in the French King's loans in Lyons, when Henry of Rantzau, the statesman and Maecenas of Holstein, hastened to bring his capital to Antwerp, when the total of dealings in money transacted in one year on the Antwerp Bourse was put as high as 40 million ducats. We must now try to go more deeply into the real nature of proceedings which had such great results.

Fairs and Bourses. The development of the international Bourses of the sixteenth century is only a fragment of the enormous cultural process which began with the dawn of any form of trade and must continue as long as trade lasts – the process of local concentration of trade on the formation of markets.

A market arises from the fact that many dealers meet at the same time in a given place to exchange commodities and that they compete with one another for this purpose. In so doing they perform a piece of productive work. They overcome the hindrances to trade and the supply of commodities arising from the fact that many goods are not available at the time and place where they are needed. We need not deal here with the causes of the latter fact, but only with the difficulties to be overcome in the future development of markets.

The formation of markets has both natural and artificial hindrances to contend with. Natural hindrances consist first in the feebleness of trade itself, and secondly in the imperfection of its tools, the roads, transport, and the news service. Next comes the hindrance caused by robberies, by ceaseless wars and feuds, by the never-ending customs barriers of the olden times, and much else of the same kind. To this must be added the intentional restriction of competitors by regulations of the states, municipalities, religious and other confraternities, guilds, etc. As long as trade has to contend step by step with such great difficulties, the formation of markets also must remain imperfect: to the greatest degree and for the longest time in the case of goods which have to be brought to market in order to be dealt in, while in the case of goods when this is not necessary a market is much more easily formed.

The steady pressure towards trade concentration in the Middle Ages triumphed over these difficulties sufficiently to form yearly markets or fairs, i.e. markets which recurred at long intervals from one to at most four times a year. The extent of the trade, the condition of the roads and means of transport proved adequate, at any rate, in the case of many commodities for these markets. Trade in them also enjoyed a certain amount of freedom: freedom from disturbance through violence as well as from the influence of the measures to restrict competition imposed by the Church, the State, the municipalities, and others. Trade concentration in the Middle Ages was really confined to those commodities which had to be taken to market, i.e. to goods in the narrower sense. It was then only within the market itself that there were houses for buying and other appliances, intended not so much in the economic interest as in that of civil control. On the other hand, in exchange business – as we have seen in our introductory section – trade-concentration even in the Middle Ages in certain isolated instances went so far as to produce Bourses. Exchange business on the Bourse soon had as its appendage Bourse transactions in loan capital for commercial purposes.

We cannot here enter in detail into the development from fair to Bourse in the case of trade in commodities properly speaking. Sufficient to say that the increase of trade, the improvement in communications, and the grant of complete trade freedom to certain markets helped to give a Bourse character to trade in commodities in these markets from the close of the Middle Ages; and the fairs gradually lost their former importance. Contemporaries at first regarded this as a dangerous anomaly; but they quickly became accustomed to it, and we soon find Lodovico Guicciardini calling Antwerp a 'continuous fair.'

The development of exchange business was on rather different lines. It had been customary from early times to specify a fair as the term for all large engagements and to discharge these together with any which had been undertaken during the progress of the fair at its close. This custom came about from the same causes which produced the fairs. There was a shortage of ready money, which was practically unobtainable except at fair times. It was difficult and dangerous to transport it. Cash transactions and sending ready money about were to be avoided as far as possible. Debits were set off against one another at the end of the fairs. Exchange business, more especially the money changing rendered necessary by the excessively depreciated currency and the in-

numerable different coinages, was relieved at fair times of the burden-
some restrictions imposed upon it at other seasons. In short, the fair in
the Middle Ages became the usual term for all large payments; and payment was already effected to a large extent by clearing-house methods,
i.e. without money actually changing hands.

This arrangement soon affected exchange business. Like other engagements bills were for choice met at fair times. Accordingly, such
bills as matured at fair times were always the easiest to buy and sell;
while, conversely, bills on certain markets were easiest to get and to
dispose of during the fair payments.

The use of bills reduced the amount of specie payments between
different places, just as the clearing-house system at the fairs reduced
them at a given place. The chief intermediaries in both cases were the
dealers in exchange.

The whole system of mediæval fair payments was a help to credit
transactions in general and, of course, first and foremost that of the
merchants. We have seen in the introduction how the Italians as early
as the thirteenth century found it more profitable to draw bills on a
large fair than to borrow. In the centuries following the bill of exchange
became more and more an instrument of commercial credit, which by
its means began successfully to evade the ban on usury. Indirectly,
that is, through the agency of merchants, such operations on occasions
even relieved the fiscal monetary needs of princes.

It might be thought that fair-time payments, like the fairs themselves,
must gradually have lost their importance at the end of the Middle Ages.
The exact reverse was, however, the case. The amount of specie in circulation increased, but the need of currency increased at least in the
same proportion. The transport of specie was still difficult and dangerous, though less so than in mediæval times. The inconvenience and risk
of sending ready money increased with the amount sent. The restrictions which the local authorities imposed on money changing and the
penalties for any infraction of the official valuation of the currency had
almost entirely lost their effect, but the false coining of the princes continued briskly. The merchant class was now much more sensitive to
these ills, but it learnt more and more how to render them harmless.
For this end it developed money surrogates (bills and clearing-house
payments), and created, in close connection with these, unalterable con-
ventional fair currencies. A belated effect of the ban on usury here
played a considerable part. The ban had, in fact, lost the greater part
of its influence, but the merchants for long held it necessary to protect
themselves against chicanery by giving the forbidden transactions an
unexceptionable form. The fair bill of exchange was recognized as such
a form, and in the sixteeneth century the theory of canon and com-

mercial law had devised for it a strong shield of fine-drawn justifications and distinctions.[1] Everything, however, turned on the necessity for the greatest possible trade concentration. While even the fairs at Antwerp and Lyons lost most of their importance in the sixteenth century, the fair payments in both markets in the first two-thirds of the century, but more especially in the second third, acted as clearing houses for the whole of Europe.

The Antwerp and Lyons fair payments were the usual dates for the discharge of liabilities. It was usually very difficult to obtain large amounts of money capital at any other time. The transactions, however, which gave rise to these payments were now for the most part concluded outside the fairs. In this respect the development was the same as in the case of the trade in commodities. The more money and credit business increased and the more the means of communication improved – and here it is a question of news rather than transport – the more this trade could move freely to its centres even apart from fair times, the more continuous did it become and the more did it assume the character of Bourse business. We shall see later exactly what we understand by this. Here we must deal with the external form given to capital transactions by all the influences we have mentioned in the world Bourses of the sixteenth century.

The Forms of Commercial Capital Transactions. We have dealt fully with these forms in the two preceding chapters. We know that two forms were principally used as a modest disguise for the loan at interest. These were the Ricorsa bill and the Depositum.

The Ricorsa bill, originally Recambium, a transaction which was only intended to allow recourse on the drawer of the bill by the holder in case of default, was certainly not much used before the sixteenth century as a cloak for loans. This was done at first chiefly in the way which we come to know in the case of Antwerp from the Report of the Paris jurists in 1530, and in the case of Lyons from Davanzati's description. This 'Ricorsa bill in two Acts' was not only a credit instrument, but also contained a strongly speculative element, as no one could foresee the exchange rate at the time of the re-exchange. Accordingly, there was a possibility of making a profit, not only on the interest, but on the difference in the exchange rate. This element was only got rid of when later the two acts of the Ricorsa bill were amalgamated in the Genoese bill fairs. The same result was meanwhile attained by the second form employed in the commercial credit business of the two world bourses, the Bourse deposit.

The Bourse deposit was at bottom nothing other than the loan from

[1] Cf. e.g. Endemann, *Studien*, I, 157 ff., 278 ff.

fair to fair, which must have been fairly frequent even in the Middle Ages. Its name 'depositum' arose in the sixteenth century from the necessity of justifying from the ecclesiastical point of view an indispensable kind of business. It was indispensable because of the rapid extension of capital transactions in the two world bourses. Hence it came about that Charles V in 1540 imposed a tax on interest in the case of transactions of this kind, and by this act the authority of the state made a wide breach in the wall of the mediæval ban on usury.

The Bourse deposit took the form either of a bill or – in the Netherlands – of a bearer bond, which for this purpose in 1537 was subject to the same rigid rules as to form which characterized the bill. Both these forms were only two different varieties of the fair bill, which, as we have seen, owed its economic importance to the fact that it provided a form to commercial credit to which exception could not be taken.

The Importance of the World Bourses for Public Credit. The world Bourses of the sixteenth century, on the one hand, made it easy for the South German and Italian merchants to turn their attention to finance business, and, on the other hand, they helped princes to raise large loans at interest. The process here carried out was a special case of the formation of markets.

In the first decades of the sixteenth century large financial dealings were still chiefly transacted in Augsburg, Genoa, and Florence, where the business houses, with the most important money capital at their disposal, had their head-quarters. They were concluded after negotiations with individual firms, without direct competition of one house with another: thus not in the characteristic market manner. The payments resulting from such engagements were, for the most part, made in Lyons or Antwerp, where the whole world in any case had either to make or to receive payment.

Even in this period, however, it happened on occasion that merchants in Lyons or Antwerp lent to princes because they had money over after a fair payment and took the opportunity of profitably employing it till the next fair with a financial official who might be at the fair. But there was as yet no regular Bourse business of this kind. The same holds good of the occasional loans which the princes in the case of a specially pressing call for money had raised in Lyons and Antwerp. These loans were more or less compulsory, and were secured by three or four different interlocking guarantees, and the pawning of the Crown jewels and what not. It needed the influence of the most distinguished statesmen as well as threats of every kind before they at last came painfully into being. Loans such as these were not really Bourse loans – a fact proved by the violent and frequent fluctuations in their rate of interest.

The twenties and thirties of the sixteenth century saw a gradual change, due to the fact that the Florentines settled in Lyons, and certain South Germans, like Hans Kleberg and Lazarus Tucher, learnt how to meet the monetary requirements of the powers struggling for the first place in the world. The years 1542–3 and 1551–2 were critical in this process of development.

For once we can time an important stage in economic development exactly because political forces here came into play to an even greater extent than economics; and political effects tend to be catastrophic, as opposed to the slow, almost imperceptible action of economic forces and interests. The first impulse to the market formation we are here considering did not count from the side of supply, from capital seeking investment, but from demand, the princes and their need of money. We see this in the case of Lyons from the fact that Francis I himself, after 1542, several times had to resort to indirect measures of confiscation in order to raise loans. The war between Charles V and Francis I, which began in 1542, demanded armaments on a scale never before seen. The French King put two armies in the field, and one of these was said to be eighty to a hundred thousand strong. These were not Swiss and Germans alone, but Swedish and Danish mercenaries also; for Francis had made alliances with the Kings of Denmark and Sweden. He had also allied himself with the Turks and so had forced the Hapsburg brothers on their side to raise several large armies. On sea, too, large forces were raised on both sides. King Henry VIII of England also prepared for war, and all Europe bristled with arms.

This all required money on such a scale that the princes finally gave up the last shred of their dislike of floating loans bearing interest, which now became a regular means of covering extraordinary expenditure and were soon used for ordinary current expenses as well. Loans both so frequent and so large could not be raised either compulsorily from the princes' subjects nor yet voluntarily with the different business houses who had hitherto helped them out of their difficulties. In this extremity two men first and foremost recognized the proper method: Gaspar Ducci in Antwerp, and the Cardinal de Tournon in Lyons. They had recourse, not to separate merchants, but to the Bourses.

Meanwhile, the supply of money capital in both markets had greatly increased in consequence of the large changes in world trade, which we already know. Many South German and Italian merchants had settled permanently in Antwerp and Lyons, where they greatly helped in bringing in their countrymen into financial dealings which promised much profit and appeared safe. The same thing was done by the Antwerp and Lyons agents of the great business houses, which let themselves be carried away only too easily, till at last the agents had it all their own way and the factories in the two world Bourses were converted into head offices. The trading companies now attracted from every side the free money capital of the small holders of capital, and for these they paid a much lower rate than what they were able to get in financial dealings. On the Bourses themselves the great financiers borrowed more and more outside capital, which could not else have found employment and was therefore relatively cheap.

The supply of money capital in liquid form was more and more concentrated in Lyons and Antwerp, and the princes and their financial advisers were not slow to profit by this. In France, especially, this was cleverly done. It was published abroad that anyone taking up the King's loans would get far higher interest than could be had otherwise in Lyons on bills or deposits. This meant the beginning of the Public Subscription Loan, a system which underwent important developments in Lyons. The South German and Italian financiers here again took an active part.

In Antwerp also a subscription loan was opened as early as 1542. It was, however, without interest and was only an occasion for the display of loyalty in face of the threatened invasion by the French. In Antwerp it did not become a system. Even Ducci, who then played the chief part in financial dealings in Antwerp, had to pay a rate far in excess of the market rate in the case of the large loans he raised for the Emperor and the Netherlands Government. It was, however, lower than it had been before – a sure sign that the supply of capital was increasing more quickly than the demand. This impression is strengthened when we consider that the city of Antwerp and the King of Portugal at this time were making demands on the money market much greater than ever before, and that the English Crown was now beginning for the first time to borrow largely in Antwerp.

Gaspar Ducci attained his end chiefly by the issue of great masses of the bonds of the Receivers General. The causes of the favour now extended by the Antwerp Bourse to a class of investment which it had before regarded with justifiable suspicion must be the subject of our investigation later. We cannot discover Ducci's methods in detail; we may, however, be sure that his intention of selling such bonds was always known on the Antwerp Bourse generally and at once, and that he used many artifices, not always of a desirable kind, to increase the success of these issues. At any rate, the business in bonds of the Receivers General was done through the market; the demand was directly competitive.

The ambition to share in the Antwerp and Lyons financial dealings affected an ever-widening circle, until finally even the most violent increase of the demand did not exhaust the supply, and whole classes of the European peoples were seized by a regular mania or craze for the possession of these magic parchments known on the world Bourses as King's Bonds, Court Bonds, or Bonds of the Receivers General.

The last great war which Charles V had waged against France and her allies from 1552 onwards, and which Philip had to continue after his father's abdication, made claims on the Bourse which hitherto would have been regarded as unthinkable. The system of employing mercenaries now reached its highest point, as may be seen from the fact that from 1552 onwards there were standing regiments of Swiss in the service of the French Crown.[1]

In 1552 Gaspar Schetz in Antwerp was appointed by the Brussels Court as the first financial agent proper; and at the same time Thomas Gresham appeared as the representative of the English Government in their financial dealings on the English Bourse. This marks a further stage in the process of development. The princes, when they wished to raise large loans in Lyons or Antwerp, at first used to send their highest finance officers; later they more and more frequently made use of the agency of the merchants resident at the Bourse centres and of brokers. At the beginning they conferred on these agents only titles and honours, a sort of semi-official position; now they gave them out and out an official position, while in Lyons the Governor-General, the King's Governor, acted as his chief financial agent.

So we find at the close of the development, on the one hand, official representatives of the most powerful European monarchs permanently accredited to the world Bourses; and, on the other hand, we note that the Antwerp and Lyons agents of the great financiers are the real leaders. It would be hard to conceive a more striking proof of the irresistible influence of the market.

The Commonalty of the Bourse and Bourse Opinion. The complete freedom enjoyed by trade in Antwerp and Lyons in the sixteenth century was far the most powerful incentive to business concentration, more important than the improvement in communications, which began to take the lead in this direction in the nineteenth century. Freedom to trade took away most of their meaning from the mediæval privileges of isolated foreign 'nations' and welded the members of those nations who crowded into the centres of international business into a merchant class, more or less homogeneous both as to its rights and its duties. It was this liberty, in the first place, which made business on commission possible, and so enormously extended the numbers of those who could share in the advantages of the market. Finally, it was this that destroyed the rigid mediæval organization of local trade and created the modern Bourse. On this last process we must concentrate our attention, restricting ourselves in the main to dealings in capital.

[1] Max Jähns, *Heeresverfassungen und Völkerleben,* 2nd ed. (1885), p. 256 ff.

The mediæval Bourses, as we have seen in our introduction, were local assemblies of merchants mainly for the purpose of dealing in bills of exchange and loans of capital for commerce. The transaction of this business was the common object which brought together merchants of different kinds who otherwise would have had nothing in common. The Bourse enabled these different dealers to deal directly with one another in buying and selling bills and loans of commercial capital.

In the Middle Ages the Italians had control of business of this sort, as they were the only people who dealt in these on a sufficient scale to form a market. Accordingly, mediæval Bourses were permanent assemblies of Italian merchants, which members of other nations only took part in when they had to do business in bills or capital on loan. Generally speaking, they remained in their houses or warehouses or their own special assemblies, in which Bourse business proper either did not exist or only came about on occasions.

This was the state of things about 1500 even in Bruges, the city which in the Middle Ages was the strangers' town *par excellence*. The different nations were then held apart by jealously guarded special privileges and by the vested interests of the natives, who reserved for themselves certain agency services (innkeeping, brokerage, etc), even if they did not, as was the custom everywhere else in the Middle Ages, entirely prohibit dealings of the 'visitors' amongst themselves.

Meanwhile, Antwerp created a Bourse for the merchants 'of all nations,' abolished all restrictions on their trade, brought them into immediate daily communication, and created what the Paris jurists in their memorandum of 1530 called the 'Bourse commonalty,' i.e. an assembly of business men of different nations for a common purpose, the transaction of business of a given kind, an assembly whose members accordingly had certain interests in common with one another. As to the kind of business which formed the common end, it is sufficient to say here that dealing in exchange remained the chief business of the Bourse.

Within the Bourse there was formed what we call the feeling of the Bourse, i.e. a common public opinion as to certain important elements of Bourse business formed from the subjective views of the different habitués of the Bourse from their immediate contact with one another, a feeling which soon came to be a most powerful influence in determining these elements.

These are the credit of those admitted to the Bourse, and the quality and price of the commodities dealt in. Dealing not organized as a market knows no public opinion on such matters. Every buyer or seller is forced to form his independent judgment. He has, of course, certain clues for his guidance in other similar transactions or in other individual views which he has noticed had been held by others before on such points. He does not, however, know what these are at the moment of the transaction; and in view of the great difficulty of forming a correct judgment on such subjects, this is what is finally decisive, especially for trade whose essence is that its operations must be quickly carried out.

Every market creates a market opinion. Among the traders who visit the market a general view grows up as to certain important elements of the business of the market, and this market opinion immediately acquires an independent meaning for the purpose of this business. In the case where the market is not yet full-fledged, as in the mediæval type of fair, the significance of the market opinion is only imperfectly developed, first because those who form it are few in number and then because, generally speaking, it can only come about two or three times a year. Conditions are quite different in the daily business of the Bourse. The opinion of the market or the Bourse here becomes a factor of the first importance.

It seems fitting here to discuss the influence of the Bourses on the development of the international news service.[1]

Long before diplomacy had sufficiently perfected its system to get the necessary political news on its own, an abundance of political and other news reached the centres of trade. From early times the merchant, in order to ply his trade, had had to have accurate information as to current events which largely determined such things as the safety of the roads, the course of commodity prices and the credit-worthiness of other merchants. The merchants' letters of the earlier period, therefore, regularly contained news of this kind often in great detail. These were the first 'newsletters,' which at a later time were composed by professionals and soon were printed – a development which began about the end of the sixteenth century.

In the mediæval fairs news of all kinds came in with the merchants themselves, and passing from one to the other formed the real basis of public opinion. Where a daily Bourse developed, the news service also became permanent. Already during the Middle Ages the best information as to the course of events in the world was regularly to be obtained in the fairs and the Bourses.

This statement applies in a far higher degree to the world Bourses of the sixteenth century. In order to see this we need only look at the dispatches of the Venetian envoys collected in the Diaries of Marino Sanuto or the reports of the English diplomatic agents, to notice how much of their news originated either directly or indirectly from Antwerp

[1] Cf. Ehrenberg, 'Geschriebene Hamburger Zeitungen im 16 Jahrhundert' in *Mitth. d. Vereins, f. Hambg. Geschichte*, Bd. VI, Heft 1, No. 8. See also *Dialogues Flamen-Françoys*, recueilliz par Gerard de Vivre, Rotterdam, 1607.

or Lyons. It is astonishing how much at that time diplomacy was indebted to trade for its news service. We have already referred to the
fact that it was Thomas Gresham's close and important connection with
the Antwerp Bourse which caused Queen Elizabeth and her statesmen
regularly to be better informed than any other Government of the
time as to everything that happened in Europe.

It will be evident without more comment that a news service of this
character must have great influence on the formation and meaning of
Bourse opinion in the world bourses.

We must now enter in detail into the meaning of this Bourse opinion
in so far as is necessary for our own particular purpose. In so doing we
disregard altogether the large question of speculation in commodities
and its importance for the Bourse business of the sixteenth century and
must once again limit ourselves as we have done before to the traffic
in bills and loan capital.

*Bourse Opinion and Commercial Credit Transactions. The Ditta di
Borsa.* In the case of individual isolated credit transactions, that is, in
those not effected through a market, every person who gives credit has
to form an independent judgment as to the credit-worthiness of the
person to whom he gives it. This is always an extremely difficult task,
and it becomes quite impossible when the persons concerned live in distant places only to be reached with enormous difficulty when means of
communication were bad. On this account, therefore, the mediæval
fairs served international credit business as a device for measuring
solvency. At the beginning of the fourteenth century the Florentine
merchant Balduci Pegolotti says of the Champagne fairs: 'Anyone who
fails to meet his engagements at the fair settling days is held for bankrupt. He completely loses his credit and cannot show his face at the
fairs.'[1] This system for assessing solvency had, however, the important
defect that it acted both too seldom and too late. The Bourse remedied
the defect in so far as that was possible. The Antwerp Coutumes codi-
fied customary laws, contain regulations as to persons who are 'called
insolvent by public report on the Bourse.'[2] This, however, was only a
negative criterion, the economic importance of which cannot be rated
very high. The Bourse, on the other hand, was most important for commercial credit transactions because Bourse opinion furnished commercial credit with the idea of the good solvent Bourse firm, or Ditta di
Borsa, as a positive permanent conception which could be turned to
account in business.

The Romanic commercial language of the Middle Ages designated

---

[1] Pagnini, *Della Decima e delle altre gravezze, etc.*, IV, 239.

[2] 'By openbaren gheruchte ter borsse voor insolvent befaemt,' in *Coutumes, dites
Impressae*, v. 1582 (Coutumes d'Anvers ed. Longé, II, 412).

ditta (dica, dicta from dicere) a commercial promise to pay a guarantee or security, and also the document containing such an engagement or the signature or trademark which made it valid in law. More especially the security given by the Romanic above all the Italian exchange dealers and bankers for the engagements of their deposit clients was called by this name. As this security was effected by book entry, by transfer in the bankers' books from one account to another, book entry also bore the same name. The modern Italian meaning of the word in the sense of a business firm appears to have arisen in the sixteenth century, and this is certainly true of the specific meaning which is in question here. The South German business correspondents of the sixteenth century use the word 'ditta' very frequently in the sense of a commercial borrower in bills or deposit business on the Bourse, and they use the expression 'Buone ditte' when they wish to designate these borrowers as credit worthy. Finally, the term 'Ditte di Borsa' is used to mean those borrowers who are generally accounted solvent on the Bourse.

The Bourse opinion of the international Bourses of the sixteenth century held as 'good' beyond all doubt a large number of business houses of different nationalities, whose representatives did business on the Bourse every day and borrowed largely. In this way individual lenders were spared the difficult task of examining the credit-worthiness of these houses, if they gave them credit. It is obvious that this greatly facilitated the development on the Bourse of a regular large business in bills and commercial loan capital. For in this business the fact that credit-worthiness had been established acted as an authoritative decision as to the quality of the object dealt in. From now onwards there was a large mass of commercial claims all similar in quality standardized, and these formed the object of a regular Bourse business. As the credit-worthiness of a sufficient number of Bourse firms had been considered as above suspicion (even if this was not so in actual fact), the parties, disregarding the difficult question of quality, could concentrate on settling the prices of bills and loan capital, and these prices could become real Bourse prices.

Bourse Opinion and Public Credit. What we have just said of commercial credit holds good also of public credit. In this case also Bourse opinion had the effect of levelling or standardizing the differences of quality between the different debts. Here, however, there were certain deviations due to the special nature of public credit in early times.

As we have seen, most princes in the 'Age of the Fugger' had originally very little personal credit. Accordingly, the quality of a debt owed by a prince was not determined, in the first place, by the credit-worthiness of the debtor, but by the kind of security which he offered the creditor, i.e. the nature of the guarantee or the pledged revenues. This quality was extremely various in the different debts.

The real value of the engagements of the same prince varied in accordance with the amount of authority the creditor was given in regard to the pledged revenues, and also with the nature of the revenues with reference to the time and place where they were collected and the willingness and capacity to pay on the part of those liable to taxation. It varied also with the result of the harvest and also with the political and other general conditions of the country whose prince was borrowing. In the same way, when it was a case of a claim secured by a guarantee, this depended on the personal qualities and credit-worthiness of the guarantor, whether the surety was one or another of the high nobility, the Diets or the different cities.

The position was complicated when there were various guarantors, whose mutual liabilities were not clearly defined. Even the forms of the notes of hand, the signatures and seals which they bore, particular phrases in the text and the like were regarded – whether rightly or not – as bearing on the real value of the claims, and were often in consequence the subject of long negotiations between the debtor and the creditor. This leaves out the times when the princely debtor was old or ill and people feared that his debts would not be recognized by his successor.

It needs no further proof that in view of such disparities in the quality of debts contracted by princes it was only by exception that there could be any question of Bourse loans, and that generally the loans were not raised through the market, but concluded with individual business houses. Yet it was exceedingly difficult for a single firm to judge of the quality of the security offered. Even the largest Italian or South German Company was unable to find out with certainty the true value of the security offered; for example, on Spanish revenues, even if they had permanent representatives in Spain and were kept in close touch with Spanish conditions, even if they chose their chief agent in Spain with the greatest care and gave him very wide powers, yet the final decision had to be made in Italy or South Germany. The true value of a claim on Spanish revenues had to be assessed in Genoa or Augsburg. This was impossible, and had it been possible the effect would have been only momentary. How could Genoa or Augsburg know whether the King of Spain would not one day see himself compelled by unforeseen circumstances to repudiate the claim?

While on the one hand the dissimilarity of the different princely loans tended to keep princes' loans in the stage of isolated transactions outside the market, this was in the long run impossible because the task of estimating the real value of the different loans was too much even for the largest isolated firms.

This situation tended steadily to standardize the business in royal loans and to concentrate it on the Bourse, a development which we can follow in sufficient detail in the case of Antwerp and Lyons.

In Antwerp it is most clearly shown in the ever-growing popularity of the bonds of the Receivers General. As we know, these were private obligations issued by the Receivers General on Government account. Since the Government gave no special security, the quality of the bonds was entirely determined by the capacity to pay of the Receivers General, i.e. of officials who had all been merchants originally and who continued to be regarded as such on the Antwerp Bourse. They were treated on the Bourse as Ditte di Borsa, and it was the opinion of the Bourse as to their capacity to pay which determined the value of the bonds.

It is necessary, however, to distinguish different stages in this development. In the earlier period, i.e. up to about 1542, the opinion of the Bourse was unfavourable to the bonds of the Receivers General. It had not yet become habitual to judge their quality merely with regard to the commercial capacity to pay of those who issued them. There was a demand for notes of hand of the feudal lord, and if possible a special additional pledge. The liability of the Receivers was not yet regarded as a sufficient substitute for other security. After 1542, however, Gaspar Ducci began to raise very large amounts on the Antwerp Bourse on bonds of the Receivers General alone, a sure sign that Bourse opinion had changed in regard to these issues. If we ask what had caused this change of front there can only be one answer, namely, that Ducci managed to convince Bourse opinion that the Receivers General were Ditte di Borsa, and the bonds of the Receivers General became in consequence completely standardized or fungible, were regarded by Bourse opinion as engagements of an even quality, which could be bought by the public without special investigation in each case.

Bourse opinion was not wrong in holding that the quality of the bonds of the Receivers General was alike in each case, its mistake was merely in regard to the quality itself. The Receivers General were completely unable to discharge the enormous liabilities they undertook. The quality of the bonds was not good, but very bad.

This, however, did not become evident till the great financial crisis of 1557. Until then the bonds of the Receivers General had borne the chief part in the enormous movement of capital concentrated in Antwerp, and they owed their importance in the last resort to the fact that they were perfectly standardized (fungible). It was this which made it possible to form Bourse opinion as to the quality of the bonds, and so facilitated the growth of a regular Bourse business.

In the case of other loans of princes and cities in Antwerp – as, for example, in the 'Court Bonds,' the obligations of the English Crown, the Portuguese Crown, the city of Antwerp, etc. – we can point to the same development, though we cannot refer it to its causes with equal certainty. We only note the fact that here also Bourse opinion acted more and more as the factor which determined quality, and that the individual capitalists were obviously for the most part led better in their views and in their action by the opinion of the Bourse and that few among them were able to escape its influence.

The development in Lyons was analogous. The capitalists who lent their money to the French Crown through the agency of the Lyons Bourse, from about 1542 onwards, ceased on account of the high rate of interest to attach any special consequence to securing their claim by a special pledge. This was, in fact, usually granted even at a later date; but from 1550, at any rate, the King's bonds were regarded on the Lyons Bourse as an investment of more or less even quality throughout, and the amalgamation of the different Bourse loans into one known as Le Grand Parti was an important step in the process of standardization.

After this the special pledge, if any, was scarcely taken into consideration by Bourse in assessing the value of the loan. This depended rather on general considerations, the material for which was taken from the news service concentrated in the Bourse. This, however, brings us to a fresh subject which we cannot treat at present.

Bourse Quotations and Bourse Rate of Interest. 'The price at which the merchants deal in bills they call the Bourse price, for no man ascribes its establishment to himself, but to the commonalty of the Bourse, i.e. the commonalty of the place where the merchants assemble.' In this way the Paris law faculty in the year 1530 rightly defines the function of the Bourse in settling prices in bill transactions. This settlement of the price had already acquired a Bourse character in many markets in the Middle Ages; but even in Bruges the Italians still controlled the transactions of the exchange Bourse, which was merely the daily Bourse assembly of the Italian merchants. Subjects of other nations usually had to apply to them, if they wished to buy or sell bills.

We know how the change came about in Antwerp and Lyons, and that the Italians lost their monopoly. Exchange dealing in both markets now assumed the character of world Bourse business, that is to say, the supply and demand of international exchange dealing was concentrated there on such a large scale that daily direct mass transactions were now possible between the subjects of the different nations.

At the same time, the standardization of commercial credit made such strides that in normal times there were enough Ditte di Borsa – that is, enough Bourse firms regarded as solvent beyond question – to make possible large daily transactions in bills which were considered as being all alike of good quality and which therefore needed no further examination.

The manner of making the price each day was built up on this basis. An accurate description is given of this also in the Paris memorandum, evidently from information supplied by an Antwerp merchant: 'The broker who has been commissioned by a merchant to buy a bill on Spain seeks out on the Bourse one of those "rich and powerful merchants" who no longer deal in commodities, but in money and exchange. The broker then asks him whether he will draw a bill, and if so on what terms? He in his turn answers by asking "What is the Bourse price?" If he is content with the price the broker names, the business comes to pass.'

The process was, of course, often different from the one described. The crucial point is that the making of the price is no longer an individual act, but is controlled by the opinion of the Bourse. The price which Bourse opinion settled as the right price, either once a day or under certain circumstances several times a day, for the bills of a certain kind issued by solvent Bourse firms, this price is the Bourse price for that kind of bill. It is noted in the business letters and the price bulletin. The smaller Bourses followed its lead, and it became the basis for exchange dealing between the different markets.

As a matter of fact, transactions were often concluded on the Bourse at rates more or less widely divergent from the general Bourse prices. These cases, however, were determined by special circumstances, such as extra risk, inexperience of one of the parties, clumsiness on the part of the broker, and so on. Transactions of this sort were more or less individual prices made in the Bourse business, but even they could not entirely escape the influence of the Bourse price for the standard type of the kind of bill in question.

The 'Conto,' the official list of quotations which was settled in Lyons during each fair pay day, was at bottom merely the officially attested result of an inquiry undertaken four times yearly under the supervision of the authorities as to Bourse opinion in regards to the price of bills. The importance of the 'Conto' was, as we have explained in an earlier chapter, chiefly legal, but the Bourse price itself was an economic phenomenon of the first order, to which we must give a special discussion later.

The Bourse rate of interest was arrived at in the same way as the Bourse quotations for bills. In this case also we have to do with a phenomenon the beginnings of which stretch back a long way into the Middle Ages. We have shown in the introduction that in the thirteenth century, in the Champagne fairs, there must have been a sort of market rate of interest; and that the Italians, in the fifteenth century at any rate, had learnt empirically the rules which produced ebb and flood in the capital markets. This knowledge became common property of the European merchant class as a whole in the sixteenth century with the growth of the practice of borrowing and lending money capital in the market. The standardization of commercial credit here had the same effect as in exchange dealing. In Antwerp and Lyons there arose a Bourse rate of interest for loans of solvent firms from fair to fair, and this rate was sanctioned by the secular authority in the Netherlands with the fixing of a maximum of 12 per cent.; and it used the transparent veil of the 'Depositum' as a protection against ecclesiastical attacks. As the interest payable at the time on Bourse deposits was also notified abroad in the Bulletin of Bourse quotations, the parallel with the exchange quotations is perfect.

The Bourse rate of interest applied only to the Ditte di Borsa; other debtors paid higher rates. This is true especially of Bourse loans to princes, the rate of which regularly was far in excess of the Bourse rate. This was, however, rather apparent than real. The rate itself was not higher, but only the insurance against risk. For a long time the fluctuations here were very wide. In the case of these loans, even on the Bourses, the price was made as an isolated instance. It was only from 1542 onwards that it assumed a Bourse character, and thenceforward the rate for the princely loans on the Bourse was fairly parallel with the ordinary Bourse rate. For every kind of princely or other public loan (Bonds of the Receivers General, Court Bonds, Obligations of the English Crown, etc.) Bourse opinion fixed a rate of insurance against risk which depended on the view taken of the quality of the kind of loan. The amount of this premium varied only within bearable limits.

On the other hand, another movement set in which appears to be exactly contrary, but which in the last resort is to be referred back to the same causes. There began to be fluctuations in the capital value of the princely debts already in circulation.

This phenomenon had its roots far back in the Middle Ages. The shares in the early Italian Monti had been subject to fluctuations in price. In the case of the world Bourses of the sixteenth century we are able to give, at any rate an approximate, date for the first scarcely noticeable beginnings of the price fluctuations which have since characterized Bourse business. We saw that in the Lyons Bourse in 1530 the 'King's Bonds' were sold at a slight discount of between $\frac{1}{4}$ and $1\frac{1}{2}$ per cent., which increased in the next few years to a discount of between 4–6 per cent. After the State bankruptcy of 1557, this grew to 15 per cent., and then increased still further. We cannot follow out this development in the case of Antwerp, though we know that here too at a later time bonds of the Receivers General could only be sold at a heavy sacrifice. The fact, which no one disputes, that it was the fluctuations in price which first brought about regular Bourse business in the already existing King's Bonds, may at first sight appear astonishing. People might be inclined to think that claims regarded as possibly doubtful would be less dealt in than those which Bourse opinion held as sound. A closer consideration soon shows the reason of this phenomenon.

While the credit of the French Crown was regarded as unimpeachable, the original creditors who had the 'King's Bonds' on account of their high rate of interest held them as long as possible; and persons anxious to invest in these securities had accordingly to apply to the agents of the French finance administration and take over new bonds at par. In the year 1550 many well-informed creditors of the Crown did not regard its credit as entirely unassailable, and accordingly sought to dispose of their holdings, if not at the face value, then at a small discount. This is the germ of the 'Baisse' tendency of our present Stock Exchanges. This discount, on the other hand, produced a widespread inclination to buy 'King's Bonds,' and thus called into being a 'Hausse' tendency (rising market). The struggle between these two opposing tendencies gave rise to the Bourse opinion as to market value of the 'King's Bonds,' that is, their Bourse price. This was reported by the habitués of the Bourse to their foreign business associates, who were also holders, but the official Bourse bulletin did not publish it till long after.

Speculation and Arbitrage in Capital Transactions. Bourse prices and Bourse rates of interest are, as we now know, the product of Bourse opinion. What, then, is Bourse opinion? The expression 'opinion' might easily produce misconceptions, especially since we have heard that Bourse opinion is bound to investigate the quality and also to fix the price of certain offers of capital on loans, bills, etc., and that in this task it based itself on the news service concentrated in the Bourse. Hence, involuntarily we may come to think that the question here is one of competition in ascertaining the truth, the 'true price,' or the like. The canonical doctrine of usury had been strongly influenced by such views, e.g. in its judgment on the fair bill. Even at present such ideas are not yet completely dispelled, though they are, of course, quite erroneous.

Bourse opinion is not like perhaps, for instance, scientific opinion, meant to serve truth, but to serve trade. The Bourse habitués want to make money. That is their private economic aim. In order to carry out their private purpose they form a market and so discharge a public economic duty. The market would not be formed if the habitués did not want to make money. The wish to make money is the indispensable condition for the performance of the special tasks performed by Bourse opinion, the settlement of Bourse prices, and so on. The performance of a service necessary in the interests of public economy is not necessarily dependent on the attainment of the individual's private aim, or vice versa. Experience seems rather to show the contrary. It is an important consequence of our economic system which everywhere hands over economic – that is, social – functions to the egoism of the individual guided by his own intelligence, because in this case both the common feeling of the community and a mechanism guided by pure compulsion are inadequate.

The money-making instinct which Bourse opinion is formed to serve is guided by intellect. The Bourse habitués try before concluding their transactions to get clear as to all the points telling for or against the attainment of their business objective. Such points are, however, only to a very small extent of such a nature as to allow conclusions to be drawn which are both sure and instantly realizable. For the most part they are only of a kind to produce guesses, opinions on which the Bourse opinion bases itself. This, again, is a necessary consequence of our whole economic system. The more it rests on exchange of commodities, the more its uncertainty increases; for on this account the individual is in conduct of his business dependent on other individuals, often at a great distance, and on foreign markets; and he is obliged ever increasingly to bring the future into the circle of his calculations.

Here we reach the point where we can look back on our concrete conditions and can link up with what we have said as to the difficulties experienced by individual lenders in credit transactions carried on outside a market in ascertaining the quality of princes' acknowledgments of indebtedness.

The change which came about when Bourse opinion took over the business of valuing quality, was not that these difficulties decreased but that the whole process was completely revolutionized. Bourse opinion, generally speaking, no longer troubled much about the special securities which had given the individual lenders so much anxious thought. What it considered important was the debtor's general capacity to pay and good will, rightly judging that in the last resort these points were decisive in the case of credit to be given to princes. Bourse opinion could not act otherwise; for the news which reached the Bourses in great quantity was not of a kind to render easier any special judgment as to the security of individual princely notes of hand, but rather to help a general judgment as to the political and economic situation or the financial condition of princes. Bourse opinion was a better judge of these general conditions than the individual business house, and this is specially so in the case of the conclusions to be drawn as to the future. The Bourses of Antwerp and Lyons foresaw in time the impending crisis of 1557, but this did not prevent the South German merchants from lending right up to the bitter end enormous amounts of capital to the Kings of France and Spain who had long been really bankrupt.

We must here discuss parenthetically the expression which the sixteenth century used for the business which aims at the systematic exploitation of future events, especially future prices. We call this 'speculation,' but in the sixteenth century this idea was confused with that of 'arbitrage,' i.e. the business based on the exploitation of present price differences between different Bourses. In fact these two ideas could not be kept entirely distinct, for an arbitrage must be speculation if it aims at making a profit on rapidly changing differences of price between centres such as Antwerp and Lyons, when it took a month to get an answer back from one to the other. Peri therefore is quite right when, in 1640, he speaks as follows about 'arbitrio.' Profit, he says, is the aim to all trade. The activity directed to this end is subject to chance, which mocks at every calculation. Yet there is still ample space for reasonable calculation in which the possibility of adverse fortunes is never left out of account. This mental activity engaged in the service of business is called 'arbitrio,' which Peri defines in conclusion as 'una discreta opinione di guadagno, posciache delle cose incerte dassi l'opinione e delle certe la scienza.' He gives it expressly to be understood that speculation on future price alterations is covered by his statement, and he mentions in one breath both transactions of this kind and arbitrage proper whether in exchange, specie, money capital, or commodities. Here we need only deal with arbitrage and speculation in exchange and borrowed capital. The business men who engaged in operations of this kind had first of all to be possessed of what Peri called 'scienza,' i.e. a knowledge based either on experience or reliable information as to those matters whose influence either on Bourse prices or rates of interest could be predicted either with certainty or with a high degree of probability. We know already that the Italians in the Middle Ages had cultivated this 'science' with success. Its results were more or less perfectly imparted by the sixteenth century to business men of other nations. Unfortunately, however, the upshot was not great, for even in the sixteenth century the sum of the unknown factors in Bourse business greatly exceeded the known. These gaps had to be filled as best they might in some other way, and here we meet once more the ubiquitous activities of Bourse opinion.

Bourse opinion drew from its continually flowing stream of news certain general conclusions as to future development and kept these conclusions in mind in fixing the present Bourse price of exchange or loan capital, a process which in present Bourse parlance is called discounting (Escomptiren) future events. In so doing Bourse opinion was always liable to serious errors and was sometimes purposely misled. For, in the first place, the prices of exchange and loan capital depended to an extraordinary extent on incalculable factors, e.g. the frequent alterations of the currency, which not only influenced exchange very greatly, but produced general ease in the money market when expected and a general tightness after the event. These also make the large field of public policy even more incalculable in the sixteenth century than now.

Moreover, the number of speculators without any special knowledge or judgment of their own has always been particularly large in this class of transaction. For most holders of liquid capital, either small or large, could at one time or other do business directly or indirectly in exchange or loan capital and they were often inspired so to do on a considerable scale by the merchants of their acquaintance who were in relations with Lyons and Antwerp. This mass of persons, being incapable of judgment and unversed in affairs, were easily led by the wish for easy profits, and so obtained a fatal influence on the prices both of exchange and loan capital.

Finally, in the case of clever conscienceless habitués of the Bourse the temptation to mislead Bourse opinion was particularly strong. On the one hand were the risks of continual losses because the course of future prices was incalculable, and on the other the lack of judgment on the part of speculators. Above all, however, there was the prospect, not only of enormous profits, but also of high distinctions, honours and titles, if they succeeded in catching masses of free capital for the political ends of powerful monarchs. This temptation was too much for people of the type of Gaspar Ducci.

From 1552 onwards a real madness or 'mania' for the Bourse loans of Antwerp and Lyons seized on the masses all over Europe, and the last vestiges of the science which should be at hand in all speculations was discarded, and a fever for profiteering rushed like a runner gone mad through the richest domains of all the old painfully gathered capital to meet the inevitable crisis.

This, however, is not our final judgment as to the world Bourses of the sixteenth century. We reserve that to the end of this chapter. We must first consider a factor which is often put in the forefront of all discussions as to the Bourse, though we would assign it a more modest rôle. We mean what is called 'Mobilization.'

Mobilization of Loan Capital. Mobilization in the widest sense of the word is the process by which the transfer of economic goods of every kind is made easier by the creation and development of 'securities' which can be used in circulation. German economic doctrine, in so far as it uses the word at all, restricts it to the case of landed property. In all other cases of fixed capital the process is the same as for landed property; and even in the case of circulating capital, including all consumption goods, the nature of mobilization is the same. Its essence is that it creates a circulation of values, the only difference being that this is the only possible form of circulation for fixed capital, while in the case of circulating capital it goes on alongside of the circulation of commodities.

A landed estate is mobilized by the issue of mortgages, a mortgage by the issue of sub-mortgages to bearer, a state loan by the issue of divided bonds, and a trading or commercial undertaking is mobilized by conversion into a company and the issue of shares; a ship's cargo by the pledging of the bills of lading; warehoused goods by the issue of warrants; a bank balance by the issue of cheques; the bullion reserve of a note-issuing bank by the issue of bank-notes; a commercial balance abroad by the drawing of a bill; a bill by its endorsement, and so on. In each case the value of an economic commodity is put into circulation, by being incorporated in a document, or this same document, either through some addition or through the issue of new documents, is given greater currency.

This is, however, not as a rule the usual definition for such documents, which at the beginning were meant for evidence of title. The general need for mobilization, however, gradually transformed them into means of circulating value, 'securities.'

We cannot, however, enter into the meaning and nature of the circulation of values in general, but must concentrate our attention on the mobilization of loan capital. As the name tells us, loan capital belongs to the great circle of groups of economic goods which do not, like consumption goods, serve to the immediate satisfaction of human needs. It serves rather to produce new goods, and taken as a whole it may be designated from the point of view of the individual 'sources of income,' or from the economic point of view generally as 'capital' in its widest sense.

Loan capital in order to produce income must be lent out, that is, must be the object of an exchange for which it is pre-eminently fitted owing to its nature as money capital. Before this exchange is completed it is liquid, or free to be lent out for any purpose. Claims are not so easily exchangeable as monetary capital. The degree to which claims are exchangeable depends on circumstances present in very variable degrees. We have already seen what are the two most important of these circumstances. These are the economic nature, the standardization (or fungibility) of the claims and the economic organization of the business done in such claims. There is also a third factor to be mentioned, the external form of the claims, and in close connection with this the legal forms in existence for exchange transactions in claims.

Forms and legal principles which facilitate the alienation of claims are undoubtedly of great importance in the development of this business. The business will in one way or another call into being such forms and legal principles, if it has urgent need of them. On the other hand, the most favourable forms and legal principles cannot evoke a highly developed business in loan capital, if the other factors are absent. This is particularly easy to prove in regard to the international Bourses of the sixteenth century.

Let us take first bearer bonds. The bearer clause is very old, but in the Middle Ages it was not meant to help the selling of the claim, but its enforcement through a representative. This does not, however, exclude the possibility that such securities might be transferred; but there was quite definitely no trade in bearer bonds in the Middle Ages or the searching investigations into such papers would certainly have revealed some trace of such documents.[1]

On the other hand, it is no less certain that in Antwerp in the first decades of the sixteenth century there was a regular trade in Bearer Acknowledgments of Indebtedness. This is evident from the often quoted order of Charles V of 7th March, 1536 (7). It is here expressly stated that in the Antwerp fairs goods were often sold against Bearer Acknowledgments of Indebtedness, and these were often transferred before they fell due without any formalities to third parties. Thereupon the drawees often refused payment on maturity and this gave rise to many lawsuits. This shows also that the habit of giving these bills in payment was of recent growth, for otherwise either the legal uncertainties due to the debtor's attitude would have been removed or payment of this kind would have been discontinued. This latter alternative was not adopted, and the order of Charles V first declared the Bearer Acknowledgment of Indebtedness for a binding obligation of the same sort as a bill of exchange.[2]

The regular trade in bearer securities remained at first confined to the Netherlands, while in England bills payable to order, and in France those where no mention is made of bearer or order came gradually into use as a means of mobilizing claims.[3]

In Antwerp the Bearer Acknowledgment of Indebtedness, as we know, was used in deposit transactions on the Bourse, and it could either be pledged before maturity – the fact which originally brought it into being – or could be sold at a discount. This bearer bond was probably

---

[1] Goldschmidt, *Universalgeschichte des Handelsrechts*, I, 390 ff. Brunner in *Ztschr. f. Handelsrecht*, XXII, 41 ff.

[2] Plac. de Brabant, I, 515. Antwerp, 'Gebodboecken' in *Bulletin des archives d'Anvers*, vol. I, e.g. p. 276 (1563), p. 326 (1576), p. 344 (1579), etc.

[3] Cf. for England Malynes, *Lex Mercatoria* (1622), ch. 11 and 12; Child, *A new discourse of trade* (1693), p. 7, 106 ff. 'Billets en blanc,' 1601, in *Docum. histor. inédits*, vol. IV, p. xxiv. Cf. Goldschmidt, l.c. p. 397.

the kind of acknowledgment of indebtedness which could be passed from hand to hand with a discount in regular exchange business.[1] The Bearer security accordingly first came in as a means of mobilizing loan capital in the sixteenth century. The bill, on the other hand, still remained frozen in mediæval immobility. The first traces of bill endorsements and bill discounting did not appear before the end of the sixteenth century, and only gradually developed during the seventeenth. We need not discuss here the economic causes of this development, which hitherto has only been dealt with by jurists. In short, therefore, during the whole time when the international Bourses of the sixteenth century were most flourishing there was not sufficient need for the mobilization of claims embodied in bills to call forth the necessary external forms. When in Antwerp at the beginning of the sixteenth century the need to mobilize commercial claims was more felt, the long-established form of the Bearer bond was used and the bill retained its ancient form.

The correctness of our view is upheld if we consider credit transactions with the Government. All Netherlands bonds of the sixteenth century which I have ever seen contains the bearer clause. Yet these bonds, with the possible exception of those of the Receivers General, did not change hands so often as those of the French Crown, which had no bearer clause and could only be transferred, may be proved from speciments in the archives of the South German nobles – with an almost incredible amount of formalities. French transfers were long-winded documents in an old-fashioned difficult Chancery style drawn up in the presence of the parties by a notary and witnesses. They contained a complete recital giving the text of the original bond. If the whole claim were not transferred, this remained in the hands of the person who in name was the sole creditor, and all transfers had to be endorsed on the back of it. The original bond was usually issued in duplicate. Each one usually carried a whole series of transfers, some referring to capital and arrears of interest, others to capital without interest, or only a part of the interest, and others to interest alone.

All this did not prevent a lively business in the 'King's Letters.' In Lyons, from about 1550, they became in fact the object of large and regular dealings on the Bourse. This business took matters into its own hands by dispensing often with formal transfers and using letters and other more or less informal documents till perhaps at last the fifth or tenth buyer fulfilled the necessary formalities. This naturally gave rise

---

[1] Cf. e.g. Tartaglia, *Trattato di numeri e misure* (1556), I, 193 ff. 'Discontes ou Rabats,' Michel Cognet, *Livre d'arithmétique*, Antw. 1573. For 'escompte' in the seventeenth century, see Cleirac, *Usance du négoce ou commerce de la banque et des lettres de change* (1656), p. 153.

to many disputes, but the Bourse business continued till the destruction of Lyons' commercial prosperity brought it to an end.

Conclusion. Our investigation is like climbing a mountain, terrace by terrace. We here reach a point where we may turn and look for a moment at the view, but we are still far from the summit.

The mediæval beginnings of capital Bourses practically did nothing but help the capital transactions of the merchants in the markets. They had not as yet the power of attracting to themselves capital scattered about the world. Such capital, in so far as it was invested at all, was in part lent direct to different princes and in part had found its way – also indirectly – into the coffers of the numerous cities, or, finally, a small proportion had reached the Italian business houses, who put it out at a great profit.

Through a thousand small channels, small driblets of capital had flowed through the narrowly fenced-in fields of mediæval industry, sometimes fructifying and sometimes getting lost in the sand. A few larger streams had indeed come into being, but not yet any great central basins. We know, however, that the need for such large concentrated masses of capital was growing very rapidly.

We have seen that in the 'Age of the Fugger' this need was at first satisfied by the great financiers, who at the beginning used chiefly their own resources and then gradually came to rely more and more on borrowed capital.

Meanwhile the international transactions of Europe, whether in commodities or exchange, had quickly concentrated in Antwerp and Lyons. This brought large masses of capital to both markets, and a market rate grew up for the best commercial paper Ditte di Borsa, so comparatively low that the large financiers were able to satisfy their credit requirements both easily and cheaply.

Princes needing money had in their turn tried in early days to borrow in the international markets. They, however, had to learn that it was no simple matter to collect liquid capital for their purposes. They had at first to pay extraordinarily high rates of interest, and even then could only collect small sums with great difficulty. For a long time, therefore, they had to try to satisfy their extraordinary credit requirements by other means, an attempt in which they were only partially successful.

A change came about when leading financial experts in their service began to attract capital from all sides for their loans in the market, and consciously to increase and turn to account the inclination already present in many quarters to wish for a high return on their money without any effort.

The boom in capital transactions which now began in both markets was certainly of an unhealthy type. Its causes, whether moral or economic, were equally dubious, and the same is true of its immediate effects.

Yet all the same these capital transactions in the world markets of the sixteenth century constitute a forward step of enormous importance in civilization. For the first time business in the different markets had brought together capital from every side on such a scale as to satisfy the largest demands of the most important princes, and to reduce by half the rate of interest on their loans.

This made it possible to raise large masses of capital at moderate rates for all the modern developments of civilization and for all the national ends of the different peoples.

This was the first step on the way to reduce the power of the individual financier within bearable limits. Though the financiers might successfully avail themselves of the advantages offered by the world markets and so at first increase their own power, yet the world Bourses have more than anything else helped to make impossible the state of things prevailing in the 'Age of the Fugger.' After they arose, it was no longer possible even for the most powerful individual financier to determine the course of the world's history.

CONCLUSION
FROM THE TIME OF THE FUGGER TO THE PRESENT

I

THE DEVELOPMENT OF NATIONAL DEBTS

NOW that we have got to know about the rise and fall of the financial powers and the world Bourses of the sixteenth century we must briefly trace out till the end of the period the form of public credit in those countries where the South German and Italian financial magnates succeeded in preserving some of their importance even after the first crisis. We must add to this a sketch of the further development down to the present time. Only in this way is it possible for us to form a final judgment in the historical and industrial significance of the Age of the Fugger.

Spain. We can describe Spanish finance in a few words; it passed hopelessly from one crisis to another. State bankruptcy and compulsory consolidation became usual financial methods. The former occurred at intervals of about twenty years – 1557, 1575, 1596, 1607, 1627, 1647. So far as concerns the compulsory consolidation always connected with them it is enough to mention an expression of Peri. He characterizes a new kind of Spanish Juros as a kind of compulsory payment (*una sorte di pagamento dato e ricevuto da qualch' anni in qua per necessità*). He adds that they can only be sold at a great loss, since there is such a large quantity of them, and since they are only paid in copper, although they purport to represent silver money. Hence it came to pass that at the beginning of the seventeenth century Spain had a copper standard in spite of its inexhaustible silver mines in America.

The individual crises are not sufficiently interesting to require a detailed account of them. On the whole they are similar to that of 1575–77. The state bankruptcy of 1596 was put an end to after a year and a half by a compulsory consolidation.[1] The number of financial associations affected was again only small. But behind them was an excessively large number of sub-shareholders who, as in 1577, had also to accept payment in depreciated Juros. To carry this out the financial associations distributed the Juros to their shareholders, then again to theirs, and so on, till the last small capitalist was reached – an operation which was called 'Tanteo' (settlement). When this at last was finished the Spanish financial officials declared that the total debt was much smaller than had been supposed. This naturally gave rise to endless difficulties and disputes. The credit of the Crown was for a time

---

[1] Cf. Canga Arguëlles, *Diccionario de hazienda* v°: *Acreedoros al Estado*; Häbler, *Die Finanzdekrete Philipps II;* Scaccia, *Tract. de commerciis et cambiis*, § 2, Gl. 5, No. 269 ff.

destroyed, which more than anything else contributed to compel them to the unprofitable peace of Vervins. The political situation was similar, only much more unfavourable for Spain than at the time of the peace of Cateau Cambresis (1559). After making the most powerful efforts to attain the hegemony of Europe, Spain only succeeded in ruining itself.[1]

When Philip II died he had three times broken his word to his creditors. Under his successors the business was managed even much worse. It is related that in 1601 the King's confessor was the actual manager of the finances, which consequently were in hopeless disorder; that the Court officials could not be paid, and so on. Four years later it is said that all the sources of income were mortgaged. If we ask how it was that in spite of this the Crown could wage war and build costly palaces, the answer must be that the secret was that almost no one was paid. Often the money for the King's table was lacking. The most necessary payment to the troops were provided by the Genoese, who for this took mortgages on the revenues for 5–10 years in advance.[2]

In November, 1607, once again payments to the creditors of the Crown were stopped. In this, as was usually the case in these State bankruptcies, the theologians gave a helping hand to justify the breach of faith. It took a year before the usual agreement was come to. Meanwhile, in spite of the suspension of payments, the Crown was in such financial difficulties that it could no longer carry on the war in the Netherlands and had to conclude a twelve years' truce.[3]

But in the following year too the Asientos for Flanders and Italy went their way. The Genoese, as always, had to come to the rescue, to save their old claims; and the Crown required strong garrisons and many officials to hold the southern provinces of the Netherlands or Italy. The confusion of the finances became more and more desperate. When shortly before 1613 the celebrated writer Garcilasso de la Vega made a pressing request to Morales, the King's secretary, to let him know, for the purpose of his great work on the wars of the Spanish in America, what was the amount of the royal revenues, Morales said that no human being, not even the King himself, was in a position to do that; the King was most anxious to know what his revenues were, but the measures which he had ordered for this purpose had not yet been taken in hand; it was, moreover, an almost impossible task.[4]

[1] Ranke, *Frz. Geschichte*, II, 31. Barozzi e Berchet, *Relaz.*, ser. I, vol. I, p. 70. See letter of Venetian envoy.

[2] Cabrera, *Relac. de las cosas sucedidas en la Corte de España desde 1599 hasta 1614*, p. 117 ff.; Barozzi e Berchet, l.c. I, p. 329 ff.

[3] Cabrera, l.c. p. 354; Fugger Archives, 43, 4 and 2, 5, 16.

[4] From French edition of the works of Garcilasso de la Vega, *Histoire des Guerres Civiles des Espagnols dans les Indes*. Paris, 1658, I, 18.

When the war started off again both in Italy and in the Netherlands, when the German branch of the Hapsburgs in the Thirty Years War had to be rescued from the heavy straits they were in by means of large subventions, the Spanish finance degenerated into mere robbery, which reached its height in the years 1627 to 1632. In 1627 exchequer payments were again stopped. Further, the Crown repeatedly confiscated the silver coming from America for private people, and even contemplated seizing the deposits of the banks. Copper money was alternately coined and debased. In short the Fugger agent was entirely right when he wrote to his masters that might went before right. There was no longer government, but only tyranny. Naturally all credit was destroyed, the people, impoverished, partly as a result of the terrible rise in prices due to the bad currency, were straightway abandoned to starvation. In Italy the situation was the same. In Genoa, where everybody had an interest in the Spanish claims, the ruin began to be general. The great Genoese banks had come to the end of their resources, the Fugger were completely ruined.[1] It seemed that the end of the Spanish monarchy had come, and yet things went on just as before. A few expressions of the Venetian envoys will suffice to show this. In 1647, when again the assignations of all Assentists, except those of the four largest financial houses of Genoa, were annulled, the royal revenues were mortgaged till 1654. They had not shrunk from mortgaging many of them twice over to different creditors. A Venetian, telling of these things in 1653, observes with bitter scorn that in order to understand how the richest country in the world had become the poorest one must first be convinced that no people in the world were so ignorant of the art of good government as the Spanish. In 1673 we hear of 40 per cent. interest which the Crown had to pay, and in 1686 Spanish finance is depicted as a horrible chaos enveloped in impenetrable darkness. In 1700, when Carlos II, the last of the Spanish Hapsburgs, died, there was not enough money in the Royal Treasury to defray the cost of the funeral and the Masses for his soul.[2] In this condition Spain came under the sway of the Bourbons. They did not save the unhappy country. This is intelligible enough, because the ruling house was never able to conduct for any length of time a wise financial and industrial policy in its own rich and powerful native land. It is unjust to make the Hapsburg dynasty primarily responsible for the financial mismanagement and the other misery which Spain had to endure during their rule. The

[1] In addition to Peri cf. Fugger Archives, 2, 5, 17, also *Mercure Français*, v. 1630 ff.; Barozzi e Berchet, I, 647, for Italy,ª Cautú. *Sulle stor. d. Lomb. del sec.* XVII. (Comment. ai Promessi sposi de i Aless. Maznoni), Milano, 1832, and *Miscell. d. stor. ital.* V, 147 ff.

[2] Barozzi e Berchet, II, 178, 202 ff., 242, 284, 390, 529 ff., 660, 682. Cf. also Mignet, *Négoc. rélat. a la succession d'Espagne*, t. II.

reign of Ferdinand and Isabella, nominally the golden age of Spain, began with a State bankruptcy and ended with such a burden of debt outstanding that Charles I (V) had repeatedly in vain to be reminded to liquidate them 'to disburden the souls of the Catholic Kings.' Even in more recent times Spain has kept true to its habit of going bankrupt about every twenty years; for since 1820 under the Bourbons and the republic there have been State bankruptcies in the year 1820, 1837, 1851, and 1873. It is plainly an inner necessity which outlives centuries. The comparison can be drawn further. How remarkable it is, for instance, that the last good security which remained for the Fugger's claims in Spain was the Almaden quicksilver mines which they worked themselves, and that there mines in the most recent times again proved to be the only security which was undoubtedly good to the Spanish creditors who had the sufficient foresight to obtain a mortgage on them and to manage the mines themselves! Further, it was the Rothschilds, the Fugger of the nineteenth century, who took over the working of the Almaden mines as a result of their financial transactions with the Spanish Government. In fact the history of Spanish finance is instructive for anyone who is willing to learn from it.

France. We already know that during the wars of religion French finances continually went from bad to worse, and that finally, about 1575, in Lyons the Crown could not obtain any more loans. In the next year part of the dividends on the rentes of the State had to go unpaid. This aroused the greatest discontent in Paris. Soon after we hear that in Lyons the obligations of the French Crown were offered at 30 per cent. of their face value. In the circles of the German creditors of the State this was attributed to the machinations of individuals, and complaints were made to the Government and to the Augsburg Council that Oswald Seng and Christopher Neidhart had depreciated their obligations to the damage and contempt of the credit of the French Crown. Finally, in 1580, all the assignations given to the creditors were recalled, and even the officials were no longer paid.[1]

This bankruptcy was on a level with that of the Spanish Crown five years earlier. But, unlike that of Spain, there soon appeared in France new financiers of Italian origin, like Diaceto, Rucellai, Sardini, Martelli, Rametti, and others, who again did business with the Crown, which certainly, as in Spain, got the worst of it. The Chancellor Chiverny, the Intendant of Finance d'O, and other highly placed persons took part in these transactions. It even occurred that a financial syndicate gave

---

[1] Desjardins, *Négoc. dipl.*, IV, 71, 323; Monfalcon, *Hist. mon. de Lyon*, II, 417. Bodin, 1577: 'A présent le pluspart (i.e. of the State creditors) veut quitter l'interest et le sort principal s'il se trouve qui veuille donner trente pour Cent une fois payée.' Cf. Augsburger St. A. Handelssachen No. 26 (22) and No. 28.

the King himself a douceur of 25,000 écus in order to obtain a profitable lease.

This was the time when the hatred of centuries of the French for the Italian financiers again burst out, when the estates assembled at Blois in 1576–7 brought forward to the King the complaint we already know of against the foreigners. 'They fall upon our country (it runs) with a pen behind their ear or with a dagger at their side, this is all they possess when they arrive; but they know how to acquire boundless riches with it.' In fact they interfered with the foreigners, made it difficult for them to trade or set up banks, did not allow them to be officials of the State or the Empire. But their ability and their capital could not be dispensed with. In spite of the empty Treasury they always knew how to track out new financial methods, which certainly got the dubious nickname of 'inventiones sanctae crucis.' To exclude the competition of the French farmers of taxes Rametti and his syndicate offered in 1584 to pay off 800,000 écus of the King's debts, on which the profitable lease of the Gabelle was made over to him because the French had not command of such a sum.

This was the time when Bodin and others loudly denounced the continual borrowing by the Crown, when Nicolas Barnaud, under the pseudonym of Fromenteau, showed that since Henry II ascended the throne to the end of 1580 loans of not less than 128 million livres had been incurred.[1] The Crown perceived that it was necessary to do something to re-establish its credit and seriously considered liquidating its debts. This produced comparative quiet at home for a period of some years, which did not cease till 1586. Then this offer of the Rametti was a welcome one. The German creditors treated through Marx Kraffter with some Swiss about the sale of their claims. They were offered 25 per cent. for them and this would have gone to 40 per cent. But the Nurembergers would not accept this 'Miseria,' and demanded 75 per cent., 'since now there is peace in France and the King will pay off all his debts.' They had soon to rue their excessive cleverness; for the King paid back only 70,000 £ in all, that is only a few per cent. The civil war broke out again, and in the last years of Henry III the mismanagement reached its highest point.

'More than ever before,' a contemporary tells us, 'the Rentes in the Hôtel de Ville of Paris remain unpaid to the destruction of many poor widows and orphans.' Unquestionably the irritation of the citizens of Paris at this was one of the causes of their going over to the camp of the League which was then fighting against the Crown. Certainly this was the chief cause of the 'Day of Barricades' (1588). When finally at the

---

[1] *Le Secret des Finances de la France* (1581), I, 13. For what follows, see Scheuerl Archives in Nuremburg.

end of the year the leader of the League, Henri de Guise, was murdered, when eight months later the King suffered the same fate, it was naturally once more all up with the credit of the Crown; there was no longer a recognized King. Already after the death of the Duc d'Anjou (1584) the opinion had been correctly expressed in the circles of the German creditors that it was very risky that 'the debts of the French Crown now only stood on two eyes.' When these were shut, when an assassin's dagger struck down the last of the Valois, the creditors of the Crown, as we see from one of the Fugger letters, lost their credit. This particularly affected the Florentines. We already know that at that time the Capponi – the last of the great Florentine banking houses in France – passed into other hands.

It took about six years after the death of Henry III before the Bourbon Henry IV could really feel himself to be King and before the condition in the State had again been got into a certain amount of order and thus made possible a serious financial reform, which now was taken in hand by Sully. He has been justly praised for carrying through this reform; but it cannot be denied that the most important part of it was a State bankruptcy. A considerable reduction was compulsorily made in the rate of interest of the State rentes, some down to 4 per cent.; and many millions of debts were not recognized as legitimate. In vain the rentiers and other creditors protested; among them some who had been reduced to great straits by these measures. On the main point Sully remained inexorable.[1] If we reflect that in 1596 the King had expressly recognized his liability for his predecessor's debts, from a moral standpoint the whole measure appears to be hardly any less dubious than one of the Spanish bankruptcies. Yet it was necessary, and in contrast with Spain, Sully did not content himself with the inevitable breach of faith, but took pains to introduce economy, order, and honourable dealing into the management of the finances.

But this state of affairs vanished again. On the murder of Henry IV and the fall of Sully a new period of financial mismanagement began; this lasted till Colbert took office. French finance at that time only differed in degree, but not in kind, from that of Spain. We cannot here depict the whole development, and must content ourselves with emphasizing a few characteristic details.[2]

[1] We have had to use *Oeconomies royales*, Coll. Petitot, ser. II, vols. 1–9, though Ranke doubts them. Roth, *Gesch. d. Nürnberger Handels*, II, 21. *Archiv. des Nürnberger Handels Vorstandes*.

[2] Cf. Gramont, *Le denier royal* (1620); Bazin, *Histoire de Louis XIII*; Mercure Français (1617 ff.): Barozzi e Berchet, *Relaz.*, ser. II, vol. II; *Journal d'Ormesson*, ed. Chéruel. Moreau, *Choix des Mazarinades*; Bresson, *Hist. financ. de la France*; *Défense* de Fouquet (1665); Ranke, *Franz. Geschichte*, Bd. II; also Bailly, *Forbonnais*, etc.

The extravagance of the favourites Concini and Luynes was followed by Richelieu's far more costly Imperialism. Since the financier Herwart had succeeded in 1630 in inducing the troops of Bernhard of Weimar to pass over into French service, the Crown had continually to maintain an army of 100,000 men. This was the first standing army of importance in Europe. Then came the boundless corruption of Mazarin, whose finance ministers helped him to plunder the public treasury. The complaints from which French finance was then suffering, were still the same as they were in the sixteenth century; on the one side the crushing burden of military expenditure and the outrageous prodigality of the Court; on the other side – farming of taxes, bargaining for offices, the splitting up and dishonesty of the financial administration. This produced a deficit which increased like an avalanche, and a floating debt which increased just as fast. There was nothing new in the grievances of the people which it condensed into criminal charges against the financiers. For example, in 1661 Fouquet was accused of putting in the accounts invented and unnecessary payments, of himself lending money to the Crown at high rates of interest, and having an interest in farming the taxes, that he allowed himself to be bribed by the farmers of taxes, that he mixed up the monies of the State with his own, that he had bought up worthless State debts and put them down at their full value, and generally that his administration was bad. Fouquet was entirely in the right when in his defence he declared those were mostly old-established abuses and he had only obeyed the orders of Mazarin who took each year 25 to 30 millions for secret expenses. Fouquet had to advance them and justly observed, 'It was *my* money when it left my chest and became the King's money when it passed into the hands of his Eminence.' Here we get to a development, which, it is true, was then by no means new, but which took on in France a quite different character: we refer to the nature of the relation between the minister who directed the finances and the people with money who supported him.

At all times, at any rate since François Ier, there were two classes of moneyed people which could satisfy the needs of the Crown for loans. There were the well-to-do bourgeois (aisés) and the professional money-lenders, who now were usually called 'partisans' because they had 'partis' (monetary transactions) with the Government. The means of the former class were utilized partly by compulsory loans (taxes des aisés), partly by issuing rentes; those of the partisans by the farming of taxes and the anticipations always connected with this.[1] Of these two classes the partisans were by far the most influential, because the Government had the most pressing need of them. So long as the taxes were farmed and anticipations were necessary no financial administra-

[1] *Journal d'Ormesson*, ed. Chéruel, I, 214, 415.

tion could be carried on without their help and credit. But on the other hand the partisans were dependent on the financial administration, which gave them the opportunity of making very great profits, and which could leave their claims unpaid if they refused further assistance. From this gradually the minister who directed the finances had his own retinue of financiers. By the sixteenth century, both in Spain and France, there were important tendencies to this. Under Sully, who tried to avoid anticipations, the partisans for a time retired to the background. In return Sully was the chief of a family clan which was politically important. On the other hand, under his successors the train of followers depending on financial interests developed more and more, this finally, under Mazarin and Fouquet, acquired political importance. At this time the expression 'partisan' took on a new meaning, which it has retained to the present time; meanwhile the original meaning was lost. The word was used as a common expression for 'unconditional adherent.' This means that the finance minister domineered over his partisans, owing to the fact that he himself more and more became the chief banker of the State and that his credit was decisive for the Crown. Sometimes this had been the case earlier; yet as a rule the person who directed the finances of the State played a tolerably insignificant rôle compared to the financial magnates. But now he became their chief; yet he could not make himself independent of the Crown and the chief minister. Fouquet was accused of trying to do this and it caused his fall. But a serious political danger could scarcely be avoided. The change which at that period came over that class of professional financiers is of profound significance; first the foreigners were gradually replaced by Frenchmen. What the hatred of centuries of the French for the Italian moneylenders could not do, was now brought about by their own exhaustion in combination with the increasing ability of the home competitors. The end of the Italian financial business in France is marked by the unrest of the Fronde and the State bankruptcy of 1648. The last foreigner who played a conspicuous part in French finance was the South German banker Herwart – who certainly was already considerably gallicized and who was active at the beginning of Colbert's time. On the other hand, at the end of Mazarin's time the great majority of the Partisans were French. They were almost entirely people of the lower classes, creatures of the Finance minister, partly even lackeys and the like, who associated together and in the main worked with the money of private people, to whom they paid relatively high rates of interest. They themselves charged the Crown at least 15 per cent., but under some circumstances this went up to 50 per cent. or 60 per cent. This is the humble origin of the Parisian world of finance. It is obvious that such people had to be unconditionally attached to their protectors the Finance ministers, who therefore as a rule treated them kindly, helped them in money difficulties and often kept them from bankruptcy.[1] On the other hand, there were among them people like that Giradin who at Fouquet's request made advances to the Crown up to 3, 4, or 5 millions, and apparently without any profit to himself, in view of the interest which he himself had to pay, and without any security except Fouquet's promise to pay. He directed a large financial syndicate which in 1655 took over the lease of the Gabelle.

The people got no advantage from the fact that the Italians were replaced by French Partisans. They were just as oppressive as farmers of the taxes; as creditors of the State they took at least as much interest and as satellites of the influential courtiers they belonged to a class which the people was more and more accustomed to regard as parasites. They were hated as arrant bloodsuckers. Through their position, as we saw, they had a great advantage over the other class of creditors – the rentiers; for as a rule the State treated them much better than the rentiers, who not infrequently had to complain that their dividends were not paid in full. In addition the Partisans carried on an extensive trade in offices and liked to remember their friends and relatives with the fattest places. This naturally again gave occasion for more oppression. So it is not surprising that by 1615 the name Partisan was hated throughout France. This again led to lively complaints of the estates and Parliament against the financiers and to the repeated appointment of commissioners of investigation as there had been before. They could call individuals to account, but could make no change in the system. The revolt of the rentier of Paris in 1638 and the unrest of the Fronde in 1649 had just as little success, but we must delay a moment over the latter.

In 1648 the financial position was as bad as could be imagined. The revenues of the Crown were anticipated three years in advance. Thereupon the Parliament obtained the institution of a chambre de justice against the Partisans, and in October there resulted a general suspension of all money orders which had been given to them. It was a State bankruptcy quite in the style that was usual in Spain. Payment of the dividends should not be stopped, but should have priority over the claims of the Partisans. Yet the rentiers soon had to complain again, and this was easily made use of by the discontented nobles of the Fronde to stir up Paris against Mazarin's Government. At this critical moment the Crown had absolutely no credit; the Partisans neither would nor could help. Every possible suggestion for getting money was made. Taxes which had been imposed and compulsory loans were not paid. Turenne's army got no pay and threatened to go over to the Fronders.

---

[1] See *Catalogue des Partisans*, or Moreau, *Choix des Mazarinades*, I, 113, 179, 287; *Défense* de Fouquet, II, 98, 133, 207, 236, 246, 296, 312 ff.

The Court sent off the banker Herwart to appease Turenne and satisfy his troops. He failed in the first; to the extreme horror of the Court Turenne set out on his march to Paris. But he soon found himself deserted by his troops, whom Herwart had alienated by paying their arrears of pay. Voltaire was right in saying that this event showed that only the man who has money is the lord. This was the last occasion when a financial magnate, quite the dramatic style of Jakob and Anton Fugger, interfered in the course of the history of the world. The praise too which Mazarin lavished on him in the presence of the King before the assembled Court is also in the style of the heroic age of capitalism which we have called the age of the Fugger. Mazarin declared that Herwart had rescued France and preserved the King his crown; that this service ought never to be forgotten. In fact Herwart, as we have already related, though he was half a foreigner, and a Protestant into the bargain, advanced to one of the highest positions in the financial administration and later still higher, till Colbert made an end of his career. Just as Herwart was the last French financier of the old stamp, so Turenne was the last French general, who, at any rate in his earlier days, had a good deal of the Condottiere in him. Only after Mazarin's death did he become exclusively a faithful servant of his lord. Now came the time when Louvois got the army completely out of the hands of the war speculators into those of the King,[1] as Colbert had tried to do with the finances and the financiers. Colbert's aim was to reform the whole financial administration; he wished to centralize it and by doing so to increase the revenues of the Crown and at the same time to bring them into harmony with the expenditure, so that anticipations would no longer be needed. He further intended to liquidate the funded debt entirely: partly because it was charged on the best and most certain revenues, and also because whenever the payment of the rentes in bad times got in arrear, this gave the agitators an occasion for stirring up the rentier against the Government. He called the rentiers idlers who consumed the fruits of their fellow-citizens' labour. Bodin a century earlier held the same opinion; the great theorist was a hundred years in advance of the great man of action.

But Colbert himself had soon to abandon such wide aims and make it his chief object to suppress the power of the Partisans more and more. He could not get on without them; but he turned them into pliant tools. He said once, 'A financier should behave towards the finance ministe like a soldier towards his general; he should never leave him so long as he lives.' He tried with all the means in his power to carry this principle into financial practice.[2]

[1] Jähns, *Heeresverfassungen und Völkerleben* (1885), p. 261.
[2] Clement, *Lettres et mémoires de Colbert*, II, p. cxcix.

What Colbert achieved is a matter of history. Above all, by raising and consolidating the duties he greatly increased the revenues of the Crown; so he changed France into an uniform large economic area and began to replace the predatory and short-sighted fiscalism of earlier times by a consideration for the people's welfare based on a broader outlook. By this he, at any rate on the Continent, became the pioneer of a new economic system. That his object was primarily fiscal in no way detracts from the great reformer's services. But, as every one knows, his economic and financial policy had soon to stop, because it was thwarted by the unbridled imperialistic policy of his master. This is best seen by following out the development of the public debt. One of Colbert's first measures was to reduce the rentes, in which he followed in Sully's foot-steps except that he proceeded in a much more inconsiderate way. In 1660 he at first kept back a third of the rentes then due on the Hôtel de Ville at Paris. Further reductions followed, till it was finally appointed that all the rentes created under Fouquet, whose present holders had bought them considerably under par, should be compulsorily repaid at a rate which left the holders almost nothing over, and Colbert even wanted to bring into account against the capital the rentes already paid. The rentiers protested; there were riots in Paris; there was a slight mitigation, so far as in determining the rate at which the rentes were to be paid off, the procedure had some fairness. A commission, in con-junction with the Paris magistracy and taking into account the changes since 1st January, 1639, fixed the rate. That occurred in 1664. In the next year Colbert reduced the legal rate of interest to 5 per cent., and amongst others gave as his reason for this measure that the high rate of interest introduced by the money changers ('le change et rechange de l'agent') and the exorbitant profits of the rentiers promoted idleness and hindered the development of Trade, Industry, and Agriculture.[1]

In this way Colbert at first succeeded in disburdening the Treasury. Yet his proceedings were just as much a State bankruptcy as Sully's were and they excited the same hatred of those affected by it. What was worse was that in the long run he could not get on without new enormous loans, especially since the disastrous war of 1672 – a land-mark in the industrial and financial history of the seventeenth cen-cury – and with a heavy heart must again enter on the precipitous path of borrowing.[2] Before he decided to do this, he had not hesitated to resume the traffic in offices on a large scale, and incited the financiers by placing the offices at their disposal at 16 per cent. below their nominal selling value. But as the many millions which the war required were not to be got in this way, Colbert in 1672 had to proceed to an

[1] Clément, II, introd. xlix. and 756.
[2] Bailly, I, 462 ff.; Vührer, I, 96; Clement, vol. II.

issue of rentes, and in the next year to floating loans and anticipations. During the ten years of his administration he often had to turn again to credit. But his procedure was essentially different from that of the former Finance minister; and here again he appears to us as the pioneer of a new epoch. To avoid the costly intervention of the financiers, Colbert in 1674 formed a State central savings bank (Caisse des Emprunts), into which anyone could pay money. The State paid 5 per cent. interest and promised to repay the capital on demand, which was secured on the rents from the tax-farming. In this way it became possible for the State to obtain at a low rate of interest considerable floating loans – usually 14 millions, but later as much as 20 million livres. Colbert also reformed the method of getting money as a funded debt, by applying to the rentes the principle of publicity which he had formerly only used in connection with floating debts. Since 1679 Colbert issued the rentes for public subscription and attained brilliant results. Earlier Paris had been the chief market for the rentes issued by the State; now the provinces and foreign countries were drawn in, and Colbert even knew how to manage skilfully the modern technique of oversubscribing. In 1679 in 18 days 2 million rentes (= 34 million capital) were issued, on which he then offered for issue a further $5\frac{1}{2}$ million rentes and repaid old debts which carried a higher rate of interest.

There were similar operations in 1682 and 1683. Pressure and dodges were used to induce the holders of rentes announced for repayment to accept rentes at a lower rate of interest instead of cash.[1]

By 1680 Colbert had represented to the King that credit had already produced 40 millions; he dared not strain it any further, otherwise the deposits would be withdrawn from the Caisse des Emprunts and they would be on the verge of bankruptcy. In the next year he pointed out emphatically the misery of the people due to the pressure of taxation and that the new outbreak of war must cause an enormous increase in the burden of interest. He continued his warnings, but without success, and when he died in 1683 the budget was again disorganized. Under his successors French finance again took the devious path which had led Spain to economic ruin. They led France to the Revolution.[2]

England in the Seventeenth Century. Where France and Spain retained the mediæval character of their financial arrangements down to the threshold of modern times, in England a successful attempt was made in the sixteenth century to reform the financial administration fundamentally. Gresham had given it a strongly national character, and had endeavoured to permeate it with the commercial principles of

---

[1] Bailly, I, 465, 477; Vührer, I, 103 ff.; Clement, vol. II, introd. and pp. 102, 372.
[2] Cf. Boisguillebert, *Le Détail de la France* (1697) in *Daire*, p. 236; also *Factum de la France* (l.c. p. 296).

honour, order, and economy. This succeeded to a remarkable extent. The foreign moneylenders gradually vanished from England, whose capital proved to be sufficient to satisfy the needs of the Crown in many difficult situations. On the Continent too its credit remained unshaken during the most severe crises, because Queen Elizabeth differed from other monarchs, by never breaking her word to her creditors, as she justly boasted in 1576.[1]

But in the long run Gresham's financial programme did not prove suitable for all contingencies. As a rule Elizabeth could not raise a loan without using compulsion. In the later years of Elizabeth, Privy Council loans (compulsory loans) were the most common way of meeting temporary extraordinary financial needs. But after Gresham's death she was so economical that she left only an insignificant burden of debt for her successor, but as a set-off a valuable treasure in jewels, which she partly had received as presents; for, as soon after a Venetian envoy pointedly remarked, 'Her Majesty liked getting more than giving.' [2]

Under Elizabeth's successor James I, and still more under Charles, the finances again fell into terrible confusion, and the burden of debt increased noticeably. At the death of James many salaries were in arrear. The absolute amount of the floating debt – there was no funded one – appears moderate in comparison with that of France and Spain; but it was much too big for the English people, especially as the Crown continued its practice of forced loans.[3]

But what Elizabeth could presume to do, called forth general indignation if attempted by her successors. The first compulsory loan which Charles I wished to raise (1626–7) led to the Petition of Right, and the King promised that he would never again exact compulsory loans. In fact there were no more of the old kind. Certainly the King more than once put more or less strong pressure on the City of London, to induce them to consent to loans in which anyone could participate at his pleasure. These loans bore a certain resemblance to those which the French Crown raised in Paris. But they were not sufficient for the financial needs of the Crown. Especially in 1640, after the conflict with Parliament had begun and he had against their wishes decided on the Scottish war, his financial position was so gloomy that he was compelled to embark in the sort of business that only half bankrupt merchants do. He bought 2,310 sacks of pepper from the East India Com-

[1] Nares, *Memoirs of Burghley*, II, 64.

[2] Green, *Calendar of State Papers*, 1547–80, p. 531 ff.; 1581–90, pp. 471, 554, 576 ff., 580, 585 etc.; 1598–1601, p. 538 ff. Cf. *Journaal van Anth. Duyck ed. Mulder*, III, 23; Barozzi e Berchet, *Relaz. d. ambasc. venet.*, ser. IV, vol. I, p. 106.

[3] Very various figures are given for the Floating Debt. Cf. *Parliam. Debates*, 1610 (Camden Soc.), introd. ix, xv; 1625, p. 102, *Calendar of State Papers*, 1619–23, p. 110; Ranke, *Engl. Geschichte*, II, 194 ff.; Sinclair, II, 42,

pany on long credit for £63,283 and sold them at once for £50,626 cash. This cost him nearly 17 per cent. in interest. He seized for £120,000 silver which had been delivered by Spanish and other merchants at the mint to be coined, and, to the annoyance of the owners, retained one-third as a compulsory loan which later was duly repaid with interest. The King also tried, but without success, to obtain money in Spain, France, and Genoa. On the other hand, Harrison, a tax farmer, advanced him £50,000 at 8 per cent., which was then the usual rate.[1] But when in 1642 the war broke out Parliament issued an appeal for gold and precious metals and promised 8 per cent. interest. There was a threat of punishment for non-compliance, so that it was a kind of compulsory loan. In fact, although the King naturally forbade it, large sums, nominally several millions, of gold and precious metals came out of the whole country. On that the King turned to the Universities, which had remained faithful to him, and got from them equally large quantities of money and gold and silver plate, although Parliament tried to prevent it. During the Revolution recourse was several times had to such means.[2]

Cromwell too could not dispense with floating loans. In his time it was the goldsmiths, who already had been bankers for decades and now were the bankers of the Government, who regularly granted advances on the revenues.[3] In this way these first professional credit brokers which the English have produced, obtained in the State finance an important position, which was enhanced under the Restoration.

When in 1660 Charles II negotiated with General Monk about the restoration of the monarchy, the first step was to raise money from the English Royalists and in Amsterdam to cover the arrears of pay of the former revolutionary army and take it into his own service. To secure his rule Parliament granted him £1,260,000 to pay his debts. But he soon got involved in new ones which increased like an avalanche through his extravagance and the great demands of the war against the Dutch. The advances made by the city were totally insufficient. The attempt in 1665, at the outbreak of the unfortunate first war against Holland, to raise a loan by direct subscription was a failure. It became more and more often necessary to call in aid the expensive assistance of the goldsmiths, among whom Sir Robert Vyner was the chief financier of the Crown. The goldsmiths procured the money at 4–6 per cent. and charged the Crown 8–10 per cent. Repayment was to be made out of

[1] *Calendar of State Papers*, dom. ser., 1640–1, p. 522; Ruding, *Annals of Courage*, I, 392, Gardiner, *Fall of the Monarchy of Charles I*, vol. I, 347, 377; II, 44.
[2] Ruding, I, 396 ff.; Sinclair, I, 171.
[3] It is a mistake to put the beginning of the goldsmiths' business as bankers later. Malynes speaks of it in his *Lex Mercatoria*, 1622. Cf. the pamphlet, *The Mystery of the new-fashioned Goldsmiths or Bankers discovered* (1676).

the taxes which had been granted as soon as the Exchequer received them.[1]

But soon here, too, the whole danger of the sort of finance became evident. In 1672, when the floating debt had grown to £1,328,526, the notorious 'shutting up the Exchequer' ensued. The Crown had to suspend payment. This was the first State bankruptcy of England since 1339, and it was the last.[2]

Charles II did just what the Kings of France and Spain had often done. The bankruptcy was settled in the same way. The King had simply taken away from his creditors the special revenues on which they had a charge. In place of this he burdened the total revenues of the Crown with a perpetual annuity of £79,711 (interest at 6 per cent. on the floating debt) in favour of the creditors. That is he compulsorily reduced the interest to an average rate of 6 per cent. and converted the floating debt into a funded debt of perpetual annuities – the first that England had had.

To be sure, after 1684 this annuity was not paid, because the Crown had got into worse and worse straits. Its credit was destroyed, especially since Parliament in 1681 had expressly forbidden the raising of floating loans on the revenues of the Crown, and even threatened with punishment the sale or acceptance of tallies and anticipations on these revenues.[3] The Crown might dissolve Parliament and at first suppress the Whigs politically, yet they had the capital in their hands. They could not prevent the Crown from once again stopping payment of interest; on the other hand, they could prevent new loans being authorized, and the age of compulsory loans was long past.

In one of its main points Gresham's financial programme had been carried out. The nationalization of the money capital available for the objects of the State had been permanently attained; but not under economy and honourable dealing.

England's development in financial policy had not prospered better than that of France. If we reflect that at the time when England went bankrupt, France, thanks to Colbert's activities, enjoyed good credit, and further that it was out of that bankruptcy that there was the beginnings of a funded debt, which France had already had for 150 years, we come to the conclusion that France was at a higher stage of financial development than England. It was the Revolution of 1688 which brought about the decisive change. But before we occupy ourselves with

---

[1] *Calendar of State Papers*, dom. 1660–1, p. 69; 1664–5, p. 43 ff., 73; 1667, pp. 256, 288, 319, 371, etc.; Ranke, *Engl. Geschichte*, IV, 282. *Calendar*, 1667, p. 204.

[2] Sinclair, I, 195; II, 44 ff.

[3] Chandler, *Debates*, II, 97.

that we must turn to the country which exhibits the highest point of development in the seventeenth century.

The Netherlands. If we wish to pay due admiration to the eighty years' fight for freedom of the little Netherlands against Spain, a world power, we must not forget that a good part of it belongs to the State credit of the Netherlands. All honour to the steadfastness of the people and the genius of the House of Orange; but these alone had not sufficed to attain victory. Here, more than anywhere else, *pecunia nervus belli.* The Dutch navy at first brought in more money than it cost; but the war on land had to be conducted with mercenaries, and to equip and maintain them the Dutch could no more get on without credit than the Spaniards.[1] Scarcely had the final peace with Spain been concluded, when the costly naval wars against England and then the desperate struggle against Louis XIV followed on. This caused the Dutch national debt to increase more and more; and although it is not possible to reconcile the very different accounts of its size, yet there is no doubt that in proportion to the population it was sufficiently large. Nevertheless during 1640–55 they succeeded in reducing the rate of interest on the funded debt from $6\frac{1}{6}$ to 4 per cent.; and even at the worse times, when the existence of the Republic hung on a hair, as in 1585 and 1672, it was ultimately possible to borrow the money necessary to defend the country. The Republic had always kept faith with its creditors, which could not be said of any of its mighty enemies. In 1672, when the French had conquered the greater part of the country, it is plain that without its credit the Republic would have been lost. For the breaking of the dams – a desperate expedient – could only bring momentary deliverance. It was the agreement for subsidies with the Emperor, the Elector of Brandenburg, etc., that secured the permanent existence of the Republic.

What made it possible for the Netherlands to do this? The short answer is – by means of those facts which in the introduction we adduced as the foundations of the credit of the mediæval cities. The Republic of the United Netherlands was pre-eminently an association of towns. Its credit in the first place rested on that of the individual provinces, and this again on that of the towns. Every town and every province formed a corporation whose members the burghers were associated together for their benefit, even if they were no longer (like the burghers of earlier times) liable both in their persons and their goods as sureties for the debts of the community.

Further, the Netherlands was a mercantile State. From the beginning

---

[1] Material for the economic history of the United Netherlands is very scanty till the eighteenth century. Cf. the newspaper '*De Koopman*,' III (1771), 169 ff., and a still shorter account by Weeveringh, *Geschied. d. Staatsschulden* (1855).

its burghers were on the average very rich, and thanks to their spirit of enterprise and times being favourable, they quickly acquired new great riches far in excess of the capital wanted for their undertakings.[1] Hence as a rule in the Netherlands there was much more capital seeking investment than trustworthy people willing to borrow it; but their native town and their native country unquestionably belonged to this class.

In 1620 a Venetian ambassador reports: 'The province of Holland alone has a debt of 40 million gulden, on which it pays $6\frac{1}{4}$ per cent. interest. They could easily pay it off if they raised the taxes, but the creditors do not want this. I hear that the merchants, especially in Amsterdam, have so much liquid capital that the State can always borrow as much as it wants from them.' The report of Sir William Temple, who knew the Netherlands well, half a century later on the usefulness of the rentiers for the Republic is well known. Among this class, above all, were the regents of the States, the provinces and the towns. Their interests were therefore very permanently united with that of the common weal, for which they devoted not only their capital, but also their intelligence and power of work. There were then scarcely any idlers among the Netherlands rentiers. Investment in home securities was then so popular that it was often considered a favour to be allowed to invest in them; and repayment was a source of regret and even called forth tearful remonstrances from the creditors, because in no other place could the money be put out so quickly and safely.[2] About the same time the *Dutch Mercury* stated that in the province of Holland alone there were 65,500 who had or were able to invest money in annuities. It is just this large number of would-be investors that is the most powerful force with which we have to do here. For once this had made it possible for the Netherlands, not only to borrow in their own country, but also to purchase foreign assistance. This made it possible to treat the State debt from the beginning as a funded one, to employ the old plan of the sale of annuities, and in this way to ensure that the creditors had no right of calling in as well as the low rate of interest.

Two other circumstances made this the easier. One was the old habit of the Dutch to make provision for their old age by buying life annuities and perpetual annuities as a provision for their widows and surviving children; this tendency, which later degenerated into a propensity to do as little work as possible and live on unearned income, which in its

[1] Guicciardini, *Descritt. d. Paesi Bassi* (1566). Van der Chys, *Geschied. d. Stichting v.d. Vereenigdeo O. J. Compagnie,* 1857. *Journ. v. Anth. Duyck ed. Mulder,* III, 295.
[2] *Observations upon the United Provinces,* French edn. v. 1674, p. 211 ff., 327 ff. Cf. Laspeyres, *Geschichte d. volksw. Anschauungen d. Niederländer,* p. 216 ff.

turn produced new consequences of far-reaching importance.[1] The other, which favoured the development of the funded debt, was on the part of the borrowing State. Its need for capital differed from that of other States. It only comparatively seldom was called forth by a sudden transitory deficit, but chiefly by the long-drawn-out strife for the freedom of their country. What in the main caused the incessant need of credit for the Spanish Crown – the great distance of the country where specie money was needed from that where it was at their disposal – did not come into the consideration of the Netherlands. Here both lay close together. The financial administration also worked much more quickly. So it was only comparatively seldom that the Government had to obtain large floating loans, and naturally so far as possible avoided a financial expedient, by using which their enemies bled to death.

Certainly since 1672, in addition to the long period or perpetual annuities, obligations for a shorter period – usually a few years – were more or less frequently issued. But this was not a proper floating debt, of the kind we have come to know in France, Spain, and England; this is clearly shown by the fact that the rate of interest was often the same as that of the annuities. But it was a floating debt when borrowed on the Bourse at ½ per cent. per month, or when the Treasurer in the old manner obtained money on his own responsibility to cover up a temporary deficit in the Exchequer; but the country was not liable for this.[2]

In general, not only did the financial officials preserve a great deal of their half-mediæval character, but also for a considerable period there were many elements in the methods of the financial administration which were scarcely compatible with the character of a modern State. Thus, in spite of many complaints and several popular risings, farming the taxes was not abolished till about the middle of the eighteenth century, while the traffic in offices was little in vogue.[3]

But the former peculiar complication of the public credit of the Netherlands lasted on. There were debts of the State on its own account and on account of individual provinces, and, vice versa, debts of the provinces on their own account and on account of the State, and in addition debts of the separate towns, many of which equally served to provide the needs of the State. The debts of the State and the provinces were again subdivided territorially according to the 'Comptoiren' where they were taken up. For – and this is again a quite modern feature – as a rule the loans were not issued through 'Negociatie,' but advertised, and it was left to those who wished to invest to subscribe directly at the

---

[1] Cf. Laspeyres, p. 248 ff., 254 ff.

[2] '*De Koopman*,' III, 178; *Gr. Placc. Boeck*, I, 1506. Grossman, *Die Amsterdamer Börse vor 200 Jahren*, Haag, 1876.

[3] Laspeyres, pp. 231 and 238.

'Comptoiren' of the State. This was always the case with the regular
annuities, but particularly in later times the borrowing on bonds was
often arranged by negotiation with wealthy brokers. But they had
nothing like the same importance in public finance as the contemporary
financiers in Spain, France, and England.

The motley picture of the public debt was reinforced by the many
kinds of annuities (life annuities, annuities for 30 or 32 years, etc.),
bonds and lottery loans. On the other hand, that fatal splitting up
which persistently underlay the borrowing of foreign States, because
most of the loans were charged on definite services, is almost completely absent. Even in situations of danger and need it was only necessary for State, provinces or town to pledge their 'Corpus.' Confidence in
their capacity to pay only faltered in certain specially critical moments
and then was always soon restored. Confidence in the honesty of their
financial administration also remained unshaken, at any rate during the
flourishing time of the Netherlands. In the eighteenth century, however, this was not so. As soon as the hated farming of the taxes was
abolished, there was general complaints that the financial administration was dishonest and corrupt. The chief cause was, unquestionably,
the secrecy which surrounded all the methods of public finance. To
the end the Republic had never published its budget, nor had the provinces and towns published theirs. The amount of the debt could as a
rule only be guessed at. The anonymous writer who refers to this in the
newspaper *De Koopman* (1771) compares with it the publicity of the
affairs of the English debt and observes ironically: 'The British will
know too much, their statesmen say too much, and display what they
know in all the public gazettes.' [1]

But in spite of this deficiency the management of the debt of the
Netherlands in the seventeenth century approximates most closely to
that of the modern State. It forms the most important link between
the national modern State and the city States of the Middle Ages.

The Netherlands were the first European State for which the financial
magnates had no longer the importance characteristic of the 'Age of
the Fugger.' This development did not depend only on the character
of the State, but also prevented the development of Amsterdam into a
money market of world importance. We shall later have to go into
details of this side of the development.

England in the Eighteenth Century. Although since the reign of Elizabeth there had been a remarkable increase in the prosperity of the
English people, when the Stuarts were finally expelled the finances of

---

[1] Some facts were published even in the Netherlands. Cf. *Rapporten ende
Memorien over de finantien van Holland: der Extract nit het Register der secreete
Resolutien van de Heeren Staaten van Holland en Westvriesland*, 25 Nov., 1678.

England were in the most deplorable condition. The Stuarts were not merely bad managers, but by their thoughtless absolutism they forfeited the willingness of the English people to make sacrifices which was readily forthcoming after the Restoration.[1]

We already know how bad was the situation of the finances of the English Crown, especially since the bankruptcy of 1672. After the revolution their position was in no way better, but worse than ever. For while the expenses increased enormously as a result of the war with France, Parliament, which had just succeeded in getting financial control, showed itself, under the influence of long and bitter experience, niggardly in its grants. It took some time before the English decided to make the necessary sacrifice to protect its national interests. When at last the grants flowed more copiously, the demand increased still more and compelled the nation to shift a great part of it on to posterity. The eighteenth century, which elevated England to a world power, also imposed on it the most gigantic national debt in the world. Only by its credit was it possible for England to become a world power. But the new English debt was essentially different from those of the older world powers.

At the outbreak of the revolution England had no funded debt, except the floating debt compulsorily funded after the bankruptcy of 1672, on which the interest, however, was not paid. No change was made in the first years after the revolution. Meanwhile floating debts of the old kind were contracted. Parliament went back to its old practice of inserting a 'borrowing clause' in its grants. On the strength of these grants the Exchequer gave tallies and the interest on these, and if possible the capital was paid back out of the supplies granted. The main money-lenders after, as they had been before, the revolution were the gold-smiths, by now mostly already called 'bankers.' They paid up to 6 per cent. interest, the legal maximum on the deposits piling up with them in increasing amounts, while the Government had to pay them up to 10 and 12 per cent. Further tallies were given to the purveyors of the Government in payment. Since, however, the revenues out of which the interest and redemption money should come were often paid only very incompletely, and often did not amount to so much as the tallies charged on them, and since, further, on account of the novelty and uncertainty of the political situation capital for the most part kept away from Government loans, the creditors of the Crown, when they wished to dispose of their tallies, often lost 20–30 per cent.[2]

[1] Macaulay, *History of England* (IV, 319), and Sinclair (*History of the public revenue of the British Empire*, II, 12 ff., 57) are very inadequate as to the origin of the English Public Debt. See G. Cohn, *Finanzwissenschaft*, p. 683.

[2] Locke, *Consequences of the Lowering of Interest* (1691); Child, *New Discourse on Trade* (1692); Godfrey, *Short Account of the Bank of England* (1695).

This was still a method of finance at a lower stage of development than that of France at the time. But now there came a fundamental change.

The first decisive step towards financial reform was the introduction of the 'funding system' after 1693. Bolingbroke asserted later that it was occasioned by the wish of the aristocracy, who had attained to power, to interest as many people as possible together with their property in the new regime.[1] It is possible that this had had something to do in the motive again reappearing in the history of finance, but unquestionably the financial need combined with the new Government was decisive. When the way was once found, the need of the English people for capital (or for investing their capital) followed on.

Macaulay has expressed surprise that England was so late in following the example of France and the Netherlands in the matter of funded loans. This surprise only again shows how difficult it is for great historians to judge simple economic events. A funded debt could not be formed so long as the King and Parliament were fighting for the mastery. It was only after the revolution that the English State became what the Dutch Republic had long been – a real corporation of individuals firmly associated together, a permanent organism. It was only after this that a proper national credit could develop in England, as, on the other hand, in France it was due to the fact that the mere word of the monarch could make his subjects liable for his debts. But there was this important difference between the national credit of England and that of France and the United Netherlands – it was public. England was the first country to introduce this great fundamental principle; as we have seen, its importance was early recognized in the Netherlands. To form a correct estimate of it we have only to think of the uninterrupted disappointments which, if business is secret, must necessarily be the fate of every attempt to find out the financial position of the State. A financial system such as has since that time developed in England could only gain by the light of publicity, while in most other lands there must have been a well-justified fear of the opposite effect.

Certainly it was a long time before the English State without great exertions could get funded loans of very considerable size – a sure sign that at first the need for an opportunity of investment cannot have played an important part in the whole development. But then it went so much the faster. In a little over a century there had been formed the largest national debt in the world. The nominal amount was £900,000,000.[2]

[1] Sinclair, II, 56. Cf. Ranke, *Franz. Geschichte*, IV, 267.

[2] Cf. Grellier, *The Terms of all Loans raised for the Public Service* (3rd ed. 1805), and Redington, *Calendar of Treasury Papers*, vols. I, II; Baxter, *National Debts*.

Meanwhile there had been some activity in reforming the floating debt, which perhaps had an even wider bearing than the introduction of the funding system. The most important methods were – the founding of the Bank of England in 1694 and the introduction of Exchequer bills in 1696.[1]

The financial distress of the English State had a good deal to do with the founding of the Bank of England. The whole capital of the Bank was lent to the State and since then has formed an essential part of the national debt. Properly speaking the procedure was the reverse. All these people, who together lent the State £1,200,000, were incorporated under the name of 'The Governor and Company of the Bank of England.' Just as in the case of the old Italian Monte here are closely connected together the three great institutions – the funded debt, the joint stock company, and the Bank – which then after that began to develop separately. But the immediate financial advantage which the State derived from the foundation of the Bank was of considerable practical importance only because the Bank from the outset was serviceable to the State. On the other hand, the proper permanent use which it afforded only gradually developed to its enormous importance of the present day.

At first the Bank began to discount the Exchequer tallies as it did short-term merchants' bills. Till then, as we know, these could only be disposed of at a heavy loss, which amounted to 30 per cent. for tallies on revenues in the far future. For a short time the Bank succeeded in causing the tallies to circulate like money at or only a little below par. Yet as the financial distress continued, and in connection with this there were great differences in the quality of the individual revenues on which the tallies were charged, soon there were more or less considerable fluctuations in the price of these notched sticks, and their old-fashioned form made them inconvenient for circulation.

These disadvantages, and that of a deficiency of a good circulating medium due to deterioration of the coinage, were removed by the issue of Exchequer bills, which had a far-reaching effect on the development of the financial system. Just as annuities represent the modern type of the funded debt, so the Exchequer bill does that of the floating debt.

The main way in which Exchequer bills differed from the tallies (which still continued) and from the former assignations of other countries, was that they very soon were charged, not on separate, but on the total revenues of the Crown, except at first the land tax and the malt tax, which were added later, so that there was no longer any particular

---

[1] v. Philoppovich, *Die Bank von England im Dienste der Finanzverwaltung des Staates,* Vienna, 1885. Rogers, *The First Nine Years of the Bank of England,* Oxford, 1887.

test of their quality, and their value depended merely on the confidence in the nation's capacity to pay. This confidence was so well founded that the Exchequer bills soon circulated as money at par or a little below, while at the same time the tallies charged on particular funds were again 25–30 per cent. below par. Certainly everthing possible had been done to make the Exchequer bills a circulating medium.[1]

The old notched sticks for arbitrary disparate amounts were replaced by endorsable paper bills for definite round sums of £5 and upwards. The State undertook to accept these bills in payment of taxes, while it did not compel anyone to take them, but offered them for public subscription.

Further particular places for the redemption of Exchequer bills were instituted, and since 1707 the Bank of England was charged with this; at the same time the obligation of the State to accept the bills in payment of taxes remained. Much later the issuing of the Exchequer bills was handed over to the Bank. But meanwhile the Bank gradually took over the whole management of the State's Exchequer business proper. This again had far-reaching consequences.

From early times the receipt of monies from the Crown and the keeping of the accounts was centralized in the Exchequer, while in the sixteenth century the Treasury developed for the financial administration proper. But in England this centralization was also strongly biased by that independent, half-business position of the individual financial officials, as we found was the case with the Dutch Receivers General (Rentmeisters) in the seventeenth century, and it was mostly completely destroyed by the fact that each separate branch of the revenue formed a separate fund, on which particular outgoings were charged, without any adjustment between the many funds.

This remnant of the financial system of the Middle Ages was gradually got rid of in the eighteenth century and partly in the nineteenth century. We cannot follow out this development in detail. It is enough that the accounts became more and more centralized at the Bank of England, till finally the Bank received all the national revenues, held all the cash balances of the State, and made all payments on its account. The Bank, thanks to its central position in the financial system, could do this almost without using any cash.

In this way the accounts of the English State are kept in a way that leaves nothing to be desired in the way of order, economy, and integrity, and which at the same time continually performs the greatest services by making available enormous quantities of capital which otherwise would have remained idle.

Although all these advances in the financial system were requisite to make possible the gigantic achievements of the English national

---

[1] Redington, *Treasury Papers*, I, 545, 552; II, 35 ff.

credit, yet the organization of a free market for capital has contributed just as much. Now, in conclusion, we must return to this.

II
THE DEVELOPMENT OF DEALING IN SECURITIES

Amsterdam. The business of the Antwerp Exchange after its decline was at first distributed among a whole series of towns; but about the beginning of the seventeenth century it became evident that Amsterdam was the chief successor of Antwerp and that the Amsterdam Exchange, which was then held in the open air on the New Bridge and only after 1613 in its own building, had developed into a true world exchange.[1] Unfortunately we cannot here depict this process in greater detail or enter upon the progress of the technique of dealing in goods and bills in conformity with exchange regulations in Amsterdam. We must confine ourselves to relating the development of the business of the Amsterdam Exchange in what are called funds, stocks, or stock exchange securities (fonds, effecten, effets publics, fonds publics).

It is above all things important to establish that in Amsterdam it was not Government securities, but shares which earliest became the objects of regular stock exchange dealings of the modern kind.

As we saw during the flourishing time of the Republic, the credit of the States General and of the separate provinces and towns was so well established, and the number of would-be investors so large, that the annuity loans of the former could be raised by direct subscription. Presumably also at any time it was easy to find purchasers at par. Floating loans for a long time seem only to have been raised in moderate amounts, and what business there was moved on the old lines. In any case, we are not told of regular stock exchange dealings in Dutch Government securities before 1672–3. But shares in the East India Company were dealt in as soon as it was founded in 1602.

The Dutch East India Company arose from the need of concentrating large amounts of capital to carry on the trade with the East Indies. As in the Middle Ages the Italians had founded 'Monte' for the loans of their Republic, and had also used them for commercial undertakings, and as the same had occurred at the great world exchanges of the sixteenth century for the large loans of the European monarchs unconnected with business undertakings, now at first in the Netherlands, very soon after in England, and soon in the other countries of Europe, similar aggregates of capital were formed, which had no fiscal aims.

In the Netherlands the collection of a large capital stock was made essentially easier by the fact that it was an undertaking of the greatest

[1] Cf. B. Wagenaar, *Amsterdam in zyne opkomst* (1765), IV, 89.

national importance, and therfore supported by the Government to the extent of its power. But this alone would not have been enough to bring together the millions required; the desire for profit must be stimulated to take on itself the unavoidably high risk. For this reason the company obtained the majority of the East Indian trade, which gave a prospect of a high return on the capital which flowed into it; since all citizens of the United Netherlands could subscribe, this had the desired result.

The founders of the East India Company had no further intentions. Nothing has yet come to light which indicates that from the outset they had drawn the Amsterdam Bourse into the circle of their interests and aims. But it fell out at once that the Bourse and the Company were each of the greatest importance to the other.

The first impulse to dealing in the company's shares on the exchange was due to the favourable 'opinion' of the prospects of the company when the subscription lists were closed. This caused the numerous persons who had not subscribed to seek to buy shares on the exchange, and since this could not be done at par, they offered a premium which within a few days rose to 14–16 per cent. Probably there were many stages. Anyhow, there were bulls and stock exchange opinion of the value of the shares. This rose higher and higher till bears came on the scene. In the struggle between bulls and bears, which from the beginning brought with it the use of dubious methods for influencing the course of exchange, there arose gradually regular stock exchange dealings. This became possible partly because the importance of the Amsterdam Exchange increased greatly, partly because the share capital of the East India Company was very considerable and easily subdivided into quantities of any size in terms of similar (fungible) parts. There was probably from the outset a business advantage in dealing in round sums, and a natural striving to have the objects dealt in as completely fungible as possible finally led to the result that in business there was a fixed unit of 500 £ Fl. or 3,000 fl., and this unit finally counted as a 'share.'

From the beginning the speculation in shares was preferably in futures. This brought a new element into the development. The nature of the speculation as a means of gain depending on taking advantage of future price changes, made it appear extremely desirable to postpone the fulfilment of the bargains. In the case of bears, who had sold shares which they did not possess, this was an absolute necessity.

Speculative future dealings made possible a twofold simplification of the technique of dealing. First, speculative dealings could be realized before the date of delivery. Secondly, settling days made it possible to use the same procedure that had done so much in methods of payment, namely, set off. Both together resulted in an incalculable increase in turnover, since now only a little ready money and stock were required for very large dealings.

The development of futures was only possible in such goods as had reached a high degree of standardization or could reach it by a development just described. Forward dealings involve the possibility of replacing any individual amount dealt in by any other of the same commodity at the same future time. This preliminary condition was, with an important exception, promised by the East and West India shares.

The companies were divided into chambers: the East India into 6, the West India into 5. This divisions had been of great importance in raising the capital. Each chamber had a definite quota. The Amsterdam chamber alone held half of the East India and four-ninths of the West India capital. Each chamber had further a corresponding share in directing the undertaking and in the profits. This also applied to the shares of the different chambers. In spite of this, from the outset their price differed considerably. This, as was reported in 1609, and often subsequently, was merely due to the fact that there was not a regular stock market for the shares of all the chambers. At first there was only a large market at all times for the Amsterdam and Zeeland shares (later on only for the former). For this reason, when the East India shares had risen to 600 per cent. and more, they stood 30–150 per cent. higher than those of the other chambers.

The regular dealings on the exchange with the shares of the Amsterdam Chamber could not have arisen because this or that shareholder had to dispose of his shares on a given occasion and that some one bought them to enjoy the dividends; for in neither respect was there any difference between the shares of the different chambers. It was the fact that from the beginning speculation was concentrated on the Amsterdam shares, since the first and largest speculators resorted daily to the Amsterdam Bourse. This shows that it was speculation which made the first modern stock exchange.

The peculiar technique of modern stock and share dealing owes its development to the Amsterdam speculation.

While the dealing in shares at Amsterdam quite early took on a modern stamp, this appears to have been the case comparatively late with dealings in Government securities. At any rate the earliest information we have about it comes from the critical years 1672 and 1673, which were epoch-making for the development of dealings in Government securities.

The earlier funded debt of the Netherlands was chiefly due to the great war of liberation, which made it necessary to have a standing army. After the peace of Westphalia the army and the influence of the statholder of the House of Orange which rested on it was more and more diminished by the ruling oligarchy, and the force for expansion became concentrated more and more on sea power. This development reached its highest point under Pensionary de Witt (1653–72).

But while by this the Netherlands lost their powers of defending themselves on land, their increasing sea power made the English more and more jealous, when de Witt with the help of Sir William Temple succeeded in 1668 in stirring up England and Sweden to conclude the Triple Alliance with the Netherlands and to carry through the peace of Aix la Chapelle in the face of France and Spain. This again excited the scorn of Louis XIV, who by gaining England and Sweden broke up the Triple Alliance and completely isolated the Netherlands, which in May, 1672, was simultaneously attacked by England at sea and France on land: the first military power of Europe united with the first (after Holland) sea power against the first trade and money power of the world at that time.[1]

The French quickly conquered half the land, while the other half was only with difficulty saved for the moment by opening the dykes. The State lost the greater part of its services; at the same time the naval forces of England and France brought trade to a standstill. Credit was destroyed, and the general panic was so great that many rich merchants brought their families and what property they could take with them into safety abroad, especially to Hamburg.

The defenceless land must have fallen to the French after the first hard frost of winter if it could not succeed in getting allies, and this required large payments of subsidies. In April, 1672, before the invasion of the French, a subsidy agreement was concluded with the Elector of Brandenburg, and in September there was another with the Emperor, thanks to the indefatigible efforts of his ambassador Lisola. But the States General had no ready money to pay subsidies and their credit had gone.

After the invasion of the French the Netherlands Government securities could be bought at the Amsterdam Exchange at 30 per cent. In September after the alliance with the Emperor and an imperial Brandenburg army advanced to help, the rate rose again to 60, 75, even to 95 per cent., and then adjusted itself accurately according to the course of the war. For example, in the following winter when the French pressed forward over the ice to Amsterdam, it sank again to 50 per cent., but as soon as the thaw came rose again to 75 per cent. So it went on. Netherlands Government securities which before the war had led a quiet, unnoticed existence at par were now a speculative security whose course was the barometer of European politics.

As already mentioned, the States General could not arrange to pay

[1] Cf. Grossmann, *Die Amsterdamer Börse vor zweihundert Jahren* (1876), p. 7, and also his *Der Kaiserliche Gesandte Franz von Lisola im Haag* (1873).

subsidies in cash and they only had credit so far as their allies obtained military successes. But things were not very rosy. The imperial Brandenburg auxiliary troops under Montecuccoli wandered about undecidedly in the neighbourhood of the Rhine. He wanted to make use of the Dutch subsidies to maintain a standing army; while the great Elector certainly wished honourably to help the Dutch, but he was not in a position to do it alone, and grumbled bitterly that the subsidies were not paid. The States General wanted to make it palpable to their allies that the amount of their subsidies depended on their successes, so they did not borrow the necessary money, but placed bonds at the disposal of the Emperor and the Electors, so that they had to bear the loss on exchange due to their dilatory methods of making war. But neither in Berlin nor in Vienna had people any idea of the nature of stock exchange securities. They thought that Netherlands bonds (*apochae, appochen, assignationes, actiones, axionen,* i.e. *aestimationen*) had at any time their par value. But the imperial ambassador Lisola had to soon inform them that this was impossible, and that it was difficult to find buyers at a much lower rate, because the whole world was scared at the dismal way the war was conducted. If the army would march on in force, the money would stream in. But he preached to dumb ears. The Emperor and the Electors indignantly asked: what was the good of the bonds if they could not be realized?

Lisola tried first to raise the 'inner value' of the bonds. For months he busied himself to make them desirable for buyers, by inserting very advantageous clauses in them. When this produced only a partial result – his bonds stood higher than the others – he tried other means. Finally the states of the province of Holland declared themselves ready to sell a part of their domains if Lisola could find buyers. But it was all in vain. For lack of money the great Elector had to withdraw for a time from the coalition, as for the same reason the King of Denmark had already done, though he was ready to perform something if a subsidy agreement was concluded. The Emperor concluded a new subsidy agreement in which it was stipulated that the states should increase their subsidies to make up for the loss on exchange of the bonds.

Thus the Amsterdam Exchange had once more justified the saying 'pecunia nervus belli,' and Montecuccoli, the Emperor's general, the eager advocate of a standing army, had learnt by experience that Trivulzio's bon mot – three things were required for war: money, money, money – hit the nail on the head. But the 'money' which had such a mighty effect no longer had the form it had in the 'Age of the Fugger.' It was no longer a single financier, but the whole Amsterdam Exchange, which affected the course of history, and, as Grossmann has truly said, the general interest was represented in opposition to the self-interested cunning of the Emperor, who was compelled to follow suit. Thus it became possible to found a new effective coalition against Louis XIV.

The Netherlands bonds were in form little suited for stock exchange dealings. Each bond had to be written, and its tenor was just as little fixed as the amount of the separate bonds. All the same they were speculated in. The bonds of the States General in the critical times we have depicted were quoted considerably lower than those of the individual provinces, among which those of Holland were the favourites. In December, 1762, they stood at 30 per cent. higher than those of the State.

In the following decade Amsterdam slowly developed into an international stock exchange. One of the first foreign loans to be brought out there was that of $1\frac{1}{2}$ million gulden, which the Emperor Leopold I borrowed in Amsterdam in 1695. The great Amsterdam firm of Dentz was then entrusted with the sale of the quicksilver from the imperial mines at Adria. Over a 1,000 barrels of it were warehoused with them. These the Emperor pledged and Dentz undertook to pay the interest out of the proceeds of sale. But the States General were the real agents who issued the invitation for subscriptions. Their Receiver General guaranteed the payment of interest. This was a new hybrid form between the simple payment of subsidies and the independent loan – a rather more complete one than that we have learnt of in the year 1672. The first stock exchange list that has come to light from Amsterdam dates from the year 1747. It already exhibits 25 different kinds of home State and Provincial bonds, 3 home shares, 3 English shares, 4 English Government securities, 6 German loans, and 3 securities, whose character is not clear, in all 44 kinds of securities. By the end of the century the number increased to some 80 home and 30 German securities.

The rate of interest on the Amsterdam Exchange, which at the beginning of the eighteenth century had fallen to 2, or even $1\frac{3}{4}$ per cent., rose gradually, as a result of the many foreign loans to $2\frac{1}{2}$, 3 and 4 per cent. in the course of a century. The author of the able *Recherches sur le Commerce* (which appeared in 1779), to whom we owe this information, estimates the total of foreign loans borrowed in Amsterdam up to 1770 at about 250 million gulden.

Paris in the Sixteenth and Seventeenth Centuries. In the Middle Ages Paris was already a place of exchange of some importance; it was then thrust into the background by Lyons, and did not begin to flourish again till the last third of the sixteenth century, when Lyons had declined.[1]

---

[1] See *Dict. de Jean de Garlande*, and Géraud, *Paris sous Philippe-le-Bel*, p. 594, and *Actes de Louis VII*, No. 84, etc. Cf. *Ordonnances des rois de France XV*, 205, and Lacombe, *Histoire de la Bourgeoisie de Paris*, I, 127.

The Venetian ambassador Lippomano briefly alludes to the Paris Exchange in a report to his Government of 1557. This contains a description of the 'Parais,' that venerable mighty building which under the *ancien régime* was the seat of justice, administration and finance. There in the centre of the machinery of State, not far from the centre of Commerce, the Pont au Change, Lippomano tells us, numerous business people of all sorts used to collect together in the morning and afternoon.[1]

The Exchange is again found there on a plan of 1652, whose superscription contains the observation that in addition to two galleries with many brilliant shops there is also in the Court of the Palais 'the merchants' exchange, or the place where they come together every midday to conclude exchange business.' It is very similar on a plan of 1714, 'La place du change, where the exchange brokers assemble, is in the Court of the Palais by the conciergerie.' To-day the brokers on the Paris Bourse are still called 'Agents de change,' since originally their main business was acting as agents in exchange transactions.[2]

In that corner of the Court of the old Palace there was also from quite early times carried on other financial transactions, such as those in bonds of the Crown. If Sully denounced the buying and selling of royal bonds at low prices, this traffic must have been partly concentrated in the Paris Exchange. Since 1639 the State annuities had a changing price. In 1661 there is mention of a business in 'Billets de l'Épargne,' and somewhat later in various kinds of State bonds.[3] But this was not regular stock exchange dealings. This is shown first by the fact that such is never mentioned, but also positively that Hautchamp, the contemporary chronicler of the Law period, expressly places the beginning of a regular speculative dealing in securities in the beginning of the eighteenth century.

The shares in the trading companies which had arisen in France in the seventeenth century were similarly not regularly dealt in. A whole series of such companies were formed from the first East India Company in 1604 to the St. Domingo Company in 1698, and amongst others the two large East and West India Companies founded by the Government in 1664.[4] But none of these companies had vitality, and there is no trace that their shares were dealt in on the Bourses like those of the Dutch Companies. In short, even in the seventeenth century France did not possess a proper stock exchange.

[1] *Relaz. d. Ambasc. Venet. ed. Tommaseo*, II, 596.

[2] Cf. *Histoire générale de Paris*, also *Evelyn's Diary*, ed. Bray, p. 46.

[3] Forbonnais, I, 223, 243, 246; Bresson, I, 266; *Journal d'Ormesson*, II, 4; Clément, *Colbert*, II, introd. lv., 755 and 766; Barozzi and Berchet, *Relaz.*, II, p. 529.

[4] See Savary the younger, *Dict. Univ. de Commerce* (1741), under the article 'Compagnie.'

London to the Revolution of 1688. The shares of the East India Company were in a different position; we know their price from time to time. In the years 1617–34, when the business of the Company was going badly, the shares were sold at 30 per cent., 40 per cent., and more, below par. In 1664 they were dealt in at 70 per cent., though the 'inner value' of the shares was estimated at 130 per cent. But in 1677 the price rose to 245 per cent., in 1680–3 to 300, or even 500 per cent.[1] Manifestly the increasing prosperity of the Company animated the dealings in its shares. Yet it is not possible that at that time there was a regular market; for in 1677–81 there were increasing complaints that only a very few people got the benefit of the enormous increasing profits of the East India trade. A petition of the ablest merchants on the Exchange of London to the King in 1681 is very instructive.

From it we learn that the number of shareholders was 550, but that the greater part of the shares were held by about 40 persons. In 1666, when the East India trade began to flourish, no one held more than £4,000 shares, but in 1681 there were several holdings of £50,000 and one of over £100,000. Since the number of shares was very small and the profits very high, shares seldom came on the market, and tended more and more to get into the hands of a few individuals. The high price operated in the same way. The Company, which in its reply did all that was possible to represent the situation favourably, made no attempt to deny those interesting assertions of the London merchants, and we can therefore take it as established that in 1681 there were no regular dealings in East India shares. Things do not seem to have altered until the revolution. There was a general lively desire to buy East India shares, but it was not satisfied.

London after the Revolution of 1688. In London as in Amsterdam it was not Government securities but shares in companies which gave rise to regular stock exchange dealings. Macaulay describes what happened as follows. He starts from the fact that during 1661–88, thanks to the brilliant industrial development in England, large amounts of capital were ready to be invested, which could not be used because of the high price of land and houses and the lack of other ways of laying it out. This of natural necessity caused the formation of many joint stock companies after the revolution.

Macaulay has made use of an interesting weekly called *A Collection for Improvement of Husbandry and Trade*, issued by a certain Houghton from 1692 to 1701. This contains a true chronicle of the business

---

[1] Malynes, *Lex Mercatoria* (1622), I, ch. 19, mentions Joint Stock Companies. Cf. Anderson, *History of Commerce*, II, 89, 126, 165, 170, 173, 178 ff.; and in the *Discourse of Trade, Coyn, and Paper Credit* (1697) there is a copy of a petition which 'the ablest merchants on the Exchange of London' handed to Charles II in 1681.

in stocks and shares. But Houghton describes the rise of this some-what differently from Macaulay. He said that the war against France since the Revolution had brought the trade by sea to a standstill. So the owners of capital bethought themselves how they could use their capital profitably in such a way that it would be possible for them again to have it available at any time in case of need, and that this was more easily achieved by investing in shares than in buying land, houses, or goods. He shows how extraordinarily English industry was advanced by this. Macaulay quite rightly has amplified this view, which clings too much to a direct immediate cause for the outburst of a long pre-pared industrial development. But he forgot to investigate why the outburst in this development occurred just then, directly after the Revolution. Further, like Houghton, he has overlooked the fact that from the beginning the general wish to make capital profits was more operative than the need for investment to get interest. Finally and most of all, Macaulay has left unnoticed a very important factor, which Houghton had touched on – the increasing demand for capital in trade and industry.

In the century before the Revolution of 1688, but particularly during the Restoration except the very last years, trade and commerce in England had begun to develop vigorously and still was far from having reached its zenith. The English nation, who under Queen Elizabeth had been a people of sheep breeders and cloth makers and dealers and whose ships had only just begun to go farther than the neighbouring seas and coasts, by the time of the fall of the Stuarts possessed a diversi-fied industry on a large scale and a world-wide trade. In all spheres there arose a versatile and bold spirit of enterprise, always seeking to appro-priate new territories, and at home there was an astonishing increase in inventions of all kinds, helped by the zeal for science. There was a good deal of immature vague adventurousness and not a few fraudulent captains of industry. Yet this seething flood of enterprises and projects was a necessary element for the creation of the Great Britain of to-day.

The shaking off a hated dynasty, the security and peace which fol-lowed, the establishment of a government of freedom corresponding to the wishes of the people, which was guaranteed by the conspicuous influence of the acquisitive middle classes – all this must have had an active influence on the spirit of enterprise. The growth of industry was checked by the political disputes during the last years before the Revo-lution and by the uncertainty of the new conditions during the first years after. But about 1691 it went forward with redoubled strength.

Then came the war with France. At first certainly English shipping suffered severely from the French privateers, in 1693 at one time 300 English ships destined for the Levant were lost. But, as Houghton observed, this stopping of sea trading had a favourable effect, so far as the spirit of enterprise was diverted for the moment to more industrial undertaking at home. Then the war compelled the English to become independent of many French articles and this, and receiving many fugitives from religious persecution, gave a great impetus to the development of the English manufacture of linen, glass, hats, knives, silks, etc.[1]

All this required large amounts of capital to be concentrated, and the easiest and possibly the only way to get it was to promote joint stock companies. On the other hand, the English people were much more inclined to invest in such conditions. Some time before the Revolution the difficulty of obtaining shares in the East India Company had given rise to lively complaints. Since then the position of the business had become much less favourable and the price of the shares had fallen again to 150 per cent. Nevertheless in 1691 there was a general movement for doubling the capital of the Company, and as the Company refused the proposal of founding a new company arose. In 1694 the capital was doubled, and yet four years later a second company was founded.

Before 1691 there were only three large joint stock companies in England. The others which from time to time had been formed had vanished again. These three were the East India Company, the Africa or Guinea Company, and the Hudson Bay Company. The capital of the first was £740,000, of the second £111,000, and of the third £110,000. But in 1691, or perhaps in 1692, there all at once came into existence about a dozen new companies for making paper, glass, linen, and silk goods, two copper mining companies, and several diving and salvage companies to get up lost treasure. By 1694 the number was at least 53, among which were 5 copper and 3 lead works, 4 machine works, 5 saltpetre works, 4 water works, 2 coal mining, 4 diving, and 3 salvage companies, 3 paper works, 4 linen factories, and so forth. The shares of the Bank of England were first dealt with in on 24th August, 1694.[2]

The fluctuations of price were very considerable and the whole stock exchange technique, which had already been so precisely formed in Amsterdam, was introduced into London ready made by skilful dealers. But the English were very apt scholars. With fiery zeal they mastered the new kind of business, anglicized all the stock exchange terms and added many more. English names, and some of persons of high position, became preponderant among the large speculators.

[1] Anderson, *History of Commerce*, II, 198.
[2] Cf. Houghton, *A Collection for Improvement of Husbandry and Trade* (1691); Angliæ Tutamen (1695); *Hatton Merchant's Magazine* (3 ed. 1699); Redington, *Treas. Pap.* II, 39; *The Anatomy of Exchange Alley or a System of Stockjobbing* (1719, reprinted in Francis, *Chronicles and Characters of the Stock Exchange*, p. 359 ff.); Mortimer, *Every Man his own Broker* (1761 and later). Extract in G. Cohn's *Jahrb. f. Nat.-Ök. u. Statistik*, v. 1866.

At first stock jobbing was carried on at the Royal Exchange; but since this aroused irritation, it was transferred to Exchange Alley, close by, and which it completely occupied, as well as the coffee-houses there and in the neighbourhood.

About the same time there was dealing in the various kinds of floating debt, Tallies, Exchequer Bills, Navy Bills, Malt Tickets, etc., which was not essentially different from stock jobbing proper, i.e. dealing in stocks and shares. But we do not hear of regular dealings in annuities, or funded Government annuities, which generally at first did not play a prominent part.

This state of affairs lasted till 1711. At that time the floating debt amounted to £ 10,000,000. It was at such a large discount that the Lord Treasurer the Earl of Oxford decided on a much condemned method of getting rid of the floating debt. He made use of the widespread inclination of the public to take shares in undertakings which promised to be profitable, especially those for realizing the fabulous hoards of the precious metals in Spanish South America, as well as the popularity enjoyed by the deep sea fishery as nursery of English sea power. So in 1711 he founded the South Sea Company (South Sea was the sea on each side of South America), with a capital of £10,000,000, which the Company was to lend to the State for funding its floating debt.[1]

The South Sea Company was to trade with the Spanish colonies in South America and engage in fishing. These ostensible objects it only partially fulfilled; on the one hand, it caused untold harm, through giving rise to unlimited speculation. On the other, it did great service to the State, and the period it introduced of the notorious South Sea Bubble gave a great impetus to English industry.

We can only point to a few outstanding facts for the reason for this view. It was with the finding of that £10,000,000 by founding the South Sea Company that the English Government entered vigorously on the path of raising funded loans and found the right way of placing the largest loans. No one before had ventured on a financial operation of such magnitude. Now they knew it was quite possible, if the requisite bait was used. For decades such bait was required to obtain the enormous sums which the kingdom needed for its position in the world. Only the nature of the bait was changed, and there was no repetition of the unprincipled encouragement of the gambling spirit as at the time of the South Sea Bubble. Yet this forms an important section in the history of the national debt.

As regards the importance of the South Sea Bubble for English industry it is enough to notice that Manchester and Birmingham, the

[1] Anderson, *History of Commerce*, II, 254 ff.; also v. Philippovich, *Die Bank v. England im Dienste der Finanzverwaltung des Staates*, p. 58.

seats of the cotton and iron industries, made their first great progress during this period. No doubt the foolish excesses of the period of mania reacted terribly on industry. But what was left was so valuable that the final judgment of the time should not be so disapproving as it mostly has been hitherto.

From the very first stock jobbing in England was the target of the loudest complaints, much more so than in Amsterdam. There was no enormity of which stockjobbers were not guilty, no national disaster for which they were not answerable. Change Alley was called a den of thieves, people spoke of the 'vile infamous practice of speculating in the funds.' The stockjobbers, it was said, had ruined the credit of the nation, they had betrayed the country to the French, etc. But was the horrible corruption of the time of Marlborough, Bolingbroke, and Walpole, the rotten men of English society, as we see it in Hogarth's pictures, really a result of stock exchange speculation? Or was not the unusually devasting effects of the dealing in Change Alley merely a symptom of the unusual demoralization, credulity, and unlimited avarice of the English at that date?

The State interfered in 1697 with speculation by prohibiting any-one who was not a sworn broker to act as agent in stock and share dealings. All futures in shares and Government securities were forbidden. But this Act had just as little effect as Sir John Barnard's Act of 1733.[1]

In 1719 a speculator, threatened with legal interference, replied: 'There is only one way to get rid of us – pay off the national debt and wind up all joint stock companies. Then they need not hang the stock-jobbers, but themselves.'

He was not so far wrong. England would not have been the Great Britain of to-day, it would not have conquered half the world, if it had not incurred a national debt of £900,000,000 between 1693 and 1815. It would not have become the richest country in the world without the 30 to 40 thousand joint stock companies with a capital of at least 4 milliards which have arisen in Great Britain. Neither the national debt nor the joint stock companies would have been possible without a strong stock exchange.

Paris in the Eighteenth Century. In spite of a good deal of outward similarity the origin of the Paris dealings in securities is essentially different from the English development we have just described. What in England was called 'stockjobbing' was called 'agiotage' in France: it means the business of making a profit from the rise and fall of certain securities. But while in England the dealing was in shares, the French agiotage was at first dealing in something between Treasury notes and paper money.

[1] Cf. Ehrenberg, *Die Fondsspeculation und die Gesetzgebung* (1883), p. 13.

The Caisse des Emprunts, founded by Colbert, had issued 'Billets,' not charged on particular revenues, whose value depended solely on the unlimited responsibility of the General Tax Farmer. These billets were always promptly paid, and the Caisse des Emprunts, which was discontinued again, left a good name behind it.

So in 1702 an office was established with the same name, but of an essentially different nature. In 1700 all French coins were called in for recoinage. The directors of the mint had given tickets for the coins delivered to them until the new kinds of money were issued; these tickets were equally promptly redeemed and were gladly taken in payment like good paper money. So they were called 'Billets de Monnaie.' At that time of the most pressing financial needs – it was the beginning of the war of the Spanish Succession – the process must have operated in a remarkable seductive way on the Finance Minister Chamillart, who lived from hand to mouth. In 1702 he again founded a Caisse des Emprunts, ordered a general recoinage, and had increasing quantities of new 'billets' issued through the new office. They carried interest and were not, it appears, meant to be paid off within a short period. In any case the purveyors of the State were soon paid in these; as they tried to dispose of them as quickly as possible and enormous quantities of the billets came into circulation, the billets gradually fell to the extent of 50, 60, 75 per cent. There were regular dealings called agiotage in them, concentrated in the Rue Quincampoix, where most of the Paris bankers had their offices. Soon other Government securities were dealt in, but it was a long time before there was dealing in the State annuities.[1]

When now Law in 1716 to 1719 founded his various great undertakings, the dealings in the Rue Quincampoix developed with fevered rapidity. The first chronicler describes the 'système' well in a few words: 'Formerly the dealings in the Rue Quincampoix were carried on in the houses, without a great concourse of people. But when the system had begun to cause general wonder the Mississippi Agioteurs collected in the streets. After the first progress of the system had aroused opinion for and against it, information was given them and offers were made like those on the exchanges of London and Amsterdam, where the businessmen came together regularly every day. The numbers increased with the growing popularity of the West India (Mississippi) shares.'[2]

The Law mania is so well known that we need not go into further details. The place for dealings was shifted from the Rue Quincampoix to the Place Vendôme, then to the Hôtel de Soissons, then to the Rue

---

[1] du Hautchamp *Histoire du Système des Finances sous la Minorité de Louis XV* (1739), I, 184. Cf .Melon, *Essai polit. sur le commerce* (1734), quoted in *Daire*, p. 791 ff.; Ranke, *Franz. Geschichte*, IV, 264, 332.

[2] du Hautchamp, l.c., I, p. 191.

St. Martin, till finally, in 1724, the King decreed that an official exchange should be established, under special regulations. It was meant for dealings in bills of exchange, commercial documents, goods, and public secutities. Exchange dealing in Paris thus obtained legal existence and a home.[1]

At the same time the sworn brokers – the agents de change – obtained a new organization, whose main features are preserved to the present day. The place of their activities was henceforth the official Bourse, which till the Revolution was in the Rue Vivienne, close by the Palais Royal. There they had a special room – the Parquet – for business. The unauthorized brokers and the small speculators set up in the neighbourhood, at first in the Palais Royal. This is the origin of the 'Coulisse.'

The rise of stockjobbing in Paris had unquestionably at first overwhelmingly disastrous consequences. It encouraged the gambling instincts of the people, and the extravagance and megalomaniac of the French Court, and for a long time only enriched a parasitic class of financiers. In the eighteenth century it only gave passing assistance to the State finances, and trade and commerce obtained very little permanent advantage.[2] But there was a fundamental change in the nineteenth century.

Externally, then, from many points of view English and French stockjobbing developed similarly in the eighteenth century; on second thoughts, their nature and methods are quite different.

The German Exchanges. Long before there arose stockjobbing on an exchange, Germany possessed a tolerable number of Bourses, some of ancient growth, others established *ad hoc*. In the first half of the sixteenth century there were already Bourses in Augsburg and Nuremberg, in the second half in Hamburg and Cologne. They are first mentioned in Lübeck in 1605, Königsberg in 1613, Bremen 1614, Frankfurt am Main 1615, Leipzig 1635, etc. We have exchange lists of prices for Hamburg of 1592, Frankfurt of 1654, Leipzig of 1711, Breslau and Nuremberg of 1715.

At all these places bills of exchange was the main business, which, however, also included different kinds of money loan capital for merchants, and at the seaports many kinds of goods, marine insurances and freights. But stockjobbing did not begin in Germany till the eighteenth century.

The Law period of gambling affected Hamburg, where some insurance companies were founded in 1720 and gave rise to speculation in their shares for some months; but this and the companies vanished

---

[1] *Histoire du Visa* (1743), II, 112 ff.
[2] Cf. Ehrenberg, *Die Fondsspeculation und die Gesetzgebung*, p. 24.

again.[1] Then for nearly a century there was no further regular stock-jobbing in Hamburg, but about 1810 the shares of the Insurance Company founded after 1765, the only joint stock company there, were offered for sale by public auction in considerable quantities several times a year. But in Vienna there was a genuine stock exchange which may be regarded as the earliest in Germany.

We know how difficult it was for the Emperor's envoys to the States General to make his Court understand the working of the dealings in securities at Amsterdam. The loans which the Emperor since 1695 raised in Amsterdam, at first with the guarantee of the States General and afterwards without it, might have gradually taught the Court of Vienna the use of a Bourse for the credit of the State. But, on the other hand, they made the unpleasant observation that the bonds of States that were continually over-indebted, and those of the Vienna State Bank at hand were often sold at low rates, which was considered as usury.[2] Both these facts together finally determined the Government to take in hand the establishment of a public stock exchange. The contents of the Patents of 1771, which we shall shortly mention, show that they had before their eyes the Paris procedure of 1724.[3]

In 1761 there appeared an ordinance 'that a public exchange be established in Vienna and place fixed where buyers and sellers of public securities can meet and conclude their sales and purchases by means of sworn brokers, and to learn from an official list the price at which all public securities stood on the previous day.' But it was ten years before (by a Patent of 1st August, 1771) the Vienna Exchange was really established.

The Exchange was meant only for dealings in bills of exchange and securities. In 1783 brokers for goods were appointed to be there, but this was given up after three years.

Anyone who had business could enter, until (following the French example) a decree of 27th November, 1810, directed that entrance tickets should be issued, to be delivered only to 'Austrian manufacturers and wholesale and retail dealers belonging to a public guild.' After that foreign merchants only had 'complimentary tickets,' without the right of dealing on the Exchange. Nevertheless, in 1817 Cibbini complained

[1] Amsinck, Die ersten Hamburgischen Assecuranz-Compagnien und der Actien-handel im Jahre 1720 (*Ztschr. d. Ver. f. hambg. Geschichte*, IX, 465 ff.).

[2] v. Mensi, *Die Finanzen Österreichs von 1701–40*, Vienna, 1890, pp. 48, 57, 249, 350, 634, 733–5.

[3] Cf. Hilberg, *Das erste Jahrhundert der Wiener Börse*, Vienna, 1871; *Sammlung der österr. Verordnungen und Gesetze 1740–80*; Cibbini, *Untersuchung über die Bestimmung einer Börse und ihren nützlichen oder schädlichen Einfluss auf den öffentlichen Credit*, Vienna, 1817; Liebhold, *Die Börsen-Ordnungen der Städte Wien und Berlin*, Frankfurt am Main, 1826.

of the 'violent admixture of the unauthorized' in the business of the Exchange, whereby 'the quiet merchant is disturbed in his intended course of business and becomes confused.' *Procul este profani* would be a very suitable inscription at the entrance of the Exchange! People who were not merchants should only be admitted twice a week.

Unauthorized exchanges were strictly prohibited; yet there is scarcely any place where dealings in the streets, cafés, etc., have sprung up more luxuriantly than in Vienna. These dealings were chiefly concentrated in the Stephansplatze, later at the corner of the Weihburg and Rauhensteingasse, and then at the Listner coffee-house in the Grünangergasse. They were not only strictly prohibited, but had no legal validity. But in the course of time these dealers on the kerb made a formal association and expelled any member who wished under cover of the law to get out of his business obligations. Finally the present 'Effecktensocietät' or 'Abend börse' developed out of it.

Shouting down the quotations was strictly prohibited, but that only means the attempt to influence the price à la baisse by calling out loud, etc., and not, as was ordered in France in 1724, all negotiation which was too noisy. Neither the one nor the other had any effect and Cibbini in 1817 complained that they were impracticable.

One characteristic of the Vienna Bourse is that since the Patent of 1771 a Government official was there to look after the business. This was copied from the French, since in Paris the policing of the Bourse was handed over to a royal official, and not, as in other markets, to the merchants themselves, and at the present day the policing inside the Paris Bourse is done by a Police Commissary. But the Commissary of the Bourse in Vienna had apparently more extensive powers and duties. To him was assigned 'the careful inspection of all business that went on at the Bourse,' i.e. besides turning out unauthorized persons, hammering defaulters, he had to give the sign for the close of business and see that prices were not forced down, and also to see that the chief object of the Government in establishing the Bourse was attained, namely 'taxing the harmful money monopoly and usury.' Yet the Patent for this purpose only provided in Section 30 that at the close of business the brokers should assemble before the Commissary to settle the mean prices for bills and securities. This provision is not in the Paris regulation. But there was no result, and it could hardly have been seriously expected because a semi-invalid subaltern called Schweinsgruber was appointed the first Imperial Royal Bourse Commissary.

In 1817 Cibbini had great hopes from a suitable choice of the Commissary of the Bourse, and his observations are sufficiently interesting to be given in full. 'The more difficult the conditions ruling on the Bourse are, the more important is the election for this post, the more remarkable are the qualities of temper and mind necessary for a man who is to manage it profitably for the common good. This would be the place for Manlius Curius Dentatus, who, when the Samnites laden with gold surprised him roasting turnips, was so far from being ashamed at his moderation that he had the pride to say: Malo haec in fictilibilibus meis esse, et aurum habentibus imperare. Yet he is allowed to get rid of this antique coarseness by a little modern polishing of the roughness of the exterior. Firmness of character, power of observation, and facility for utilizing every occurrence, are more necessary for him than wide knowledge of business. For in this respect it would be very advantageous if the Commissary had associated with him two experienced traders of staid disposition who would help him with advice in the various cases and share the oversight with him.'

But if we ask what tasks Cibbini will attribute to this man of remarkable qualities, except being a censor of the manners of the Bourse and presiding over the giving of the list of prices by the brokers, we get a very inadequate answer. He should, Cibbini thinks, 'as often as on the exchange there is an unusual fall or rise in public securities, make a report, with the assistance of the two Bourse Councillors, to the provincial government in which he should give the certain or conjectural fundamental causes, or at least the occasions for this change.'

Among the many Bourse Commissaries in Vienna since 1771 there must presumably have been at least one or more who, if he was not Curius Dentatus, yet zealously tried to do his duty. It would be very interesting to know what such a man did.

At first the Vienna price list contained 16 kinds of securities, bonds of the State, of the Vienna City Bank and of the individual Austrian provinces. Yet there was little regular dealing in them. In 1799 the number had risen to 24, and in 1805 to 27. The Bourse had a humble existence in hired rooms on the Minoritenplatz, and later on the Coal Market. The subsequent period of defeat, State bankruptcy and pegged prices enlivened the stock exchange dealings. But the life which gradually sprang up after the peace of 1815 was not a healthy one. In 1818 the first shares, those of the Austrian National Bank, appeared on the list; till 1842 they were the only ones. In the 'fifties the Bourse had an enlivening influence on business in the Bruck era, which on 11th July, 1854, introduced more freedom into the organization of the Bourse.

In Berlin there was a Bourse for dealing in bills in the first decades of the eighteenth century. The industrial policy of Frederick the Great and Frederick Wilhelm I promoted it. This is also shown by the fact that the Crown granted it a house close by the Royal Schloss, a position which is almost the same to-day. The Berlin Bourse is the only one in

Europe in which the direct interest of the monarchy for the good of business found a permanent expression in the position of the building used by the Bourse.

Frederick the Great also manifested his interest by founding a series of trading companies, whose shares could at any rate to some extent be bought on the Bourse, long before Government securities were dealt in there. We know that the shares of the Emden Herring Fishery Company, founded in 1769, and of the Maritime Trading Company, founded in 1772, were dealt in on the Bourse soon after they came into existence, but it is questionable whether this happened regularly.[1] The exchange prices of Prussian Bonds were published from Amsterdam and Frankfurt from 1794–6, and from Berlin from 1806. The Berlin stock market did not become of considerable importance till 1820–5, and did not become of international importance until the founding of the German Empire.[2]

The oldest Regulations of the Berlin Bourse in 1739, before securities were dealt in, allowed anyone to go there, but contained many other restrictions which were not got rid of until the regulations issued after stock exchange dealings had become part of it.

This is seen most clearly in the treatment of Jews. In 1739 they could only enter if they had to speak with Christian merchants, but they were not allowed to act as brokers except one whom they were to propose and who was sworn by the head of the merchants' guild. The Regulations of 1805 gave them the right of joining the corporation of the Bourse and to choose one of the four overseers of the Bourse. There was no distinction between Christians and Jews as regards visiting the Bourse and acting as brokers. In the Regulations of 1820 Jews are no longer mentioned. This is not the place to go into other developments: it is enough to say that they were in the direction of greater freedom and self-management.

The first years after the Treaty of Vienna were epoch-making for the dealings of the German Bourses, which did not before 1817 possess speculative dealings and a developed technique as had existed in Amsterdam for 200 and in London and Paris for 100 years.[3]

The main cause of this development was without doubt the large loans which most States had to borrow after the conclusion of peace. But another cause, which hitherto has not been sufficiently observed,

---

[1] Nicolai, *Beschreibung de Königl. Residenzstadte Berlin und Potsdam*, 1786, I, 464, 467; Metrà, *Il Mentore Perfetto de Negozianti* (1794), II, 235.

[2] Krug, *Geschichte d. Preuss. Staatsschulden*, pp. 32, 50, 80, 109–10, 233, 245; Weeveringh, *Handleiding tot de Geschiedenis der Staatsschulden*, II, 848.

[3] Bender, *Über den Verkehr mit Staatspapieren*, 1825 (2, A. 1830); v. Gönner, *Von Staatsschulden, deren Tilgungsanstalten und vom Handel mit Staatspapieren* (1826). Cf. Ehrenberg, *Fondsspekulation und Gesetzgebung*, p. 53 ff.

had also been active. Since the decline of Amsterdam after the French conquest of Holland, Frankfurt am Main developed into an important centre for international stock exchange dealings. But how that came and what effects it had is for the moment not completely clear, but the Books of the Rothschilds contain the main material for it. All that concerns the Rothschilds belongs to a new section in the history of finance. So we must stop here.

III
RETROSPECT

We have arrived at the highest point of a period of world history. We will try to stay there a short while. Our starting-point was the increased demand for capital for war purposes towards the end of the Middle Ages; at first this was an exclusively economic event, a part of that industrial development which, as regards exchange, is called 'Transition from barter to money and credit,' and as regards production as 'The rise of capitalism.'

As the savage's club remains the same instrument whether used for killing beasts or men, so capital is a store of goods available for human activity whether this is production of goods or carrying on war. Under some conditions war is a business. It is as a rule merely destructive as a means of dynastic policy. Such were the wars of Charles V, Philip II, Louis XIV, and Napoleon I. But it was not quite the case with the wars of Frederick the Great, and not at all with the Netherlands war of liberation, and England's naval wars in the seventeenth and eighteenth centuries. These acted like expensive improvements which make it possible to attain a higher degree of industrial civilization. Yet whatever the aim of the war was, it had to go through the same process of development as industry, only some centuries in advance.

We have already worked out in the introduction that military service which had become a profession through feudalism, in the thirteenth and fourteenth centuries became a trade through the pay system, and in the fourteenth and fifteenth centuries a heavy industry through muskets and cannons. But the princes who were conducting the war could not carry it on either on the technical or economic side. So the technical side had to be given over to the Condottieri, professional war speculators, and the business side to private undertakers, the Financiers (traitants, asentistas, partisans). From Maximilian I to Louis XIV European wars were almost entirely carried on by the troops and credit of private undertakers. That is the most important characteristic of the 'Age of the Fugger.' The German and Italian financial magnates, who owed their development to this, obtained an extraordinary influence over princes and nations, even on the whole course of the history of the world – the only point in the development which lay outside business. But the more they poured their capital and fellow-countrymen into the Danaides' sieve of those dynastic wars, the more they became dependent on the princes whom they served with their credit. This ultimately caused their ruin. Long before this happened the isolated financial magnates had been unable to satisfy the growing demands of the princes for capital. So the Bourses of Antwerp and Lyons were utilized. Thanks to the free trade on this Bourse, an important traffic in capital was concentrated there, a Bourse rate of interest arose, and also a Bourse opinion of the credit which could be given to the merchants frequenting it, and of the princes who asked for credit there. For the first time in this way they got credit proper and the possibility of raising large loans. Such loans were made fungibles and objects of speculation. This formed a Bourse price, and strengthened extraordinarily the power of the Bourse to attract capital. The overstraining of credit led to severe repercussions, the bankruptcy of princes and many trading houses. When the former with their own hands again completely ruined the world exchanges by religious and fiscal oppression, new and terrible crises resulted. At last what remained of financial dealings in this world which was industrially going to pieces became concentrated in the Genoese fairs, where it was given an excellent organization. But its continuance rested on the credit of the great Genoese financiers and finally on the hopelessly deranged finances of Spain; so at last the whole system had to collapse. The final result was that on the one hand there was an increasing demand for available capital, on the other the possibility of concentration of great quantities of capital with individual intermediaries on the exchanges, and a new technique for this, but one which needed further development to deal with the increasing number of new problems.

The conditions, out of which the development we have described arose, had again gradually undergone important changes. The power of princes had in individual countries developed into a real power of the State. It had become possible for them to tax their subjects without their consent and make them responsible for the debts of the Crown. Louis XIV, who carried this to the farthest point, could now take the decisive step which made him independent of the 'war speculation.' He formed a standing army. His finance minister Colbert also tried to make him independent of the financier. That miscarried owing to the enormous increase of the financial demands consequent on the maintenance of a standing army to serve a dynastic policy that knew no bounds. Nevertheless, the importance of the financiers was considerably lessened. This was made essentially easier by the complete nationalizing of finance which had taken place shortly before.

The end which the absolute monarchy in France approached was pursued in England under Elizabeth by Gresham on the basis of his commercial experience and ideas. He had made possible a considerable development of sea power founded on the national power of capital, and had also achieved what in France (except for short periods under Sully and Colbert) was always lacking, namely order and honesty in the financial administration. But under Elizabeth's successors these achievements were mostly lost again in the struggle between the people and the Crown.

Among modern States it was a citizen State, the Republic of the United Netherlands, which first succeeded in getting a genuine State credit, and so independence as a necessary condition of its brilliant prosperity. England followed suit when the final victory of Parliament put an end to the civil war. In both countries the State, after the pattern of the mediæval cities, took on the form of a corporation whose members were responsible for the engagements of the State.

In this way the Netherlands and England were able to raise large funded loans at a low rate of interest, to keep a large navy and utilize the armies of military States by paying them subsidies. These subsidies are an interesting link between the period of the Condottieri and that of a standing army. The Netherlands and England could very well themselves have maintained large armies, but they did not want to, because they feared it would endanger popular freedom. So they confined themselves to maintaining large fleets, and when they wanted a large army, particularly in the wars against France, they bought German help, or at any rate German troops, as in the war against the United States. On the other hand, the subsidies for the German States, in particular for Brandenburg Prussia, but also for Austria, were at first a very important method of supporting a standing army and thereby attaining their own ends. But these were only transition phenomena, and only to be regarded as exceptions to the regular development of militarism. The regular method was for the States to form and organize the necessary forces for their own interest. War changed from being a large-scale industry into a business of the State.

The standing armies and large navies of the seventeenth and eighteenth centuries required capital far in excess of that wanted for war in the age of the Fugger. If then the credit of the individual financial magnates had proved insufficient to supply the necessary capital, so now that was completely the case. The army and navy required the credit of the State, and this in its turn required the stock exchanges.

In the sixteenth century the Bourses had showed their central significance for dealing in credit, and especially public credit, which finally almost remained alone and had produced severe crises through its too luxuriant growth. But from this time of crises a large new Bourse developed in Amsterdam. Its power of attracting available capital was conversely directed, not to public credit, not for the benefit of the State and its undertakings, but for private businesses.

By the sixteenth century, partly through the 'Regalism,' partly through trading companies, the State had become more and more capitalistic. But the final decisive step was taken at the beginning of the sixteenth century.

In Italy in the Middle Ages there had been formed pure capital companies of the creditors of the State who farmed the taxes. These had shares which were fungible, and therefore could be dealt with like stock exchange securities. But these Monti or Fonds, which were Government loans, joint stock companies and banks all in one, and represented the highest stage of development of Italian State finance, were not copied completely in the rest of Europe in the sixteenth century. There certainly were formed Government funds for the loans of princes and States, and also various kinds for business purposes. But in the meantime only the former were large enough and sufficiently fungible to be dealt in in the exchanges, and the private undertakings did not reach this state of development until the beginning of the seventeenth century, and then they certainly got much farther.

It was the trade with the East Indies, which till then had been carried on as a royal prerogative, which first required large capital stock. Thus joint stock companies arose in some countries; but at first stock exchange speculation in the shares only developed in the Netherlands East India Trading Company and only in the shares of its Amsterdam 'Chamber.' But as regards these the modern technique of stock exchange speculation was soon completely built up. Industry followed suit as soon as its development gave occasion to form large and concentrated capital stocks. In England this occurred soon after the Revolution of 1688. Then came the dealings in Government securities. In 1672 in Amsterdam this already had a speculative character, but not noticably more than it had in the sixteenth century. In England and France this did not occur before the speculation period of 1720; then the speculation in Government securities became almost like that which had for a long time been the case with shares.

The mainspring was always the need of unusually large amounts of capital, which could only be satisfied by exciting the desire for gain of the greatest possible number of people and thus bringing together many small amounts of capital. This desire for gain was chiefly speculative. Without speculation the requisite quantities of capital could not be collected. The stock exchange and its technique are due to speculation. The object of speculation has always required that its whole attention is concentrated on the making of prices. The objects dealt in must be very numerous and possess a high degree of fungibility, so that at any time transfers of any size without testing the quality are possible. When for this reason there are regular stock exchange dealings then from the combined opinion of the Bourse towards a fall or a rise there is an attempt in fixing the price to approximate as far as possible to the prospective development of the factors which determine the prices. It is liable to great error and intentional misleading. If one or the other or both occur a devasting crisis is the result. This again has often caused the State to interfere in the external form of speculation, but it has never achieved anything by doing this.

All human contrivances have their dark side. The excessive power of individual financial magnates attained dangerous dimensions in the age of the Fugger. The large stock exchanges put an end to that, but produced other evils. But this alone should not determine our judgment. We ought rather to ask whether these undertakings of States and individuals which required the formation of large capital stocks with all their consequences have or have not promoted the development of human civilization. To ask this question is to answer it.

INDEX